German Exile
Literature in America
1933–1950

German Exile Literature in America
1933-1950

A HISTORY
OF THE FREE GERMAN PRESS
AND BOOK TRADE

Robert E. Cazden

AMERICAN LIBRARY ASSOCIATION
Chicago 1970

International Standard Book Number 0- 8389-3098-0 (1970)
Library of Congress Catalog Number 76-98639

Printed in the United States of America

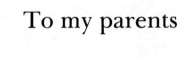
To my parents

Contents

Tables

Preface

GERMAN EXILE LITERATURE IN AMERICA 1933-1950 investigates the publication and distribution of German-language books and periodicals in the United States from 1933 through 1950—reading matter produced for (and usually written by) refugees from Nazi Germany. The arrival of these emigrants—including not only scores of writers, scholars, and scientists, but also labor leaders, journalists, and politicians—proved to be a seminal event, affecting many facets of American life. At the same time the literary artifacts of this migration are of the greatest interest to anyone concerned with twentieth-century German culture. In the present study I intend, first of all, to shed light on this most recent chapter in the long history of German-American cultural interchange and to place the Free German book trade within its proper setting, pursuing the destinies not only of books but also of the men who made them. The appendixes to this study have yet another purpose and one that may appeal to the more pragmatic reader, be he librarian, bookdealer, or collector—to provide an initial (if necessarily tentative) record of Free German printing in the United States.

Originally prepared as a doctoral dissertation for the University of Chicago in 1965, the manuscript in its present form has been considerably amended and revised. The Editorial Board of the Association of College and Research Libraries Monographs initiated the publication of the revised work and brought it to the attention of ALA's Publishing Services for its subsequent publication by the American Library Association. Acknowledgment is gratefully made to the ACRL Monographs

Board: J. Periam Danton, Louis Shores, Eileen Thornton, Howard W. Winger, and David W. Heron, editor.

Many persons and institutions have provided either source material or information without which my work could hardly have been completed. First of all, I would like to express my deep appreciation for the generous and invaluable assistance of Herman Kormis of New York City. I am also greatly indebted to Walter A Berendsohn (Stockholm) for the privilege of obtaining a microfilm of his unpublished manuscript, "Die humanistische Front, Teil 2."

Acknowledgment is made to the following publishers for their kind permission to quote from their publications as cited below: American Academy of Political and Social Sciences: Eduard Heimann, "The Refugee Speaks," *Annals* (May 1939); American Council for Nationalities Services: George N. Shuster, "Those of German Descent," *Common Ground* (Winter 1943); Aufbau-Verlag (Berlin): Walther Victor, *Es kommt aber darauf an, sie zu verändern* (1962); Heinrich Mann, *Briefe an Karl Lemke und Klaus Pinkus* (1964); Franz Carl Weiskopf, *Unter fremden Himmeln* (1948); Walter A. Berendsohn (Stockholm), unpublished manuscript of "Die humanistische Front, Teil 2"; Bouvier & Co. Verlag (Bonn): Dietrich Strothmann, *Nationalsozialistische Literaturpolitik* (1960); R. R. Bowker Co.: *Publishers' Weekly,* issues of Nov. 11, 1939 and July 14, 1945; Christian Science Publishing Society: George Pate, "Free Germans in the U.S.," *The Christian Science Monitor,* Nov. 14, 1942; Claassen Verlag (Düsseldorf): Heinrich Mann, *Briefe an Karl Lemke und Klaus Pinkus* (1964); Joan Daves Agency (New York City): Bertolt Brecht, *Gedichte 1941–1947* (1964); Verlag Kurt Desch (Munich): Karl Jacob Hirsch, *Heimkehr zu Gott* (1946) and Hermann Kesten, ed., *Deutsche Literatur im Exil* (1964); Dietz Verlag (Berlin): Albert Norden, *Die Nation und wir* (1964); Dr. Joseph E. Drexel (Nuremberg): Werner Wille, ed., *Aufrecht zwischen den Stühlen* (1956); Faber & Faber, Ltd. (London): Prince Hubertus zu Loewenstein, *After Hitler's Fall* (1934); S. Fischer Verlag (Frankfurt am Main): Thomas Mann, *Briefe 1937–1947* (1963); Klaus Mann, *Der Wendepunkt* (1960); The Free Press: Philip Selznick, *The Organizational Weapon* (1960); Harper & Row: Maurice R. Davie, *Refugees in America* (1947); Harvard University Press: Ralph F. Bischoff, *Nazi Conquest through German Culture* (1942): Alfred Kantorowicz (Hamburg), author of *Vom moralischen Gewinn der Niederlage* (1949); Alfred A. Knopf, Inc.: Thomas Mann, *Briefe 1937–47* (1963); Walter Krieg Verlag (Vienna): *Das Antiquariat* (Nr.1/2, 1963); Paul List Verlag (Munich): Ludwig Marcuse, *Mein zwangzigstes Jahrhundert* (1960); New World Club, Inc. (New York): *Aufbau,* Interview with Friedrich Krause, Dec. 5, 1941, and Manfred George, "Ueber den Aufbau," in

Aufbau Almanach (1941); Günter Olzog Verlag: J. C. Maier-Hultschin, "Struktur und Charakter der deutschen Emigration," *Politische Studien* (Nr.67, 1955); University of Pennsylvania Press: Carl Wittke, *Refugees of Revolution* (1952).

I would also like to thank the following persons for their valued contributions: Kurt Pinthus, Karl O. Paetel, Mary S. Rosenberg, Selmar Schocken, Hellmut J. Freund of S. Fischer Verlag, Peter Thomas Fisher, Dr. H. Rumpel of Europa Verlag, the editorial staff of the *Aufbau,* Margaret T. Muehsam of the Leo Baeck Institute, Gabriele Tergit of the P.E.N. Zentrum deutschsprachiger Autoren im Auslande (London), Mrs. Miriam Minnick of the Oregon State University Library, Associate Professor Howard W. Winger of the Graduate Library School, University of Chicago, and the late Oskar Maria Graf and Paul Mueller.

ROBERT E. CAZDEN

Introduction

The term "Free German Literature" (*Freideutsch* as opposed to *Reichsdeutsch*), *Exil-Literatur,* and *Emigranten-Literatur* have all been used to designate the mass of German-language publications written or published by émigrés from Germany and Austria[1] during the period of Nazi rule. The emotional and pejorative overtones adhering to these labels differ in each instance. For the purpose of this book, Free German seemed the more useful term since it encompassed, besides German-language books written by émigrés and published outside Germany, *all* books in German published by émigrés. This distinction is important, for the latter category may include not only books banned by the National Socialists, but also editions of respectable classics, such as the writings of Goethe, Schiller, and Rilke, issued by émigré publishers in many lands.

The presence of Free German publications in the United States during the period covered by this study (1933–1950) suggested a number of problems that warranted further scrutiny:

> Who were the American publishers of Free German literature and what were their motives?
> How were these books and newspapers distributed and by whom?
> How were Free German books that were published in Moscow, Buenos Aires, Karlsbad, Stockholm, Mexico City, and elsewhere brought into the United States?

It soon became evident that these questions could not be answered without thoroughly analyzing the role of the German-American

1

anti-Nazi community and its associated political groups; for after 1933 the fate of the new emigrants and the already established German-American population became inextricably entwined.

Several necessarily incomplete bibliographies of Free German books were compiled during the early years of the emigration: the *Almanach fur das freie deutsche Buch*[2] in 1935 (one of the first) and the five-year bibliography issued in 1938 by the émigré journal, *Das Buch* (one of the best).[3] In December of 1944 the German writer and bookseller Walter H. Perl, then with the Academic Book Service (New York City), stated that he was undertaking the task of compiling a bibliography of all publications of exiled German writers; but this project proved to be abortive.[4] The following year it was announced that Kurt Pinthus and Franz Carl Weiskopf were collecting information toward a comprehensive account of German literature in exile to be published by the Aurora Verlag of New York. The result of this venture was Weiskopf's relatively short outline that appeared in the Russian Zone of Berlin in 1948.[5] About this time a similar work, edited by Richard Drews and Alfred Kantorowicz, was published in the American Zone and enjoyed wide popularity.[6]

The first extensive discussion of exile literature and its publishers to appear at the end of the war was Walter Berendsohn's *Die humanistische Front,* much more complete than earlier works but understandably quite subjective in approach. Unfortunately only the first part of Berendsohn's manuscript, covering the period up to 1939, ever saw publication.[7] Between the years 1947 and 1962, a number of important bibliographical articles were written by Karl O. Paetel and Wilhelm Sternfeld on the German exile press; and the year 1962 also saw the arrival of Sternfeld's long-awaited bibliography compiled under the sponsorship of the Deutsche Bibliothek and the Deutsche Akademie für Sprache und Dichtung at Darmstadt. In spite of severe limitations, this remains the most complete bibliography to date.[8] An excellent supplement to Sternfeld is the copiously annotated exhibition catalog (first published in 1965) compiled by Werner Berthold of the Deutsche Bibliothek.[9] Matthias Wegner's recently published dissertation, *Exil und Literatur: Deutsche Schriftsteller im Ausland 1933–1945,*[10] is the most up-to-date general survey on the literary emigration and contains a good bibliography. The publishing history of the emigration remains largely unwritten.

A brief clarification is called for regarding the use of the terms "émigré," "immigrant," and "exile." (It should be noted that the literature is quite inconsistent on this point.) In all cases the use of the term "immigrant" implies one who has entered the United States through normal channels with the intention of applying for citizenship. "Émigré," on the other hand, retains the meaning of one who was forced to leave his native land (for political or other reasons), has no clear intention of becoming a citizen of another country, is still keenly interested in the internal affairs of the mother country, and hopes, perhaps vainly, to return under more favorable conditions. The word "exile" has similar connotations. The difficulty lies in the application of these terms. Many persons active in exile politics, or in Free German publishing, opted for American citizenship after the end of World War II; conversely, others· who sincerely intended to remain American citizens changed their minds and returned to Europe. The post-1933 German-American press also evades a simple labeling of either immigrant or émigré. A newspaper like the *Neue Volks-Zeitung* (New York), for example, which was the American voice of the German Social Democrats in exile, was at the same time the leading paper of the German-American labor movement.

Two other points should be brought to the reader's attention. Most important is the practice followed herein of translating all quoted German texts into English (the responsibility for any errors and insufficiencies is the author's). It must also be borne in mind that the written language of the German Americans has many peculiarities. The original orthography is faithfully reproduced in the citation of books and articles; organizations are consistently referred to by the most commonly used form of the name, e.g., Deutsche Arbeiterklubs (instead of Deutsche Arbeiter Clubs).

Notes

1. All German-speaking writers and journalists, whether claiming German, Austrian, or Czech citizenship, are considered part of the German emigration for the purposes of this study. It was by chance that Thomas Mann, for instance, was provided with a Czech passport and thus was not subject to restrictions imposed on enemy aliens in the United States. Only when dealing with the Austrian press, with its particular national aims and friendly alien status, will this study consider the Austrian emigration separately.

2. Prag: Kacha Verlag, 1935.

3. *Fünf Jahre freies deutsches Buch 1933-1938* (Paris: Verlag Strauss, 1938).

4. *Aufbau* (N.Y.), Dec. 29, 1944, p.5.

5. *Unter fremden Himmeln: Ein Abriss der deutschen Literatur im Exil 1933-1947* (Berlin: Dietz Verlag, 1948). Weiskopf, a prominent German-Czech Communist writer and journalist, was made Czech Ambassador to Sweden in 1950 and Ambassador to China in 1953. He died in 1955. Pinthus was a leading editor and literary figure in Germany before 1933, particularly noted for his efforts on behalf of German Expressionism. Until recently he has resided in New York City.

6. *Verboten und verbrannt: Deutsche Literatur 12 Jahre unterdrückt* (Berlin: Heinz Ullstein-Helmut Kindler Verlag, 1947). This compilation was first published in a shorter version as a special number of the West Berlin periodical *Sie*. Kantorowicz was a

well-known Communist journalist who spent the war years in New York. In 1957 he fled from East to West Germany. For further details see his autobiographical *Deutsche Tage-buch* (Berlin: Kindler, 1959), 1:321.

7. Zürich: Furopa Verlag, 1946. The manuscript of Part 2 is deposited in the Deutsche Bibliothek, Frankfurt am Main. Hereafter, these volumes will be cited as Berendsohn 1 and 2.

8. Wilhelm Sternfeld and Eva Tiedemann, *Deutsche Exil-Literatur 1933-1945: Eine Bio-Bibliographie* (Heidelberg: Schneider, 1962). A new edition is planned. See my review in *Library Quarterly* (July 1963).

9. *Exil-Literatur 1933-1945,* Zweite Auflage (Frankfurt am Main, 1966).

10. Frankfurt am Main: Athenäum Verlag, 1967. See also Hans-Albert Walter, "Die Helfer im Hintergrund: Zur Situation der deutschen Exilverlage 1933-1945," *Frankfurter Hefte,* 20:121-32 (Feb. 1965).

I

European Background
1933 – 1940

German Emigration – Diversity and Factionalism

With good reason the ominous litany of events that led to National Socialist rule in Germany has been subject to intensive historical investigation; for 1933 saw the dissolution of all German political parties, the adoption of official anti-Semitic programs, and the initial steps taken toward transforming the Weimar Republic into a ruthless totalitarian state. The flight of displaced scholars and scientists, of politicians and labor leaders, Jews and non-Jews alike, was perhaps the earliest manifestation of the new regime to attract the attention and concern of the outside world. The activities of the many privately funded organizations that assisted in the relocation of these refugees showed that the world was not entirely indifferent to their fate.[1]

It is almost impossible to generalize about the German emigration of 1933 since, in addition to the relatively small group of political émigrés, one can speak of an ethnic, confessional, literary, and scientific emigration, although the boundaries separating these groups were often fluid.[2] This multifariousness led Karl O. Paetel to confess: "Whoever in Germany today takes on the job of writing a doctoral dissertation on 'The Intellectual in the German Emigration' must, after a dozen attempts, lay down his pen in discouragement. He realizes that the German Emigration as a descriptive term is a fiction."[3]

German Jews, both confessional (*Glaubensjuden*) and "Jews" according to Nazi interpretation, made up the largest single group of emigrants.

Of the 721,654 *Glaubensjuden*—the population of *Grossdeutschland* (Germany, Austria, and the Sudetenland) in 1933—it is estimated that about 350,000 succeeded in escaping.[4] Often overlooked, however, is the fact that a large, although indeterminate, number of Catholics and Protestants also felt obliged to leave Germany. The former High Commissioner for German Refugees under the League of Nations, James G. MacDonald, described these exiles as being among "the political and intellectual leaders under the German Republic—Democrats, moderate Socialists, pacifists, liberal professors, journalists, Catholic priests and Protestant pastors . . . some of the finest intellectual representatives of democratic Germany."[5]

The factors which determined the decision for physical emigration from Germany—as opposed to the so-called inner emigration, the withdrawal from public affairs—were the ethnic, the political, and the ethical-religious. It was usually a combination of these that placed the individual in a situation admitting of only one apparent solution. Only in rare cases was emigration a free, conscious protest action. Intellectuals were certainly not the only victims, for Nazi racial policies were applied without favoritism: "Thus were hundreds of thousands, mostly belonging to the middle class, and representatives of the most diverse occupations, placed before the choice of concentration camps or emigration."[6] Continental Europe, Palestine, and the United States were favorite destinations during the early years, the politically active émigrés preferring to settle in neighboring France and Czechoslovakia.

Prague was the base from which the exiled leadership of the German Social Democratic Party (SPD)[7] operated until 1938, when Nazi pressure on the Beneš government forced a new move to Paris. At Karlsbad, on the German border, the party's newspapers, pamphlets, and books were published and distributed. In the early optimistic years, the SPD and other political groups in exile engaged in a variety of illegal activities, including the smuggling into Germany of camouflaged anti-Nazi literature. As the Hitler regime consolidated its powers, these clandestine operations declined rapidly in frequency.

The SPD, the Social Democratic Party of Germany, in spite of being the nation's largest political party for forty years, played a rather ineffective role during the years immediately preceding 1933. Although the party was able to salvage sufficient funds and personnel to carry on in exile, it was soon split by dissension. Not only did the SPD bring with it all the old ideological quarrels of the Weimar era, it was also faced with a new revolt—the younger generation against the older clique of party professionals. From these internal conflicts arose numerous splinter groups whose fluctuating relationships to one another have been carefully described.[8]

The interparty controversy was centered around three major points of disagreement:

1. The charge that the SPD was "Reformist" and had abandoned the party's original revolutionary ideals
2. The claim that the *Sopade* [executive committee of the SPD in exile] was the legally elected representation of the German Socialists in exile, denied by proponents of a new, illegal party within Germany, one without any connection with the old leadership[9]
3. The positions of the various Socialist groups toward cooperation with the Communists.

Point three became an acute problem after 1935 when the Communist International (Comintern) abandoned its attacks on the Socialists and strove to form a People's Front of all anti-Nazis regardless of political affiliation. It was the SPD position, adamantly held throughout the emigration, that no cooperation was possible with the Communists. Between the fixed poles of Communist and SPD policy, there hovered the innumerable parties and sects of deviationist Socialists and Communists. Among Socialist groups worthy of note were the *Sozialistische Arbeiterpartei* (SAP),[10] the *Internationaler Sozialistischer Kampfbund* (ISK), the *Revolutionäre Sozialisten Deutschlands* (RSD), and the group calling itself the *Neu Beginnen* (New Beginning).[11] Characteristic of these left-wing splinter groups was their changing attitudes toward cooperation with the Communists as well as their criticism of official SPD policies and tactics. Indeed the SAP, organized in 1931 as a new focal point for German labor, practically fell to pieces during the emigration over the former issue. The Communist Party, too, had its own opposition groups to deal with, not to mention the German Trotskyites, members of the *Fourth* (Trotskyite) *International*. Outside of the Marxist-Leninist sphere entirely were the *Black Front* movement of Otto Strasser, a former associate of Hitler, and Karl O. Paetel's *Gruppe Sozialistische Nation,* one of the remnants of that peculiarly German phenomenon, National Bolshevism.

Paris, in the mid-thirties, was already the headquarters of a number of émigré groups in Western Europe, including the German Communists and, after 1938, the German and Austrian Socialists expelled from Czechoslovakia.[12] But all this feverish activity was to come to an abrupt and bitter end. Only two years later, at the outbreak of World War II, the French government interned all German nationals, Nazis and anti-Nazis alike. The quick disintegration of the French army worsened the plight of the imprisoned émigrés who feared, justifiably so in many cases, that they would be turned over to the incoming Germans. Those fortunate enough to escape found sanctuary where they could: in Palestine, North and South America, Mexico, Australia, New Zealand, the U.S.S.R., Shanghai, Turkey, and the Union of South Africa.

Free German Publishing in Europe

On May 10, 1933, the Nazis instigated the burning of thousands of books judged inimical to the National Socialist philosophy and program—a symbolic cleansing of the German *Volksseele*. Consigned to the flames were works of Jewish authors (almost en masse) and books of Marxist, pacifist, "internationalist," or pro-Bolshevik content. Many writers of international reputation were included, such as Karl Marx, Heinrich Heine, Sigmund Freud, Heinrich Mann, Bertolt Brecht, Sholem Asch, Stefan Zweig, and Erich Maria Remarque (not to mention the German editions of Upton Sinclair). The continued publication and distribution of such literature from 1933 to 1945 required an active German press and book trade beyond the political limits of the Third Reich.

During the early years of Nazi rule it is estimated that between 250 and 1000 well-known authors were forced to flee their native land; the great majority of Jewish and Marxist writers had emigrated or were arrested immediately after January 30, 1933.[13] Newspapers and publishing houses owned by Jews were soon furnished with new owners and often new names. It did take a little time to eliminate all the undesirable books from the German market:

> Directly following the first clean-up measures and the first wave of emigration, publishers such as S. Fisher, Rowohlt, and Insel tried to save their stock of books written by émigré authors from confiscation. These writers now abroad were requested by their publishers not to compromise themselves by associating with any émigré literary periodical.[14]

The government was soon in complete command, and on October 10, 1933, the *Reichsstelle zur Förderung des deutschen Schrifttums* issued the following warning: "Whosoever in Germany today buys the books of those authors now living abroad and publishing the most slanderous lies and incitements to war against Germany is guilty of treason."[15]

During the first seven years of the emigration, until the outbreak of war, the German anti-Nazis living abroad felt it their mission to enlighten world opinion regarding the true nature and goals of the new German barbarism. This was the object of most polemic literature of the period. Of a different caliber were the detailed reports published by the *Sopade*,[16] the foreign bureau of *Neu Beginnen,* and the newspaper *Das*

Neue Tageblatt,[17] all of which were regularly scanned by newspapers and government officials in Europe and America. Much of the information therein came, or so it was claimed, from sources inside Germany.

It would be incorrect to categorize all Free German literature of the period as being strictly anti-Nazi propaganda. Berendsohn[18] and Wegner have judiciously analyzed this nonpolemical literature which includes works of such major writers as Thomas Mann, Robert Musil, Stefan Zweig, Franz Werfel, and Bertolt Brecht. The production of historical novels was especially large, Berendsohn counting seventy-one published up to 1939. This escape to the historical novel on the part of writers like Lion Feuchtwanger and Alfred Neumann elicited sharp critical attacks in the émigré press which urged that literary energies be devoted solely to the struggle against Fascism.

Works of scholarship and scientific interest were not entirely neglected, although circumstances were hardly suitable for such endeavors. The firm of A. W. Sijhoff, Leiden, was one of the few commercial houses publishing German scientific works outside the Third Reich (and Switzerland). More often a publishing venture was organized to propagate the work of one man or group, such as the Imago Press, London, publisher of Freud, and the Verlag für Sexualpolitik, Oslo-Copenhagen, publisher of Wilhelm Reich. The make-up of the Free German book trade faithfully mirrored the political fragmentation of the emigration so that one finds, alongside the commercial or trade publishers, an impressive array of firms run by German Communists and supported by the Soviet Union, and a third group of lesser magnitude in the orbit of the German Socialists.

The Communist International in Moscow, working with the Communist Party of Germany (KPD) and other national parties, financed the publishing of a vast number of German-language newspapers, periodicals, and books. At least seventy-four German-language journals were published under the party aegis in countries other than Germany. Within the Soviet Union itself many German books were published[19] as well as two major literary journals: *Das Wort* (1936-1939), nominally edited by Bertolt Brecht,[20] Lion Feuchtwanger (both of whom later emigrated to California), and Willi Bredel, and *Internationale Literatur* (1930-1945), which absorbed *Das Wort* in 1939.

Paris was the headquarters of the communications empire administered by Willi Münzenberg, the dazzling magician of Communist propaganda. A founder of the German Communist Party and later of the Communist Youth International, his crowning achievement was the International Workers' Aid, the first Communist "front" organization. Through the so-called Münzenberg Trust, which controlled innumerable newspapers, journals, and book-publishing houses as well as the distribution of Soviet films, he became, for a time, one of the most influential men in the international Communist movement. Under his imprint — Éditions du Carrefour (which continued the work of the Neuer Deutsche Verlag in Berlin) — appeared many German-language books and journals including the best-selling *Brownbooks*.[21] During his Communist period that ended with his disenchantment with Stalinism in 1937, Münzenberg's publications were distributed through ordinary party channels in the United States. After leaving the Communist Party in 1937 and until his internment by the French in 1940, he was associated with the non-Communist Deutsche Freiheits Partei and published in Paris the important Free German newspaper, *Die Zukunft* (October, 1938–May, 1940) and a number of books under his new imprint, Éditions Sebastien Brant.

German Socialism in 1933 meant, in addition to the old established Social Democratic Party of Germany (SPD), an aggregation of sometimes cooperating but more often mutually suspicious splinter groups. The most important publisher among the Socialists was naturally the propaganda arm of the SPD in exile — Graphia Verlag (Karlsbad). Publications were of modest dimensions, mostly brochures devoted to Socialist theory or the current world situation. More important were the nineteen newspapers and journals, including *Neuer Vorwärts* (1933–1940) and the *Zeitschrift für Sozialismus* (1933–1936). The publication programs of the various splinter groups were usually based upon a newssheet, a theoretical journal, and a vigorous pamphlet literature.

Commercial or trade-book publishers not dominated by any political party or clique were the backbone of the Free German book trade.[22] Certainly some of them had strong political sympathies: for example, Emil Oprecht, owner of the Europa Verlag (1933–) and a leading Swiss Socialist, or Wieland Herzfelde, whose Malik Verlag in Berlin (1917–1933) stood very close to the German Communist Party (but was never part of it) and who continued publishing from Prague until 1938.[23] Oprecht and Herzfelde were, strictly speaking, commercial publishers rather than party propagandists. Perhaps the best known of any Free German publisher was Gottfried Bermann-Fischer whose Bermann-Fischer Verlag (Vienna, Stockholm, New York) Herzfelde once labeled the "right-wing of exiled publishing houses."[24] Under Nazi pressure the justly famous S. Fischer Verlag (Berlin) was "reorganized," and in 1936 Samuel Fischer's son-in-law and heir was allowed to leave Germany taking with him rights to those authors deemed undesirable.[25] After a first attempt to set up shop in Switzerland was opposed by that government to protect, it was said, the interests of the Swiss book trade,[26] Bermann-Fischer was successful in establishing his new firm in Vienna (May, 1936). But the days of Vienna were numbered, and within two years the harried publisher again had to flee, leaving behind a book stock of some 400,000 volumes as booty for the Nazis. Undeterred, he soon regrouped his forces in Stockholm with financial aid from the Swedish firm of Albert Bonniers. Production in Sweden continued until 1948 although Bermann-Fischer, because of his anti-Nazi activities, was forced to leave the country with his family, finding refuge at last in the United States. His American career (1940-1946) is treated in a subsequent chapter.

Two Dutch firms located in Amsterdam and later to become close associates of Bermann-Fischer—the Verlag Allert de Lange and the Querido Verlag—were early and important purveyors of Free German literature. During the summer of 1933 Emanuel Querido (1871-1943), quickly responding to events in Germany, established a German-language affiliate of his firm under the leadership of Fritz H. Landshoff, former director of the Kiepenheuer Verlag, Berlin. The new Querido imprint soon won international prestige with *Die Sammlung* (the first literary journal of the emigration)[27] and a roster of celebrated authors, such as Albert Einstein, Erich Maria Remarque, and Emil Ludwig. By chance, it was a former associate of Landshoff at the Kiepenheuer Verlag—Walter Landauer (1902-1944)—who took charge of the German division of Verlag Allert de Lange. "The Allert de Lange firm . . . is the exact complement, the counterpart in mentality and policy, of the Querido Verlag, the difference being that Allert de Lange lays more emphasis than Querido on works of history, political theory and economics."[28] Querido, De Lange, and Bermann-Fischer in Stockholm jointly launched a very popular paperback series, the *Forum Bücher*, which included such titles as Heinrich Mann's *Die kleine Stadt* (1939), Franz Werfel's *Die vierzig Tage des Musa Dagh* (1939), and a Heine anthology, *Meisterwerke in Vers und Prosa* (1939). So successful were these little books (outside Germany) that the Nazi critic Willi Vesper in exasperation demanded a counterattack by National Socialist publishers: "Long enough have we allowed the German book market to be dominated by emigrants and Jews," he complained.[29]

Distribution of the books of all three firms was by 1939 consolidated in the hands of the Allert de Lange Verlag, but not for long; in the spring of 1940 the Germans occupied Holland and thus gave a sudden coup de grâce to émigré publishing in Amsterdam. The entire De Lange stock as well as 100,000 volumes of Querido and Bermann-Fischer books were lost, including most copies of *Das Vermächtnis*, the last published work of the Alsatian novelist, René Schickele. The few extant copies of this little book, which was warmly recommended in the press of several countries, were examples sent out for review.[30] On the other hand, when Landshoff of Querido returned to Amsterdam in 1947, he found still intact the unbound sheets of several books which finally received a delayed publication.[31]

Publishers were destroyed as well as their books: Emanuel Querido and his wife were gassed at Auschwitz; Walter Landauer starved to death in Bergen-Belsen. Fritz Landshoff did manage to escape to New York, joining Bermann-Fischer in setting up the L. [for Landshoff] B. Fischer Publishing Company. Landshoff had originally planned to transfer the Querido Verlag to Batavia, Dutch East Indies, but this move was thwarted by the Japanese invasion. A 1941 edition of Remarque's *Drei Kamaraden* is mute testimony to the world's derangement at that time; although the book was printed in Stockholm, the title page bore Batavia as place of publication, while Landshoff, the publisher, was already established in New York.

As the only neutral German-speaking country in Europe, Switzerland was a natural market as well as a producer of Free German literature.[32] The leading Swiss publisher of anti-Nazi books was the previously mentioned Emil Oprecht of Zürich, a close friend of Thomas Mann and publisher of Mann's literary periodical, *Mass und Wert* (1937–1940). After 1933 Oprecht spent most of his time building up his international book service (Oprecht & Helbling) and two publishing houses devoted to Free German literature: Oprecht Verlag (belles-lettres) and Europa Verlag (political and social criticism). The industry of the Oprecht group was one of several factors which led to a remarkable upturn in Swiss book production, an increase of 100 percent from 1936 to 1945 according to one commentator (who also proudly claimed that during those years Switzerland "truly represented German culture, science, literature, and art").[33] Official German pressure on the Swiss government to confiscate outspokenly anti-Nazi books reached a critical point in 1938 when the Swiss did, in fact, suppress one Europa publication — Hans Wyl's *Ein Schweizer erlebt Deutschland*. That same year, to counter the threat of future German intimidation, Oprecht opened an affiliate in New York City under the direction of Friedrich Krause, the German émigré bookseller.[34] More than 128 books bearing the imprint New York/Zürich were issued by the Europa and Oprecht Verlage between the years 1938 and 1945.[35]

World Acceptance of Free German Literature

The first reaction of the Western democracies to the book burnings of 1933 was one of shock and anger. Protest committees were formed in England and the United States. H. G. Wells was made chairman of a Society of Friends of the Burned Books. In 1934, significantly on May

10 [the first anniversary of the Nazi book burning], the Deutsche Frei-
heitsbibliothek was formally opened in Paris.[36] Supported by German
writers in exile led by Alfred Kantorowicz and Heinrich Mann, the
library's aim was to collect copies of all books banned in Germany.
Immediately after the annexation of Austria by Germany in 1938, dealers were forced to clear their shelves and either destroy or conceal
books of proscribed authors. A group of students at Williams College
(Massachusetts) cabled Vienna for an opportunity to purchase the
banned books. The borough president of Brooklyn offered to pay trans-
portation costs to obtain them for the Brooklyn Public Library. Not to
be outdone, the *Yale Daily News* urged a mass intercollegiate protest,
and the Library of Congress was asked to intervene.[37] This sympathetic
response toward the victims was matched by at least passive acceptance
of Nazi goals by many Germans and non-Germans living abroad. Thus
the stage was set for an international battle of the books.

The Nazis devised several methods of undercutting the market for
Free German books. According to Herzfelde, Propaganda Minister
Goebbels encouraged the dumping of Nazi-approved publications on the
foreign market at 25 percent reduction in price. Further, many thousands of volumes of "undesirable" literature confiscated in Germany
were also dumped at bargain prices, hurting the sales of émigré publishers and, at the same time, bringing into the Reich much-needed
foreign currency.[38] Still the German book export program, under government control after 1933, met with continued rebuffs in its attempt to
propagate National Socialist literature. The authorities, learning from
experience, soon gave priority to those categories of exports for which a
demand still existed, namely scientific and technical books and confessional literature—the latter primarily destined for Spain and the South
American continent.[39]

On the other hand, the popularity of Free German literature on the
world market was dramatically shown by comparative translation statistics compiled for the years 1933–1945. Of 1247 German-language
books translated in 24 countries, 683 were titles by banned *(verbotene)*
authors, 172 were by undesirable *(unerwünschte)* authors, 329 were
books considered classics; and only 63 were written by authors encouraged *(geförderte)* by the German government. For the United States the
breakdown on translations from the German was: 59 books by banned
authors, 15 by undesirable authors, 9 considered classics, and only 5
by Nazi-supported authors.[40] Before 1939, when the European market
was still open, rather high production figures also confirmed the popularity of many Free German best sellers—20,000 copies of Lion
Feuchtwanger's *Die Geschwister Oppenheim* (Amsterdam, 1933) were

sold within one year. Bermann-Fischer's editions of Thomas Mann, Stefan Zweig, and Franz Werfel also averaged 20,000 copies each.[41] Hans Liepmann, whose own book *Das Vaterland* (Amsterdam, 1933) sold 22,000 copies, wrote that about one-half of all Free German books published as of 1936 had gone through two or more editions and that one-quarter sold more than 3,000 copies.[42]

Nazi propaganda was continually attempting to discredit the persistently growing body of émigré literature. Friedrich Krause recounted, in a talk before the Roland Society of New York, that a manuscript purporting to be the memoirs of General von Schleicher (Hitler's predecessor as Chancellor) had been secretly offered to an émigré publisher, but upon inspection was turned down as a forgery. Had the book been published, the numerous false statements it contained would have been ammunition for the Nazis to impugn the integrity of the publisher[43] and, by inference, of the entire émigré press.

The fall of France in 1940 signaled the end of this first and most productive period of Free German publishing. The traditional centers of European culture were now exchanged for more exotic towns and strange outposts. As the war progressed, numerous small presses, often one-man operations, sprang up in Palestine, Tanganyika, Brazil, Chile, and Cuba. Although a few publishers of significance did develop in Argentina and Mexico—Editorial Cosmopolita and El Libro Libre, respectively—the United States became the new rallying point for the German émigré book trade.

Notes

    1. See Maurice R. Davie, *Refugees in America* (New York: Harper, 1947); Norman Bentwich, *The Rescue and Achievement of Refugee Scholars* (The Hague: Nijhoff, 1953); Stephen Duggan, *The Rescue of Science and Learning* (New York: Macmillan, 1948); Arieh Tartakower and Kurt R. Grossman, *The Jewish Refugee* (New York: Institute of Jewish Affairs, 1944); Varian Fry, *Surrender on Demand* (New York: Random, 1945); Helge Pross, *Die deutsche akademische Emigration nach den Vereinigten Staaten: 1933–1941* (Berlin: Duncker & Humblot, 1955); John Charles Wetzel, "The American Rescue of Refugee Scholars and Scientists from Europe 1933–1945" (unpublished Ph.D. dissertation, Univ. of Wisconsin, 1964).

    2. Erich Matthias, *Sozialdemokratie und Nation* (Stuttgart: Deutsche Verlags-Anstalt, 1952), p.18.

    3. Karl O. Paetel, "Das deutsche Buch in der Verbannung," *Deutsche Rundschau,* 76:757 (Sept. 1950).

    4. Mark Wischnitzer, "Die jüdische Wanderung unter der Naziherrschaft 1933–1939," in Heinz Günther (ed.), *Die Juden in Deutschland 1951/52–1958/59* (Hamburg: Gala Verlag, 1959), p.135.

    5. Quoted in American Friends Service Committee, *Refugee Facts* (Philadelphia: 1939), p.11.

6. Pross, op. cit., p.14.

7. The executive committee of the SPD in exile was commonly known as the Sopade and was appointed May 4, 1933, when the party was still functioning in Germany. Of the original committee members, Friedrich Stampfer, editor in chief of the *Vorwärts* (the party's leading newspaper) and Paul Hertz, a left-wing Socialist, later emigrated to the United States. See Lewis J. Edinger, *German Exile Politics* (Berkeley: Univ. of California Pr., 1956), p.26-42.

8. See Edinger, op. cit., and Matthias, op. cit., as well as Karl O. Paetel, "Die deutsche Emigration der Hitlerzeit," *Neue Politische Literatur,* 5:465-82 (June 1960).

9. A parallel situation arose when the Austrian Socialists (SPÖ) were forced to go underground after the Feb., 1934 revolt. For details and comparison of the two situations see Joseph Buttinger, *In the Twilight of Socialism: A History of the Revolutionary Socialists of Austria* (New York: Praeger, 1953) and Otto Bauer, *Die illegale Partei* (Paris: Editions "La Lutte Socialiste," 1939).

10. See Babette L. Gross, "The German Communists' United-Front and Popular-Front Ventures," in Milorad M. Drachkovitch and Branko Lazitch (eds.), *The Comintern: Historical Highlights* (New York: Praeger, 1966), p.130-31; Hanno Drechsler, *Die Sozialistische Arbeiterpartei Deutschlands* (Meisenheim am Glan: Anton Hain, 1965).

11. Probably the most important oppositional Socialist group critical of the old party. Their platform demanded renewal of socialist ideals and a radicalization of party policies. They strove for unity among all workers' organizations including, if possible, the German Communist Party (KPD). The leader of the *Neu Beginnen* group, Karl Frank, alias Paul Hagen, emigrated to the United States and was quite influential in both German and English-speaking circles.

12. Arthur Koestler describes German Communist activities in Paris during this period in his memoir, *The Invisible Writing* (New York: Macmillan, 1954).

13. Dietrich Strothmann, *Nationalsozialistische Literaturpolitik* (Bonn: H. Bouvier, 1960), p.73, 90.

14. Ibid., p.71. Letters sent by Thomas Mann, René Schickele, and Alfred Döblin to their publisher Gottfried Bermann-Fischer expressing their disapproval of Klaus Mann's periodical, *Die Sammlung* (Amsterdam, 1933-35) were written for this purely economic reason, but the Nazis published copies in the *Börsenblatt* hoping to stir up trouble among the émigrés (which to some extent it did). See Matthias Wegner, *Exil und Literatur: Deutsche Schriftsteller im Ausland 1933-1945* (Frankfurt am Main: Athenäum Verlag, 1967), p.68-71 and Hans-Albert Walter, "Der Streit um die 'Sammlung,' " *Frankfurter Hefte,* 21:850-60 (Dec. 1966).

15. Wilhelm Sternfeld, "Die Emigrantenpresse," *Deutsche Rundschau,* 76:250 (April 1950).

16. The *Deutschland-Berichte der Sopade* (Prague), 1934-37 and (Paris), 1938-40, were familiarly called the "Grüne Berichte" because they were printed on green paper; issued monthly in German, French, and English editions. The full series totals some 10,000 pages.

17. Edited by Leopold Schwarzschild and a continuation of the *Tageblatt* (Berlin). Published continuously through May 11, 1940, it was doubtless the most respected political journal of the emigration, numbering among its contributors Konrad Heiden, Ludwig Marcuse, Joseph Roth, Thomas Mann, Sigmund Freud, Harold Nicolson, and Winston Churchill. See Hans-Albert Walter, "Leopold Schwarzschild and the *Neue Tage-Buch,*" *Journal of Contemporary History,* 1, No. 2:103-16 (1966).

18. Berendsohn 1:108-50.

19. The best coverage of these Russian imprints may be found in *Deutsche Nation-*

albibliographie, Ergänzung I: Verzeichnis der Schriften, die 1933-1945 nicht angezeigt werden durften (Leipzig: Verlag des Börsenvereins des deutschen Buchhändler, 1949). The most frequently appearing imprints are: Moskau: Verlagsgenossenschaft ausländische Arbeiter in der UDSSR; Engels: Deutscher Staatsverlag (Engels on the Volga, an area heavily populated by Germans); Rostow am Don: Asow-Schwarzmeer-Gauverlag; Kiew: Verlag für nationale Minderheiten.

20. Brecht, at least, carried on his editorial duties by mail from Denmark, declining to remain in Moscow. When asked why not, he would smile and say: "I could not get enough sugar for my tea and coffee." Martin Esslin, *Brecht: The Man and His Work* (Garden City, N.Y.: Doubleday, 1960), p. 168.

21. The first *Braunbuch über Reichstagbrand und Hitler-Terror* was translated into twenty-three languages, and 600,000 copies were distributed by 1935. Helmut Gruber, "Willi Münzenberg: Propagandist For and Against the Comintern," *International Review of Social History*, 10, Part 2:191 (1965). For other studies in English on Münzenberg see: R. N. Carew Hunt, "Willi Muenzenberg," *St. Antony's Papers*, No.9 (London: Chatto & Windus, 1960), p.72-87; Jorgen Schleimann, "The Organization Man: The Life and Work of Willi Münzenberg," *Survey: A Journal of Soviet and East European Studies*, No.55: 64-91 (April 1965).

22. The following survey of publishing is by necessity incomplete. On the considerable publishing that went on in Czechoslovakia, for example, consult Gertrude Albrechtova, "Zur Frage der deutschen antifaschistischen Emigrationsliteratur im tschechoslowakischen Asyl," *Historica*, 8:177-233 (1963).

23. For the history and bibliography of the Malik-Verlag see: Deutsche Akademie der Künste zu Berlin, *Der Malik-Verlag 1916-1947* (Berlin, 1967).

24. *Direction* (Darien, Conn.), 2:2 (Dec. 1939). Because Bermann-Fischer remained in Germany until 1936, and because of the flurry caused by letters from Thomas Mann and others written at his behest (see note 14), there was some suspicion of his move to Vienna. His most violent critic, Schwarzschild of *Das Neue Tageblatt*, actually insinuated collusion with the Nazis and expressed fear that Bermann-Fischer with his roster of world-famous authors would be financially disastrous to smaller émigré firms. This, of course, was proved quite untrue. See Wegner, op. cit., p.84-85.

25. Hugo von Hofmannsthal, Arthur Schnitzler, Jakob Wassermann, Thomas Mann, Franz Werfel, Carl Zuckmayer, Alfred Döblin, André Maurois, and George Bernard Shaw.

26. S. Fischer Verlag, *Vollständige Verzeichnis aller Werke, Buchserien und Gesamtausgaben mit Anmerkungen zur Verlagsgeschichte 1886-1956* (Frankfurt am Main: 1956), p.37.

27. *Die Sammlung* (1933-1935), edited by Klaus Mann. Aldous Huxley, André Gide, and Heinrich Mann were patrons. For Amsterdam publishing see: Karl H. Salzmann, "Amsterdam als Verlagsort der deutschen Emigration," *Börsenblatt für den deutschen Buchhandel* (Leipzig), 116, Nr.23:186-87 (1949).

28. Erika and Klaus Mann, *Escape to Life* (Boston: Houghton, 1939), p.199.

29. From an article in *Neue Literatur* quoted in *Volksfront* (Chicago) [a Communist newspaper], Jan. 28, 1939, p.3.

30. *Aufbau* (Berlin), 2:1081 (Oct. 1946).

31. Joseph Roth, *Leviathan;* Bruno Frank, *Sechszehntausend Franken;* Alexander M. Frey, *Der Mensch;* Salzmann, *Börsenblatt für den deutschen Buchhandel* (Leipzig), 116:187 (1949).

32. It was, however, very difficult for an émigré author to obtain a publication permit from the Swiss police and most Free German books published in that country were written by nonresidents. This situation gave rise to the practice of *Negerarbeit* as it was called, the

publishing, under the names of Swiss authors, the works of German emigrants living in Switzerland. See Wegner, op. cit., p.51.

33. J. Svehla, "Von Schweizer Verlegern und Buchhändlern, " *Der Schweizer Buchhandel,* 6:335 (June 15, 1948).

34. From an interview with Krause quoted in the *Neue Volks-Zeitung* (N.Y.), Oct. 29, 1938, p.2.

35. Two other firms associated with Oprecht—Verlag Der Aufbruch and Verlag Die Gestaltung—used the same double imprint occasionally. The joint *Verlagsverzeichnis* of Europa/Oprecht for Spring, 1948 still carried Zürich/New York on the title page.

36. The library issued a *Mitteilungsblatt* from 1935 to 1937; with issue No.14, the title was changed to *Das Freie Deutschland.* See Werner Berthold, *Exil-Literatur 1933–1945,* p.174–75.

37. *Publishers' Weekly,* 133:1746 (April 30, 1938).

38. Hans-Albert Walter, *Frankfurter Hefte,* 20:126 (Feb. 1965).

39. Strothmann, op. cit., p.127.

40. Ibid., *Appendix, Tabelle Nr.8.* Since the table is headed *Titelauswahl,* his statistics are not to be taken as definitive.

41. Walter, loc. cit.

42. "German Authors Write in Exile," *New York Times Sunday Book Review,* Oct. 23, 1936, p.8.

43. *Aufbau* (N.Y.), March 15, 1940, p.9–10. The publisher was possibly the Europa Verlag for whom Krause was employed as reader until 1938.

II
German-American Background

As the largest national minority group in the United States—
6,873,103[1] in 1930, 4,950,000[2] in 1941—German Americans have been
the subject of an extensive body of descriptive literature although inter-
pretive studies have been scarce.[3] From earliest times, the successive
waves of German emigration can be superficially categorized as religious, economic, or political in origin; for example, the trans-
planting of Lutherans from Saxony to Missouri in 1838, the agricultural
migration of the nineteenth century, and the arrival of the "For-
ty-Eighters"—that amalgam of republicans, nationalists, and extreme
radicals. These and many other groups of German immigrants were
large and cohesive enough to maintain their separate identities by establishing their own newspapers, schools, and organizations. Active though
the political immigrants were, even more cultural autonomy was attained
by the larger, more homogeneous religious communities such as the
Lutherans and the German Catholics. The point to be made is that long
before 1933, German America was made up of many often unreconcil-
able groups. As Ralph Bischoff has written:

> All previous periods of German-American history had been, to a great
> extent, dominated by splits within the ranks of German Americans
> themselves, in particular between the old immigrants and the new, and
> between those who were church-minded and those who classed them-
> selves as freethinkers and organized themselves into *Vereine*. . . . In the
> latter half of the nineteenth century the conservatives and the German
> churches were on one side, and the liberals, socialists, and freethinkers

were on the other, and not even the cementing force of a common origin and heritage could bridge this chasm.[4]

From the political and social diversity of German America we may, for argument's sake, identify four strata: the dominant conservative middle class and agricultural groups; the liberal, more highly educated minority (the most rapidly assimilated); the labor movement (the predominantly Socialist subculture of the large cities);[5] and the German Jews.

By the end of the nineteenth century, middle class German Americans had reached new heights of material prosperity, though at the cost of a certain cultural complacency. A tendency to recreate the cultural surroundings of the Germany from which they emigrated resulted in a slowly evolving "Biedermeier" culture, always several decades behind that of the mother country. Their literary tastes followed suit. According to Hawgood: "Attempts to introduce twentieth century German literature to the Germans in America of nineteenth century immigrant stock, such as those in the hill country of Texas, have been made without much success."[6] That these strictures did not only apply to the hill country of Texas is brought out by George N. Shuster, former president of Hunter College of New York:

> If you step into the Milwaukee Public Library, you will find a good collection of German drama. All the earlier plays of Hauptmann, Sudermann, and the rest are there. But no titles more recent than 1914 are on the shelves. The interesting fact is not so much that no additional books were purchased after the war but that nobody cared to ask the librarians to buy more.[7]

In contrast to the conservative elements (and also to the closely knit Socialist subculture of the cities), the "democratic" or "liberal" minority — college professors, lawyers, physicians, artists, and writers — were most inclined to break out of the German-American isolation.[8] Germans inspired by the ideals and institutions of American democracy (exemplified by Carl Schurz) were anxious to take part in politics and preferred to be thought of as Americans of German descent rather than German Americans. Yet, until the experiences of World War I, particularly the unexpected and often violent anti-German sentiments of their fellow citizens, the greater part of the German community in America remained isolated and entrenched behind the protective walls of their mother tongue and inherited culture.

Progressives, Jews, and Radicals

The limitations of this chapter prohibit any discussion of German-American life on the eve of 1933 except where pertaining to those groups sympathetic to the majority of emigrants: the liberal anti-Nazi elements of the middle class (organizationally as weak in the United States as in Germany), the German Jews, and especially the disunited Left.

During the 1920s and 1930s it seemed that to many Germans living in the United States the traditions of American democracy were less attractive than reviving nationalist, racist, and authoritarian ideologies on the one hand, or Marxist and anarchist ideologies on the other. The Roland German American Democratic Society was one of the few liberal, non-Socialist organizations that continued to function after 1914. Erwin H. Klaus (president of the society in 1941) complained of the apolitical character of the German immigrant at the turn of the century and of the formless nature of the progressive German-American forces.[9] Klaus confessed that he could only find three "progressive associations" worthy of note: The Deutsch-Amerikanischer Reformbund (because of its support of Robert La Follette in 1924), the Turnvereine (gymnastic and social societies),[10] and the Deutsch-Amerikanischer Bürgerbund of Milwaukee. His list intentionally does not take into account any Marxist, freethought, or labor groups. The Roland Society itself deserves notice for its sympathetic cooperation with labor and émigré groups throughout the thirties and forties.

The situation of the German Jew within the German community of mid-nineteenth century America is described in a positive manner by the historian Carl Wittke:

> The cultural assimilation of Germans and German Jews in the United States is attested by the fact that Jewish Forty-eighters, whatever the country of their origin, became part of the German-American community, and were accepted as fellow champions of the republican traditions of 1848. Jews moved in the same cultural milieu with Germans in the United States throughout most of the nineteenth century. They belonged to German *Turnvereine,* and several Jewish Turner were prominent leaders of these gymnastic societies and vigorously advocated their radical programs. Jews belonged to German-American literary clubs, and generously supported the German theatre. . . . In the decade before the Civil War, conventions of Jewish organizations conducted their business in the German language.[11]

A less cheerful picture of relations between Germans and German Jews in America — one that points up latent and overt antagonisms — may be found in the writings of Rudolf Glanz.[12] However, the bond of a common language and culture was strong enough to hold these two segments of German America together with some degree of amity, at least until the rise of National Socialism. The year 1933 marked an abrupt change in this relationship. The public utterance of Nazi anti-Semitic polemics in many German clubs and fraternal groups soon resulted in a mass exodus of German Jews from these organizations. A statement by Victor Ridder, publisher of the conservative *New Yorker Staatszeitung,* revealed that in his view before 1933, 20 to 25 percent of all members of German-American organizations were Jews, and they left when the (Nazi) Friends of the New Germany started its activities.[13] Thus did events in Germany cast their shadow over German-American life.

GERMAN SOCIALISM IN AMERICA

Socialism, anarchism, labor unions, and workers' singing societies were all part of the German-American urban milieu which, despite the present interest in labor history and radical movements, seems hardly to have beguiled the historian (and this lack of any accessible account is the main reason for the following detailed survey). Does this dearth of interest reflect the irrelevancy or unimportance of the subject? Probably not if the Socialist Labor Party (SLP) is taken as a case in point.

Until the end of the nineteenth century the party, founded in 1877 and for many years dominated by Germans, issued its convention proceedings and propaganda in both German and English, and maintained close contact during the 1880s with the then outlawed German Social Democratic Party (particularly with party leaders living in Zürich and London)—a relationship that included exchange of publications. The later history of American Socialism was also affected by the presence of numerous immigrant groups among which the Germans remained the largest. Under the doctrinaire leadership of Daniel DeLeon (and with its large foreign-born membership), the SLP did not seem capable of transforming itself into a mass party. In 1900, Eugene Debs and other opponents of DeLeon formed the Socialist Party, making a pointed appeal for the support of native-born American workers. This "Americanization" of the Socialist image, in turn, led foreign-born workers, those who did not speak English or who preferred to use their native tongue, to resort to "more or less independent organizations."[14] By 1917 these foreign-language federations sheltered about 40 percent of the total party membership. It is hard to disagree with Draper's conclusions that: "A large part of the history of the American Socialist movement has remained shrouded in comparative obscurity because the language barrier has hindered an adequate study of these relatively autonomous organizations."[15]

Spokesman for most of the German-language federations and societies in the New York area and the leading Socialist daily in America, the *New Yorker Volkszeitung* could boast of a long and checkered career. Founded in 1877 by an association of dedicated immigrant workers drawn predominantly from the bakery, meat handling, brewing, and metal trades, the paper flourished under the editorial direction of Alexander Jonas, Carl Adolf Douai, Hermann Schlueter, and Ludwig Lore.[16] Though the *Volkszeitung* was long a bulwark of the Socialist Labor Party, it also had strong trade union backing, which was no doubt influential in the paper's decision to bolt the De Leonites and give its support to the fledgling Socialist Party. That was in 1900. Continued backing by German-language unions and Socialist groups raised the newspaper to a position of eminence it enjoyed even after its transformation into the weekly *Neue Volks-Zeitung* in 1933.

From 1919 to 1931 with Ludwig Lore as editor, the *Volkszeitung* became trapped in a situation that was nothing if not ambiguous. For Lore was one of the founders of the American Communist Party and from 1919 to 1925 had made his newspaper the de facto mouthpiece of the new movement among German-American workers. The fact that the *Volkszeitung* still drew its financial support from professedly Socialist organizations and unions, many on the conservative side at that, gradually led to strained relations between these groups and the Lore clique. Even after 1925, when Lore was officially expelled from the Communist Party, he continued to be active in various Communist oppositional sects until he bowed out of radical politics for good in the early thirties. This clash of radical and conservative elements among the German Socialists was one of the decisive factors in Lore's forced resignation as editor of the *Volkszeitung* in 1931.[17] The paper's vacillating ideological commitment has led one commentator to refer to it simply as an organ of the Communist Party, a position that needs some qualification.[18]

Numerous German and bilingual trade union journals bear witness to the preponderance of Germans in certain trades and crafts[19] as well as to traditional Germanic feelings of solidarity. These trade unionists also supported the very influential Arbeiter-Kranken- und Sterbekasse (now Workmen's Benefit Fund), a medical and life insurance cooperative founded by German-American workers in 1884. By 1937 the Krankenkasse had almost 50,000 members.[20] Always in the vanguard of left-wing Socialist endeavor, the organization gave its support to most Communist-led Popular Front activities (1935–39) among German Americans. The pivotal figure in these machinations was Otto Sattler,[21] the esteemed editor of *Solidarität,* organ of the Krankenkasse. Sattler by 1935 was undoubtedly the Nestor of the German-American labor movement and ideally suited for such largely honorary positions as president of the German-American League for Culture (Deutsch-

Amerikanischer Kulturverband), a large anti-Nazi organization whose policies reflected the interests of its Communist members. Always the ubiquitous godfather, Sattler was present at the birth of many German-American clubs and newspapers of either Communist or Socialist parentage. Though he was often attacked as a tool of the Communists, it must be emphasized that in the 1930s his pronounced anti-Fascist stance restrained a number of German Americans from succumbing to Nazi intimidations and blandishments. Most probably he saw himself in the role of mediator among the warring factions of the German-American labor movement.

The anti-Nazi camp also included a number of Socialist organizations whose nominal interests were recreation, sports, and other of the non-political amenities of life. Many of them date from the nineteenth century, such as the Freidenkerbund,[22] the Turners, the Naturfreunde,[23] and the Arbeiter Sängerbund. Their members made up a dependable audience for anti-Nazi publications and the pages of their organizational newspapers were always open to contributions from exiled comrades — an opportunity often seized for the diffusion of radical political sentiments. An exemplary case was that of the émigré journalist Walther Victor, whose short and stormy tenure as editor of the *Sänger Zeitung* (organ of the Arbeiter Sängerbund) lasted only a year (1942), long enough for his readers to rebel against an inflammable radicalism coupled with blunt criticism of their musical abilities.[24]

COMMUNIST PARTY OF AMERICA

The intricate and often melodramatic story of the birth of the Communist Party of America (CPA) has been given its definitive presentation by Theodore Draper. To a greater degree than in the Socialist parties, the foreign-language groups were dominant during the formative years of American Communism. Draper estimates that as late as 1921, "the overwhelming majority of both members and sympathizers, probably as high as 90 percent, were foreign-speaking."[25] ·

For a number of reasons the Germans, while the largest foreign-language group in the United States, were one of the weaker groups in the CPA. During the years 1922 through 1925, membership figures in the German section were respectively, 463, 461, 422, and 350.[26] The strong tradition of Socialist Party activity and the influence of older labor leaders kept many German Americans out of the Communist camp at this time. Changing tactics, the attempts during the 1930s and 1940s to develop a mass party with its attendant army of sympathizers, resulted in a corresponding membership increase in the foreign-language groups, although national figures are not available.[27] During this same period both Communists and Socialists were rivals for the loyalties of the incoming emigrants.[28] Little headway was made by the Communist Party with the rank and file, but the party attracted a group of sympathetic intellectuals, some of whom were already members of the German Communist Party (KPD). The CPA in cooperation with its exiled German comrades and sympathizers did succeed in controlling or disrupting most of the organizations jointly established by German Americans and émigrés.

One indication of Communism's lack of appeal to the German-American worker was the nonexistence of a Communist German-language daily paper.[29] In 1935 the CPA claimed nine foreign-language dailies: two Finnish, two Lithuanian, and one each in Hungarian, Yiddish, Russian, Slovak, and Ukrainian.[30] Repeated attempts to establish a German daily always met with failure (more details on this in Chapter V). Despite this seeming lack of support, the party went to great lengths to influence the German-speaking worker, not primarily to create a strong German-American wing of the party, but to maintain a sounding board for Soviet propaganda.

The so-called "Third Period" of Comintern policy was operative in the United States for roughly seven years (1928–1935). Characteristic of this policy was the violent opposition to all existent Socialist parties (in Communist parlance, "Social Fascist") and non-Communist unions as well as a belief in the imminent demise of capitalistic society. This struggle against capitalist and "Social Fascist" alike meant abandonment of a policy of working within existing labor groups for a new policy of open opposition to the non-Communist Left.

The "Third Period" also had its impact on German-American life. With the usual pomp and circumstance, new Communist singing societies (Arbeiter-Sängerchöre) and gymnastic groups (Arbeiter Turn- und Sportbunde von Amerika) were organized. A rival to the well-entrenched Krankenkasse, the International Workers' Order, was greeted with indignation by the non-Communist press.[31] A Communist version of the Freidenkerbund, the Arbeitsgemeinschaft proletarischer Freidenker, for a short while issued a monthly bulletin, Die Stimme, a very modest publication.[32] Most of these new organizations were short-lived, vanishing only to reappear in a new guise, a response to the changing political environment. Not until Stalin's reversal of the "Third Period" line (in the United States sometime in 1935) did the Communists actually enter into the anti-Nazi struggle, abandoning their former ploys, such as dual unionism, for a new grand plan—a Popular Front against

Hitler under the tutelage of Soviet Russia. This period of German-American history, which coincided with the arrival of the new émigrés, will be treated in Chapter 5.

German-American Apathy in 1933

The disappearance of the German Americans as a political bloc after 1920 was directly attributable to the anti-German hysteria that accompanied America's entry into the First World War. Once bitten, twice shy became the rule of conduct for the bourgeois German-language press:

> The German press no longer was active politically and tried to avoid controversial issues. The disastrous experience of the war years had convinced many publishers that it was wise to have no editorial policies. By 1940, papers like the *Cincinnati Freie Presse,* the *Wächter und Anzeiger* of Cleveland, and the *Tägliche Tribüne* of Omaha contained almost no editorial comment.[33]

Studies of the German-American press show quite a high degree of either pro-Nazi or neutral sentiment; the fear of provoking advertisers (including German firms) and occasional acceptance of subsidies from the German government after 1933 no doubt helped to reinforce this attitude.[34] Even during World War II, as Joseph Roucek pointed out, "Only a few German newspapers with woefully small circulation [were] aggressively anti-Nazi. The great majority [tried] to sidetrack the issue of the war, a difficult feat in any language, but particularly so in German."[35] Like the press, the academic world was attacked for neutrality or pro-Nazi leanings. Gerhart Seger, later editor of the *Neue Volks-Zeitung,* wrote in 1940 that of the ninety-three academic institutions at which he lectured, only on three occasions had the German departments taken an official part in the proceedings—at the universities of Washington, Nebraska, and Michigan. Seger further classed the German-American population at that time as being 5 percent pro-, 5 percent anti-Nazi, and 90 percent indifferent.[36]

Most impartial observers of the German-American community (or *Auslandsdeutschtum*) would agree with Seger and not indiscriminately accuse it of being pro-Nazi; but neither, one must add, was there any great wave of sympathy for the anti-Nazi refugees. The relationship of the German anti-Nazi exiles to the *Auslandsdeutschtum* in the United States can be described then as singularly unharmonious.[37] The latter did not provide the kind of support which, for example, émigrés from Italy, Poland, France, and Czechoslovakia found and were "on the whole opposed or indifferent to the efforts of the anti-Nazis."[38] To combat this indifference and to counteract pro-Nazi propaganda were two chief reasons for disseminating Free German literature in the United States; it was the indeterminable number of anti-Nazis among the German Americans plus the new arrivals who would form the readership base for these publications.

And how large was this body of emigrants? Accurate statistics cannot be derived exclusively from the records of the Immigration and Naturalization Service since aliens may have entered on immigration quotas, visitors' or emergency visas.[39] In his usual thorough fashion Maurice Davie has investigated the many problems involved and finally arrived at a cautious estimate of 218,298 German and Austrian refugees admitted to this country from 1933 through 1944. Of these about 110,000 had declared themselves as Jewish. This latter figure seems in line with later estimates of between 100,000 and 150,000 German and Austrian Jewish immigrants for the same span of years.[40] If we accept Davie's calculations, we must admit that the Jews represented only slightly more than one-half of the German-speaking emigrations. It is believed that the true percentage of Jews was higher than that, probably closer to 75 percent.[41] Unfortunately, there has yet been no study of the non-Jewish elements of the emigration.

Notes

1. Carl Wittke, *The German-Language Press in America* (Lexington: Univ. of Kentucky Press, 1957), p.282.

2. Heinz Kloss, "German-American Language Maintenance Efforts," in J.A. Fishman, ed., *Language Loyalty in the United States* (The Hague: Mouton, 1966), p.213.

3. Exceptions being: John A. Hawgood, *The Tragedy of German-America* (New York: Putnam, 1940) and Heinz Kloss, *Um die Einigung des Deutschamerikanertums* (Berlin: Volk und Reich Verlag, 1937).

4. Ralph F. Bischoff, *Nazi Conquest through German Culture* (Cambridge: Harvard Univ. Pr., 1942), p.158–59.

5. See Guenther Roth, *The Social Democrats in Imperial Germany* (Totowa, N.J.: Bedminster Pr., 1963) for similar developments in Germany. He expands upon the concept of a Socialist subculture in great detail.

6. Hawgood, op. cit., p.272.

7. George N. Shuster, "Those of German Descent," *Common Ground,* 3:31 (Winter 1943).

8. Dieter Cunz, "Rise and Fall of the German Americans in Baltimore," *Common Ground,* 7:65 (Spring 1947).

9. Erwin H. Klaus, "Die fortschrittliche deutschamerikanische Bewegung," *Aufbau Almanach* (New York, 1941), p.73–82.

10. "The contributions of the German Turner (Turnvereine) to American political and cultural history are among the most important of the immigration of the nineteenth century.... The Turnvereine [gymnastic societies]... became centers of German radicalism in the abolitionist movement of the 1850s." As time went on, they lost their militant radicalism and developed into primarily social organizations. Carl Wittke, *Refugees of Revolution* (Philadelphia: Univ. of Pennsylvania Pr., 1952), p.147–48.

11. Ibid., p.88–89. Of the many relevant studies, see in particular Eric E. Hirshler, ed., *Jews from Germany in the United States* (New York: Farrar, 1955).

12. *Jews in Relation to the Cultural Milieu of the Germans up to the Eighteen Eighties* (New York: The author, 1947), and "German Jews in New York City in the 19th Century," *YIVO Annual of Jewish Social Science,* 11:9–38 (1956/57).

13. Quoted in the *German American* (N.Y.), April, 1944, a militant anti-Nazi newspaper supported by the Communist Party.

14. Theodore Draper, *The Roots of American Communism,* (New York: Viking, 1963), p.32.

15. Ibid., p.67.

16. Jonas, a well-known Social Democrat from Berlin, and Douai (1819–1888) were the first editors. Douai, who came to New York in 1852 after stops in San Antonio and Boston, directed the *Volkszeitung* from 1878 to 1888. He also started the first German kindergarten in America. Another editor during the 1880s was Serge Schevitsch, exiled Russian nobleman and husband of Helena von Racowitza over whom Ferdinand Lassalle fought a fatal duel. Schlueter was also a leading Social Democrat who came to the United States in 1888 and became the historian of the German-American labor movement. Lore (1875–1942), who studied under the economist Sombart, came to the United States in 1905; by 1915 he was executive secretary of the German Socialist Federation in New York and in 1916 succeeded Schlueter as editor. He joined the *New York Post* as an anti-Nazi journalist in 1934.

17. See p.32 for further details.

18. Nathan Glazer, *The Social Basis of American Communism* (New York: Harcourt, 1961), p.80. According to Glazer, the Communists claimed the *Volkszeitung* as their own at the fourth annual convention of the party held in 1925. He further states that after a few years, ca. 1927, the paper "was no longer appearing." Actually, the *Volkszeitung* was never an officially Communist-financed publication; and after 1925, of course, the Communists, following Lore's expulsion, could no longer claim it—but the daily continued to be published without interruption until Oct. 12, 1932.

19. Most notably, furniture workers, bakers, restaurant workers, cigar makers, and printers. The German typographical union, Typographia, published the *Buchdruckerzeitung* monthly until 1940. For additional data see Lloyd G. Reynolds and Charles C. Killingsworth, *Trade Union Publications* (3; Baltimore: Johns Hopkins Pr., 1944–45).

20. Karl J. R. Arndt and May E. Olson, *German-American Newspapers and Periodicals 1732–1955* (Heidelberg: Quelle & Meyer, 1961), p.396.

21. Sattler was born in Emmendingen, Baden, in 1872 (d.1950), learned bookbinding, studied philosophy and literature at the University of Zürich, and traveled extensively for fifteen years. He became a journalist in the United States and published volumes of poetry and travel sketches in German. As an authority and lecturer on German-American history, he was widely known in all parts of the country. On Sattler's earlier career, see William Frederic Kamman, *Socialism in German American Literature* (Philadelphia: Americana Germanica Pr., 1917), p.115–17.

22. The Freidenkerbund von Nordamerika (after 1933 known as the Free Thought League of North America) issued the weekly *Freidenker* from 1872 to Oct. 25, 1942.

23. An international Socialist sports and social group founded in Vienna (1895). See Werner Jurkowski, "Geschichte und Aufgaben der Naturfreunde in USA," *Deutsches Volksecho* (N.Y.), July 8, 1939.

24. See Appendix II, p.186–87.

25. Draper, op. cit., p.272.

26. Glazer, op. cit., p.50.

27. The New York State party in 1938 alone claimed 600 members in its German-language group (Communist Party of America, New York State Committee, *Proceedings of the Tenth Convention* [New York, 1938], p.276).

28. Stefan Heym, editor of the Communist *Deutsches Volksecho,* affirmed the need to develop organized political groups for the newcomers, "who are to a man thoroughly unpolitical creatures." Such a Communist-dominated organization exclusively of immigrants never materialized *(Deutsches Volksecho,* June 19, 1939).

29. Apart from the *Volkszeitung* for the years 1919–25. According to the independent Socialist newspaper *Kampfsignal* (N.Y.), 20,000 subscribers would have been needed to support a daily among German workers (July 29, 1933).

30. Glazer, op. cit., p.84.

31. *Kampfsignal,* Feb. 18, 1933, in a front-page article titled: "Perfidie gegen die eigene Klasse!"

32. Its circulation was probably only one to two hundred copies per issue. Cf. the case of the *Labor Defender,* the national organ (for German-Americans as well) of the Comintern-controlled International Labor Defense. According to a statement in the Communist Party organ, *Der Arbeiter* (N.Y.), issue of Jan. 22, 1929, the circulation of the *Labor Defender* was only 200 copies per issue in the winter and 150 in the summer!

33. Wittke, op. cit., p.283.

34. In 1941 a presidential committee reported that 90 percent of the German-American press was pro-Nazi. Louis L. Gerson, *The Hyphenate in Recent American Politics and Diplomacy* (Lawrence, Kans.: Univ. of Kansas Pr., 1964), p.121. The case of Val. S. Peter may also be cited; editor of the *Tägliche Omaha Tribüne,* owner of an extensive chain of German-language newspapers and a number of travel bureaus, he was charged both with receiving a regular subsidy from the German Consulate and for aiding Nazi prisoners of war in Canada before Pearl Harbor. While not criminal acts, they indicate the vulnerability of the conservative German-American community to National Socialist intrigues. See O. John Rogge, *The Official German Report* (New York: Yoseloff, 1961), p.342.

35. "Foreign Language Press in World War II," *Sociology and Social Research,* 27:464 (July, 1943).

36. As quoted in Berendsohn 2:219.

37. For several reasons: besides the problem of anti-Semitism, there was, according to Helge Pross, a good deal of anti-intellectual *ressentiment* on the part of the German minority which was "overwhelmingly Christian, and socially belonging mostly to the lower middle-class" *(Die deutsche akademische Emigration nach den Vereinigten Staaten: 1933–1941,* p.32). The emigrants also were not escaping from an invading army – Hitler *was* the legal head of the German state.

38. Lewis J. Edinger, *German Exile Politics* (Berkeley: Univ. of California Pr., 1956), p.252.

39. The President's Advisory Committee on Political Refugees, active from July, 1940 to July, 1941, issued emergency permanent visas enabling 2000 members of the German intelligentsia to enter the United States. Maurice R. Davie, *Refugees in America* (New York: Harper, 1947), p.31–32.

40. Julius and Edith Hirsch, "Berufliche Eingliederung und wirtschaftliche Leistung der deutsch-juedischen Einwanderung in die Vereinigten Staaten (1934–1960)," in American Federation of Jews from Central Europe, Inc., *Twenty Years . . . 1940–1960* (New York, 1961), p.44.

41. Donald Peterson Kent, *The Refugee Intellectual* (New York: Columbia Univ. Pr., 1953), p.17.

III
German Socialist Press in the United States 1933–1945

The Nonaligned Left

Émigré German Socialists in America were represented by one major party, a handful of splinter groups, and a number of isolated spokesmen. In descending order of importance they were: The SPD (the party recognized by the American Federation of Labor as the official representative of German labor); the coterie around Karl Frank (alias Paul Hagen), left-wing Socialist and leader of the New Beginners in the United States whose personal influence extended far beyond the limits of his organization; the homeless Left, émigrés unwilling to go along with the SPD or the Communist Party and powerless to act on their own. To this latter group we can add those German immigrants of pre-1933 vintage who were likewise estranged from the major workers' parties. From the periphery of German-American radicalism (and this is of special interest for us) two periodicals arose—the *Kampfsignal* and *Gegen den Strom*—which, during the crucial 1930s, served much like the chorus in Greek tragedy, supplying a running commentary on the intrigues and misadventures of exile politics.

The *Kampfsignal* (N.Y.) first saw the light of day in December, 1932, and on the thirty-first day of that month the Communist Party organ *Der Arbeiter* (N.Y.) with heavy mockery greeted the birth of a "new German humor magazine." Continuing in the same vein, the next issue of the *Arbeiter* contained within a suitable black border an expression of sorrow over the sudden death of the *"Krampfsignal* [sic]." The announcement was premature, however, since the new publication did eke out a precarious existence (largely through the support of the Krankenkasse and a few sympathetic labor unions) until November 1934. The *Kampf-signal* arose from the ashes of the old *New Yorker Volkszeitung,* the Socialist daily that in October of 1932 had succumbed to a severe case of internal dissension. In charge of the new periodical was a crew of young and radical German Americans including many former supporters and colleagues of Ludwig Lore (e.g. *Kampfsignal* editor Selmar Scho-cken) who found a new political lodestone in A. J. Muste's Conference for Progressive Labor Action.[1] The *Kampfsignal* was also "fraternally" related to the Sozialistische Arbeiterpartei of Germany (SAP), whose party newspaper in Berlin bore the same name.[2]

Both the SAP and the Conference for Progressive Labor Action were motivated by the idea of giving new direction (still within the Marxist context) to the disunited political labor movement in their own countries. By 1933 the *Kampfsignal* was caught up in the burgeoning anti-Fascist front in the United States, vainly opposing its threatened domination by Communist Party members. Its hope of becoming the German-American voice of non-Communist radicalism was stifled by the competition of the far more powerful *Arbeiter* and *Neue Volks-Zeitung.*

The same fate awaited what was to be the last attempt at creating an independent German-language radical periodical in this country — Richard Bek-Gran's *Gegen den Strom.*[3] Bek-Gran came to the United States after World War I, working first as a salesman in a German-American bookstore and later teaching in a progressive school in Peekskill, N.Y. He joined the Communist Party in 1930. After an active career in the German Bureau, he left the Party in 1937, and following one familiar pattern of Communist disillusionment gave us in *Gegen den Strom* a unique account of the Party's work with German Americans. The journal, during its short life, attracted both "reformed" Communists as well as dissidents of other stripes including an-archo-syndicalists and disappointed liberals such as Rudolf Brandl. While the content of *Gegen den Strom* is often highly interesting — there are, for example, several detailed accounts of Communist infiltration in German-American organizations — the intent is always polemical; and these "factual" reports must be read with caution. As spokesmen for the disestablished Left, both the *Kampfsignal* and *Gegen den Strom* give us the opportunity to view émigré politics from another vantage point.

The SPD in the United States

When the vivacious Reichstag delegate Toni Sender and the Social Democratic journalist Gerhart Seger, author of the first eyewitness report on German concentration camps,[4] arrived in the United States in 1934 for an extensive lecture tour, there was already in existence an embryo organization of the SPD in exile. One year earlier a Deutsche Sprachgruppe had been established (or more accurately revivified) by the New York branch of the [American] Socialist Party,[5] a conservative group for which the exiled Social Democrats felt a natural affinity. The Sprachgruppe met regularly, initiated lectures, and developed into a regular SPD club which soon made useful contacts in many areas of American life.[6] It remained through 1945 the political organization with the broadest membership base and the most immediate appeal for the newly arrived emigrant in New York.

Blossoming from the friendly contact between émigré and American labor leaders, the German Labor Delegation was constituted as the official representation of German labor in the United States. It enjoyed from the first the patronage of the American Federation of Labor and its president, William Green.[7] Most leading Social Democrats in exile were members of the Delegation; the well-known editor and publicist, Friedrich Stampfer, who arrived in 1940, was considered spokesman for the group. The Delegation carried out three functions: (1) it solidified contacts within refugee groups; (2) after the war it worked on programs for a "New Germany"; and (3) it was recognized as the "authority" to present SPD views to the American public whenever called upon. The *Neue Volks-Zeitung* was the German-language organ of the SPD in exile, but the Delegation occasionally issued other publications in German and English.[8]

Two organizations, the German American Congress for Democracy and the Association of Free Germans, sounded suspiciously alike in name but actually had quite different functions. The GACD was conceived as a nonparty coordinating body, a link between the SPD and other German-American groups that was intended to serve as a strong anti-Communist force in conscious opposition to the Communist-dominated Deutsch-Amerikanischer Kulturverband. It was, needless to say, the national organization most resolutely supported by the *Neue Volks-Zeitung*. The Association of Free Germans, on the other hand, was composed exclusively of German émigrés and only former members of the Weimar Republic coalition parties—the SPD, the Democrats, and the Zentrum Partei. No former Nazis or Communist Party members *under any circumstances* were allowed into the Association—a move to eliminate Otto Strasser, Hermann Rauschning, and Karl Frank (the leader of the New Beginners and a former KPD member) from possible participation.[9] As the German Labor Delegation was considered the official voice of German labor, so the Association of Free Germans demanded recognition as a German government in exile:

The organization assured itself of the strong backing of American labor by forming an energetic Committee of Sponsors with William Green, A.F. of L. president at its head and having at its disposal a first rate propaganda apparatus set up years ago by the Social Democratic Party and the vigorous German American Congress for Democracy — embarked on its campaign at the time the United States actively entered the war. This campaign consisted in the suggestion to the American people that the Association of Free Germans, Inc., is the sole and most worthy representative of democratic Germans.[10]

The newspaper that served as the organ of the SPD and its affiliated organizations was the then weekly *Neue Volks-Zeitung,* a new version of the long-time standard bearer of German-American Socialism, the *New Yorker Volkszeitung*. After fifty-five years (on October 12, 1932), the venerable paper was forced to shut down; this event came only one year after its controversial editor Ludwig Lore had departed. As has already been noted, the radicalism of Lore was at variance with the conservative Social Democracy of many of the *Volkszeitung* supporters. By 1930 the situation became even stickier and rumors of fraudulent dealings by Lore were in the air (he was later publicly accused of embezzlement). A retrospective editorial in 1933 stated that a special committee had found Lore guilty as charged but that he had been allowed to resign without public disclosure. This, at least, was the official version. The accusation may have been largely an attempt to discredit Lore who was extremely popular with the German-speaking workers.[11]

By December 17, 1932 the first issue of the *Neue Volks-Zeitung* was on the newsstands. The paper, sponsored by the Progressive Publishing Association, Inc., whose members represented a variety of German-American Socialist and labor organizations, was now solidly conservative Socialist in its views, following the position of the so-called "Old Guard" of the American Socialist Party. Siegfried Jungnitsch was the acting editor until the appointment of the German Social Democrat, Gerhart Seger, in May of 1936. Born in a time of crisis for Germany, the *Neue Volks-Zeitung* (through 1936) maintained a close relationship with exiled SPD compatriots, many of whom were regular contributors from Europe. When Seger took on the direction of the newspaper, he was ably backed up by an experienced staff of émigré Social Democrat journalists and politicians such as Rudolf Katz, Julius Epstein, and Friedrich Stampfer. The book reviewing chores were handled with polish and expertise by émigré writer Karl Jakob Hirsch (under the pseudonym of Joe Gassner).

This "take-over" by émigré politicians of the leading German-American Socialist weekly did not pass without some criticism from the resident population. One disgruntled German-American radical pulled no punches:

> He [the émigré politician] hasn't the slightest realization that he is not in his blessed *Weimarisch* Berlin, but in a new world ... and with his unseemly protestations, helps his enemies and hurts his friends. Nothing bothers him. He makes use of the God-given organizations in the good old U.S.A. as he did his own in Germany, which he ruled from top to bottom. That our country is another country and that its people are different, that his own countrymen who indeed speak his language, don't even understand him, disturbs him not at all. With the words, ICH BIN EMIGRANT, he sets himself above everyone else and no one contradicts him. That he and his arrogance endanger the old workers' organizations and can destroy them, must be made clear before it is too late. He speaks of unity and means his own party and its hangers-on. He speaks of a People's Front and means Weimar and its ill-starred Republic. He speaks of the future but he has bartered away the past, our history, our life and the lives of our families ... he has the unheard of audacity to pose as our leader ... Many times he burns his fingers and then disappears and works as a wirepuller through his faction. But always he is the same—a parasite.[12]

"The Oldest Anti-Nazi Newspaper," "Published in USA Since 1932—Banned Germany Since 1933," these were masthead mottoes from the years 1941 and 1942 presenting the *Neue Volks-Zeitung* in the role of an émigré SPD paper. Actually the majority of its readers were still drawn from an earlier generation of German-American workers. The *Neue Volks-Zeitung,* just like its predecessor, was supported in the final analysis by the numerous German-American Socialist and trade union groups, many of whom used the paper as a kind of organizational news bulletin. One page entitled "Aus der Arbeiterbewegung" was set aside for this very purpose, allowing one to follow the day-to-day activities of the Roland Society, the singing societies, the Naturfreunde, and a host of other clubs and unions—some seventy in number. Circulation fluctuated from 21,850 in 1934 to 17,632 in 1949, with a low of 9068 in 1946.[13] Although the majority of readers were inherited from the defunct *Volkszeitung* as were many of the advertisers, the paper also appealed to numerous émigrés; the exact proportion is not open to verification.

Seger remained editor to the very end in 1949, though by that time most of his colleagues had returned to Germany. When the rejuvenated *Volkszeitung* "died" for the last time, it marked the end of an era of American Socialism. A lot of the fighting spirit had left the paper with the departure of its staff of exiles. It was once again primarily a German-American Socialist paper, and as such doomed to extinction

since, in the words of Daniel Bell: "By 1950 American socialism as a
political and social fact had become simply a notation in the archives of
history."[14]

New Beginners in the U.S.A.

Shortly after the outbreak of war, Karl Frank (using the name Paul
Hagen) began his fund raising and propaganda work in the United
States.[15] He was one of the few New Beginners of rank to reach the
United States (Paul Hertz, formerly on the SPD Executive Committee,
was another); the majority of those who escaped from France had made
their way to England. The British and American branches soon went
their separate ways. In 1941, the New Beginners and other émigré
Socialist and trade union groups in Britain succeeded in forming a united
front—the Union of German Socialist Organizations in Great Britain
—while in New York, the obdurate rivalry between the German Labor
Delegation and the New Beginners and their two chief strategists,
Stampfer and Frank, prohibited a similar development.

The continuance of their *Reports from Inside Germany* was of paramount importance for the New Beginners as this was their only means
of counteracting SPD influence in the various host countries. In addition
to their London-based *Reports* (1939–1941), these exiled Socialists issued a French and—until April, 1940—a Norwegian edition. In the
United States, Frank's organization (the American Friends of German
Freedom) published *Inside Germany Reports* (1938–1945) a venture
that exhibited somewhat more survival power.[16] The German-language
reports issued by the New Beginners (*I.B. Berichte*) ceased in 1940, and
Kurt Kleim records that the last two numbers were issued from New
York.[17] Frank and his associates were able to convince many Americans that their group of left-wing Socialists represented a strong underground party in Germany, a proposition that by 1940, at any rate, was
wholly unfounded. Even in 1934, when Lore could refer to them as the
"living embryo in the dying body of Germany's labor movement,"[18] a
more reliable estimate of the party's true strength was a membership of
not more than 300.[19] The Berlin group led by Hermann Brill was the
most active unit and a reliable source of information during the early
years—but after the mass arrests in 1935, it virtually ceased to exist.[20]

One fact that plagued some New Beginners (especially Karl Frank)
was their earlier affiliation with the Communist Party in Germany,[21] and
denunciations of Frank as a crypto-Communist were a recurring feature
of exile politics in the United States, whether in the pages of the *Neue
Volks-Zeitung* or in Ruth Fischer's vitriolic anti-Communist sheet, *The*

Network.[22] The Hagen-Frank cause célèbre reached a climax in May of 1940 when a special committee of seven Socialists, called together to examine these charges, was abruptly dissolved amidst mutual recriminations and without issuing any "official" statement.[23] The final years of Frank's political career in the United States (he later retired into private life as a psychologist) were marred by the ultimate triumph of his enemies who effectively prevented his return to postwar Germany: "The continuous accusations of the German Labor Delegation that he was a Stalinist agent and adventurer, together with the attacks of the Communists, of the ex-Communists around Ruth Fischer and of the Vansittarts,[24] had succeeded in that the American authorities had denied him an exit visa, as a security risk, although many influential personalities intervened on his behalf."[25]

Conclusion

Only the *Neue Volks-Zeitung,* of all its contemporaries in the United States, can in any sense be considered a German émigré paper. The New Beginners, whose resources were put to use elsewhere in attempts to influence the thinking of English-speaking Americans, published no German-language periodical; both the *Kampfsignal* and *Gegen den Strom* were produced by, and largely for, the pre-1933 generation of German radicals. It was in the editorial offices of the *Neue Volks-Zeitung* that the former powers of the SPD — Stampfer, Katz, Grzesinski, and Aufhäuser — found a new, if more limited, outlet for their talents. The presence of this elite clique of experienced journalists and politicians certainly did add lustre and vitality to the paper, but it was transitory, giving a false sense of renewed vigor to the dying world of German-American Socialism; for unlike the earlier waves of German emigration to America of the 1880s and early 1920s, this latest did not bring with it the necessary new blood — the flock of young workers needed to keep the movement alive. The old *Volkszeitung* did manage to escape the fate of other Social Democratic papers like the *Milwaukee Vorwärts* (which had ceased publishing in 1932, unable to weather the great depression), but it was only the special circumstances engendered by World War II that enabled the *Neue Volks-Zeitung* to endure as long as 1949.

Notes

1. "Muste gathered around him a group of brilliant labor intellectuals like David Saposs, the economist, and J. B. S. Hardman, former leader of the Jewish socialists." In 1933 the CPLA was transformed into the American Workers Party which promptly fell

victim to what Daniel Bell has termed the "cannibalism" of the American Trotskyites. Daniel Bell, "The Background and Development of Marxian Socialism in the United States," in Donald Drew Egbert and Stow Persons; eds., *Socialism and American Life* (Princeton: Princeton Univ. Pr., 1952), 1:385. See also Muste, *The Essays of A. J. Muste* (Indianapolis: Bobbs-Merrill, 1966), p.162–74.

2. The *Kampfsignal* (Berlin) was banned by the Nazis in March, 1933. Kurt Rosenfeld and Jakob Walcher (one of the founders of the KPD) were the best-known SAP leaders who came to America.

3. March, 1938–Oct./Nov., 1939.

4. *Oranienburg* (Karlsbad: Graphia, 1934). Gerhart Seger (1896–1966), a pilot in the German Air Force during World War I, became on his return to civilian life a militant Socialist and ardent pacifist (at one time he was Secretary General of the German Peace Society). In 1930 he entered the Reichstag, and in 1933 was one of the first to be imprisoned by the Nazis. After a dramatic escape from Oranienburg he made his way to the United States. Editor from 1936 to 1949 of the *Neue Volks-Zeitung* (N.Y.), Seger's later years were devoted to writing and a continuing involvement in American politics. See Felix E. Hirsch, "Gerhart Seger: in the Tradition of Carl Schurz," *American-German Review*, 33:26–27 (April/May 1967).

5. After 1936 the New York group split from the Socialist Party and became the nucleus of the more conservative Social Democratic Federation.

6. In 1936 the chairman of the Deutsche Sprachgruppe was Rudolf Katz, later an associate editor of the *Neue Volks-Zeitung*. The board of directors included Max Brauer, former mayor of Altona; Wilhelm Sollmann; Albert Grzesinski, former Police President of Berlin; and former Reichstag members Siegfried Aufhäuser and F. W. Wagner.

7. Michael Kuehl, "Die exilierte demokratische Linke in U.S.A.," *Zeitschrift für Politik*, 4:281 (July 1957). The committee of AFL advisors to the Delegation included Green, George Meany, and David Dubinsky.

8. In particular: *Letters on German Labor* (N.Y.), July–Sept. 1943.

9. *Aufbau* (N.Y.), Jan. 16, 1942, p.7.

10. George W. Pate, "Free Germans in the U.S.," *The Christian Science Monitor,* Nov. 14, 1942, p.5.

11. *Neue Volks-Zeitung,* Dec. 16, 1933, p.4.

12. Hannes Schmidt, "Unsere Emigranten," *Gegen den Strom,* 1:12–13 (May 1938).

13. Karl J. R. Arndt and May E. Olson, *German-American Newspapers and Periodicals 1732–1955* (Heidelberg: Quelle & Meyer, 1961), p.385. Like its predecessor the *Neue Volks-Zeitung* had both a New York edition and one for national distribution. *Neue Volks-Zeitung,* Sept. 13, 1941, p.4.

14. Bell, op. cit., p.405.

15. The most extensive study of the New Beginners is Kurt Kleim, "Der sozialistische Widerstand gegen das Dritte Reich dargestellt an der Gruppe 'Neu Beginnen' " (unpublished Ph.D. dissertation, Univ. of Marburg, 1957).

16. No issues were published in 1942.

17. Kleim, op. cit., p.256.

18. Ludwig Lore, "German Socialism Underground," *New Republic,* 80:8 (August 15, 1934).

19. Erich Matthias, *Sozialdemokratie und Nation* (Stuttgart: Deutsche Verlags-Anstalt, 1952), p.292.

20. Hans J. Reichhardt, "Neu Beginnen," *Jahrbuch für die Geschichte Mittel-und Ostdeutschlands,* 12:186 (1963). Maier-Hultschin charged that most of the later *Reports* issued by the New Beginners from abroad were "creations of fantasy." "Nochmals: Neubeginnen," *Politische Studien,* 6, Nr.70:49 (1956).

21. Frank had left the KPD in 1921, worked in various Communist opposition groups and joined the SAP in 1932. He entered the SPD soon afterwards and immediately became a leader of the young radicals (the New Beginners) within the parent party.

22. Ruth Fischer was a leading personality in the KPD during the 1920s. Unlike her brother Gerhart Eisler, she did not remain in the party. Both spent the war years in the United States. *The Network* (1944–45) specialized in uncovering German Stalinists among the émigrés.

23. Pro-Frank members were Gustave Richter (i.e., Joseph Buttinger), Max Hirschberg, and the American, John Herling; on the other side were Rudolf Katz, William Karlin and Max Brauer. Paul Brissenden was the American chairman, and Serafino Romualdi vice-chairman, later acting chairman upon Brissenden's resignation. The immediate cause of the affair (soon lost sight of) was the accusation that Frank had written letters to American Socialist and Jewish leaders intimating that conservative SPD exile Wilhelm Sollmann held anti-Semitic views and should not be supported by their organizations. A transcript of these proceedings carried on in English — a remarkable 316-page document to be found in the *Paul Hertz Papers* on microfilm at the Hoover Institution Library (reel 17) — gives a vivid picture of the acrimonious relations between the old-line Social Democrats and the New Beginners. A report on this secret inquiry in the *Neue Volks-Zeitung*, June 28, 1941, p.3, is not completely accurate.

24. After Lord Vansittart, whose *Black Record* (London, 1941) attempted to prove that the Nazis were only the natural product of German history and that the real guilt lay in the inherently warlike character of the people — thus anyone believing in the collective guilt of the German nation, an opinion shared by a number of émigrés, e.g., Emil Ludwig and Friedrich Wilhelm Foerster. See Matthias, op. cit., p.268–81.

25. Kleim, op. cit., p.273.

IV
German Communists
in the United States
1933–1945

The Decade of the *Arbeiter* (1927 – 1937)

This chapter does not pretend to be a thoroughgoing analysis of the Communist Party's role during the emigration; rather its purpose is to give the reader an overview of organizations, newspapers, and personalities connected with German-American Communism, unquestionably one of the vital shaping forces of émigré political life. To gain a proper understanding of the organizational and propaganda methods utilized to attract the German-American worker (and later the new emigrants), it is necessary to go back to 1927, the year the German Bureau of the Communist Party of America (CPA) issued its first official newspaper.

The language bureaus were the operational bases for work with foreign minorities in the United States, directing the activities of the foreign-language branches – local units made up entirely of members with the same language background. These branches were nothing more than the old semiautonomous language federations.

In 1925 the Communists initiated a very serious campaign to subordinate the language branches to the will of the Central Committee (later National Committee) and so create a unified, homogeneous party; one of the steps taken was to change the name of the basic organizational unit from branch to fraction. According to the 1925 party Constitution, a fraction was made up of "all members of the party speaking the same language *within* a subsection, section or city organization."[1] Though the party disapproved of strong independent foreign-language federations, it still was tenaciously trying to mold foreign-born workers—be they Italians, Germans, Finns, or Greeks—into trained political activists. It was an uphill road as Comrade "F. Brown" intimated in a speech before the eighth convention of the CPA in 1934, quoting a report from Youngstown, Ohio (the language group is not identified):

> There is a very low level of political understanding, irregular attendance and participation in the so-called general Party work, a shrinking from any activity that is not within the narrow shell of 'society doings'. Their activities in the main are those of the old line of federationalism—that is, limited to associating with their old friends, seeing the same faces year in year out, having a dance and lecture here and there and, of course, giving financial support to their language press.[2]

The German Bureau, under the direction of the Central Committee, controlled all work among the German Americans including the official German-language press. The determination of the Bureau to develop a strong newspaper arose from the special function allotted to the press by Communist tacticians. As Philip Selznick has remarked:

> The communist press is more than a medium for the dissemination of party propaganda. An incidental potentiality for mobilizing the membership is explicitly recognized and exploited. The great emphasis on the importance of the party press—far in excess of that normal in political organizations—is due as much to the organizational utility as to the propaganda potential of the material issued.[3]

A voice of the German Bureau, however it may have been disguised to conform to the many changes in party line, existed uninterruptedly from 1927 to 1945.[4] In addition, an internal bulletin of a strictly confidential nature was apparently circulated among the members of the Bureau and leaders of language branches. To round out the picture, all the organizational gambits of the Bureau, the anti-Nazi groups, the youth clubs, the Proletarian Freethinkers' League, et al., had their own German-language membership bulletins.

The years 1928 through 1935 were, roughly speaking, the period of ultra-Leftism in international Communist policy, a time when the party was strongly in opposition to all existent Socialist groups and non-Communist trade unions in the United States—they also coincided approximately with the life span of the first official German-language party newspaper, *Der Arbeiter* (1927–1937). The ousting of Ludwig Lore, editor of the *Volkszeitung*, from his post as Secretary of the German Bureau and his expulsion from the Communist Party at the fourth party convention in 1925[5] indicated to party leaders that the time was now ripe for a purely Communist German-language newspaper, since the *Volkszeitung* was no longer at their disposal.

Der Arbeiter was on the stands by September 15, 1927, and from the outset suffered from inadequate financial support; this led to the establishment of a network of worker's organizations whose real purpose would be to support the new Communist paper. The tactics of party bureaucrats were almost crudely opportunistic as they urged the undermining of such existing groups as the Freidenkerbünde—main branches in Philadelphia, New York, Milwaukee and Chicago—and their transformation into Arbeiterbünde. In a confidential *Rundschreiben an die deutsche Distrikt-Büros* (as quoted by E. W. Mareg) these aims are baldly stated:

> We know that these organizations for the most part are dominated by older Social Democratic elements; therefore we must go forward towards the formation of fractions and through perseverance enlarge our influence. The social and political oppression of foreign-born workers in this country will help us in winning over these workers. The official organ of the Arbeiter-Bünde is to be the *Arbeiter*. Not only will it contain official announcements, but the *Arbeiter* must be utilized to strengthen the clubs and for propaganda. By these means all club members will become interested in the *Arbeiter* and it will be possible to turn them into recruiters [for new subscriptions].[6]

It was easier to give instructions than to see them carried out; only four Bünde ever reached even a rudimentary stage of organization, and only the Philadelphia Bund showed any real signs of life. The entire maneuver had to be considered a failure.

The growing strength of Adolf Hitler and his party in Germany aroused a wave of opposition among German-American workers and an increasing desire for an organization exclusively devoted to the anti-Fascist struggle. At that time, Mareg was assigned the job of creating such an organization in the Yorkville section of New York. From its founding (December 6, 1932), the Deutscher Arbeiterklub (DAK) of Yorkville enjoyed an immediate success largely due to its complete dissimilarity to the old Bünde. Temporarily, at least, no attempt was made to turn the club into an openly Communist organization. Possession of a clubhouse increased the feeling of group identity, and this provision was made mandatory for the creation of any new Arbeiterklub. The DAK Yorkville grew rapidly, and soon there were branches in downtown New York, the Bronx, Brooklyn, and even an independent Burgenlander (Austrian) chapter in Yorkville. By 1934 the movement spread outside the city with the founding of a Hudson County and a Newark DAK. The German Bureau was quite ready to take full credit for these successes. Again, the Communist fractions in the clubs rammed through motions requiring the creation of an *Arbeiter* press fund and of shock troops for soliciting new subscriptions. Every member was obliged to become a subscriber to the paper and a weekly payment of four dollars was demanded from each club treasury. It is clear that such heroics must have raised some doubts among the members as to the purpose of their organizations.

In the autumn of 1933, Robert Bek-Gran, then a member of the CPA, was sent on a tour through the industrial centers of the East and Middle West to recruit more subscribers and to help develop new Arbeiterklubs. The number of clubs now demanded a coordinating leadership, and the first national conference of the Arbeiterklubs, held on March 24 and 25, 1934, created the Föderation der deutschen Arbeiter Klubs von Nord-America.[7] On May 1, 1934, the federation began issuing a mimeographed *Mitteilungsblatt der deutschen Arbeiter Klubs;* after eight months it had enough support to warrant a photo-offset edition. Shortly before the 1935 national conference, the Federation had planned to print a news bulletin. At this juncture, the omnipotent Central Committee of the CPA decided the bulletin should henceforth be issued as a supplement to *Der Arbeiter.* Bek-Gran and Mareg argued that this was contrary to the purpose of the clubs which were intended to present the appearance, at least, of independent workers' organizations. They were overruled by the party, however, and by the end of 1935 the Arbeiterklubs lost whatever veneer of independence they had possessed. This was the reason (again following Mareg's account) why the two originators of the Arbeiterklub movement left the party. The clubs remained in existence under various changes of name until the middle 1940s. Disenchanted remnants of the DAKs later united to form the (New York) Club Deutscher Antifaschisten in 1938, publishers of *Der Anti-Faschist* (a monthly journal), and chief support of Robert Bek-Gran's new sounding board for the alienated German-American Left—*Gegen den Strom.*

The Anti-Nazi Front

The formation of nationwide anti-Nazi organizations of German Americans and émigrés offered the Communists new opportunities to control or, at least, to influence the policies of the anti-Hitler forces in this country. The first such attempt was the ill-fated Antifaschistische Aktion (AA).[8] In February, 1933, 150 delegates from some sixty German-American labor organizations met to establish this national federation of anti-Nazi groups. The Communists, true to their disruptive ultra-leftist tactics, unhesitatingly aimed at immediate control of this new organization. An effective device used to undermine the AA, nominally open only to corporate members, was the encouragement of "illegal" individual memberships, thus allowing a phalanx of party workers to infiltrate the parent federation. German Americans were invited to join the Antifaschistische Liga which was foisted upon them as a quasi-official agency of the AA. As a result of this opportunistic policy, non-Communist groups, led by the Socialist Party-Deutsche Sprach-gruppe, one by one abandoned the obviously partisan organization. The representatives of the *Neue Volks-Zeitung* left in a huff when the AA made support of *Der Arbeiter* a prerequisite for continued membership. The last achievement of the Antifaschistische Aktion, as if in mockery of its original ideals, was the publication of the one and only issue of the newspaper *Einheitsfront* (the United Front) in August, 1934.

Greater and more enduring success was to be the lot of the CPA during the Popular Front years (1935–1939), because for once the party line was in harmony with the dominant mood of the American people. The triumph of the Nazis in Germany had brought home the necessity of a new Comintern policy of unity among the anti-Nazi forces, and this involved a fundamental change in tactics. As Howe and Coser have pointed out: "What was new, and, from a Marxist point of view, a grave heresy, was the readiness of the Communist parties to subordinate the class struggle at home to the strategic needs of the Soviet Union."[9] It was a far cry from the anti-capitalist jeremiads of the twenties to the strange new statements now appearing in the Communist press. Strange, indeed, when in 1938 the New York State Communist Party advised its German fraction to join the Steuben Society, not long before the object of its scorn:

> Who is the spokesman of the German people? ... Is it the *Volksecho* [the Communist newspaper]? Is it the Kulturverband [Communist domi-nated anti-Nazi organization]? We hear so much about the Steuben Society and other German organizations. I wonder how many German comrades realized the importance of belonging to such an organization which speaks in the name of the German people.[10]

This apparent willingness to work together with Socialist and bourgeois groups to form an anti-Nazi front resulted in two crises that marked the years 1937–1941: the creation of a new Popular-Front-oriented German Communist newspaper, the *Deutsches Volksecho* (N.Y.) and its struggle with the *Neue Volks-Zeitung;* and the Communist usurpation of control over the Deutsch-Amerikanischer Kulturverband.

The *Deutsches Volksecho*[11] was the official continuation of the *Arbeit-er* as organ of the CPA German Bureau, a fact it soon took pains to disguise. In format and content it presented an odd contrast to its predecessor. The new paper, wrote the editor with pride, "combines the advantages of the American tabloid with the best features of good German and American journalism."[12] It was the only lavishly illustrated

German-American paper of the Left and the only one to carry a proletarian comic strip (in English)—*The John Smiths,* drawn by Harold
Magin. In content no longer doctrinaire, it attempted to woo all segments of the German-American Community for the common cause and
to this end included many features in English—a woman's page, a young
people's corner, and full sports coverage. Although still Communist
controlled, the *Volksecho* accepted paid advertisements from German-American businessmen and even campaigned for more advertisers.
Under its brash young editor, Stefan Heym,[13] the party went all out to
produce a really American style paper. Members of the liberal establishment flocked to the support of the new anti-Nazi weekly and the
editor could point with satisfaction to a list of American sponsors that
included Malcolm Cowley, Arthur Garfield Hays, Max Lerner, Vito
Marcantonio, Joseph Freeman, and others.[14] Nevertheless, before long
the *Volksecho* was in serious financial difficulties, even though it boasted
of a circulation twice the size of the old *Arbeiter.*[15] The increased cost of
producing this imitation *New York Daily News* was a drain on the party
treasury, especially since most German-American labor organizations
were still in the Social Democratic camp. It is no wonder then that the
party-owned printing establishment, the Uptown Cooperative Press,
Inc., went bankrupt.[16]

The *Volksecho*, in a vain attempt to gain the leadership of the
anti-Nazi movement, fomented a campaign to establish a unity paper
(Einheitszeitung)—one daily German-language paper to lead the fight
against Fascism. The gauntlet was flung down in Cleveland where, in
September, 1937 at the National Congress of the Arbeitersänger (workers' singing societies), the Communist faction pushed through a motion
to create a single daily newspaper by merging the *Deutsches Volksecho*
and the *Neue Volks-Zeitung.*[17] It was further suggested that both papers
should immediately begin negotiations to that end, for in this way only,
the motion went on, lay the possibility of a daily paper embodying the
principles of the Peoples' Front. At the Cleveland gathering, Gerhart
Seger, editor of the Socialist *Neue Volks-Zeitung*, objected that the
Volksecho was a Communist paper and not the straightforward
anti-Nazi organ it claimed to be. The *Volksecho* replied:

> It goes without saying that the Communist Party as a workers' organiza-
> tion that honestly supports the United Front is concerned with the
> journalistic torch bearer of this United Front in the German-American
> arena, the *Deutsches Volksecho*. This is not only the right but the duty of
> any organization which supports the United Front.[18]

During the next few months this Cleveland program received the
support of a number of German-American groups, most of them controlled by Communist members.[19] The reply of the Social Democrats

came in a speech by Seger to the general assembly of the Progressive Publishing Association, the publishers of the *Neue Volks-Zeitung*.[20] Seger stated that the duty of the Progressive Publishing Association was to propagate the ideas of scientific socialism by adhering to the principles and directives of the Socialist International. More to the point, he argued that the *Neue Volks-Zeitung* was not only an anti-Nazi paper but primarily the organ of the Socialist German-American worker who was the principal financial support of the paper. Merging the two papers could only lead to the *Neue Volks-Zeitung* losing its true identity. Seger, drawing on experiences gained in Weimar Germany and in America (with the Antifaschistische Aktion and the Deutsch-Amerikanischer Kulturverband), also feared Communist control of the proposed paper. At any rate, by the end of 1939 the question became academic for after September 16 the *Volksecho* vanished, suddenly and unannounced, obviously unable to carry off the 100 percent political about-face called for by the Nazi-Soviet Pact signed three weeks earlier.

The second clash between Communist and non-Communist Germans in America was over the Deutsch-Amerikanischer Kulturverband. Since the debacle of the Antifaschistische Aktion, the German anti-Nazis lacked any organizational basis. To remedy this situation, members of the Krankenkasse arranged a conference of progressive German Americans in September, 1935, the result of which was the creation of the Deutsch-Amerikanischer Kulturverband (DAKV). Like the AA, the Verband was a federation of existing German-American organizations, but it differed from its precursor by admitting bourgeois groups and barring any political party from membership. Thus the founders of the DAKV hoped to prevent another Communist coup. After the election of officers was completed,[21] the conference was presented with a series of grandiose plans for the future. It was announced that a bulletin would soon be issued as well as a series of *Flugblätter für Kultur* and a more ambitious *Schriften für Kultur:* "If it is practical for propaganda purposes these may be issued in the vernacular [i.e. English]."[22] The delegates were also regaled with visions of Kulturverbände arising in all the countries of South and Central America, culminating in a Deutsche Weltbund für Kultur. Unfortunately, before 1936 was over, the Verband had become politicized and under the influence of the Communist Party.

As president-elect for 1936, Gerhart Seger represented those anti-Nazis determined to keep politics out of the Kulturverband. According to one obviously partisan account, Seger accidentally discovered a secret document that revealed the party's intention of turning the DAKV into a front organization by eliminating all non-Communists from positions of influence. This was the alleged reason for Seger's resignation as president that year, although he himself declined to clarify the matter.[23] Otto Sattler became the new and perennially reelected president of the Verband, and by the end of 1936 many important national offices were occupied by party members or fellow travelers. The DAKV also continued its policy of appointing internationally respected Germans or German Americans as honorary president or chairman (e.g. Franz Boas, Frank Bohn, and Thomas Mann).

The decisive events in securing total Communist control over the organization were acted out not in New York but in Chicago, and the shadow Svengali who called the tune (according to the Social Democrats) was the editor of the *Volksfront* (Chicago)—a man who called himself Martin Hall.[24] The *Volksfront* began publishing in 1934, first as a monthly, then a weekly, the voice of the German Bureau in the Middle West. By 1938, the paper had begun calling itself the official organ of the Kulturverband, a completely unauthorized move by Hall and most offensive to the majority of German Americans. It was Hall's influence on Otto Sattler (again, according to Brandl who was for a time an official of the DAKV) that prompted the first national conference of the Verband in 1938 to move the seat of its executive from New York to Chicago—away from its many critics. The final touch was Martin Hall's election as national secretary,.which made him the administrative head of the organization.

The strength of the Communists and their sympathizers in the Verband was made painfully clear to the rank and file members at the second national convention held in Cleveland (September, 1939). Otto Sattler, in a rare show of spirit, proposed a motion that would have sharply condemned the recent Stalin-Hitler Pact. The Resolutions Committee after due deliberation, shelved the motion without bringing it to the convention floor, explaining that "because of the unclear world situation it would be impossible to render a balanced judgment upon the treaty."[25] During the altered ideological climate of 1939 and 1940, many old faces and institutions were allowed to quietly fade away—the *Volksecho* in September, the *Volksfront* by the end of December, 1939. Martin Hall was removed from the limelight and sent forth from Chicago to begin a new career as national organizer for the Kulturverband.[26]

It is a delicate task to describe the participation of a number of prominent left-wing émigrés in Popular Front activities without unconsciously leaving the impression that they were members of the KPD and following party directives. This was certainly not the case with men of the stature of Kurt Rosenfeld and Alfons Goldschmidt, who were convinced that the only way to defeat Hitler and create a new Germany was to cooperate closely with the Soviet Union and consequently with the national Communist parties. Bearing these circumstances in mind, let us see (our examples being Rosenfeld and Goldschmidt) how the non-Communist émigré functioned in Popular Front affairs.

Kurt Rosenfeld (1877-1943) a lawyer by profession (after 1918 attached to the Prussian Ministry of Justice), was long active in German Socialist politics, a career that included thirteen years as a member of the German Reichstag. In 1931 he was instrumental in founding the SAP, an act of disillusionment with both large Marxist parties, the SPD and KPD. Rosenfeld came to the United States in 1934 (his traveling companions included Willi Münzenberg and British Labourite Aneuren Bevan) with the immediate intention of touring the country on behalf of Münzenberg's National Committee to Aid Victims of German Fascism. One of his first public performances took place in Madison Square Garden—a rerun of Münzenberg's highly successful mock Reichstag Fire Trial, an open indictment of Adolf Hitler.[27] In 1936 Rosenfeld became literary adviser to the American Committee for Anti-Nazi Literature, a group chaired by William E. Dodd, Jr. He also headed the Volksfrontgruppe Deutscher Emigranten which, in early 1938, was primarily interested in arousing public support for an imperiled Czechoslovakia.

Rosenfeld was not without his enemies—usually Social Democrats of conservative mien or Trotskyites who disapproved of any fraternization with representatives of the Stalinist International. In such a light we may view the rather uncomplimentary remarks which appeared in the *Kampfsignal* (N.Y.):

> Upon his arrival in Paris last February, 1933, Kurt Rosenfeld reported in to the K.P.D. but apparently there were other plans for him. In the meantime, he and Münzenberg had probably come to the reasonable conclusion that it would serve their purpose if he toured the land as a "revolutionary neutral" and represented Münzenberg's interest.[28]

The last two years of his life brought Rosenfeld to the forefront of émigré political life as founder and first president (1942) of the German American Emergency Conference. This was a major gathering of left-wing Germans, many of whom were Communist Party members. In all his ventures Rosenfeld strove for a broad anti-Nazi front disregarding party allegiances, and that stance brought him into close contact with radicals of every stripe.

Alfons Goldschmidt (1879-1940), a trained economist who specialized in Latin American affairs—founder of the Economic Institute for Latin America in Berlin—was always closely associated with radical political movements in Germany. In 1918 he became economic advisor to the *Weltbühne*, the most influential journal of the German intellectual

Left. Goldschmidt's friend Kurt Hiller, the independent Socialist journalist and pacifist, said of him, "In his heart very close to the Leninist ideology, although never a party man, he found it hard to renounce when it degenerated into the Stalinist ideology."[29] Hiller went on to describe Goldschmidt as a dynamic person combining special knowledge with social consciousness, an outstanding stylist, speaker, and teacher.

Arriving in the United States after a short stay at the University of Mexico City, Goldschmidt soon became involved in the fortunes of the *Deutsches Volksecho*. Rudolf Brandl, already cited as a biased and unfriendly witness of Popular Front activities, penned a description of this affair which is worth preserving as an example of anti-Communist sentiment among the émigrés:

> When the bankrupt Communist *Arbeiter* slipped into the garments of the *Volksecho*, Alfons Goldschmidt using old personal connections, forayed into a New York circle of German Jews—the jestingly named Rosenbaum Concern—Deutsch-Jüdische Männerbund, Deutsch-Jüdische Damenbund, Loge Freundschaft—in order to entice it away from the *Neue Volks-Zeitung* and to incorporate its members into the group around the young "liberal progressive sheet." His efforts failed—the victims refused upon reflection to throw away clear water in exchange for a rather muddy liquid.[30]

Further evidence of his intimate association with the Communist paper is contained in the *Deutsches Volksecho* for June 25 and October 29, 1938. Up until the former date, the newspaper was published by the Deutsches Volksecho Publishing Company. In the June 25th issue this was altered to read: Alfons Goldschmidt, Publisher. By July 16, the corporate name had changed to the Pastorius Publishing Company; the October 29th edition was more explicit and bore the imprint: Pastorius Publishing Company, President Alfons Goldschmidt. A short episode in itself, Goldschmidt's connection with the American Communist press can serve as a good example of how prominent left-wing intellectuals were drawn into Popular Front adventures.

Hitler-Stalin Treaty, August, 1939—June, 1941

If the signing of the Nazi-Soviet pact on August 24, 1939 was a shock to the American party, it was all the more acutely felt in German-American and émigré circles. While the *Daily Worker*, after taking a deep breath, once again continued to fight the party's battles, the German Bureau by the end of the year had given up both its weekly papers. The German émigré population in particular had little use for a Communist newspaper under the circumstances that then prevailed.

Biding its time, the German Bureau turned its attention to other segments of the German-American population.

To preserve the continuity of communication between the German
Bureau and the ordinary worker, the modest *Mitteilungsblatt* of the
Föderation Deutsch-Amerikanischer Klubs (the old Arbeiterklubs re-
christened in 1936) was expanded and given a new name, *Unsere Zeit.*
In no sense a newspaper of mass appeal, it served to mark time until one
could be feasibly published. Its readership was limited almost exclusively to members of the German-American clubs. Total printing
costs for the two and one-half year period ending in July of 1942 were
only $1654.25[31] — a good indication of its meager circulation. A new
venture for the CPA was the organization of German-American youth.
Unaware of the imminence of the Nazi-Soviet *rapprochement,* the party
founded the German American Youth Association in June, 1939.[32] The
following November saw a hurried reorganization and the appearance of
a new voice of German-American youth, the *Youth Outlook.* Quite
cleverly, the title and entire front page were printed in English, with
most of the German text on the inside. The sentiments expressed were
quite predictably in tune with the new Communist policy of neutrality,
peace, and a plague on both your houses. The anti-Nazi Popular Front
was dead; the new slogans were "Keep America Out of War" and "The
Yanks Are Not Coming."

The "Great Patriotic War" 1941 — 1945

GERMAN AMERICAN EMERGENCY CONFERENCE

Hitler's invasion of the U.S.S.R. in June, 1941, brought with it a new
turn in Communist policy. Fearing a possible capitalistic alliance, to
dismember the Soviet Union, the Communists pressed for immediate
American entry into the war. For almost two years the party press
exhibited the most uncompromising pacifism only to become overnight
"the most outspoken interventionist force in American life."[33] This was
bound to shake the German-American Communist press out of its dol-
drums. Even the DAKV bestirred itself to some semblance of action
after withdrawing into semi-obscurity during the years of the Pact:

> The D.A.K.V. . . . is after long inactivity again appearing before the
> public. An informative and instructive pamphlet prepared members,
> friends and affiliated groups for a series of events and publications which
> were to prove that the mass of German-Americans were enemies of the
> Nazis. . . . Hundreds of German-American workers were recently assem-
> bled at the Naturfreund Camp outside New York and heard a forceful
> speech by Oskar Maria Graf. A gathering of far-reaching importance will

be held in December at the Yorkville-Casino, the center of the German-American section of New York—the opening event in a large-scale "enlightenment" campaign among German-Americans throughout the country.[34]

The organ of the Deutsch-Amerikanische Klubs, *Unsere Zeit,* still the only German-language weekly in the Communist camp, began to prepare its readers for the necessity of a larger and better paper, something on a par with the defunct *Volksecho:* a newspaper not perforce aimed at the limited audience of club members, but one encompassing the labor movement as a whole, appealing also to the émigrés and with special features for women and young people. In March, 1942, such a paper was in the first stages of realization when, under the direction of Kurt Rosenfeld, the first meeting of the German American Emergency Conference (GAEC) was held. This new group was planned to bring together all elements of the anti-Nazi emigration as well as representatives of German-American labor, but SPD adherents held back, allowing the mantle of leadership to fall upon members of the CPA and the KPD.

To the American public at large the conference was a rousing success, certified, as it were, by a list of such eminent sponsors as Franz Boas, Walter Damrosch, and Lillian Hellman and supported by Otto Sattler, the Krankenkasse, the DAKV, and numerous other German-American labor organizations. To realize their professed aim of unifying all German Americans in the fight against Nazism, the members of the GAEC founded a new German-language paper.[35] The *German American* was publicly confirmed in its party lineage by the blessings of the Föderation Deutsch-Amerikanischer Klubs transmitted through its organ, *Unsere Zeit:*

> We can today say with conviction that both publications, *Unsere Zeit* and the *German American . . .* agree to such an extent in their common appeals to the German-American, that it would be foolish to issue two such similar journals side by side. . . . It has been decided to unite both of them to form a more substantial monthly periodical in the hope of some day being able to give the German-Americans a weekly paper.[36]

Communist Party control of the paper is undeniable. The ranking representative of German-American trade unionism who supported the GAEC was Michael Obermeyer of the International Alliance of Hotel and Restaurant Employees and Bartenders, a "key Communist trade-union leader in the hotel and restaurant industry of the New York region."[37] Obermeyer was also the chairman of the Victory Committee of the German American Trade Unions, a front organization that supplied the first two editors of the *German American*. A close look at the regular contributors from 1942 to 1945 reveals a hard core of KPD publicists, all émigrés: Albert Schreiner, Max Schroeder, F. W. Weis-kopf, Alfred Kantorowicz, Albert Norden, and Gerhart Eisler (alias Hans Berger). Furthermore, according to a fellow exile, the actual editorial direction of the paper lay in the hands of Eisler and Schroeder,[38] the nominal editor (trade unionist Rudolf Kohler) serving merely as a straw man.

COUNCIL FOR A DEMOCRATIC GERMANY

The final scene of the political tragicomedy that reached its climax in 1945 — one last attempt to create a Free German representation in exile — was once again flawed by the recurring struggle between Communists and Socialists. Only this time the usual provinciality of previous quarrels, whose impact was hardly felt beyond the émigré enclave itself, was shattered by the direct involvement (for the first time) of one of the great powers. Attempts at building an effective organization to represent a "Free Germany" in exile had consistently proven futile, and the exiles, especially those representatives of the workers' parties — the SPD, KPD, and smaller groups — wasted most of their energy in fighting among themselves without giving too much thought to possible affiliation with middle-class and conservative anti-Hitler forces.[39] The formation of the Moscow Nationalkomitee Freies Deutschland in July, 1943, with the Communist poet Erich Weinert as chairman and Count Heinrich von Einsiedel,[40] a direct descendant of Bismarck, as vice-chairman, followed by the rapid proliferation of Free German Committees in England, France, Sweden, Switzerland, and above all in Latin America, began a new and final phase of the German political emigration. For the first time a foreign power was attempting to manipulate anti-Hitler forces for its own purposes. The Moscow committee was made of two wings, a group of prisoners of war led by a sprinkling of German Communists, and (for propaganda efforts within Nazi military circles) the Bund Deutscher Offiziere headed by two captured Nazi generals.

In Mexico City the soldier-novelist Ludwig Renn and his associates[41] guided the fortunes of the Soviet-sponsored movement throughout Latin America. Everywhere the Free German Committees had attracted, at least temporarily, the support of prominent exiles, writers, politicians, and scientists[42] and it seemed only a matter of time until such a committee would be conjured up in the United States. A front-page article in the *Aufbau* of October 15, 1943, mulled over a dispatch from the Overseas News Agency that a Free German Committee was about to be established in New York City. The article suggested two possible organizational patterns that might be followed: an openly Communist committee, on the model of Moscow, London, and Mexico City, or a more inclusive representation, not openly under Communist control.[43] What did occur was the formation of a nonpartisan committee to bring togeth-er Catholic, Protestant, Communist, Socialist, and "bourgeois" spokes-men in equal proportions. Thomas Mann was first approached as a possible leader, but he, like former Chancellor Brüning, declined to participate.[44] Still, preparations for such a committee went on apace, and a chairman of stature was found in the theologian, Paul Tillich. The new organization, known as the Council for a Democratic Germany, suffered under certain disabilities. On the one hand, the German Social Democrats (with a few notable exceptions) refused on principle to col-laborate in an endeavor with which Communists were associated.[45] On the other hand, Jewish intellectuals were opposed to the Council whose views, they said, smacked of German nationalism.

A bilingual declaration dated April, 1944, was the first public procla-mation of the Council. This was no ordinary émigré group, but a con-scious attempt to create a "shadow cabinet" for a liberated Germany.[46] One did not join the Council but was called to represent this or that political tendency; the members sympathetic to the Communist position on the treatment of Germany[47] were in the minority and could not change the Council into another Free German Committee. They were strong enough, though, to block any chance of unity within the Council by their unwavering support of Allied policy toward Germany as devel-oped at the Yalta, Teheran, and Potsdam meetings. This meant support of territorial decisions in favor of the Soviet Union such as the new Polish German border, the removal of the German population from East and Southeast Europe, and the deindustrialization of Germany antici-pated at that time. The Council was thoroughly divided on all these points and could take no unified public stance. To attain even an adviso-ry role on the international scene, the Council needed at least the appearance of unity; they could not (as they did) present in one issue of their *Bulletin* (February, 1945)[48] six different and contradictory posi-tions on the German question and hope to survive.

Finally, on October 10, after six more months of wrangling, Karl Frank and most of the non-Communist members left the Council en masse. Paetel rightly ascribes the inefficacy of the Council not only to factional struggles but to the unreality of its claims to represent the oppositional forces within the Third Reich. The fact that not one of the representatives of the "other Germany" on the Council had any con-nection with or inkling of the July, 1944 conspiracy—in spite of its failure, the only serious attempt on Hitler's life—robbed it of any legiti-mate moral and political right to act as a representation-in-exile of the German resistance.

As a brief postscript (in lieu of a formal summary), it should be reiterated that there were two Communist parties: the CPA which from its inception had worked diligently with German Americans, and the few actual members of the KPD who came to these shores.[49] Given the structure of international Communism, it was no surprise that the two groups immediately joined together in their propaganda and organizational efforts, whether directed at German-American labor, the émigrés, or all anti-Nazi Germans living in the United States. The success of these ventures varied with the changing international situation and the strength of the opposition parties. But one thing is certain—the full story of the émigré press and book trade cannot be told without coming to grips with the Communist sector and all its works.

Notes

1. Italics mine. Quoted in Theodore Draper, *American Communism and Soviet Russia* (New York: Viking, Compass Books Ed., 1963), p.161.

2. F. Brown, "For Improving the Work of the Party among the Foreign-Born Workers," *The Communist* (N.Y.), 13:706 (July 1934). See also Robert Jay Alperin, "Organization in the Communist Party U.S.A. 1931-1938" (unpublished Ph.D. dissertation, Northwestern Univ., 1959). He writes: "Rather than being alienated from the traditions of their national backgrounds, members of language mass organizations appear to have been absorbed in them, engaging in singing and dramatic activity to the exclusion of cultivating a wider corps of sympathizers and building the Party" (p.382).

3. *The Organizational Weapon* (Glencoe, Ill.: Free Pr., 1960), p.48.

4. *Der Arbeiter* (New York), 1927-1937; *Volksfront* (Chicago), 1934-1939; *Deutsches Volksecho* (New York), 1937-1939; *Unsere Zeit* (New York), 1940-1942; *The German American* (New York), 1942 to date. Numerous foreign language editions (including German) of rival factional papers were undoubtedly published during the early 1920s. Only a few samples have survived, e.g., the organ of the United Communist Party of America, *Der Kommunist* (New York), issue of 10 Juli 1920 in the National Archives, Record Group 85, U.S. Dept. of Labor, Bureau of Immigration, 54885/34.

5. Draper, op. cit., p.148.

6. Quoted in E. W. Mareg, "Geschichte der Deutschen Arbeiterklubs," *Gegen den Strom,* 1:9 (May 1938). The following discussion of the Arbeiterbünde and Arbeiterklubs is largely based on Mareg's account which appeared in the April, May, June, and Aug. issues. Mareg was a former member of the German Bureau and claimed to be the originator of the Arbeiterklub movement. As a former party member, Mareg's views as expressed in 1938 are perhaps biased and somewhat bitter; unfortunately there is no other account of these organizations that can be used for comparison.

7. Mareg was elected general secretary; R. Bek-Gran, organizational secretary. *Gegen den Strom,* 1:13 (Aug. 1938). *Der Arbeiter* of Sept. 29, 1935, estimated the membership of this new federation at 1200 but, considering the source, this figure might be inflated.

8. The name Antifaschistische Aktion was also chosen by the German Communist Party in 1932 for a last-ditch attempt to organize a united front resistance to the Nazis. The American version was possibly a related propaganda device. In current East German historiography the stature of the AA looms large. For the American adventure, see *Der Arbeiter,* Jan. 22, 1934; *Kampfsignal,* June 24, 1933 and May 12, 1934; and *Neue Volks-Zeitung,* Nov. 4, 1933, p.16.

9. Irving Howe and Lewis Coser, *The American Communist Party* (New York: Praeger, 1962), p.323.

10. Communist Party of the U.S.A., New York State, *Proceedings of the Tenth Convention* (New York, 1938), p.276.

11. *Deutsches Volksecho*, published from Feb. 20, 1937 to Sept. 16, 1939.

12. Ibid., Aug. 28, 1937.

13. See p.168–69.

14. Ibid., June 17, 1939.

15. The *Volksecho* in its first issue already claimed 35,000 readers, undoubtedly an exaggerated figure.

16. It declared itself bankrupt and was sold at auction on April 9, 1938. The press had a colorful past dating back to 1923 when it was started by a group of Czech Communists in New York. In 1934 it was purchased by the *Arbeiter. Gegen den Strom*, 1:15 (May, 1938).

17. Reported in the *Deutsches Volksecho*, Sept. 11, 1937.

18. Ibid., Sept. 18, 1937.

19. The German group of the International Labor Defense of Detroit, the Bronx and Yorkville sections of the DAK, etc.

20. *Neue Volks-Zeitung*, Nov. 6, 1937, p.7.

21. Officers elected for 1935 were Otto Sattler, president; Karl Meyer of the Sänger-bund, first chairman; John E. Bonn, director of the Neue Theater-Gruppe, second chairman; Herman Kormis, secretary. Kormis, proprietor of the Modern Deutsche Buchhandlung, the leading German Socialist bookstore in New York, was a victim of Communist intrigues that caused his premature departure from the Verband.

22. *Der Arbeiter*, Oct. 6, 1935.

23. An attempt to elicit Seger's own account (before his death in 1967) was not successful. The document in question was a confidential bulletin of the German Bureau, *Wocheninformationsbriefe*, Vol. 3 (1936), "Unsere prinziepielle [sic] Stellung zum Deutschamerikanischen Kulturverband und unsere Aufgaben." Quoted by the rabidly anti-Communist Rudolf Brandl, "Der 'Kulturverband' und seine Sippe," *Gegen den Strom*, 2:10 (Oct.-Nov. 1939). A manuscript history of the DAKV in my possession, compiled by several anti-Communist Germans in New York (ca. 1937) including Herman Kormis and Robert Bek-Gran, does confirm the existence of such a document.

24. Martin Hall was identified by Rudolf Brandl in a polemical anti-Communist pamphlet as being one Hermann Jacobs, former chairman and Moscow delegate of the Kommunistische Jugend Deutschlands. The same identification was given in the testimony of Benjamin Gitlow, formerly a CPA official, before the House Committee on Un-American Activities. See Brandl, *That Good Old Fool, Uncle Sam: A Refugee Sounds a Warning* (New York, 1940), p.13, and U.S. Congress, House, Committee on Un-American Activities, *Investigation of Communist Activities in the New York City Area*, 83rd Cong., 1st Sess., 1953, Part 6, p.2130–31. Gitlow's account is not accurate on all points.

25. *Volksfront* (Chicago), Sept. 30, 1939; *Deutsches Volksecho*, Sept. 16, 1939.

26. See Howe and Coser, op. cit., p. 387–407, for a description of the disintegration of Popular Front organizations at that time.

27. The first "Trial" was held in London. Taking part in New York (besides Rosenfeld) were Münzenberg himself, Franz Höllering (an émigré author), Aneurin Bevan, and Allan Taub (lawyer for the International Labor Defense). *New York Times*, June 9, 1934, p.2. See also, Babette Gross, *Willi Münzenberg* (Stuttgart: Deutsche Verlagsanstalt, 1967), p.280.

28. *Kampfsignal*, Sept. 15, 1934.

29. Kurt Hiller, *Köpfe and Tröpfe* (Hamburg: Rowohlt, 1950), p.274–75.

30. Brandl, *Gegen den Strom*, 2:18 (Oct.-Nov. 1939). The social organizations men-

tioned belonged to the German Jewish Congregation (Deutsch-Israelitische Kultusgemeinde) and the German Jewish Center founded in the late 1920s under the guidance of Rabbi Max Malina. See p.61–62, 64.

31. *Unsere Zeit*, Sept., 1942. This last issue of the paper contained a complete financial report for the twenty-six-month period, June, 1940–July, 1942.

32. Its mimeographed newspaper was called *Das Neue Leben* and only three numbers were published, June–Aug. 1939 in an edition of 1,000 copies each. *Volksfront*, Sept. 9, 1939.

33. Howe and Coser, op. cit., p.407.

34. A report by the Communist publicist, Alfred Kantorowicz, then living in New York, first printed in the Communist newspaper *Freies Deutschland* (Mexico City), and reprinted in his *Vom moralischen Gewinn der Niederlage* (Berlin: Aufbau-Verlag, 1949), p.210. O. M. Graf was the spokesman for the Communist-oriented exiled German writers in the United States.

35. Before the first issue of the *German American* in May, 1942, the Conference had distributed a preliminary *Mitteilungsblatt* for March and April. *Unsere Zeit*, Sept., 1942.

36. *Unsere Zeit*, Sept., 1942. Annual subscriptions to *Unsere Zeit* were completed by issues of the *German American*. All former employees of the deceased newspaper would be added to the staff of the *German American*, it was announced.

37. David J. Saposs, *Communism in American Unions* (New York: McGraw-Hill, 1959), p.86. See also *The Network* (N.Y.), July, 1944, p.11. Obermeyer was finally forced to resign as president of Local 6 in 1950 and was deported in 1953 as an alien Communist.

38. Walther Victor, *Ich kam aus lauter Liebe in die Welt* (Weimar: Volksverlag, 1961), p.138. Gerhard Eisler, the senior KPD official in the U.S. (and putative Comintern representative) was subject to Congressional investigation climaxed by a dramatic escape aboard the Polish steamer, the Batory, in May, 1949. See Draper, *American Communism and Soviet Russia*, p.387; Jacob Spolansky, *The Communist Trail in America* (New York: Macmillan, 1951), p.111–14; Hede Massing, *This Deception* (New York: Duell, 1951). Hede Massing was Eisler's first wife and a confessed Soviet agent who attained some notoriety through her testimony at the Alger Hiss trial.

39. Karl O. Paetel, "Zum Problem einer deutschen Exilregierung," *Vierteljahrshefte für Zeitgeschichte*, 4:288 (July, 1956).

40. See his diary, *I Joined the Russians* (New Haven: Yale Univ. Pr., 1953), published in England as *The Shadow of Stalingrad* (London: Wingate, 1953). For a concise study of the Freies Deutschland movement see Paetel, "Das Nationalkomitee 'Freies Deutschland,' " *Politische Studien*, 6, Nr. 69:7–26 (1956). Also valuable are the accounts of Erich Weinert, *Das Nationalkomitee "Freies Deutschland"* 1943–1945 (Berlin: Rütten & Loening, 1957) and Bodo Scheurig, *Freies Deutschland* (München: Nymphenburger Verlagshandlung, 1961).

41. The text of the Moscow Committee's inaugural conference was printed in Mexico City and from there distributed in both North and South America. For a full roster of German Communists active in Mexico City see the *Neue Volks-Zeitung*, Jan. 26, 1946, p.2.

42. For details on the English committee see the report of one of its founders, Heinrich Fraenkel, *Farewell to Germany* (London: B. Hanison, 1959). Fraenkel, not a Communist, soon quit the organization.

43. Despite the lack of a formal organization in the United States, propaganda for the Freies Deutschland Bewegung was ably taken care of by the *German American*, which also sponsored an English-language newssheet, *Germany Today*, edited by Albert Norden and devoted exclusively to such propaganda.

44. See "Kein Deutschland Komitee in USA: Ein Dementi Thomas Manns," *Aufbau*

(N.Y.), Dec. 3, 1943, p.1. Paetel reported that Brüning would have only yielded to pressure from the U.S. government. *Vierteljahrshefte für Zeitgeschichte,* 4:289 (July, 1956).

45. A crisis arose within the German Labor Delegation and the Deutsche Sprachgruppe of the Social Democratic Federation when Grzesinski, Kurt Glaser, Siegfried Marck, and Siegfried Aufhäuser disregarded official sanctions and accepted membership on the Council. See Rudolf Katz's article, "Der New Yorker Stalin-Coup," in which he accuses Tillich of being a Communist (*Neue Volks-Zeitung,* May 6, 1944, p.4.). Edinger also thought of the Council as a Communist dominated Free German Committee (*German Exile Politics* [Berkeley: Univ. of California Pr., 1956], p.236). Paetel presents a convincing defense of the thesis that the Council was never actually under Communist control (*Vierteljahrshefte für Zeitgeschichte,* 4:300 [July, 1956]).

46. Karl Frank was one of the most vigorous supporters of the Council and the Association for a Democratic Germany, as his organization was now called, was its official sponsor.

47. Felix Boenheim, Bertolt Brecht, Albert Schreiner, Albert Norden, Maximilian Scheer, Hermann Budzislawski, Walther Victor, Jakob Walcher, and Julius Lips.

48. The Council took no stand on the problems raised but allowed six of its members to present their own views.

49. Actually German Communists avoided the United States when possible as immigration restrictions against them were stringently applied. After the invasion of Russia by the Nazi armies, the United States forbade any German aliens to leave the country without special dispensation. This fortuitous event caught several boatloads of leading KPD intellectuals in New York, all of whom were furnished with special visas for Mexico (e.g., Gerhart Eisler, the poet and novelist Hans Marchwitza, Albert Norden, Albert Schreiner, Max Schroeder, Philip Daub, and Alfred Kantorowicz). On the issuing of Mexican visas see *Neue Volks-Zeitung,* Sept. 5, 1942, p.7, and also Kantorowicz, *Deutsche Tagebuch* 1:160.

V
Non-Marxist, Jewish, and Free Austrian Newspapers

The Non-Marxist Press

The world of émigré journalism falls easily into four sub-groups—Socialist, Communist, German-Jewish, and Free Austrian, but while this classification may adequately describe existing newspapers and journals it does not correspond to the total ideological climate. There is missing a category (or categories) that would take in a wide range of non-Marxist ideologies represented in pre-Hitler Germany by an equally wide range of political parties. In the emigration, however, these points of view were represented by isolated spokesmen. The strong organizations, the widely read newspapers, the incessant polemics came usually from the parties of the German Left.[1] Despite this apparent Marxist domination of émigré politics, and while it is impossible to objectively measure the political preferences of the mass of immigrants, it seems (on the basis of secondary sources) that conservatism or moderate liberalism was more acceptable to the majority than a dogmatic Socialist or Communist outlook.

A concise pen portrait of the non-Socialist political emigration is given by J. C. Maier-Hultschin:

> The middle class was only weakly represented in the emigration. There were a few liberals and it was usually a question of those who were non-Aryans or had Jewish wives—except in the cases of the Reichstag delegates, Koch-Weser and August Weber. Even smaller was the number of those from the camp of the moderate right, such as Treviranus.

Somewhat larger was the number of former National Socialists, Rauschning, Hanfstaengel or the people around Otto Strasser, who, mostly ex-Nazis, never could be considered enemies of Germany *(deutschfeindlich).* The largest group were the Catholics, and in these circles there was absolutely no enmity towards Germany. Heinrich Brüning, during the emigration, went so far as to maintain complete silence – which behaviour was taken in bad grace by his adherents.[2]

Brüning, a Catholic, and Chancellor of Germany from 1930 to 1932, was the highest ranking émigré statesman in the United States and quite probably was in contact with such groups as the broadly based but anti-Communist Deutsche Freiheits Partei.[3] Although Brüning kept his own counsel, his presumed participation in exile affairs was noted in the American press, as for example by George W. Pate in the *The Christian Science Monitor* (an article sympathetic to the German Social Democrats):

> Dr. Brüning and his group wish with the understanding of the Vatican to bring about the fall of Hitler . . . this group is becoming more popular as a result of its constant claims that it enjoys the support of the British government, its launching of rumors – thus far unconfirmed by facts – that it is in constant touch with the Reichswehr opposition and especially with the so-called "party of Generals," its closer ties with the Vatican and its numerous but generally little known contacts with rightist circles of American big business, interested in the New Germany.[4]

The multiplicity of social and political ideas cherished by the non-Socialist emigration was reason enough for an almost total absence of political organization. No group had sufficient money or cohesion to support a German-language organ of its own – with the exception of the Austrian monarchist press and Karl O. Paetel's *Deutsche Gegenwart* (which was an independent venture). Some intellectual sustenance did come from outside the United States; strongly conservative and nationalistic feelings were nourished by Otto Strasser's Free Germany movement based in Canada, while the non-Marxist moderates and Catholic anti-Nazis found support (and in turn supported) the *Deutsche Blätter,* a German émigré journal published in Chile.

THE BLACK FRONT IN AMERICA

Otto Strasser, derisively nicknamed Hitler's Trotsky by leftist émigrés, was indefatigible in his efforts to create around his person an effective nationalist anti-Nazi movement. Retaining many elements of original National Socialist theory, and with a certain affinity to the Catholic corporate authoritarianism of Dollfuss, the Black Front, as his organization was called, represented the extreme Right wing of the

German emigration. When in 1940 the necessity of leaving Europe was forced upon Strasser, he first opted for Bermuda where he girded himself for a new campaign: "to fight Goebbel's propaganda lies that Hitler was Germany . . . to found a political movement that spoke for a free Germany."[5] Thus the Frei-Deutschland Bewegung was born.[6]

The new organization got off the ground quickly, aided by 2000 dollars in royalties just collected from the American edition of Strasser's book, *Hitler and I*. By January 30, 1941, he had saturated North and South America with copies of his new manifesto in German, English, and Spanish versions.[7] These were distributed from bases in New York and Buenos Aires by former members of the Black Front. Newspapers and radio stations were contacted—in Sweden, Peru, and New Zealand; from Edmonton, Canada to Melbourne, Australia. Pressure was also exerted on the United States government for recognition as the official representative of "Free Germany." According to Pate: "On January 5, 1942 the German emigration formed a unified anti-Nazi front and asked to be admitted to the block of 26 nations . . . in reality this was simply a maneuver by Otto Strasser's Canadian group. Dr. Strasser is anxious to make former Chancellor Dr. H. Bruening the standard bearer of the opposition and the future leader of a new Germany."[8]

Supporters of Strasser included right-wing Socialist leaders acting on their own as well as conservatives. Wilhelm Sollman (SPD), a former minister in the Stresemann cabinet; Wenzel Jaksch, the leader of the German Sudeten Socialists; Brüning; Treviranus; and Rauschning were all involved in an abortive attempt to establish a "non-Marxian" front geared to Strasser's organization, a counterpoise to the Communist Popular Front of the late 1930s[9] ("non-Marxian" in the sense of abandoning the internationalism of Socialist doctrine as formulated by Marx and Engels for the "national" or "patriotic" Socialism that goes back to the teachings of Ferdinand Lassalle). Although he found many supporters in South and Central America as well as in the United States,[10] Strasser elected to settle in Canada once his stay in Bermuda terminated—a tactical mistake for the future of his movement. The Canadian government was far from sympathetic and, by 1943, any further propaganda work was officially proscribed. Strasser did seem to strike a sympathetic chord among conservative German Americans, especially in the Midwest, and reverberations of his political activities were picked up from time to time by the sensitive antennae of the émigré press.[11]

THE *Deutsche Blätter*

It was primarily through the efforts of two Catholic publicists in Chile aided by Catholic and conservative anti-Nazi groups in the United

States that the *Deutsche Blätter* became the leading German literary periodical of the war period. Founded in Santiago de Chile by Nikolaus von Nagel, Udo Rukser, and Albert Theile, and edited by Rukser and Theile[12] from its inception in January, 1943 to its demise in December, 1946, the *Deutsche Blätter* may be viewed as a descendant of such earlier émigré journals as *Die Sammlung* and *Mass und Wert*. It was often termed one of the finest of all émigré literary periodicals. In any case, it was somewhat unusual—a consciously "über-parteilich" émigré journal, uncommitted to a political party, whose pages reflected the humane and conservative sympathies of its editors. They welcomed any serious, nonpolemical discussion of world problems as well as poetry and prose of émigré writers. Its surveys of the world press and lengthy book reviews were widely appreciated (the most frequent contributor of book reviews from the United States was Karl O. Paetel, who also was editorial representative of the journal in this country).[13] The spirit of the enterprise shines through its cover motto—"For a European Germany/Against a German Europe"—followed by a text from Pestalozzi best left in the original: *Wir wollen keine Verstaatlichung des Menschen, sondern eine Vermenschlichung des Staates.*

The *Deutsche Blätter* represented the best of German cultural achievement during the emigration and found its greatest response in the United States. A Freundenkreis der Deutschen Blätter was active in arranging cultural events among the émigrés in New York City; in line with their philosophy, the members hoped to show "that men of good will could communicate with one another over common problems—removed from any group and party differences."[14] Berendsohn, after characterizing the editorial policy of the journal as "middle class, and of a strong Catholic and conservative bent," goes on to comment on the leading figures of the American Freundenkreis: "The circle around Karl Paetel and Friedrich Krause [bookseller and publisher] in New York is a fruit off the same tree. Even if we differ with them on essential points, we cannot deny our great respect for their honest endeavours."[15]

A figure of 2000 is given as the journal's circulation before 1945. The United States provided 40 percent of the readers, a figure that rose to 50 percent when German prisoners of war in the United States were permitted to accept subscriptions.[16] The *Deutsche Blätter* was the first German-language periodical published outside the United States to be allowed in POW camps; and the editors lost no time in establishing POW gift subscriptions at lower rates, to be paid for by interested readers. The *Deutsche Blätter* has been discussed in some detail because it was, after 1940, the sole nonparty political and literary journal of the German emigration—and was as much an American as a Chilean achievement. This is evidenced by the number of subscriptions, contributions, letters to the editor, and advertisements emanating from the United States, the latter certainly a telling point.

KARL O. PAETEL

A native of Berlin (b.1906), Paetel participated in various youth organizations, gradually entering that ideological borderland known as National Bolshevism. Its supporters, while forming no single party, cherished, in the words of Walter Laqueur:

> ... the forlorn hope of finding some synthesis between Communism and National Socialism. They agreed with Hitler's radical nationalism, though not with his anti-Bolshevism; they were quite willing to join in the Communist attack on bourgeois society, but not to accept the theory of Marxism-Leninism.[17]

Journalism was Paetel's métier until 1933 when his periodical, *Die sozialistische Nation,* was banned by the Nazis. Two years later he was forced to abandon his now illegal activities and flee the country, finding a haven after many trying years in New York, which since 1941 has been his home.[18]

At the end of the war Paetel became disturbed by the one-sided character of the information made available to American readers; this "biased" presentation could not, as in earlier years, be counteracted to any extent by an exile press that by now had almost disappeared. The *Deutsche Blätter* was practically the last. Paetel's new venture may have been conceived as a continuation in spirit of that South American journal defunct after December, 1946; for one month later, in January, 1947, the first hektographed issue of *Deutsche Gegenwart* was distributed from Paetel's home in Forest Hills, Long Island—its purpose, to bring factual reports, articles, and letters to the German-reading American public. Although the newsletter had to be abandoned in 1948, the documentary material, preserved and augmented by Paetel, grew into the Archiv "Deutsche Gegenwart," an extensive research collection housed in Forest Hills.[19]

There was no particular political direction to the enterprise; the people behind it, as Paetel himself confessed, differed on more than one issue. This is confirmed by Walter R. Boelke, one of the original collaborators:

> After the end of the war, Paetel felt the need of a periodical that would report the real situation in Germany. He was especially taken by the idea of publishing authentic material about the "inner emigration." We argued over the significance of the 20th of July and the practicality of a periodical. To be sure, the "other Germany" existed for me also, but I saw little purpose in combating the hysteria of the day with a hektographed sheet. Finally, I allowed myself to be convinced by Paetel and together

with other friends, founded the *Deutsche Gegenwart.* . . . Unfortunately, the monthly did not find the hoped for response and had to cease publication after two years . . . It seems only right to report that I was in complete disagreement with this undertaking and after the appearance of the third number severed my connections.[20]

A second German-language newsletter was issued by Paetel during this same period, a venture possibly unique in the annals of German émigré publishing. Here is his own account of the nature and purpose of the *Blätter der Dritten Front* (1947–50):

> The *Blätter der Dritten Front* were in the truest sense a private printing. It began when I sent five copies of a *Rundbrief* [circular letter] to five people [in Germany]. These five people each made five additional copies and sent them to addresses taken from a list supplied by me. The next five did the same [etc.]. . . . Thus by such a snowball system were people supplied. . . . When life in Germany became more normal the *Rundbriefe* were mimeographed in Munich and sent out to a list of recipients never numbering more than 200. The purpose of this letter was to determine through continual contact with individuals in *ca.* 26 German cities whether there was any chance for the creation of a political "Third Front" between the Right and the Left. When it was evident that for such a position only a marginal existence was possible, in agreement with my German friends, I discontinued delivery of the *Rundbriefe* and did not return to Germany.[21]

The German Jewish Press

The organizational structure of the German Jews in New York that was to meet the unexpected challenge of large-scale Jewish immigration (by 1955 numbering over 200,000)[22] had its roots in the years immediately following World War I. The pre-Hitler migration to the United States was not statistically impressive, at the most about 30,000 persons (according to Max Malina),[23] and these primarily young people looking for work. There was little contact between the older and younger generations of German-Jewish immigrants during the twenties; indeed, after the experience of World War I, only one German-Jewish organization managed to preserve its identity—the Deutsch-Israelitischer Landeswehrverein, an association of war veterans.[24]

It was also a group of young Jewish veterans who helped to form the German Jewish Club, the publisher of the *Aufbau* and the most important German-Jewish organization of the middle 1930s. Until 1932, however, the focal point of immigrant life in New York was the German Jewish Center (not to be confused with the German Jewish Club) and its affiliated congregation, the Deutsch-Israelitische Kultusgemeinde whose spiritual leader from 1926 on was Rabbi (and journalist) Max Malina. In all, Malina published three German-language papers from 1927 through February, 1939, but they were basically community and congregational organs. After 1933, the representative voice of the emigration was without question the *Aufbau,* the bulletin of the New World Club that swiftly developed into a secular paper of international renown.

The New World Club, central organization of the German-Jewish emigration in the East, dates back to 1924, to the founding of the parent German Jewish Club by a handful of immigrants who at that time thought of themselves primarily as Germans and their club as "a confession of faith in German culture."[25] But events soon made clear the illusory nature of this attitude and they, as their brothers in Germany, were soon caught up in the Jewish revival of the late twenties, the new ferment in youth, and Zionist organizations. The prospects of the German Jewish Club were greatly enhanced when, in 1932, it absorbed the aforementioned German Jewish Center, a very timely consolidation as events were to prove. The increasingly oppressive European situation and the rapid rise in membership encouraged the club leadership in 1934 to authorize the printing of a free bulletin—the *Aufbau.* It was fortunate that New York possessed both an organization and a newspaper prepared to meet and aid the new wave of emigrants from Germany.

The achievements of the club in hastening the assimilation of tens of thousands of newcomers—and in attending to their financial, social, and economic needs—are unquestionably worthy of admiration, as are the many cultural, recreational, and special interest groups sponsored by the club, but these have all been described elsewhere.[26] One discordant voice breaks the apparent smooth surface of German-Jewish unity—the caustic and vitriolic tones of Rudolf Brandl[27], editor of the *Aufbau* from 1937 through 1938. Brandl's particular bête noire was the spectre of Communist infiltration, the omnipresence of crypto-Communists and fellow travelers. Since his major polemical articles were written during the era of the Hitler-Stalin Pact—a crise de conscience for many liberal intellectuals—and since one of his favorite targets was Manfred George, the man who succeeded him as editor of the *Aufbau,* some of his grievances may be explained away on personal grounds. But it would have been unusual for any organization at that time to entirely escape attempts at Communist infiltration.[28]

When the *Aufbau* was started in 1934 as a complimentary bulletin, the position of editor was little more than an honorary one; but by the Spring of 1937 a professional journalist was needed and Rudolf Brandl was selected to fill that post. Manfred George (until 1933 the chief editor of the Berlin daily newspaper *Tempo*) took over in 1939 and immediately transformed the *Aufbau* into a tabloid weekly on a paid subscription basis. With the adoption of the motto, "Aufbau — Serving the Interests and the Americanization of the Immigrants," a new period of rapid expansion had begun. From the modest *Vereinsblättchen* with a circulation in January, 1939 of 3000, the *Aufbau* by 1940, under the guidance of George, could count 13,000 weekly subscribers plus a lively street sale. Weekly circulation figures document the continuing prosperity of the newspaper: 14,000 in 1941, 26,000 in 1942, 30,500 in 1944. An increase in advertising lineage, from 300,000 in 1940 to 850,000 in 1944, is additional testimony of the paper's solid place in the German-Jewish community.[29] Actually, world-wide distribution made the *Aufbau* a truly international voice of the German-Jewish migration.

> No foreign language journal in New York is so frequently seen as the *Aufbau* and none can boast that it is as widely read in Shanghai as in Palestine, in the African Bush as in Australia, in beleaguered London as in the peaceful capitals of South America. For the U.S. government, the *Aufbau* is the public voice of the new immigration from Germany, Austria, Czechoslovakia.[30]

In 1941 the newspaper "officially" became a national paper by incorporating in a new supplement (called *Die Westküste*) the former organ of the Jewish Club of Los Angeles, *Neue Welt*, that had appeared monthly from 1933.

The general literary excellence of the paper, the many first printings of prose and poetry[31] by authors such as Thomas Mann, Werfel, Zweig, and Brecht, the numerous book reviews, discussions of all aspects of German, Jewish, and American culture — all contribute to make the *Aufbau* an indispensable source for any literary or cultural history of the emigration. Besides the fostering of German literature, the *Aufbau* was guided by two other fundamental aims: A devotion to the needs of the German-Jewish community, and a perseverance in furthering the Americanization of its readers.

The *Aufbau*, especially after it absorbed the *Neue Welt* of Los Angeles, dominated the German-Jewish press in the United States. All of the remaining German-language papers of Jewish interest were of the type so prolific in Germany — the community bulletin or *Gemeindeblatt* — newspapers sponsored or largely supported by local congregations. The post-World War I infusion of German Jews did not readily assimilate into the existing Jewish congregations but formed their own, such as the Deutsch-Israelitische Kultusgemeinde led by Rabbi Max Malina; this pattern held after 1933 when the new immigrants reestablished in America their abandoned religious communities (there were eighteen such refugee congregations established after 1933 in the New York area alone).[32]

Rabbi Malina's earliest essay in journalism was on a small scale, a German-language *Bulletin* issued for his Kultusgemeinde in New York (1927-1933?).[33] But expansion came rapidly and in 1930 his newly formed concern (German Jewish Publishers) was able to finance publication of the *Jüdische Zeitgeist* (1930-1937) and its continuation, the *Jüdisches Familienblatt* (September, 1937-February, 1939). The *Familienblatt* represented a faction of the German-Jewish community opposed to the *Aufbau's* policy of urging rapid assimilation on the newcomers. The first issue of the new paper underlined this point: "The *Judisches Familienblatt* is an organ for all Jews, a paper that fights against that unfortunate passion for assimilation. . . ."[34] In turn the *Familienblatt* was superseded by the bilingual *Our Way in America,* a community bulletin of moderate circulation which in July of 1940 merged with yet another similar paper, the *Neues Jüdisches* [sic] *Gemeindeblatt,* organ of the Washington Heights community (further bibliographical details of the New York *Gemeindeblätter* are given in Appendix II). Documentation on the German-Jewish press outside of the New York area is virtually nonexistent but other papers did exist — e.g., the *Neue Welt* of Los Angeles and the *Cosmopolitan News* of Baltimore.[35]

The German-Jewish émigré press, both in the United States and elsewhere, should really be termed an immigrant press, since it was first of all concerned with problems of adapting to a new homeland rather than with the fate of any exiled political party.[36] The individual Jew did take part in émigré politics, but as a German rather than a Jew. The dominant view of the German-Jewish community was most clearly expressed by the editor of the *Aufbau,* Manfred George, as he condemned the continual dissensions among the German immigrants: "We are loyal to America and take seriously only the attainment of her war aims. We belong to no German or Socialist International who wish to burden the American people with their political and party strife."[37]

The *Aufbau* and its readers were soon immersed in American politics, enthusiastically supporting New Deal liberalism and keeping their distance from organized Marxism (in contrast to earlier European migrations of the twentieth century). The dominant creed of the Jewish emigrants was (in Eduard Heimann's words) a conservative liberalism:

> Their political allegiance in Germany was to a distinctly conservative liberalism, where liberalism meant the vital issue of tolerance, and conservatism meant the preservation of their prosperous condition. It must not be concluded that all German Jews were members of the upper bourgeoisie. Probably the majority came from small towns, where they used to own and manage a butcher's or dairy shop or the like.[38]

While Manfred George and the *Aufbau* represent the militantly positive, the optimistic face of the German-Jewish community, a glimpse of the shadows is captured by the gifted artist and writer Karl Jakob Hirsch:

> I had just given a lecture there [the German Jewish Club in New York City] on Heine and the emigration, which left me very unsatisfied. I remember that while reading from my manuscript, I suddenly realized how hopeless and backward-looking the German-Jewish emigration was. One lived on memories and the future was expressed in one word—America, which however, meant something different to each person. To some it meant the recapturing of past glories, to others salvation through assimilation of the American Dream.[39]

The Austrian Émigrés and Their Press

The Anschluss of Austria in 1938 by Nazi Germany was the signal for the hurried departure of Jews, labor leaders, Social Democrats, Communists, and other anti-Nazis. In the latter category we can include the monarchists (supporters of the House of Habsburg) and the remnants of the Vaterländische Front (VF)—the Austrian mélange of Fascism and Catholicism. Members of the VF who reached the United States included Guido Zernatto (poet and General Secretary of the Front) who died in New York in 1943, Hans Rott, and Richard Schueller, Rott and Schueller being former members of Chancellor Kurt von Schuschnigg's cabinet.

Assistance for the mass of refugees pouring out of Vienna after 1938 was provided by a Zentral Vereinigung Österreichischen Emigranten set up in Paris with an advisory board made up of Sigmund Freud, Franz Werfel, and Alfred Polgar. The group published the *Nouvelles d'Autriche, Oesterreichische Nachrichten* for which subscriptions were solicited in the United States.

The Austrian community in this country prior to 1933 was not large compared to the German-American, and besides it was not imbued with strong national feelings; immigrants from the Habsburg empire seemed especially sensitive to their ethnic origins and preferred to join together in Hungarian, Bohemian, Croatian, or Ruthenian associations. After World War I, the emigrants from the newly proclaimed Republic were almost all Burgenlanders from Lower Austria; these *Landsleute,* mostly from the laboring class, worked together in trade unions, social, and recreational organizations.[40]

Austrian and German emigrants belonged to many of the same organizations before 1939, but afterwards political considerations fostered the growth of independent Austrian associations. The United States had never granted de jure recognition to the incorporation of Austria into the

German Reich and consequently when war broke out with Germany, Austrians were *not* classified as enemy aliens—a fact that allowed them considerably more freedom of movement. The friendly alien status and the growing desire to protect Austrian autonomy after the war led to a proliferation of Austrian-centered newspapers as well as political action committees. These special motivations, the relative smallness of the Austrian emigration, and the nonexistence of an "Austrian-America" set the Austrian press apart from the German in one important respect: most of the Austrian papers were exclusively devoted to exile political interest—that could not be said of any German émigré paper.

The presence in wartime America of Otto von Habsburg, the head of the House of Habsburg, and former Empress Zita, his mother, added an element of Ruritanian improbability to Austrian émigré life. Capitalizing on an American proclivity for royalty in distress and a naïveté regarding the facts of Central European life, the monarchists made a bid to take over the leadership of the Austrian emigration. The U.S. War Department, at one point during World War II, proposed, or at least assented to the formation of an all-Austrian battalion (to be led by Archduke Otto) that would serve alongside American forces.

At the same time Otto, in speeches made throughout the country, insisted on referring to himself as ruler of the Croats, Slovenes, Czechs, and Hungarians—drawing (not surprisingly) an enraged response from members of these national groups living in the United States (and particularly from the governments-in-exile of Poland and Czechoslovakia). Highly vocal opposition from Austrian republicans and Social Democrats as well as from interested Americans rapidly "enlightened" official opinion, and the government had to disavow any thought of restoring the Habsburg dynasty. The denouement was reached (according to Austrian Social Democratic Julius Deutsch) when "of the tens of thousands of Austrian males in the U.S.A. only two dozen were found ready to join the Habsburg battalion."[41]

Although failing on the international stage, the monarchists, with probable financial aid from Otto, were strongly entrenched within several nominally nonpolitical organizations such as the Austrian Committee[42]—pulled together in 1941 and chaired by Richard Schueller—and the later Austrian National Committee (chairman, Hans Rott), a coordinating agency for numerous partisan groups that soon was exclusively monarchist in persuasion.[43] A most outspokenly monarchist and antilabor journal was *Austria, Organ der bürgerlichen Meinung,* in the camp of former Minister Rott and the voice of his Christliche-sozialistische Partei in 1944.[44] Rott was also in Canada for a time, working with the *Donau Echo* (Toronto) and *Voice of Austria* (Ottawa), two papers that had subscribers across the border.

Between the émigré monarchists and the Socialists stood the moderate bourgeois majority that gave birth to Austrian Action and the Assembly for a Democratic Austrian Republic, organizations dominated by the idea of an independent Austria. Austrian Action, led by Graf Ferdinand Czernin, began operations in March of 1941. Hoping to become the spokesman for all Austrians abroad, the organization tried to amalgamate with groups of exiles in other countries.[45] In the United States alone, Austrian Action established affiliates in eight major cities including Portland, Oregon, and Miami Beach, and in five Latin American countries; this after only one year of activity.[46] The official newspaper was *Österreichische Rundschau,* devoted almost exclusively to émigré life and politics — published from February, 1942 to May, 1945, at which time the organization was dissolved and its leaders returned to Austria.

A different course was followed by the Assembly for a Democratic Austrian Republic and its paper, the *Austro-American Tribune*. The Assembly began its career in May of 1942 and one month later issued the first number of *Freiheit für Österreich,* "a non-subsidized anti-Nazi paper entirely supported by donations of members."[47] In July, 1943 the Assembly underwent a transformation, merging with the Austrian Social Club to form the Austro-American Association. Changing the name of its newspaper from *Freiheit für Österreich* to *Austro-American Tribune* (an emphasis now on the New rather than the Old World) indicated a clear shift in policy: "At present," the editors explained, "there is no more important task than to assist future Americans in integrating into American life, and to give their utmost to the war effort."[48] While the primarily political newspapers of the Austrian emigration ceased publication abruptly at war's end, the *Austro-American Tribune* continued until mid-1949; although the most representative newspaper of the Austrian emigration, it was (as was the *Aufbau*) essentially an immigrant paper.

Like the German Social Democrats after 1933, the Austrian Socialists (SPÖ) were accused of theoretical rigidity, abandonment of radical Socialist principles, and domination by an old guard. Just as the New Beginners pricked the sensitivities of the SPD, so the Revolutionary Socialists (RSÖ) attempted to abrogate the authority of the old party leaders who, since 1934, were operating from Brünn on the sufferance of the Czech government. The two situations, however, were not really identical, since Otto Bauer (leader of the old Austrian party) was quite sympathetic with the aims and methods of the new underground group, and the leaders of the illegal party still retained the highest personal respect for Bauer. Although Josef Buttinger, leader of the RSÖ, declined to participate in exile politics upon his arrival in the United States, many of his co-workers held different sentiments.[49] Leafing through the well-printed pages of the *Austrian Labor Information* (N.Y.) one discovers the names of some of the most prominent Austrian Socialists of the past decades: Friedrich Adler (secretary of the Socialist International), Manfred Ackermann, Julius Deutsch (military expert of the Austrian party and a Loyalist "General" during the Spanish Civil War), Karl Hans Sailer (a rival of Buttinger's for leadership of the RSÖ), and Otto Leichter (prominent journalist and former editor of the *Arbeiter-Zeitung* in Vienna).

As the official organ of the SPÖ in exile, the *Austrian Labor Information*[50] pledged itself to the support of Austrian labor in the United States and to the interest of labor throughout the world. It is worth noting that the *Labor Information* was the only Austrian newspaper not actively behind postwar Austrian autonomy; it still cherished the old Socialist hope for a unified German and Austrian proletariat. For this reason, the SPÖ, in the United States at any rate, never joined any of the several Free Austrian federations. The paper itself was a model of sober party journalism with occasional photographs and many scholarly articles; a detailed index for the first twenty-four issues was published in April, 1944. Some of the material was reworked, translated into English, and published irregularly as the *Austrian Labor News,* a mimeographed paper. The *Austrian Labor Information* was the only German-language Marxian-Socialist journal dealing seriously with international problems of Socialism published during the post-1940 period. Whether this is attributable to the inspiration of Socialist doctrine or to the tenacity of tradition is a moot point.

After viewing the patchwork quality of Austrian émigré journalism—there were at least seven newspapers or bulletins in addition to those discussed above—one may be entitled to accept as unconscious irony a statement printed in the *Österreichisches Rundschau:* "We would like to point out that there is no such thing as Austrian disunity."[51] Attention has already been called to the strong monarchist contingent that encouraged much of this fragmentation. On the other hand, as opposed to the German, the Austrian Left was represented by only *one* newspaper, the Socialist *Austrian Labor Information.* After 1938 the "illegal" and the "old-guard" Austrian Socialists were reunited and worked together with an outward show of harmony. Contrast this with the enduring quarrels, at least in the United States, between the New Beginners and the older German Social Democrats. Amity on the Left was also encouraged by a lack of any vocal Austrian Communist clique among the émigrés in the United States (although they were active elsewhere). Finally, there was a major distinction between the

Austrian Socialist paper and the German *Neue Volks-Zeitung:* the former was operated by and for the Austrian exiles; the latter was indeed editorially controlled by a small group of political exiles, but its audience was largely made up of older German-American workers.

Notes

1. These remarks are wholly inapplicable to the Austrian émigrés (in the U.S. at least), among whom non-Marxist organizations and newspapers were by far the most numerous.

2. "Struktur und Charakter der deutschen Emigration," *Politische Studien,* 6, Nr.67:12 (1955). Gottfried von Treviranus, member of the Volkskonservative Vereinigung and Reichsminister (1930–1932), emigrated to Canada. Hermann Rauschning, president of the Danzig Senate until 1936, broke with the Nazis and fled via Poland, Switzerland, France, and England, reaching the United States in 1941. His several important books were among the best expositions of the dangers of National Socialism. Erich Koch-Weser (actually a half-Jew) was chairman of the Deutsche Demokratische Partei.

3. The German Freedom Party (based in Paris and London) was created in 1937 on a strictly conspiratorial basis and was not in any real sense a political party. It was one of the few exile groups to maintain contact with dissident elements in the German army. Among its leaders were: Karl Spiecker, former press chief of the Brüning cabinet; August Weber, industrialist and banker, member of the Deutsche Demokratische Partei; Hans Albert Kluthe, journalist and also member of the DDP; and Willi Münzenberg after his break with the Communist Party in 1937. See Gross, "The German Communists' United-Front and Popular-Front Ventures," p.132–33 and Berthold, *Exil-Literatur 1933–1945,* p.151–57.

4. George W. Pate, "Free Germans in the U.S.," *The Christian Science Monitor,* Nov. 14, 1942, p.5 et passim.

5. Otto Strasser, *Exil* (München: The Author, 1958), p.155–56.

6. Not to be confused with the Soviet-inspired Free Germany Committees of 1943–45.

7. *Hitlers Sturz durch die Frei-Deutschland Bewegung* (New York: Free Europe Radio Station, 1941), 16p.; note the fictitious imprint. Besides the English language version, *Free Germany Against Hitler,* with only a post office box number on the cover, Strasser collaborated with Douglas Fairbanks Jr. on *Hitler's Shadow Over South America,* issued under the imprint Free German Movement, Brooklyn, 1942. By this time Strasser was in Canada.

8. George W. Pate, op. cit., p.5.

9. Edinger, *German Exile Politics,* p.171–74.

10. Ohio Representative William R. Thom suggested official U.S. recognition of Strasser's Free Germany Movement. Strasser, op. cit., p.156.

11. The *Aufbau* (N.Y.) of April 17, 1942 (p.7) noted that Strasser's reception in the Midwest was aided by his brother Bernhard (a Benedictine at St. John's, Collegeville, Minn.) who had written favorably in the *Aurora und Christliche Woche* (Buffalo), Jan. 29, 1942. Turning to the original (really only a letter to the editor), we find it overtly anti-Semitic: "And now the Communists and Jews led by Herr Greszinsky have formed their own Frei Deutschland Bewegung [i.e. Association of Free Germans] naturally against my brother Otto Strasser." After the war, the *Aufbau* reported that a number of Midwestern papers—in particular the *Deutsche Wochenschrift* of St. Louis—were continuing to support Strasser in his vain efforts to build a German Catholic People's Party (Sept. 5, 1947, p.5).

12. Rukser, born in 1892, was a lawyer and journalist, founder and editor of *Das Ostrecht* which ceased publication in 1933 because of Rukser's refusal to fire his Jewish collaborators. In 1938 he emigrated to Chile. Theile (1904-) was a successful writer, journalist, and translator. He left Germany in 1933. For a list of contributors to the *Deutsche Blätter* (among whom were Thomas Mann, Carl Jung, Arnold Brecht, Hermann Hesse, and Arthur Koestler) see Berthold, op. cit., p.296.

13. He shared this post with Dr. Joseph Kaskell of New York.

14. *Deutsche Blätter,* 2, Heft 6:47 (1944).

15. Berendsohn 2:273.

16. Ibid., p.272.

17. *Young Germany* (New York: Basic Books, 1962), p.180. See also Otto Ernst Schüddekopf, *Linke Leute von Rechts* (Stuttgart: W. Kohlhammer, 1960), for the best study of the movement.

18. See "Kurzbiographie," Karl O. Paetel, *Jugendbewegung und Politik* (Bad Godesberg: Voggenreiter, 1961), p.186-89.

19. Karl O. Paetel, "Deutsche Gegenwart in den U.S.A.," *Börsenblatt für den deutschen Buchhandel* (Frankfurt am Main), 15:1007-11 (1959).

20. Werner Wille, ed., *Aufrecht zwischen den Stühlen: K.O.P. Grüsse zum 50. Geburtstag* (Nürnberg: Druckhaus Nürnberg, 1956), p.70-72.

21. Letter to the author from Karl Paetel (original in German), Dec. 29, 1963.

22. Julius and Edith Hirsch, "Berufliche Eingliederung und wirtschaftliche Leistung der deutsch-juedischen Einwanderung in die Vereinigten Staaten (1934-1960)," p.44.

23. Max Malina, *Deutsche Juden in New York nach dem Weltkriege* (New York, 1931), p.15.

24. Ibid., p.13.

25. Literally, "Ein Bekenntnis deutscher Juden zum Deutschtum," *Aufbau* (N.Y.), Jan. 1, 1935, p.1.

26. Fred Bielefeld, "Unser Club," *Aufbau Almanach* (New York, 1941), p.30-33; Ludwig Lowenstein, "Die Entwicklung des 'New World Club,' " in American Federation of Jews from Central Europe, Inc., *Twenty Years,* p.71-76; Davie, *Refugees in America,* p.112.

27. At one time an editor of the *Frankfurter Zeitung,* Brandl, prior to his departure from Germany, was Chief Librarian at the Ullsteinhaus in Berlin. He was editor of the *Aufbau* from 1937 to 1939.

28. See Rudolf Brandl, *That Good Old Fool, Uncle Sam: A Refugee Sounds a Warning* (New York, 1940), and "Der Kulturverband und seine Sippe," *Gegen den Strom* (N.Y.), 2:9-25 (Oct./Nov., 1939). In the latter, Brandl (p.18) attacked a "Marxist" organization that met in the German Jewish Club building, remarking that the boys and girls belonging to that group had developed the ability "to burst out with the anathema 'Trotskyite' in all the wrong places." His bitter, sardonic attacks are good examples of anti-Communist polemics among the émigrés (in a class with Ruth Fischer's *The Network*); but one must be wary of accepting his charges at face value.

29. Berendsohn 2:197-99.

30. Manfred George, "Ueber den Aufbau," *Aufbau Almanach* (1941), p.8.

31. Berendsohn has said that "one could compile from the *Aufbau* alone an anthology of German lyrics of the emigration." Berendsohn 2:210.

32. Hugo Hahn, "The Religious Situation of Our Generation," in American Federation of Jews from Central Europe, *Twenty Years,* p.86. See also, Alexander Carlebach, "The German-Jewish Immigration (1933-1942) and Its Influence on Synagogue Life in the U.S.A.," *Leo Baeck Institute Year Book,* 9:351-72 (1964).

33. A Sonderheft of this bulletin exists dated 1933. Max Malina, ed., *Anti-Semitismus — Hitlerismus.*

34. Sept. 1, 1937.

35. *Cosmopolitan News, Mitteilungsblätter des Phönix Club* and official organ of the New Hebrew Cosmospolitan Society; cited in the *Aufbau* (N.Y.), Oct. 1, 1939, p.12.

36. During the war, the Association of Jewish Refugees in Great Britain publicly stated that it was in no way connected with the machinations of exile political groups in London. Quoted in *Aufbau* (N.Y.), March 3, 1944, p.1.

37. Manfred George, "Deutschland Politik in U.S.A.," *Aufbau*, Jan. 28, 1944, quoted in Berendsohn 2:203.

38. Heimann, "The Refugee Speaks," *Annals of the American Academy of Political and Social Sciences*, 203:109 (May 1939). See also Hans J. Morgenthau, *The Tragedy of German-Jewish Liberalisms* (The Leo Baeck Memorial Lectures 4, New York: Leo Baeck Institute, 1961).

39. *Heimkehr zu Gott* (München: Verlag Kurt Desch, 1946), p.106.

40. The Burgenlanders formed the core of the Austro-American Trade Union Committee for Victory. *Austro-American Tribune* (N.Y.), Oct., 1943.

41. *Ein Weiter Weg* (Zürich: Amalthea, 1960), p.362. See also Gary Travers Grayson, *Austria's International Position 1938-1953* (Genève: Droz, 1953), p.42.

42. Wilhelm Schlag, "A Survey of Austrian Emigration to the United States," Otto Hietsch, ed., *Österreich und die angelsächsische Welt* (Wien: Braumüller, 1961), p.187. The *Aufbau* (N.Y.), June 20, 1941, p.2, lists the members.

43. Kurt Hellmer, "Wandlungen der Oesterreichischen Monarchisten," *Aufbau*, March 17, 1944, p.9 et passim. For a list of committee members, see *Oesterreichische Rundschau*, March 7, 1942.

44. *Aufbau* (N.Y.), Dec. 15, 1944, p.8. The editor, Octave O. Günther, a long-time resident of the United States, had, back in the days of Franz Joseph, issued a newspaper of the same name from New York City. According to Arndt and Olson, *German-American Newspapers and Periodicals 1732-1955*, p.343, it lasted from 1909 to 1914.

45. In 1944 Austrian Action joined a new Free Austrian Movement with headquarters in London and a Latin American center in Montevideo. A further example of international cooperation among the Austrians was the newspaper *Zeitspiegel*, published in London by the Austrian Centre and read in forty-one countries including the United States (as of 1944). Austrian Centre, *Five Years* (London, 1944), p.12.

46. *Österreichische Rundschau* (N.Y.), April 11, 1942.

47. A dig at Habsburg-financed monarchist papers. *Freiheit für Österreich* (N.Y.), July, 1942.

48. *Austro-American Tribune* (N.Y.), July, 1943.

49. See Buttinger, *In the Twilight of Socialism*, p.514-46, for a description of émigré politics and his own justification for leaving the party.

50. Nos.1-37, April 20, 1942 to May 1, 1945.

51. March 7, 1942.

VI
Import Trade
in Free German Books

America at Peace

On the occasion of the first German American Conference held in 1932, a group of dealers in German books decided to form their own protective association—the Gemeinschaft der Deutschen Buchhändler in New York. Led by the long established firms of G. E. Stechert, E. Steiger and Co., and B. Westermann, a total of fourteen bookdealers, among them one specialist in Socialist literature,[1] banded together for the encouragement of the German book in America. A more unpropitious time for unity could hardly have been chosen. The new organization was much too weak to weather the storm that broke during the following year.

From 1933 to Pearl Harbor there was continuing pressure on American dealers in German-language books to choose between distributing Nazi-approved or émigré publications; only these dealers who were already ideologically committed faced no such dilemma. It should be emphasized that by 1933 facilities for the import and distribution of Socialist and Communist literature in the German language were already in existence and would continue to serve as key outlets for Free German publications for years to come. Retail distribution of nonparty literature—books from the Bermann-Fischer Verlag, from Holland, Switzerland, and elsewhere—was taken over in large part by the recently arrived émigrés themselves. The established importers and retailers in the

United States were, for a long while, hesitant to make a clear choice, yet growing anti-Nazi sentiment in the late thirties made one unavoidable.

Until late in 1938 the retail trade in Free German literature was rather disorganized. American bookstores had to order directly from Amsterdam, Zürich, Prague, or Paris since there was as yet no central depository in New York to compete with such distributors of "official" German literature as B. Westermann, Inc.[2] During those early years the fight for Free German literature in America was carried on primarily by Socialist, Communist, and Jewish groups feeding a growing anti-Nazism among Americans that soon gave rise to a boycott of German goods (leading in turn to counterdemonstrations by Nazi sympathizers). America's foreign policy was becoming more and more anti-German, and no one was surprised when the government openly assisted the boycott of Nazi publications by increasing tariffs on German imports by 25 percent.[3] This action happily coincided with the establishment in New York City of two émigré concerns which aimed at centralizing the import of Free German books — the Alliance Book Corporation and Friedrich Krause's Zentrale freier deutschen Literatur — events greatly enhancing the image of this American metropolis as a new gathering place of "das andere Deutschland."

Granted that the unhampered import of Free German publications lasted until December, 1941, what was its real importance in terms of volume? The number of anti-Nazi German-language periodicals and newspapers, for example, available in the United States by subscription or direct sale was impressive. At least sixty were easily obtainable and frequently advertised — twenty-three of these were non-Communist in origin. But the circulation of the average émigré journal was, to begin with, not very large. The weekly printing of the German Social Democrats' *Neuer Vorwärts,* when published in Paris (1938–1940), averaged 5000 copies — and this was one of the most widely read exile newspapers.[4] On the other hand, Communist-backed publications, vehicles for propaganda which were continually pressed upon the German-American worker, enjoyed a much more inflated edition size. Thus the literary periodical *Das Wort* (Moscow) boasted an initial printing of 5000 in 1936, a figure that was increased to 7000 by popular demand with the second issue.[5] The poor economic position of both German-American workers and the new immigrants, at least from 1933 to 1941, inhibited widespread sales of imported journals despite their availability. Furthermore, these imports faced stiff competition from the numerous Free German newspapers actually published in America. Average circulation of imported periodicals, then, can scarcely be estimated at more than 200–500 copies per issue.

The volume of book imports is equally difficult to ascertain. If one bears in mind (1) the production figures for Free German books already cited (p.13-14), (2) the number (probably not large) of German-speaking residents who would purchase books at all, let alone any by anti-Nazi authors, and (3) the economic environment of prewar America, it is doubtful that sales of imported Free German books exceeded 500-1000 copies per title (with the exception of certain very popular works of Thomas Mann, Stefan Zweig, and Franz Werfel). The always optimistic Friedrich Krause, drawing on his several years of bookselling experience in New York, estimated that the total volume of American sales for 1941 would reach 100,000:

> On the basis of findings made during my travels through the United States, from information received from colleagues, from the sales figures of my firm and from the statements of large libraries, one may estimate a yearly sale of 100,000 Free German books in the United States. Considered as Free German literature are naturally not only all books printed outside the Third Reich but also most of the works published in Germany before 1933 that were later either burned or suppressed. . . . Whoever buys such books does his bit not only to keep the production of Free German books alive, but to see it grow. Whoever finds himself unable to purchase books should at least go to the public library and as often as possible ask for titles of Free German publications. Orders from the libraries will follow according to demand.[6]

Whether or not this was an accurate appraisal is hard to say; it certainly did not have any predictive value for the war years that followed.

America at War

The European war ended the primacy of the continent as a source of Free German publications (except, of course, for Sweden and Switzerland), and the balance of production shifted to new areas. A sporadic blossoming of émigré publishing occurred in the United States and Latin America as well as in Palestine and England. Palestine possessed a very sizable German-speaking population and was the source of a great variety of émigré publications.[7] The export of books from the British Mandate to the United States was still feasible as late as October 1942, and was again in full swing by January 1945. Free German books from Britain (after a brief hiatus of about two years) were available in America even before 1945.[8]

More important were the wartime contacts maintained between the United States and Latin America, particularly with the nearby Communist colony in Mexico City from whence German comrades, by 1939 already in control of the Liga Pro Cultura Alemana en Mexico,[9] were able to export propaganda material.[10] It was in 1942, when the supply of German publications from the Soviet Union was temporarily halted, that the Mexican émigrés came to the aid of their North American fellows. One link between the two countries was the German-language monthly, *Freies Deutschland* (Mexico City), which had in 1942 a circulation of 3900 and was distributed in both the Americas.[11] On May 10, 1942, ninth anniversary of the Nazi book-burning extravaganza, the most noteworthy achievement of the German Communists in Mexico was announced—the founding of the German-language publishing house of El Libro Libre (Mexico City). As advertised in the German-American press, the first six books to be issued were offered to Americans at a subscription price of two dollars each, three dollars after publication.[12] An impressive total of at least twenty books in German and six in Spanish were printed by El Libro Libre from 1942 through 1946.

The contributions of the Free German book trade in South America are less well known. Besides the highly esteemed *Deutsche Blätter* (Santiago de Chile), other émigré journals from below the equator could boast of a small but faithful audience in the North. *Das andere Deutschland* (Buenos Aires and Montevideo, 1938–1948), edited by August Siemsen, first appeared as a hektographed monthly, then as a printed bi-weekly; during the 1940s a fair portion of its approximately 3000 circulation was directed to American subscribers.[13] Also from Buenos Aires came the only daily anti-Nazi German newspaper printed in the Western Hemisphere, or so the editors of the *Argentinisches Tageblatt* claimed. The paper was no émigré journal (having been founded long before, in 1889) but it did wholeheartedly welcome contributions from émigré writers and was widely read in the United States.[14] From Chile came Paul Hesslein's *Wirtschaftliche Privatinformation für Chile und Südamerika* (1938–1944), half of whose 400 subscribers—including Thomas Mann, Emil Ludwig, and the conductor Fritz Busch—lived in the United States.[15]

Free German books soon began to be printed in South America after the war had all but isolated the emigrant colonies there. Two Buenos Aires firms, Editorial Cosmopolita and Editorial Estrellas, offered especially interesting lists including the first edition of Franz Werfel's *Eine blassblaue Frauenschrift* (Estrellas, 1941).[16] At the same time several adventurous South American booksellers, specialists in anti-Nazi literature, made serious efforts to find new markets in the United States by advertising in the German-American press. Here is an example: "South America's largest Antifa-bookstore, Alejandro Barna y Hijos, Buenos

Aires, international bookstore, German books, free catalogue."[17] Walter Berendsohn even reports on the activities of one E. Friedländer of São Paulo, who in 1942 attempted to unify the independent German book-dealers in both the Americas in order "to blaze new paths for the Free German Book."[18] He was not successful.

As the war in Europe entered its final months, trade with England, Switzerland, Sweden, and Palestine was once again established on a regular basis. For several years after 1945 the publishing of Free German books experienced an Indian Summer in both Europe and America—a situation which lasted until the revival of German publishing in the four Allied zones of occupation.

Channels of Distribution

GERMAN SOCIALISTS

This study now considers in some detail those persons and agencies responsible for distributing Free German publications in America, first looking at those affiliated with the German-American Left. By 1933 German-American Socialists, once the backbone of the American movement, were in difficult straits partly due to the decline in German immigration from the peak years of the late nineteenth and early twentieth centuries, but also attributable to the inroads made by the new and dynamic Communist Party. Hardly any German Socialist newspaper had been able to weather the great depression; only the *New Yorker Volkszeitung* endured, although in the revamped guise of the weekly *Neue Volks-Zeitung*. This newspaper together with the Moderne Deutsche Buchhandlung in New York were the major channels of distribution for German Socialist publications—those sanctioned by the German and Austrian Social Democrats as well as those issued by various independent groups.

The Moderne Deutsche Buchhandlung, which dates from 1932, exemplified the plight of German-American Socialism vis-a-vis the Communist Party. The owner, Herman Kormis, maintained connections with the German-American Communists until 1935 by advertising in the party organ, *Der Arbeiter*. Neither party member nor sympathizer, Kormis incurred the displeasure of the German-language section of the CPA, resulting in the establishment of a rival Communist bookstore some few doors away.[19] Now boycotted by the Communists, Kormis was limited to advertising in the German-Jewish *Aufbau,* the *Neue Volks-Zeitung*, and the independent *Gegen den Strom. Publishers' Weekly* brought his store to national attention in an article titled

"Anti-Nazi Bookstores in N.Y."[20] The same article gave equal attention to the Communist Deutsche Zentral-Buchhandlung—oblivious, of course, to their bitter rivalry, ideological as well as commercial.

More closely identified with the trade in SPD publications after 1933 was the *Neue Volks-Zeitung*. (Socialist literature was also available directly from Vienna[21] but only until the Austrian Socialist uprising of February, 1934, and the consequent banning of the party by the Dollfuss government.) The New York German-language paper soon was able to supply all publications issued by the SPD in exile under its Graphia imprint and by 1936 added to their offerings the books of the Social-ist-minded Oprecht and Europa Verlage. As part of its untiring cam-paign against the Nazis, the paper urged all workers to boycott German books from the Third Reich and buy only Free German literature:

> No books for Christmas published in Germany after 1932! All books published in Germany since 1933 have been censored by Propaganda Minister Goebbels and are permeated by the National Socialist *Welt-anschauung*. The Free German spirit lives only in the books of émigré writers. Support these authors who have taken upon themselves the hard lot of emigration because they did not wish to submit spiritually to Dr. Goebbels. You will do your part in upholding and furthering the German spirit by keeping a sharp eye on your friends and acquaintances urging them to buy only books published outside Germany. We will supply you with every book published outside Germany at the original price.[22]

During the war the growing scarcity of Free German books and the now large number of retail dealers active in the New York area induced the paper to drop out of the book business.

Another method for distributing German Socialist literature was the book club, today so much a part of the publishing scene. In the month of August, 1924, the Educational Association of German Printers (Bil-dungsverband der deutschen Buchdrucker) in Berlin founded the Büchergilde Gutenberg to provide the German worker with inexpensive, well-designed editions of good literature. By 1933, the Guild could boast of 85,000 members,[23] as well as branches in Zürich, Prague, and Vienna. The collapse of the Weimar Republic brought with it the *Gleichschaltung* of the parent organization in Berlin under the direction of the renegade proletarian poets, Max Barthel and Heinrich Lersch.[24] With the support of the Oprecht brothers (Emil and Hans) in Zürich, Bruno Dressler, the former manager of the Berlin Guild, now guided the fortunes of the Swiss affiliate, preserving its original Socialist tradition.[25]

From 1935 to 1945 Guild membership increased rapidly and sales enjoyed a prodigious growth—from 74,800 volumes in 1933 to 2,765,000 in 1945.[26] As of 1930, the Guild could count over 1,100

foreign members, including many in the United States. Although for
1933 and afterwards, the number of American members is not ascertainable, the Guild was actively soliciting memberships in this country as
well as selling directly to the general public through the pages of the
Neue Volks-Zeitung.[27] Many Guild books were works by German and
Austrian émigrés; many were translations of American authors — Sinclair
Lewis, John Dos Passos, and Upton Sinclair in particular. One of the
most popular of German (or German-American?) writers, the mys-
terious "B. Traven," author of the *Treasure of the Sierra Madre* and
other tales of adventure, requested that his books be exclusively published and distributed by the Guild after 1933.[28] As the *Aufbau* phrased
it in 1941, the Büchergilde Gutenberg functioned as a cultural institution
in those barbarous times.[29]

THE CPA-*Literatur als Waffe*

Distribution of German Communist literature in the United States
was under strict party control; each party member was fully aware that
this was one of his most important tasks. In 1928 local German-
language groups of the CPA received the following directive:

> Next to the regular leadership there should be in every *Bund* a Literature
> Chief responsible for the sale of Marxist literature and proletarian nov-
> els. The Literature Department of the *Arbeiter* stands by ready to supply
> trustworthy comrades with valuable guides and financial support.[30]

By 1934 "anti-Fascist" replaced "Marxist" but the message was the
same:

> Work for the anti-Fascist press! Read, subscribe and recruit for the
> German anti-Fascist newspaper! Distribute these newspapers at all gath-
> erings. . . . No demonstrations without these newspapers. Circulate them
> in all mass organizations.[31]

Not only New York and Chicago were exposed to the proselyting
activities of the German Bureau; a report from St. Louis is probably
typical:

> In the schools, the colleges and in the two universities, we must make
> our influence felt, particularly upon the German teachers and their stu-
> dents. The demand for German reading material is great, perhaps we can
> make the *Volksecho* and other German anti-Fascist magazines and books
> popular. We must concern ourselves about the libraries so that they
> obtain the most important items of anti-Fascist German literature.[32]

An unintentionally comic manifestation of this passionate concern for
the printed page was the Antifa-Presseball held in 1934 to which com-

rades of both sexes were invited to dine and dance; the feature attrac-
tion—in the center of the ballroom floor—a small printing press in
flagrante delicto.[33]

Agencies for the distribution of German-language Communist literature came and went with a certain transiency, reflecting the chame-
leon-like history of the party. Advertising in *Der Arbeiter* from that
paper's first issue in 1927 (but only for a few years thereafter) was the
Modern Bookshop, whose rather commonplace name hid its exotic
origin. The shop was founded in 1925 by several Hungarian refugees
from the wreckage of Bela Kun's Hungarian Soviet Republic and was
located in the Hungarian Workers' Home, New York.[34]

A more important source was the *Arbeiter* itself. The main *Arbeiter*
bookstore was housed in the *Daily Worker* building on Thirteenth Street
in lower Manhattan, in business there since 1928. Almost immediately a
Yorkville branch was started, followed soon after by Arbeiterbuch-
handlungen in Philadelphia, Milwaukee, and Chicago. These branches
(according to Kormis) amounted to nothing more pretentious than the
private apartment of the *Arbeiter* agent in each city where material
obtained from the New York office would be sold. Periodically *Der
Arbeiter* informed its readers of the current whereabouts of their local
literature agents, for these political colporteurs were of necessity highly
mobile. Both the *Arbeiter* and its successor the *Deutsches Volksecho*
found it expedient to entice new subscribers with book bait—premiums
of such immediate appeal as the German translation of Michael Gold's,
Jews without Money (Juden ohne Geld) and a Jack London Bibliothek
in sixteen volumes, all printed in Moscow.[35]

The German Bureau made use of retail outlets other than the party
press and, as has already been observed, opened its own bookstore in
1935, a stone's throw from Herman Kormis' Moderne Deutsche Buchhandlung. The Deutsche Zentral-Buchhandlung, as it was called, was
welcomed by the party press as a store for the masses, a new headquarters for the German anti-Fascist book. In one newspaper story qualified
praise was bestowed upon the worthy efforts of privately owned stores
which were hampered by lack of organization—each store having to deal
directly with either a large number of European publishers or a cumber-
some apparatus of middlemen. To rectify this situation, the newspaper
report continued, a number of publishers of anti-Fascist literature decided to set up one central book depot thereby cutting expenses and
simplifying the work of retail book dealers—this at least was the official
pronouncement. In reality, the store was interested only in distributing
books of Communist publishers.[36] Despite party support the venture
was not a rousing success, as the *Volksecho* all but confessed in January
of 1939: "We had reported several times about attempts to centralize

the trade in Free German publications in New York. These, for reasons which as of now cannot be divulged [i.e. too much competition] were not successful."[37]

In a further attempt to entice customers away from rival dealers and at the same time to move some of its own stock off the shelves, the Deutsche Zentral-Buchhandlung (in September, 1935) started a book club for German anti-Fascist literature:

> The Deutsche Zentral-Bücherei is a book society for all Germans in America who are openly opposed to any kind of cultural barbarianism. The Deutsche Zentral-Bücherei will supply only worthwhile and finely produced books both well-documented and illustrated. Every novel will be carefully selected to be anti-Fascist as well as a work of real artistic merit. Each book will cost from two to three dollars, for members only one dollar and fifty cents. The quarterly selections will be interchangeable. From February 1, 1936 a bi-monthly *Mitteilungsblatt* will be sent free to members.[38]

By the end of 1939 the Deutsche Zentral Buchhandlung and its associated book club were at long last hors de combat. The trade in pro-Communist Free German publications picked up again in 1942, now that the United States and the Soviet Union were wartime allies. The party newspaper, the *German American* (New York), acted as a retail source for its own publications, those of El Libro Libre (Mexico City), and other friendly presses. One other dealer with radical affiliations made his debut in New York in 1944 — Wieland Herzfelde and his Seven Seas Bookshop, a pendant to his German-language publishing house, Aurora Verlag.

Commercial Distributors of Free German Books

Large scale commercial distribution of Free German literature began with the establishment of H. G. Koppell's Alliance Book Corporation and the Zentrale freier deutschen Bücher of Friedrich Krause. This made sense in 1938 for political as well as economic reasons, not the least of which was the potentially large German reading audience that included the steadily increasing stream of anti-Nazi emigrants.

Heinrich Günther Koppell, the man behind the Alliance Book Corporation, already had a distinguished European career as the organizer and first manager of Germany's largest book club, the Deutsche Buchgemeinschaft. Resigning in 1932, he spent four years in Palestine before making his way to the United States. Here he put into action an ambitious plan for the dissemination of Free German literature: a comprehensive service that included publishing of both German and English-language books, wholesale importing from Europe, a book club, and an outlet for direct retail sales.

The new firm, aptly named Alliance, was organized in 1939 with the assistance of the American house of Longmans, Green. Under their joint imprint some thirteen German-language titles were published with Longmans, Green providing distribution facilities, storage, and office space for the fledgling publisher. The majority of the books sold under the Longmans-Alliance imprint were American editions of Querido, De Lange, and Bermann-Fischer books printed in Europe.[39] At the same time Koppell had contracted to become the official agent for these exile publishers, maintaining an extensive stock of all their books as well as books of other Free German trade publishers. The Alliance catalog for 1938–1939 that offered 266 titles for sale expressed the hopes of the new enterprise:

> For the first time the millions in America who speak and read German have the opportunity to procure all books of Free German literature from a central source in the U.S.A. Our catalogue includes the works of the most famous German poets and younger, still unknown talents in exile. Swiss, Alsatians, and other authors of the German literary milieu round out the totality of non-Nazified German literature of our day. . . . German and German-American literature is struggling for its very life and spiritual freedom. The freedom loving German-Americans will certainly support an independent German literature.[40]

By 1939 Alliance was already registered in the *Publisher's Trade List Annual* under the heading—"Books in German for schools, colleges, libraries, exiles, refugees, students and teachers." Koppell was determined not to neglect any possible class of consumer. A further stimulus to sales was needed though, and again it took the form of a book club. The Alliance Book Club (ABC-Deutsche Bücher) was the most ambitious attempt thus far to develop a broad readership in the United States for Free German literature. The inaugural announcement appeared late in 1938 with a bold-faced manifesto in the *Aufbau* and a smartly styled prospectus complete with a goodwill message from Thomas Mann:

> It was with the liveliest interest that I heard of your plan to found a book society in New York that is to propagandize for and distribute German books, insofar as they are products of the German spirit free from totalitarian oppression. I am happy to extend to you my most heartfelt good wishes for the success of your plan. I consider such an organization as most felicitous, because I am convinced that there exists today in America much more-or-less latent interest for good German books which needs only to be activated.[41]

Members were required to purchase four books a year from a list of club selections and as a bonus would receive one free volume of the Forum Bücher series and the club magazine (which was never published).

Despite its auspicious beginning, the entire German-language program of the Alliance Book Corporation was dropped by July, 1940. *Publishers' Weekly* announced the fact that Alliance was going to discontinue acting as American agent for Free German publishers in France and Holland because of "unsettled publishing conditions." In the future, the firm was going to publish exclusively "English language books of American interest and English translations of European books of importance."[42] Undoubtedly the threatening situation in Europe was the determining factor, but contributing to this was the presence in New York of a second center for Free German literature. Alliance retained its separate identity only until May, 1942, when it was acquired by Ziff-Davis; by December of that year, Koppell had severed all connection with the firm.[43]

If his own account be credited, Friedrich Krause played no small part in the history of Free German publishing. As reader for Emil Oprecht's Europa Verlag, Krause claimed to have given his opinion on some 1000 manuscripts of émigré authors, 150 of which appeared in book form.[44] In 1938 he came to New York and soon opened the doors of his Zentrale freier deutschen Bücher.[45] The accredited representative of Emil Oprecht, whose books were now issued with a New York/Zürich imprint, Krause was also American agent for several other Swiss publishers. From 1938 to 1941 almost a dozen catalogs offered for sale nearly the entire range of commercial Free German literature.[46] Contrary to one's expectations, the import of Free German books from Switzerland continued even during the war years—all volumes reportedly printed and bound before shipment.[47] Indeed, after 1942, Krause had built up a world-wide clientele as a distributor of Free German publications:

> Just five years ago the Center of Free German literature was transferred to New York and has grown in importance because the war has extended its sales to world-wide markets. Every week books are being shipped to all Central and South American countries, to Australia, New Zealand, and Hawaii, to England, Russia, Palestine, and South Africa, and even to the Negro Republic of Liberia, where people ask for Free German literature.[48]

Krause also directed his attention to college and university libraries and complained that some libraries, not realizing the availability of a considerable quantity of anti-Nazi German literature, had ceased purchasing German-language books now that the country was at war.[49] It was one of the ironies of the war that the most significant addition to the American market after 1942 was the several hundred thousand German prisoners of war settled in camps throughout the country; and Krause was one of many dealers who supplied them with books. Despite Krause's leading position in the Free German book trade at the war's end (he had published under his own imprint thirteen German-language titles of note), his share of the market dwindled steadily thereafter so that by the mid-fifties he was active only as a literary agent, a vocation he had pursued since 1940.

Retail Book Trade

The number of retail bookshops handling German-language publications increased sharply in 1939 and 1940 when many émigré bookmen, including a large contingent from Austria, set up shop in their new homeland. Apart from the international book dealers of long standing, such as Stechert and Brentano's, whose interest in German publications was at best peripheral, some forty firms existed which were connected in some degree with the distribution of Free German literature (see Appendix I). Two of these were old established American firms: the Williams Bookstore in Boston and Schoenhof's Foreign Books in Cambridge, Massachusetts. The guiding hand behind the Boston and, after 1941, the Cambridge store as dealers in Free German books was Paul Mueller (died 1964), former owner of Muellers Buchhandlung in Vienna.

Of the other retail dealers, perhaps the best known was Mary S. Rosenberg who came to the United States in 1939 from Fürth, Bavaria. Starting out from a single furnished room in New York City, within five years she had increased her stock to almost twenty thousand volumes.[50] Most of her competitors flourished on a smaller scale and often gave their attention equally or predominantly to the buying and selling of used books.

After all the evidence concerning the nature and scope of the retail German book trade in the United States during these years is weighed, two conclusions are inescapable: (1) that no dealer could subsist by trading in Free German publications alone and (2) that no dealers could subsist by serving only the needs of the immigrant public. Miss Rosenberg had expressed herself on this latter point: "There is not such a thing as a book shop which specifically caters to the immigrant population because nobody could live on it. All the immigrant bookdealers I know do business with libraries and, of course, in addition to it, also with [the] immigrant population as far as they buy imported books."[51]

In a normal publishing profile for a given year, say Germany in 1932 or the United States in 1940, a large percentage of titles, and an even larger percentage of the total volume, would be classified as light fiction, or *Kitsch* in the blunter Teutonic terminology. That few books of this type were issued by Free German publishers amidst the tribulations of exile is understandable. As the books manufactured in Nazi Germany were untouchable and, after 1941, unavailable to the émigré bookseller, a large part of his bread and butter was the traffic in secondhand fiction. Despite Friedrich Krause's glowing account of the literary tastes of the German reading public in America,[52] a more sober and accurate estimate was given by the bookseller Helen Gottschalk in a talk before the women's auxiliary of the (German-Jewish) New World Club in New York: "The German-language authors most in demand are Ganghofer, Karl May and the Courths-Mahlers,"[53] she remarked, and concluded somewhat cynically, "for the bookseller there remains little scope for idealism."[54]

Secondhand fiction (and nonfiction) published before 1933 was therefore a staple of the German-American book trade. Many such books had been brought over by the immigrants themselves, those who were able to transport their private libraries to the United States. But because of economic difficulties and lack of space in their small furnished apartments, they were forced to sell their books, and the farsighted bookseller had been quick to take advantage of a temporarily depressed market. By 1945 a considerable demand for German-language books suddenly developed, credited in part to the increased prosperity of the immigrants. The *Neue Volks-Zeitung* investigating this situation[55] caustically remarked that when the immigrants first came they had no money and sold their books for ridiculous amounts, only the booksellers profited. Five years later, dealers with stock enjoyed a seller's market with the highest prices being asked for books banned in Nazi Germany.[56]

With the total collapse of Hitler's Reich in 1945, the twelve years of the anti-Nazi emigration came to an end; it took another five (an extraordinarily short time, actually) for the reorganized German publishing industry to get back on its feet. And that, of course, made the continuance of Free German publishing superfluous. In retrospect, the most characteristic feature of the Free German book trade was its international structure. By 1939 the German reading public in this country was exposed to a continuous flow of books and journals from most of the major centers in Europe. In a few years the balance of trade shifted from Europe to South America, Palestine and the United States; Friedrich Krause (and also Mary Rosenberg) came to occupy a central position in the world distribution of German émigré literature.

The Free German book trade cannot and should not be considered as a single phenomenon, but as a composite of three fairly distinct networks of production and distribution. The German Communists enjoyed the backing, financial and otherwise, of the international Communist movement; this and not any numerical superiority over the Social Democrats made the Communists so much more fertile a source of Free German publications. It was the independent publisher, though, who provided most of the serious literature and nonfiction that was the stock in trade of the ordinary retailer, the major intellectual products of the "other Germany." And it was largely due to efforts of émigré book-dealers from Germany and Austria that this literature was distributed in the United States.

Notes

1. The Moderne Deutsche Buchhandlung of Herman Kormis. The other members were W. Beyer, Brentano's, A. Bruderhausen, German Book Importing Co., International News Co., G. Kenessey, Kerekes Bros., Maurers Buchhandlung, E. Weyhe. and Rex Book and Arts Shop. See Ernst Eisele [manager of Westermann's], "Der deutsche Buchhandel in Amerika," German American Conference, *Sitzungsberichte und Erläuterungen* (New York, 1932), p.31.

2. In March, 1942, Westermann filed an involuntary petition of bankruptcy; the store was closed by the U.S. Treasury Dept. after the FBI revealed that the majority of stockholders were German nationals. *Publishers' Weekly,* March 14, 1942, p.1107.

3. Effective on April 22, 1939. *Publishers' Weekly,* March 25, 1939, p.1206.

4. Edinger, *German Exile Politics,* p.209.

5. According to *Der Arbeiter,* October 3, 1936. In 1939 the *total* American audience of German-language anti-Fascist journals were estimated at only 15,000 by the independent Socialist periodical *Gegen den Strom,* 2:3 (June 1939). But this was an unduly conservative figure reached in a fit of pique at the extravagantly large membership claims made by the Communist-controlled Deutsch-Amerikanischer Kulturverband.

6. *Aufbau* (N.Y.), Dec. 5, 1941, p.19. For a fuller discussion of the German-American book-buying public see chapter VII.

7. Publishers of German-language books located in Tel-Aviv were: "ABC" — Verlag, Aeatan, Irgun Olej Merkaz Europa, Bitaon Verlag, Matara, W. Menke, Olympia (Martin Feuchtwanger), Refta, N. Rosner, Schocken; in Jerusalem: Junge Dichtung, Dr. Peter Freund, R. Mass, L. Mayer, Romema-Edition, M. Rothschild, Willy Verkauf; in Haifa: OTH Cooperative Printing Press, Ltd. The list is not exhaustive.

8. On trade from Palestine see advertisement of Feldheim's Jüdische Buchhandlung in the *Aufbau,* Oct. 23, 1942, p.8 and *Publishers' Weekly,* Jan. 27, 1945, p.461. On books from England see *Aufbau* (N.Y.), Nov. 24, 1944, p.8.

9. The story of the German Communists in Mexico parallels in many ways their adventures in the United States. In one of their first sorties they took over the non-Communist Liga Pro Cultura Alemana, founded in April, 1938, and in addition formed the Heinrich Heine Club, a "cultural" organization similar to the DAKV. See Heinrich Heine Club, ed., *Heines Geist in Mexiko* (Mexiko: Heine-Club, 1946) which contains a list of all events sponsored by the club from 1941 to 1946.

10. The Liga published the pamphlet, *La Verdadera Cultura Alemana,* Tomo 1, 1939. Five thousand copies were available to bookdealers and organizations in the United States

at a cost of twenty-five cents per copy (thirty cents to individuals). The money received (plus profits from another pamphlet titled *El Nazismo)* was to be used to finance Tomo 2. This is an example of cooperation among foreign language groups of the CPA since the above announcement appeared in the Midwest party organ *Volksfront* (Chicago), Jan. 28, 1939. The pamphlets would presumably have been distributed among Spanish-speaking Americans.

11. *German American,* Oct., 1942. There was also a Spanish edition called *Alemania Libre. Freies Deutschland* (1941-1945) was continued under the name *Neues Deutschland* until 1946. Alexander Abusch, now an East German literary pundit, was the editor. Coworkers included stellar personalities such as famous journalist Egon Erwin Kisch, Ludwig Renn, Bodo Uhse (ex-Nazi turned Communist), Paul Westheim (art critic), and Paul Merker. The latter was an old political rival of Walter Ulbricht. For details concerning the postwar careers of these and other members of the colony see the unsigned article, "Freies Deutschland," *Wiener Library Bulletin,* 7:7 (April 1953).

12. The titles were: E. E. Kisch, *Markplatz der Sensationen;* Lion Feuchtwanger, *Unholdes Frankreich;* Anna Seghers, *Das Siebte Kreuz;* Heinrich Mann, *Kriegstagebuch 1939-1940;* Ludwig Renn, *Der Königshof* (not published under this title). Both Mann and Feuchtwanger were at the time residents of California. *Aufbau* (N.Y.), May 10, 1942, p.17.

13. Berendsohn 2:252. Like the *Deutsche Blätter,* it was allowed in American POW camps.

14. Beginning in 1941, subscriptions were regularly solicited in the *Aufbau* (N.Y.), which see for Aug. 8, 1941, p.9.

15. Published as *Die Politische Briefe* from 1938 to Jan., 1944, a "republican Catholic monthly." Berendsohn 2:276.

16. James J. Friedmann of Verlag Cosmopolita in Buenos Aires has recently completed his memoirs of that critical five-year period, 1940-1945, but the manuscript has not yet been published. A Cosmopolita imprint of 1965 — Peter Bussemeyer, *Argentien 1810 bis zur Gegenwart* — contains an incomplete listing of German books printed in Argentina.

17. *Aufbau* (N.Y.), Nov. 19, 1943, p.15. Another firm was Libreria Oscar Pollak, Santiago de Chile.

18. Berendsohn 2:263.

19. Kormis opened his store in 1932 on Second Ave., later moving to 250 E. 84th St. The Communist Deutsche Zentral-Buchhandlung was located at 218 E. 84th St.

20. June 3, 1939, p.2947.

21. In Aug. of 1933 the Wiener Volksbuchhandlung (official Austrian Socialist bookstore in Vienna) began offering both German and Austrian Socialistica for sale. *Neue Volks-Zeitung,* Aug. 13, 1936, p.7.

22. *Neue Volks-Zeitung,* Nov. 27, 1936, p.9.

23. Berendsohn 2:169. See also Helmut Dressler, *Werden und Wirken der Büchergilde Gutenberg* (Zürich, 1947).

24. *Solidarität* (N.Y.), Jan. 1934., p.22.

25. The ties of the Büchergilde to the Oprecht publishing group were very close. The Europa Verlag, founded in 1933, was originally designed to serve as the commercial outlet for the books of the Büchergilde Gutenberg, but soon began to pursue an independent publishing program. Dressler, op. cit., p.66.

26. Ibid., p.108.

27. "Büchergilde Gutenberg an organization of proletarian readers — Hermann Schroeder, agent for America." (Dec. 1, 1934, p.10). In 1946 Austrian émigré H. Felix Kraus became the Guild's American agent.

28. *Neue Volks-Zeitung,* June 29, 1936, p.10. Traven's death in Mexico City (March, 1969) has apparently unveiled his true identity as Traven Torsvan, a native of Chicago.

29. *Aufbau* (N.Y.) Aug. 8, 1941, p.12.

30. Quoted from a *Rundschreiben an die deutsche Distrikt Büros* of Feb. 26, 1928, by E. W. Mareg, *Gegen den Strom*, 1:9 (May 1938).

31. *Der Arbeiter*, Aug. 19, 1934. Among the newspapers urged upon the German-American workers were the *Arbeiter* and the *Einheitsfront*, both American papers; *Gegenangriff* (The Saar) — eight cents per issue, fifty cents for the "illegal" edition on thin paper for smuggling into Germany proper — *Unsere Zeit* (Paris, Basel, Prague); and the *Deutsche Volkszeitung* (The Saar).

32. "Arbeitsfeld und Arbeitsplan des Deutsch-Amerikanischen Klubs St. Louis Mo.," *Mitteilungsblatt der Deutsch-Amerikanischen Klubs*, 5:4 (Sept. 1937). Organ of the Federation of German American Clubs, formerly the German Workers' Clubs.

33. *Der Arbeiter*, Nov. 11, 1934.

34. Undated letter from Herman Kormis to the author (1964).

35. Advertised in *Der Arbeiter*, April 28, 1935, and the *Deutsches Volksecho*, June 12, 1937 respectively. Another source for émigré periodicals printed in the U.S.S.R. was the Soviet importing agency in New York, the Bookniga Corporation. Willi Münzenberg had his own representative in New York City from 1933 to 1938, one Andrew Kertesz, a bookseller who advertised often in the German-American press.

36. *Der Arbeiter*, June 2, 1935.

37. *Deutsches Volksecho*, Jan. 21, 1939.

38. *Der Arbeiter*, Sept. 15, 1935. Two of the earliest club selections were from the Münzenberg-controlled Éditions du Carrefour: *Das braune Netz* (1935) — an exposé of Nazi agents around the world — and the German translation of André Malraux, *Les Temps du Mépris* (*Die Zeit der Verachtung*, 1936).

39. Only two of the thirteen titles were actually printed in the United States — Thomas Mann's *Dieser Friede* (1938) and his *Achtung Europa!* (1938).

40. Alliance Book Corp., *Freie deutsche Literatur* [Catalog] (New York, 1939), p.1.

41. Alliance Book Club, *Prospectus* (New York, 1939), p.1.

42. *Publishers' Weekly*, July 27, 1940, p.247. Alliance bestsellers included: Jan Valtin's *Out of the Night;* Erich Kästner's children's books; Boris Souvarine's *Stalin;* Hermann Kesten's *Guernica;* and Hermann Rauschning's *Revolt of Nihilism*. By 1939 books of strictly American interest such as the *Face of America* series were also in the offing.

43. *Publishers' Weekly*, Dec. 19, 1942, p.2429. Koppell operated a Readers Book Service for a short while afterwards, then opened the Alliance Travel Corp. specializing in student tours. He died in 1964. Ibid., Dec. 14, 1964, p.38.

44. *Aufbau* (N.Y.), Dec. 10, 1943, p.16.

45. Sometimes called the Zentrale freier deutschen Literatur. From 1938 to 1946 he moved at least four times, after 1941 settling in uptown Manhattan (popularly termed the "Fourth Reich") where so many of the new emigrants lived. When Krause first came to the United States he was connected briefly with Koppell's Alliance Book Corp. — reportedly in charge of distribution and publicity. See *Deutsches Volksecho*, Nov. 5, 1938.

46. *Publishers' Weekly*, Nov. 11, 1939, p.1858. His first catalog listed over 250 titles, a first supplement (1938–1939) added 145 and a second supplement, *Neue Erscheinungen Frühling und Sommer* (1939), added 39 new titles. From the first his venture was supported by all anti-Nazi groups and newspapers. Krause also offered a variety of Swiss trade books for sale.

47. Letter from Dr. H. Rumpel of Europa Verlag, Zürich, April 1, 1964.

48. *Publishers' Weekly*, Dec. 25, 1943, p.2315.

49. *Publishers' Weekly*, Jan. 17, 1942, p.190.

50. *Publishers' Weekly*, Jan. 27, 1945, p.961.

51. Letter dated Aug. 22, 1962.

52. Krause published a popularity scale of German authors drawn from his own bookselling experience. At the top of the list stood Thomas Mann, followed in descending order by: Franz Werfel, von Hofmannsthal, Goethe, Stefan Zweig, Rilke, Karl Kraus, Schiller, Lessing, Kant, Nietzsche, Schnitzler, Schopenhauer, Hölderlin, Georg Kaiser, Rauschning, Otto Strasser, Fallada, Arnold Zweig, Josef Roth, Feuchtwanger, Zuckmayer, Freud, Heinrich Mann, Gerhart Hauptmann, Klabund, Wilhelm Busch, Otto Flake, Stefan George, Emil Ludwig, Bruno Frank, Alfred Neumann, Adrienne Thomas, Annette Kolb, Oskar Maria Graf, Heine, Leonhard Frank, Robert Neumann, and Oswald Spengler. *Aufbau* (N.Y.), Dec. 5, 1941, p.19.

53. The adventure novels of Karl May and the sentimental fiction of Ludwig Ganghofer and the two Courths-Mahlers, mother and daughter, were perennially in demand. Cf. Berendsohn's statistics on the most translated German writers between the years 1933 and 1938 (based on the *Index Translationum*). Frau Hedwig Courths-Mahler occupied the undisputed first place — with 134 translations to her credit — followed then by seven émigré and *verboten* authors. Berendsohn 1:155.

54. *Aufbau* (N.Y.), Oct. 31, 1947, p.13.

55. Robert Breuer writing in the *Neue Volks-Zeitung* gives three reasons for a revival of interest in German books that became evident in 1945: "Americans are learning to speak foreign languages in ever increasing numbers . . . the war brought Europe once again to the forefront of public attention . . . numerous immigrants who in the 'old country' had left their libraries and books, were taken with the urge to complement their American library with a portion of their lost books." (Feb. 17, 1945, p.7).

56. Loc. cit., e.g., a complete set of Karl Kraus' *Die Fackel* ($1000); Thomas Mann, *Der Zauberberg* ($15 for the 1st edition); Egon Friedell, *Kulturgeschichte* ($25); volumes of the *Propylean* art history ($35 each).

VII

Free German Publishing in America

The 353 German-language publications (admittedly an incomplete figure) which provide the subject matter for this chapter[1] mirror the vitality and variety of émigré life in the United States. As table 1 shows, Free German book production reached its peak in wartime and this high level was maintained through the first few postwar years. The peculiarities, strengths, and weaknesses of this roster of titles are in part traceable to the preeminence of the import trade during most of the emigration period. But even more important was the decentralization of Free German publishing in America, attested to by the existence of eighty different imprints, forty-eight appearing only once. Only six publishers can be credited with more than ten volumes apiece.

The figure of 353 may be refined even further. At least seventeen titles were published by Frederick Ungar and Mary S. Rosenberg as reprints authorized by the U.S. Alien Property Custodian. Verification of all licensed reprints was not possible since the latest official listing available was a 1944 cumulation. By December of that year the total book republication program amounted to 539 titles (mostly in German) with a strong emphasis on science and technology.[2] Of the books licensed to Ungar and Rosenberg—the only two émigrés involved in German-language reprinting—about half were in the humanities and included such items as the *Sprach-Brockhaus,* Heinrich Schmidt's *Philosophisches Wörterbuch,* and Richard Hamann's *Geschichte der Kunst.* One unlikely volume that appeared with the official license was a reprint

TABLE 1
FREE GERMAN PUBLICATIONS IN THE UNITED STATES 1933–1954

YEAR	NUMBER	YEAR	NUMBER
1933	3	1944	39
1934	2	1945	86
1935	7	1946	78
1936	1	1947	28
1937	5	1948	6
1938	11	1949	7
1939	8	1950	2
1940	7	1951	4
1941	11	1952	4
1942	16	1953	2
1943	23	1954	3
		Total	353

of the Reclam edition of Hermann Hesse, *Eine Bibliothek der Weltliteratur* (Ungar, 1945). Because of their subject matter and the fact that most of the Rosenberg and Ungar reprints were advertised in the German-American press, they were included in book production figures of Free German literature. The other 500 or more scientific reprints (none of which were advertised in émigré journals) do not fall within the scope of this study.

In estimating the edition size of Free German publications, content and intended audience are determining factors. The polemical or political pamphlet, ephemeral in nature, seldom enjoyed wide geographical distribution and only in special instances did large printings occur.[3] Bibliophile and private press productions averaged between 300 and 575 copies while the endeavors of the author-cum-publisher were, with the exception of Oskar Maria Graf, likewise limited.[4] The trade house of Aurora Verlag published each of its books in editions of between 2000 and 4000 copies,[5] and the extensive reprint list of Frederick Ungar probably had an even wider circulation although figures are not available. Schoenhof Publishers, Inc., issued several of their own books in relatively large editions of 5000 copies. However, the largest editions recorded were for a series of paperbound books destined exclusively for distribution among German prisoners of war, Bermann-Fischer's *Neue Welt* series—twenty-four volumes of German and American literature in quantities of 10,000 each.

Despite the haphazard nature of German-language publishing, an analysis by genre reveals a surprising balance. It is possible to divide the 353 titles (using very broad categories) into 201 volumes of literature (table 2) and 152 of nonfiction (table 3). A finer analysis is a more hazardous undertaking since some books may be assigned with equal justification to one or another classification. Such a dissection at any rate may prove informative. Contemporary German exile literature which accounted for 34 percent of the total book production may be further broken down into books by established authors (eighty-nine) and books by relatively unknown or unpublished authors (thirty).

TABLE 2

ANALYSIS OF THE 201 TITLES IN THE CLASS "LITERATURE"

SUBCLASS	NO. OF TITLES	PERCENTAGE OF TOTAL FREE GERMAN BOOK PRODUCTION IN THE UNITED STATES
Classics*	59	17
Anthologies	11	3
Translations into German	12	3
German exile literature†	119	34
Total literature	201	57

*Included are books by such writers as Goethe, Grillparzer, Wilhelm Busch, and Hermann Löns.

†Although reserved for works of literature written by German and Austrian writers in exile, this class also includes American reprints of books by Erich Kästner and others who remained in Germany but were forbidden to publish. For this very reason books by Kästner are listed in Sternfeld, *Deutsche Exil-Literatur* and books by Ernst Wiechert in Kantorowicz, *Verboten und verbrannt*.

TABLE 3

ANALYSIS OF THE 152 TITLES IN THE CLASS "NONFICTION"

SUBCLASS	NO. OF TITLES	PERCENTAGE OF TOTAL FREE GERMAN BOOK PRODUCTION IN THE UNITED STATES
Political	59	17
Social science, humanities	45	12
Science	10	3
Dictionaries, grammars	28	8
Immigrant handbooks	10	3
Total nonfiction	152	43

Being aware of the decentralization of Free German publishing in the United States, eighty publishers and 353 titles, only begs the question: Why was there no *one* major publisher of such books in America? It might be objected that the 110 or more volumes issued by Frederick Ungar belie this line of thought. But by émigré standards Ungar was not primarily a publisher of émigré literature. The chief function of an effective Free German publishing program—such enterprises as Querido, Allert de Lange, Bermann-Fischer, and Europa—was the dissemination of émigré literature and opinion; in essence, the publisher would act as a spokesman for Germans opposed to the Nazi regime. This was certainly not the responsibility that Ungar took upon himself. The 110 books published under his imprint were almost entirely reprints of classics, reference works, dictionaries, and translations. Only four of his books were by authors who were living or who had lived in exile, and three of those were reprints of works at least fifteen years old.[6] The question above then remains to be answered.

By the end of 1939 it was clearly only a matter of time until Free German publishing in Europe would be seriously crippled if not destroyed. The neutrality of Sweden and Switzerland was no certainty and the imminent defeat of England no harmless specter. But even prior to the outbreak of the European war the need for a large-scale publishing enterprise on American soil was openly discussed.

A most interesting if chimerical idea absorbed the attention of Thomas Mann upon his arrival in the United States. Writing to Werfel in May, 1939, Mann described his plan in some detail. Apparently the acknowledged leader of the émigré establishment believed that unhampered contact between the exiles and the opponents of Hitler inside the Reich could still be maintained. Mann's idea was to publish twenty-four paper-bound volumes a year, "written by representatives of the German spirit *for Germans* [i.e., Germans living under Hitler]." Furthermore, the publications should in no way be political in nature (a rather unrealistic conception) but should appeal to the "better instincts" of German citizens.[7] Ready and willing to underwrite the project, claimed Mann, was a committee of American friends led by Frank Kingdon, president of Rutgers University. In all innocence it was thought that 5000 copies of each brochure—to be written by such prominent exiles as Lotte Lehmann, Max Reinhardt, Paul Tillich, and Stefan Zweig—could be distributed throughout Germany by mail. The fateful course of events in Europe soon militated against fruition of this wholly impractical plan.

Another assumption current in 1939 was that there existed in the United States a sufficient number of German Americans and émigrés willing to support an extensive publishing program of anti-Nazi and Free German literature. Outspoken proponents of this idea were the German-American Otto Sattler and the recently arrived Friedrich Krause. Sattler entertained the notion of a renaissance of German literature in America, of a new German cultural center outside the Third Reich. He expressed himself most cogently on this subject in an article that appeared in the *Volksfront* (Chicago), January 28, 1939:

> Until now the German-American writer and journalist was only an outpost of German literature, a literature that had its homeland in Germany, Austria and Switzerland. German-American literature has never been nurtured, it has, even in the United States, received hardly any encouragement. Now, however, when many of the best German writers have found their new homeland in this country, the German-language press together with these writers should do everything possible to interest the German-American in German literature; and that with the help of those publishers who have also come to these shores. Our German literature can become a world center for Germans in many lands.

In a similar vein, the expatriate bookseller and publisher Friedrich Krause wrote in 1941 that he was convinced of the feasibility of printing and selling German-language books in the United States although the rewards would be, in his words, "more spiritual than financial." He pointed to the success of the Free French publishers in this country and could see no obstacles to an equally luxuriant flowering of Free German literature. "Many exiled German and Austrian writers are living here in poor circumstances," he continued, "in spite of which they courageously continue writing in their mother tongue. Many valuable and important manuscripts will be forever lost unless the production of German books in America is made possible."[8]

These and similar schemes were supported only by representatives of the anti-Nazi front, the German Jews, the radicals, and the more democratic elements of German-American society. There was, of course, another German-American literary culture whose *völkisch* sympathies were eagerly appropriated by the National Socialists[9] and whose bourgeois philistinism was roundly criticized by the German-American Left. After the trauma of World War I, this once thriving middle-class literature was in a perilously moribund state. Such publications as did appear were sponsored by various clubs, *Vereine,* and church groups. Occasional memoirs, volumes of verse, and homely meditations were often published at the author's expense and frequently issued under the aegis of the local German or English-language newspaper.[10] The *Auslandsdeutsch* literary tradition, such as it was, languished in the older German-American milieu and had nothing to do with the new literature envisioned by Sattler, Krause, and others.

Good intentions were not sufficient to spark or sustain a German-American *Sturm und Drang.* Will and talent there were in super-abundance, but certain factors weighed heavily against success — and they were primarily of a down-to-earth economic nature. First of all, if Krause's estimate of 100,000 volumes of Free German literature sold in 1941[11] (almost all published abroad) is accepted, even with reservations, and the sum of all such books imported from 1933 to 1941 is added to that, the market outlook was not overly gloomy. Little complaint in the press concerning a shortage of Free German books can be noted until after 1939. Advertisements reveal at least some measure of trade in new and used books even during wartime. And it should not be forgotten that trade with Switzerland was completely interrupted (if at all) only for a short period. The generous provision of German-language books by the public libraries,[12] especially in New York City, was also helpful in assuaging the reading demands of the immigrants.

The precarious economic situation of the émigrés has already been cited as a reason for their inability to purchase books but it may be argued, hearking back to Krause, that the new arrivals formed only one segment of a potential market that supposedly purchased 100,000 volumes in 1941. The decisive factor working against the creation of a large audience for Free German books and particularly for books printed in this country was the extensive lack of support and sympathy shown the immigrants of 1933 by millions of Americans of German extraction. To hold up the Free French publishers in North America for emulation (as Krause did) was self-delusory since the supporters of General de Gaulle could count on the goodwill of both the French-American and French-Canadian communities. The anti-émigré attitude of many American *Auslandsdeutsche* went hand in hand in some cases with an acceptance of deeply felt nationalist values in literature. For example, as late as 1947 the *St. Louis Deutsche Wochenschrift* commended to its readers Hans Grimm's *Volk ohne Raum,* a novel that had become a National Socialist classic.[13] Evidence of a hardly disguised antipathy to émigré writers is to be found in Edward Carlton Breitenkamp, *The U.S. Information Control Division and the Effects on German Publishers and Writers 1945 to 1949.*[14] Comparing the German writers who emigrated with those who remained, he states: "Since the writers of the Inner Emigration were most frequently Christian inspired, as opposed to the *Communist character of the true emigration* [italics added] their influence has grown with rift between the West and the Communist world."

The Publishers — A Survey

The record of Free German book publishing in the United States prior to 1942 is very fragmentary and elusive. Certainly the steady flow of books from abroad dulled the edge of any local venture. The two large-scale operations between 1938 and 1942, Alliance and Bermann-Fischer, were also outlets for imported Free German publications, and apart from these the horizon is virtually barren of anything but a scattering of one-book publishers. A typical case was the Freedom Publishing Company organized in August, 1941, by Stephen Naft, editor of *Living Age*. In that year the firm published the German edition of a quite important book, Hermann Rauschning's *Die Konservative Revolution*. Placing advertisements in the major German-American papers, Naft claimed to be "the only publisher in the world publishing anti-totalitarian books in the German language."[15] In the familiar vein of Krause, Sattler, and Thomas Mann, Naft cherished the hope that Free German literature might find a rallying point in the United States; but after the appearance of the Rauschning volume nothing further was heard of the Freedom Publishing Company.

The publication of Free German books by a few American trade and university presses showed early promise but achieved only peripheral importance. In 1939 and 1941 the University of Chicago Press released the American editions of books by Hans Kelsen and Richard von Mises,[16] and in 1945 Princeton University Press came out with a bilingual volume of Werfel's poetry.[17] With the exception of Victor Hammer's Wells College Press (which was really a private press), these ventures are the extent of university press involvement in Free German publishing.[18] During 1938 Farrar and Rinehart in an experimental mood simultaneously published English and German versions of Walter Schönstedt's novel, *Das Lob des Lebens*. This step was a natural outgrowth of John Farrar's interest in and close contacts among German émigré writers.[19] The novelty of dual publication was offset by the meretriciousness of the fiction and did little to change the habits of American publishers. Farrar, Benjamin Huebsch, as well as Alfred Knopf and others, persevered in their efforts to bring Free German literature in translation to the attention of the American public; the more than 200 volumes of German literature thus made available to the English-speaking reader during the emigration exerted an influence on American culture that has yet to be evaluated.

More than 75 percent of Free German books published in the United States fall within the six-year period, 1942-1947. Although the first peace-time years (1946 and 1947) were marked by the reorganization of the German book trade, Bermann-Fischer's return to Europe, and the reestablishment of the Querido Verlag in Amsterdam, they also saw 106 German-language publications bearing American imprints. From then on, due to the rapid recovery of German publishing and the dissolution of the émigré literary enclaves, Free German publishing virtually disappeared in fact as well as in name. From 1942 through 1947 the United States was host to a variety of German-language publishing ventures ranging from the mass production of cheap reprints by Frederick Ungar to the more limited output of the private presses, the purveyors of contemporary German poetry and the author-publishers. Before embarking on a systematic analysis of these publishers, it is necessary to dwell awhile on two special topics: the role of openly Socialist or Communist publishers in the United States, and the many-faceted career of Gottfried Bermann-Fischer.

THE POLITICAL LEFT AS PUBLISHER

The tripartite division into Socialist, Communist, and commercial spheres previously adopted is less rewarding in the present context; for outside of the predictable pamphlet literature the Left shied away from any extensive publishing programs. It should be borne in mind that after 1941 the Communists outwardly shed their party identification in order to merge into a unified American war effort. From "sympathetic" publishers some thirty-four titles representing nine imprints have been identified. Socialists of all persuasions accounted for only fifteen titles divided among eight publishers. The Aurora Verlag alone can be considered a serious trade publishing house; the twelve volumes that it issued were the only ones of more than transitory value produced by the German Left. This unobtrusiveness was more than equalized by the verbosity of both Socialist and Communist newspapers.

Little has been preserved of the voluminous German-language pamphlet literature spawned by the Communist section of the anti-Nazi front. Only seventeen leaflets or brochures bearing the imprint of either the *German American* or the *Deutsch-Amerikanischer Kulturverband* can be positively identified, such ephemera having a naturally high mortality rate. The record of book publishing is fortunately more durable. The supply of party-approved reading matter in the United States suffered only a brief hiatus even though European sources for German-language Communist publications were cut off by the war. In 1942 the firm of El Libro Libre was founded in Mexico City to help alleviate this isolation. These Mexican imprints added to the publications issued by the Aurora Verlag in New York (many of whose authors stood close to the Communist Party) come to a grand total of thirty-three titles, most of them substantial volumes of literature, philosophy, or history—all distributed in the United States.

The German Socialists in the United States, from conservative Social Democrats to the New Beginners, published few books of worth in German (though quite a few in English). The SPD depended primarily upon its weekly paper while the New Beginners concentrated on reaching the American public directly. Not to be overlooked are the two *Volkskalender* or almanacs published by the Arbeiter Kranken- und Sterbekasse in 1938[20] and 1939, large volumes of almost 200 pages each with numerous contributions by exiled writers.

A discussion of German Socialist publishing in the United States would be rather fruitless were it not for an interesting series of pamphlets connected with a minor but exemplary political tragedy of the Hitler period that appeared in 1939 and 1940. Max Sievers, independent Socialist, one-time president of the German Freidenkerbund and a determined anti-Nazi publicist was another political exile interested in creating a non-Marxian front patterned on the patriotic tradition of Lassallean Social Democracy. Sievers' adherents in both hemispheres were kept informed of European events through the pages of his newspaper *Freies Deutschland* (Antwerp) dispatched from Stockholm (1938-1939). During 1939 Sievers established an American distribution agency for his publications, the Public Voice Publishing Company, under the direction of one Wendelin Thomas.[21] The sudden and deadly course of the war, however, disrupted all of Sievers' projects including his newspaper, which ceased publication with the August, 1939 issue.

In the face of disaster, Sievers paid a visit to New York, perhaps with the thought of making it his new base of operations,[22] but unfortunately he went back to Europe later that same year and fell into the clutches of the Nazis, his eventual executioners. The task of the agency set up by Sievers in America was to continue the good work of the now defunct Stockholm paper, and by October, 1939, the first number of a new series[23] *(Schriftenreihe Freies Deutschland)* was on sale in New York: its purpose, to fill the breach for former subscribers to *Freies Deutschland* by reporting the world events of August to October, 1939. At least six more pamphlets were published in New York by Wendelin Thomas before contact with his European correspondents was finally severed in late 1940.

Several authors in or close to the Communist or Socialist camps also brought out their own works of poetry and prose, writers as diverse as Oskar Maria Graf, Hans Marchwitza, Josef Luitpold Stern, and Louis Roemer. They will be treated in a later section devoted to the author as publisher (see page 113).

GOTTFRIED BERMANN-FISCHER

Even during his New York exile, Bermann-Fischer remained the center of a publishing and importing complex spanning two continents so that he cannot be pigeonholed in any simple classification. Consequently a description of his activities will stand as a unit in itself, a quite properly detailed history of this quintessential Free German publisher. His story is taken up at the end of June, 1940, on the eve of his departure for the United States. After an adventurous trek from Stockholm to New York (via the Soviet Union) Bermann-Fischer, who had shared the vicissitudes of exile with many of his authors, entered the ranks of

American trade publishers. In 1941, with the backing and encouragement of the American publisher Alfred Harcourt and with F.H. Landshoff as vice-president, the L.B. Fischer Publishing Corporation was formed. The firm was exclusively an English-language house, although it issued translations of many important and provocative books of European origin (e.g., Klaus Mann's autobiography *The Turning Point,* 1942).

Upon his arrival in 1940, Bermann-Fischer toyed with the idea of starting a German-language house in New York but, as an experienced businessman, soon realized the practical limitations of such a course.[24] As an alternative he made every effort to have his Stockholm publications available in the United States. The distribution had been handled by the Alliance Book Corporation from 1938 to July, 1940, when it was taken over first by Harcourt, Brace and Co., and later by Friedrich Krause.[25]

Soon after Pearl Harbor the stock of Bermann-Fischer books was rapidly depleted as "transport from Sweden became impossible."[26] Clearly if the American market was to be supplied, Bermann-Fischer books would have to be manufactured on this side of the Atlantic. Even before United States military involvement, a program of reprinting German books was in the planning stage, as the following report in *Publishers' Weekly* would seem to indicate: "For the time being this firm [Bermann-Fischer] continues to operate in Stockholm but has decided to print in the United States the German texts of important books and distribute the books to universities and libraries."[27] The fruits of this plan were limited in number but of definite literary significance. It was actually in 1938 that Bermann-Fischer had his first German-language book printed in the United States — Thomas Mann's *Dieser Friede.*[28] Ten thousand copies were printed here though the title page mentioned only Stockholm as the place of publication. How much of this edition was distributed outside the United States is not ascertainable, though Mann, in a letter to Bermann-Fischer, leaves the impression that the copies were primarily destined for American consumption: "If you only had not burdened yourself with 10,000 copies of *Dieser Friede!* Knopf, of course, had 10,000 copies of his edition printed and is about ready for a new edition. But this is an English speaking land. Will the 10,000 copies in German also be disposed of?"[29] The only book set and printed in New York under a New York/Stockholm imprint was a volume of verse by the aged Austrian-Jewish poet and playwright, Richard Beer-Hofmann.[30] This too was distributed by Harcourt, Brace.

Bermann-Fischer undertook his most interesting publishing experiment on behalf of his most celebrated authors, Thomas Mann and Franz Werfel. His efforts were understandable, because these two novelists were the most widely read German writers of the emigration. Mann's

Goethe novel, *Lotte in Weimar,* was first published in Stockholm in 1939 and even in that eventful year an initial edition of 10,000 copies was easily sold (there were 5000 prepublication orders alone).[31] A short while after the Bermann-Fischer family had arrived in New York, the wandering publisher had announced to the press his intention of photographically reprinting *Lotte* for American distribution.[32] At the same time he stated that "a few thousand copies" of Mann's *Vertauschte Köpfe* would also be made available by the following spring (1941).[33] Other of Mann's publications reproduced in this way were *Deutsche Hörer* and *Joseph, der Ernährer,* the final volume of the *Joseph* tetralogy.[34] Since no complete bibliography of Franz Werfel has yet been compiled, collateral documentation of Bermann-Fischer's Werfel reprints in the United States is not available. The Library of Congress copy of *Jacobowsky und der Oberst* (Stockholm: Bermann-Fischer, 1945), however, does carry the note—"Printed in the U.S."—and it is almost a certainty that a reprint of *Das Lied der Bernadette* was also undertaken.

At the same time that Gottfried Bermann-Fischer was managing the L. B. Fischer Corporation and having many of his German texts reprinted in New York, he continued to direct the fortunes of his Stockholm firm. The forty-seven Free German books produced there during his American exile comprise an heroic chapter in the annals of publishing history. Not all the European editions were printed in Sweden. One copy examined of Werfel's *Jacobowsky* bore the imprint Stockholm, 1944, and also carried the note "Printed in Switzerland." It was no mean trick to see a Free German book through the press when author and publisher were isolated in the United States, the printing done in Switzerland, and the books released in Stockholm—right under Hitler's nose. During the war Bermann-Fischer, taking advantage of a Swedish-German commercial treaty, was able to transport printed sheets on sealed freight cars overland through Germany to Switzerland.[35] Manuscripts were prepared in their final form in New York and flown to Stockholm for printing, a procedure which necessarily eliminated any chance to correct proofs and consequently resulted in very unreliable texts.

Thomas Mann's correspondence illuminates the handicaps under which Bermann-Fischer was forced to work. In March, 1942, as the concluding volume of the *Joseph* series was nearing completion, Mann wrote to Hermann Hesse of his (Mann's) intention to give up what was left of the European market and have only a small German edition printed in the United States as a pendant to Knopf's English translation:

> Under present conditions of communication it is quite impossible to have any sort of a complex text printed in Europe. That was shown by

Werfel's new novel [*The Song of Bernadette*] . . . for its snobbish Catholicism and unpalatable belief in miracles, by the way, I have sternly
scolded him. The book is thoroughly disfigured by typographical errors—naturally, since he could not correct the proofs. I won't allow
Bermann to do that with the *Joseph*. A German edition will be produced
here side by side with the English so that the original version will at least
be available.[36]

Gradually Mann yielded to Bermann-Fischer's powers of persuasion.
and agreed to have the manuscript printed in Stockholm with all the
problems that this course entailed. "Dear Doctor Bermann," he wrote:

Today I am sending you the *Joseph* manuscript . . . as to our agreement
to have the book printed in Stockholm, we must abide by it. It is
naturally difficult for me to give up correcting the proofs and an accurate
first edition is scarcely to be expected. We will have to console ourselves
with the thought that soon, perhaps in two years, a reprint can be
arranged. For now, the idea that the still valuable remnant of the European market will be open to the book is important to me; and, as with
Lotte in Weimar, we have agreed to produce an edition [in the U.S.] by
photographic means. I would like your estimate of how long it will take
until the German edition appears in Europe.[37]

The Stockholm edition appeared on schedule, but paper shortages
plagued the American edition. Wartime regulations stated that a publisher could utilize in 1944 only as much paper as was consumed in
1942. The L.B. Fischer Publishing Corporation did not have access to a
supply sufficient to cover both its expanded English-language schedule
and the proposed German reprint. Bermann-Fischer tried to purchase
additional paper from some of his fellow publishers, a practice formerly
allowable but under interdict by the War Production Board in 1944.[38]
Still the book was finally released in an edition of 1800 copies, with all
the errors of the first edition intact. Mann was immensely gratified as he
wrote to Marianne Liddell: "I have more joy in the 1800 German copies
in America than in the 200,000 English."[39]

The Publishers — A Typology

Most publishers of Free German books in the United States can be
subsumed under one of four classes which, when taken together, form a
serviceable though rudimentary organizational scheme. These classes
are:

1. Large-scale trade publishers for whom publishing was a full-time business
2. Small-scale publishers for whom publishing was a sideline growing out of
   other activities, yet whose books do not bear the characteristics of
   private press or bibliophile editions

3. Private or bibliophile presses, publishers of limited editions who stressed typographic excellence and revealed a certain eclecticism in choice of texts. The line between this and the foregoing is often finely drawn
4. The author-publisher, or in the more felicitous German designation, the *Selbstverleger*.

LARGE-SCALE TRADE PUBLISHERS

Of the many émigrés who became part of the general American book trade, some were totally unconcerned with German-language publishing. This was true of Dagobert Runes,[40] founder of the Philosophical Library, and of Kurt Enoch,[41] a key figure in the expansion of the American paperback industry. There were, on the other hand, a number of American publishing houses founded by German émigrés which were involved to some extent in the production of Free German books. In addition to Alliance and Bermann-Fischer whose contributions have already been described, there are three other firms deserving mention. Each one—Pantheon Books, the Frederick Ungar Publishing Company, and the Schocken Publishing Company—has earned a special niche in both American and German publishing history.

Kurt Wolff and Pantheon Books. It is neither possible nor necessary to list all the achievements of this redoubtable German publisher since such accounts are readily available.[42] The Kurt Wolff Verlag was the leading avant garde publishing house of the 1920s, the magnet that attracted so many young writers of promise (including Kafka, Werfel, Georg Trakl, and Max Brod) and particularly many members of that heterogeneous company of authors and artists now lumped together under the rubric "Expressionist." Abandoning Germany in 1931, Wolff spent most of the following decade in southern France, involved in various publishing enterprises.

In 1941 Wolff made his way to the United States where, at the age of fifty-five, he created for himself another career, that of an American trade publisher.[43] Pantheon Books in a very short while became one of the most respected of American imprints and by the end of World War II could boast a yearly output of from 100 to 300 titles. That Wolff's perspective was European rather than German explains his share in establishing French Pantheon Books in 1942, a French-language affiliate that, under the direction of Jacques Schiffrin (originator of the Éditions de la Pléiade), published original editions of Charles Péguy, Vercors, André Gide, and Albert Camus. In Wolff's own words:

> There was only sense in [publishing books in French] during and directly after the war, that is during those years in which no French books came to the United States from France. Gide, for example, sent us manuscripts from Tunis, which we brought out in French since he was not able to send them to France and have them published.[44]

Only two books entirely in German were published under the Pantheon imprint: the anthology *Tausend Jahre deutscher Dichtung* (1949) edited by Curt von Faber du Faur, and the first German edition of Hermann Broch, *Der Tod des Vergil* (1945).[45] A bilingual selection of poems by Stefan George was published by Wolff in 1943; the introduction by Ernst Morwitz, a member of that closely knit group of devotees who helped create the George legend, gave the collection added lustre. Kurt Wolff is not to be considered an émigré publisher in any strict sense but rather, as Salzmann puts it, in the tradition of Bernard Quaritch and Bernhard Tauchnitz, "he opted for world literature whether his field of action was Germany or America."[46]

Frederick Ungar Publishing Company. A publisher whose career proceeded along quite different lines was Friedrich Ungar of Vienna, founder of the Phaidon Verlag in 1922 and director of the Saturn Verlag from 1926 to 1938. Forced to leave his native Austria in 1938, Ungar transferred his business activities temporarily to Switzerland. In 1940 he decided to proceed to America, and by October of that year he could already announce the launching of the Frederick Ungar Publishing Company[47] featuring illustrated educational books and inexpensive text editions for which the former Saturn Verlag was noted. These became Ungar's stock in trade for a number of years.[48]

The actual publishing record of the firm is very inaccessible; corroborative details have not been forthcoming from the present management. The *Publishers' Trade List Annual* for 1946 — Ungar's only entry prior to the 1950s — lists by title only a handful of educational volumes, most of them aimed at the immigrant audience.[49] Reviews and advertisements in the German-language press and lists of Ungar publications that appeared on book jackets or in trade and specialized bibliographies have had to suffice as sources of information. Even so, the remarkable total of 110 German-language titles has been identified. Most were reprints of German poetry and fiction. Few of the literary reprints available for inspection carried a license from the U.S. Alien Property Custodian, though the large amount of paper utilized during a period of strict rationing suggests some kind of official sanction.

The seventy-two volumes of German literature reprinted by Ungar are a landmark in the history of Free German publishing in America. Included in this figure are fourteen volumes of Rainer Maria Rilke, which makes him, next to Thomas Mann, the most frequently reprinted German writer in the United States during the emigration.[50] Most of these titles are not recorded in the standard Rilke bibliography compiled by Walter Ritzer in 1951, nor are all listed in the more recent (1966) catalog of the Richard von Mises Rilke collection. Although in the strict sense (as has been said before) Ungar was not a publisher of émigré literature, his achievement cannot be underrated. He provided numerous inexpensive volumes of German literature, reference books, and text-books at a time when they were obtainable nowhere else.

Schocken Books. The Schocken Books imprint was formally regis-tered in New York City in October of 1946, but the history of the original Schocken Verlag goes back to 1932. In that crucial year the German-Jewish businessman, art collector, and philanthropist Salman Schocken gave his name to a publishing house dedicated to the pres-ervation of Jewish culture in Germany. Under the calculated per-missiveness of the new German government the firm continued its precarious existence until the disasters of 1939. At that time a new Schocken Verlag was set up in Jerusalem. The New York house, headed by Theodore Schocken, one of the sons, was to be completely indepen-dent of the parent concern.

The importance of Schocken Books for German literature is secured by its being the only authorized publisher of the works of perhaps the most influential of all twentieth-century German writers, Franz Kafka. Seven volumes of the *Gesammelte Schriften* (and the English trans-lations as well) were published in New York from 1947 to 1952. Kafka's great impact upon American writers of the postwar period may be traced back to these events.

The Aurora Verlag. Before examining the nontrade and part-time publishers of the emigration, due space must be given to an undertaking with an ideological orientation and unique form of organization that made it the most widely known émigré imprint to come from the United States. The Aurora Verlag of New York can trace its pedigree back to the Germany of Kaiser Wilhelm, where, in the autumn of 1915, a brash new periodical appeared on the literary horizon. *Neue Jugend* was its name, founded and edited by the young Wieland Herzfelde, newly returned from the Western Front.[51] Herzfelde came into conflict from the outset with the German censors because of his radical leanings. After a number of tortuous maneuvers culminating in the official closure of his publishing house—the very first issue of *Neue Jugend* was num-bered Heft 7 and began with page 123 to give the impression of an officially sanctioned periodical—Herzfelde regrouped his forces in 1917 under a new name, Malik Verlag. The firm's artistic director was Herz-felde's brother (one of the original group of German Dadaists) who for reasons of conscience anglicized his name to John Heartfield. Heart-field's reputation rests primarily upon a highly ingenious application of the technique of photomontage to the graphic arts, in particular to book jackets and posters.

A host of radical writers and artists were associated with the Malik Verlag throughout the entire Weimar era, a fact which has led many commentators to label it a Communist front, but it never was officially controlled by the party.[52] One of Herzfelde's most celebrated co-workers was the artist Georg Grosz, some of whose famous print collections were published by the Malik Verlag. Radical literature of other lands, especially modern Soviet literature,[53] were staples of the Malik list as the names of Upton Sinclair, John Reed, Mayakovsky, and Gorki would indicate. The future partners in the Aurora venture — Graf, Brecht, and Weiskopf — were also published by Malik. An adjunct to the Verlag was the Malik Buchhandlung, meeting-place for Berlin's Communist intelligentsia (so too Herzfelde operated the Seven Seas Bookshop in New York). Immediately following the events of 1933, the Malik Verlag was moved to Prague, although for legal reasons it was thought expedient for the firm to be registered in London. While most of the books published between 1933 and 1939 were printed in Czechoslovakia they still carried a London imprint, as did the last Malik title to appear in Europe — Brecht's *Svendborger Gedichte* (1939), which was actually printed in Denmark. Toward the end of 1939, Herzfelde found a more permanent asylum in the United States.

One of Herzfelde's first undertakings in America was the compilation (with the assistance of the German Writers Association in New York) of the December, 1939, issue of the literary journal *Direction* (Darien, Conn.) devoted in its entirety to "Exiled German Writers." With contributions by such eminent refugees as Oskar Maria Graf, Ferdinand Bruckner, Bertolt Brecht, Ernst Bloch (the philosopher), Klaus Mann et al., and with a cover montage furnished by brother John then in England, the issue, as Herzfelde acknowledged, "brought together for the first time those of us alone in a strange land and gave us reason to think ahead to additional joint efforts."[54] The rejuvenation of the old firm was first attempted in 1942 as the result of a series of successful lectures and exhibitions sponsored by a group of émigré writers and artists that called itself Die Tribüne, Forum für freie deutsche Kultur. Herzfelde presented his plan in a widely distributed form letter from which the following details are taken:

> The unexpectedly successful reception of these [lectures] has convinced us that it is possible at this time to expand and intensify the cultural struggle against National Socialism through the formation of a German publishing house. We want to call it: Die Tribüne, Gemeinschaftsverlag für freie deutsche Literatur. The concern would be a nonprofit undertaking carried on under the prescribed legal regulations. Capital will be raised through the sale of 1,000 shares of stock — at ten dollars each. We expect that many friends of our plan will sign for more than one share. In addition, we want to organize the patrons who have attended our affairs — we have the addresses of more than 2,000 — into a Leser-Ge-

meinschaft [Readers' Circle] in order to simplify the chores of production and distribution. I will assume responsibility for the publishing end; the selection of manuscripts, however, I will not undertake alone but in consultation with colleagues in the area, such as [Berthold] Viertel, Graf, Bruckner, [Friedrich] Alexan. My work and that of my colleagues will be unsalaried.

On the first thousand copies of each publication no royalties will be paid – therefore the author will receive 30 free copies. Ten percent of all additional copies sold will go for royalties. At the present time we don't foresee publishing any books, but a *Schriftenreihe* – each small volume will be either 32 or 64 pages long. We want to inaugurate the series with a volume – *Freiheitsstimmen der Völker*. It will contain not documents of individual authors, but the declarations of people who represent such freedom movements, e.g. the *Bill of Rights, Declaration of the Rights of Man,* and similar items. This publication will set the tone of our undertaking.[55]

The project so described never materialized and Herzfelde was forced to wait three more years before he could once more play the role of publisher.

After a year of preparation, the reincarnated Malik Verlag was presented to the American public. The new firm, known as Aurora Verlag, was organized on a cooperative basis by Herzfelde and ten of the leading exiled German poets and writers in America.[56] Much of the financial backing was supplied by Mary S. Rosenberg whose "financial idealism" in this matter was praised by Kesten in the *Aufbau*.[57] Aurora's program was greeted with great enthusiasm in the German-language press, with approbation in the American press, and with a certain coolness by hard-nosed anti-Communists.[58] It appeared to many exiles as the first breath of fresh air, a long delayed expression of German intellectual vitality. Hermann Kesten found prototypes of the Aurora cooperative experiment in the old *Nouvelle Revue Française* and Insel Verlag. He agreed with Herzfelde in pointing to the shameful contradiction that, in wealthy America – a land that possessed the largest German-speaking population outside Germany, Austria, and Switzerland – no Free German book publisher had hitherto existed.[59] The *Austro-American Tribune* of February, 1945, was equally forthright:

> It is astonishing that only today a publishing house for Free German books has been formed. There have been enough German manuscripts and readers of German books in North and South America during recent years. An isolated German book was published here and there, but this is truly a German publisher with a program.

A grand total of twelve titles graced the Aurora list during the years of its American tenancy, but at the same time the firm supplied posterity with a number of tantalizing bibliographical ghosts such as: Hermann Broch, *Die Buecherverbrennung;* Georg Grosz, *Unter der gleichen Sonne;* and John Heartfield, *Faschistenspiegel.* These were announced but never published. The span of Aurora books reached from Brecht's *Furcht und Elend des Dritten Reichs* and Ernst Bloch's *Freiheit und Ordnung* to fiction and drama by such stalwarts as Feuchtwanger, Graf, and Bruckner. All Aurora books appeared in editions of 2000 or more, relatively high figures for German books in the United States. The inexpensive volumes were put together with little pretense or show, and all carried the distinctive Aurora signet (made up of the letters D and T) designed by Herzfelde in 1942 for the stillborn Tribüne publishing program. This well-publicized undertaking ended abruptly in 1947 when Herzfelde, Brecht, and Bloch made their way back to Europe—to the Soviet sector of Germany. Here the last chapter of the Malik odyssey was unfolded; by 1948 the returned exiles were ensconced in occupied Berlin affiliated with the Russian-dominated Aufbau Verlag and publishing under the name of Aurora Buecherei.[60] With these notes on the achievements of Kurt Wolff, Frederick Ungar, Schocken, and Aurora, the arena of "professional" trade publishing is left and attention is directed to those independent publishers and "amateurs" whose productions give to Free German publishing much of its variety and interest.

SMALL-SCALE PUBLISHERS

The part-time publisher, perhaps a printer, bookseller, or literary agent by profession, falls between the trade publisher and the private press. He does not partake of the more extensive resources, the easy access to channels of distribution and advertising of the former, nor does he necessarily produce the *Luxus-Ausgabe,* the signed limited edition of the latter. Four exemplary individuals will be discussed in some detail. The first three fall nicely into the category of bookseller-publishers: Mary S. Rosenberg, Friedrich Krause, and Paul Mueller of Schoenhof's Foreign Books. An account of the work of the printer Ernst Willard rounds out this section.

Bookseller-Publishers. Rosenberg, Krause, and Paul Mueller of Schoenhof's were publishers in their own right as well as retailers of Free German literature. The publication programs initiated by these three bookdealers, however, do reveal marked differences.

The name of Mary Rosenberg appears on at least six licensed scientific reprints as well as on two reference works in the fields of art and philosophy. Miss Rosenberg, who was closely associated with the Aurora Verlag and the Pazifische Presse in Los Angeles (both belles lettres publishers), apparently felt no urgent need to underwrite similar publications under her own name. Apart from the licensed reprints only three books appeared under her imprint: a booklet to advise immigrants on financial matters, a new edition of a Heine anthology edited by Hugo Bieber, and a volume of prose poems by Edward Kaufmann.[61] An edition of Werfel's poetry under the title *Schönste Gedichte* (1946) is often cited as a Rosenberg imprint,[62] but is merely an incorrect entry for the Pazifische Presse volume *Gedichte aus den Jahre 1908 - 1945,* the distribution of which was handled by Miss Rosenberg. As she explained: "I wrote in the description on the leaflet that these are Werfel's 'best poems by his own choice.' Maybe the second title comes from this description."[63]

Friedrich Krause — bookdealer, importer, and literary agent — embarked on a rather extensive program of book publishing during the years 1944 through 1946. His variety of titles and formats included deluxe bibliophile editions of Johannes Urdizil, *Der Trauermantel: Eine Erzählung aus Adalbert Stifters Jugend und Kindheit* (1945) and Kurt Juhn, *Der Hexenhammer* (1945); the valuable series of texts on the "other Germany," *Dokumente des anderen Deutschland* (4 volumes, 1945- 1946); and two volumes of German songs. Besides these, Krause also issued six other titles of political history and literary criticism in the tradition of the Europa Verlag. As early as 1942 he had dabbled in some English-language publishing, oddly enough on the subject of first aid,[64] but apparently the results were not sufficiently encouraging to inspire further experiments in this line.

Berendsohn's description of Friedrich Krause and the Freundenkreis der Deutschen Blätter as being of a middle-class, relatively conservative bent (see on p.59) is borne out by the inclusion in Krause's list of authors such as Karl Paetel[65] and the publication of such an important document of the German conservative resistance as Carl Goerdeler's *Politisches Testament.* As the story goes, Goerdeler, the former Lord Mayor of Leipzig, and one of the leaders of the unsuccessful July 20th conspiracy against Hitler, paid a visit to the United States in 1937 and at that time deposited with some friends a memoir that critically described the political and economic plight of Germany. This *Denkschrift,* together with a biographical sketch and a letter addressed to "an American politician," dated October 11, 1938, comprise the bulk of the volume which Krause published in 1945.[66] Another Krause anthology edited by Hellmut Lehmann-Haupt — *Neue deutsche Gedichte* (1947) — attempted to collect and preserve the German poetry that expressed the spirit of resistance within the Third Reich and included selections by the German Catholic writer Reinhold Schneider.

Paul Mueller of the Schoenhof Verlag (a division of Schoenhof's Foreign Books) completes the trio of bookseller-publishers. A former Viennese, Mueller had built up Schoenhof's into a major distributor of

Free German literature. His own publishing program, for all its brevity, offered the German-American public a varied list of fiction and nonfiction in inexpensive editions. The most important author on Mueller's list was Ernst Lothar, the Viennese theatrical director who was already well known to the American public as a successful novelist.[67] Only two of a planned quartet of novels were ever published in the original German: *Der Engel mit der Posaune* and *Heldenplatz,* both in 1946.[68] *Verse für Zeitgenosse,* a volume of poetry by Mascha Kalécko popular enough for two editions (1945 and 1948), and three books on nonfiction completed the Schoenhof catalog.

Ernst Willard, Printer and Publisher. Ernst Willard of New York, formerly Ernst Wilhartitz of the Frisch Verlag in Vienna,[69] remains one of the more obscure of émigré publishers. Very little information has been forthcoming about either the man or his books, many of which were not well publicized in the German-language press. Willard served as printer for a number of other émigré publications as evidenced by occasional statements in the press and in the books themselves, although the latter practice was not the rule. He also initiated what might have been one of the more grandiose publishing feats of the emigration had it gotten off the ground, the Deutscher Buch Club in Amerika.[70] In 1946 several German-American papers brought to their readers' attention a "tastefully produced brochure," the first and last issue of the *Magazin des deutschen Buch Club.*[71] "It will be some years before books will again come out of Germany and Austria," Willard logically but mistakenly predicted, and "if we are interested in the preservation and development of the German language, then we must help ourselves."[72] For this reason the new club was going to publish the best of older German literature as well as works of contemporary authors. Willard also offered to distribute the books of any other publisher, English or German, to club members. The project came to naught. Lack of response to his prospectus and the increased availability of German-language books caused the abandonment of the club. The first issue of the *Magazin* listed a large number of new titles and reprints that Willard claimed to have already in stock, but, barring further revelations, these citations must be relegated to the realm of bibliographical fantasy.[73]

Nine books including at least one in English are known to have been published by Willard; there may have been others. Most are little-known documents of the emigration that possess special importance for the historian. As an illustration, one may cite Walther Victor's autobiography, *Kehre wieder über die Berge* (1945). Victor goes into great detail about his journalistic career in Weimar Germany, details that were eliminated from the new editions of his writings now current in the German Democratic Republic. One of the most informative books on

German writers in America is Peter M. Lindt's *Schriftsteller im Exil* (1944), another Willard publication in which two years of German-language radio broadcasts, largely interviews with exiled writers, are recorded. Also worthy of attention are the memoirs of Julius Korngold, *Posthumous Erinnerungen* (1946). The elder Korngold (whose more famous son Erich became a successful Hollywood composer), one of Vienna's leading music critics, died in relative obscurity in the United States. The article devoted to him in the standard German music encyclopedia makes no mention of these posthumously published sketches.[74] In sum, very special interest adheres to the Willard publications that have come to light, and the documentation of the German emigration in America would be all the poorer in their absence.

PRIVATE PRESSES

Attention to typographic excellence, limited editions, and a certain eclecticism are three hallmarks of the private press though among German émigré publishers these criteria are not so easily applied, particularly size of edition. Nevertheless, there are three presses which may be conveniently brought together here, the Johannespresse, the press of Victor Hammer in Aurora, New York, and the Pazifische Presse in Los Angeles.

The Johannespresse. The Johannespresse and the Hammerpresse are paradigms of cultural continuity between the Old World and the New. The career of Otto Kallir, proprietor of the Johannespresse, goes back to the 1920s and the Vienna of Hofmannsthal, Richard Beer-Hofmann, Oskar Kokoschka, and Alfred Kubin. All of these writers and artists were connected with the Vienna Johannespresse, and one relationship survived a transatlantic voyage to America shaping a curious epilogue to a dead era—the friendship of Otto Kallir and Richard Beer-Hofmann.[75] Kallir had published several works from the pen of Beer-Hofmann in prewar Vienna, perhaps the best known being the *Vorspiel auf dem Theater zu König David* (1936). Caught up in the maelstrom of violent change triggered by the events of 1938, both poet and publisher (after an interlude in Switzerland)[76] found shelter in the United States. An unexpected portion of recognition, a $1000 grant from the National Institute of Arts and Letters, lightened the poet's last years. Equally flattering was the formation of a Richard Beer-Hofmann Gesellschaft in New York with Kallir as president. In this favorable climate, the poet's last work was composed, a fragment of which was published in 1944 (a complete edition was released five years later).[77] The collaboration between the two Viennese reached its fulfillment in 1963 with Kallir's edition of Beer-Hofmann's *Gesammelte Werke* published by S. Fischer Verlag.

Perhaps of equal historical significance was Kallir's association with the celebrated mathematician and Rilke collector, Richard von Mises. Their partnership produced an important addition to the Rilke canon—the three-volume collection, *Rilke im Jahre 1896*. The individual volumes bore the titles: *Ewald Tragy* (1944), *Briefe an Baronesse von Oe* (1945), and *Verse und Prosa aus dem Jahre 1896* (1946). This was only the second publication of the novella *Ewald Tragy*,[78] while the other two volumes contained poetry and letters either unpublished or hitherto uncollected in book form. The introduction and copious annotations supplied by Von Mises added to the interest of the series. The last American imprint of the Johannespresse was Beer-Hofmann's *Paula* in 1949; about that time Kallir returned to Vienna.

The Hammer Press. The accomplishments of Victor Hammer as printer, type designer, and painter have received their share of critical attention.[79] His European career reached its apogee with the productions of his well-known hand press, the Stamperia del Santuccio (first used in Florence, Italy in 1930). During all his many peregrinations, whether in Kolbsheim on the Lower Rhine, Grundlsee in Austria, in Aurora, New York, or Lexington, Kentucky, Hammer used the imprint of the Stamperia for his finest typographical work.[80] Accompanied by his son and co-worker, Jacob, the elder Hammer began his American sojourn in the small college town of Aurora, a peaceful community in upstate New York. There, from 1941 to 1949, father and son operated the Wells College Press where eighteen items in several languages were carefully and tastefully produced. The Hammer Press imprint was used on three additional titles during this period. Ten of these volumes were in the German language, either wholly or in part. But nothing in these bare statistics reveals the true literary significance of these publications (apart from their obvious artistic merits). To understand this it is necessary to focus upon the American career of Herbert Steiner, initiator and sponsor of much of Hammer's German-language work.

Little enough has been written on Steiner's achievements, although they add up to a lifetime of service to both German and world literature.

> No *"Who's Who,"* no *Kürschner* or *Kosch* carries his name, for during his lifetime, the bearer . . . has found an almost Rumpelstilskin-like pleasure in hiding his light under a barrel, artfully keeping himself in the background, in order to escape the attention of literary notoriety. . . . We thank this "secret agent" of poetry for, among other things, the collected works of Hofmannsthal, the translations of Valéry and his work as editor of *Corona*.[81]

It is indeed as the editor of *Corona* that Steiner is best remembered. In America, Steiner continued publishing along similar lines welcoming from many countries original contributions of prose, poetry, essays, and

letters so long as they were unpolitical in content and unfettered to
Aktuelles. Two numbered series were printed by Hammer under the
sponsorship of Steiner—*Mesa* and *Aurora.* The former, of which five
numbers were published from 1945 to 1955, was a continuation of the
old *Corona* in both format (which was large and elegant) and content. In
limited editions of 250 to 300 copies, the superbly designed volumes
brought together contributions in many languages, but each issue would
contain a characteristic piece by perhaps Hofmannsthal, Rilke, Heinrich
Zimmer, or Erich von Kahler.

Aurora was the name given to a series of brochure-like publications
ranging in size from ten to thirty-six pages, each devoted to a single
essay or prose work. Again, Steiner was responsible for the selection of
the texts; the printing was done at the Wells College Press. Of the seven
numbered volumes limited to 100–225 copies per title, two contained
first editions of German texts: Herbert Steiner, *Begegnung mit Stefan
George* (1942)[82] and Rainer Maria Rilke, *Briefe an eine Freundin
1918–1925* (1944). The Rilke letters have a fascinating American pro-
venance, for besides publisher, printer, and editor—in this case Richard
von Mises—Rilke's correspondent (Claire Goll)[83] was herself a resident
of the United States.

Of the remaining productions of the Hammer Press, one in particular
stands out as both a literary and a human document, Gerhart Hauptmann's *Die Finsternisse.* The tragedy of Hauptmann's declining years,
his clouded relationship to the Nazi regime, has been the subject of
much polemical writing. The background to *Die Finsternisse* is especially worth retelling because of the light it throws on Hauptmann's
friend and ardent admirer, the Silesian-Jewish textile manufacturer Max
Pinkus.[84] The funeral of Max Pinkus was held in Neustadt, Upper
Silesia, a city which had made him an honorary citizen in 1927. The only
Christians who attended the services in 1934 were Hauptmann and his
wife. *Die Finsternisse,* by the very act of its creation a quiet protest
against the National Socialist order, was composed in Rapallo, the text
written down by Hauptmann's secretary. Although the original manuscript was destroyed out of fear of official confiscation, according to
Walter Reichart three copies had been made and given to Felix A.
Voigt, Frau Voigt, and C. F. W. Behl.[85] One of these copies reached the
United States and fell into the hands of Professor Reichart who was also
granted publication rights. Already in 1946 public attention, both in
Germany and America, was drawn to "Eine unbekannte Dichtung Gerhart Hauptmanns," the title of a newspaper article by Behl, which
concluded with these words: "If this still unknown play [Dichtung] be
published, it would serve as his [Hauptmann's] legacy for the future."[86]
In 1947 this pious wish was fulfilled when the German text, together
with an English introduction by Walter Reichart, was printed for Her-

bert Steiner at the Hammer Press in an edition of 400 copies. Thus in
their common exile the printer and the man of letters combined their
talents to produce a most respectable oeuvre that should be far better
known. For while the *Corona* of the 1930s is one of the most
sought-after literary journals of the period, its offspring in America are
virtually unknown.[87]

Pazifische Presse. The only Free German press on the West Coast of
America, the Pazifische Presse is still remembered if only through the
collective fame of its authors, in particular Thomas Mann, Franz Werfel,
and Alfred Döblin. Although New York was always the mecca of
émigré life, the hub of political activity, the center of publishing, the
press and book trade, the Hollywood aggregation sparkled with the
glamor of refugee actors, directors, musicians, and writers not all, by any
means, financially secure. The indubitable success of a Thomas Mann, a
Werfel, or a Feuchtwanger should not mask the economic straits and
spiritual isolation of the unlionized, of a Heinrich Mann or an Alfred
Döblin. Circumstances certainly favored some attempt at Free German
publishing in California and it is surprising that not more was
accomplished.[88]

The Pazifische Presse was the child of two expatriate Germans, Ernst
Gottlieb and Felix Guggenheim.[89] In 1942 they conceived the idea of
perpetuating through the medium of print the memory of those exiled
writers who had found a temporary haven in California. Thomas Mann
with three titles dominated their list of publications as a matter of
course. The remaining nine titles were more or less fairly distributed
among some of the lesser stars of the literary firmament — Franz Werfel
with two books, his *Wahre Geschichte vom wiederhergestellten Kreuz*
(1942) and the *Gedichte aus den Jahren 1908-1945* (1946); a play and a
novel from the pen of Lion Feuchtwanger; and fiction from Bruno
Frank, Leonhard Frank, Alfred Döblin, and Friedrich Torberg. In their
earliest public announcement, the Pazifische Presse offered on subscription the first seven of their publications only as a set in an edition limited
to 150 copies.[90] This information seems to refer only to a deluxe signed
edition since other sources indicate that 250 copies of each were printed.[91] The eighth publication of the press, Thomas Mann, *Das Gesetz*
(1944) was issued in an edition of 500 copies. It was first offered on
subscription and then in July, 1944 was given over to Mary S. Rosenberg for distribution.[92] The next four books published[93] were completely subsidized by Mary Rosenberg who also acted as sole distributing agent. She is quite justified, therefore, to consider herself the
actual publisher of these volumes.[94] The literary significance of some
Pazifische Presse titles may be a matter of dispute but not the care that

went into the production of the first eleven volumes which were printed by Saul and Lillian Marks at the Plantin Press, Los Angeles.

THE SELBSTVERLAG

A fascinating phenomenon of the émigré book world is the *Selbst-verleger,* the author as publisher. His productions may range from the crudely hektographed, mimeographed, or photographically reproduced volumes of near print, to the professionally printed and bound book in no way inferior to a trade publication. The former class includes the more obscure, ephemeral items, the sheaf of poems or the polemical pamphlet that is rarely caught in the bibliographical net. A certain number of these publications have been recorded though undoubtedly as many or more have vanished without trace.[95] It may be stretching a point to place at the head of the list the first German-language editions of Thomas Mann's last three novels—*Doktor Faustus* (1947), *Der Er-wählte* (1951), and *Die Bekenntnisse des Hochstaplers Felix Krull* (1954)[96]—since they were issued solely for the legal protection of both Mann and his publisher, Bermann-Fischer. The existence of these "first editions" hinged upon Mann's American citizenship and the necessity at that time to protect his copyright by having a German-language edition "manufactured in the United States of America" filed in Washington prior to its release in Europe.[97] When Mann was first made cognizant of these facts in 1947, he immediately authorized a limited mimeographed edition of *Doktor Faustus* to be prepared.[98]

A more difficult bibliographical problem was posed by Bertolt Brecht's *Gedichte im Exil,* a volume of poetry supposedly published in 1943. Its existence was first vouched for by F. C. Weiskopf:

> This volume was typewritten and photographically reproduced in 1943, at a time when publishing opportunities for the exiled writer in North America were especially meager, in order to reach by this means a number of readers and friends. Thus exile brought with it a revival of the publication methods of the medieval monks—of course with the use of modern aids.[99]

No mention of the *Gedichte im Exil* is made either by Sternfeld or Walter Nubel in his Brecht bibliography.[100] Further complicating matters is a bibliographical note appended to the Aurora Verlag anthology, *Morgenroete* (1947) that gives as the source of a Brecht poem ("An die deutschen Soldaten im Osten") a volume cited as *Gedichte im Exil, 1933-1947* (New York: Aurora Verlag, 1947). No such collection was ever published by Aurora either in New York or in Berlin; indeed no comparable volume appeared until 1964. Volume 6 of the collected edition of Brecht's poetry carries the title—*Gedichte 1941-1947: Gedichte im Exil, in Sammlungen nicht erhaltene Gedichte, Gedichte und Lieder aus Stücken* (Frankfurt am Main: Suhrkamp Verlag, 1964). Here for the first time the bibliographical details are clarified:

> During the first years of his American exile, Brecht brought together three different collections of his poetry under the same title [*Gedichte im Exil*]. From the typewritten copy of the last collection dated December, 1944, Brecht had a number of photo-copies made. To a friend who was given a copy as a Christmas gift Brecht wrote: "I am somewhat abashed that I cannot present you with [my poems] in printed form, however, we must put up with this reversion to the early Middle Ages."[101]

The preceding discussion was limited to processed publications. Of the ten author-publishers of normally printed books, only the two most important figures shall be described in any detail: Oskar Maria Graf and Josef Luitpold Stern. For details on the eight remaining imprints consult the appended bibliography.[102]

Oskar Maria Graf. "Ein Dichter hilft sich selbst!" was the ubiquitous by-line of innumerable notices and advertisements that so enlivened German-American journalism after 1939. The ebullient Bavarian "Provinzschriftsteller" Oskar Maria Graf spent over twenty-five years in the United States, tramping the lecture circuit, publishing and selling his own books.[103] Following World War I Graf joined the ill-starred Munich revolutionary government of Kurt Eisner but subsequently turned to the less bloody muse of literature, a course that led from literary criticism to fiction. Graf's fame increased with publication of the autobiographical *Wir sind Gefangene* and his numerous *Bauerngeschichte,* popular, earthy tales of peasant life. In 1933 he protested against the tacit acceptance of his books in Nazi Germany and demanded that they too be cast on the bonfires.[104] While in Prague (1934-1938) he assisted in the publication of the Communist-backed *Neue Deutsche Blätter*. He reached the United States in 1939, settling down in a small Manhattan apartment.

Graf exhibited a certain naiveté (at least from the present position of unindulgent hindsight) in his political views and especially in his relation to the Communist Party. Although he considered himself a nonorganization man, his critics on the Right did little to hide their conviction that Graf was the leading Communist among German émigré writers. In the unique position of being not only a non-Jewish proletarian writer but an *Ur-Bayrischer Volksdichter* as well, Graf made an ideal figurehead for Communist-led organizations and campaigns among the German-American workers.[105] His sympathetic attitude toward Communist policies in the United States went hand in hand (as in the case of Otto

Sattler) with enthusiastic support from the German-Communist press. However, a balanced judgment should take into consideration a recent statement of faith written by Graf in 1960 which, after a very general description of Socialist ideals, concludes with these words: "Towards [these goals] I have always tried to direct my actions; and everyone who struggles for the [same ends] — whether he calls himself Communist, free Socialist or Social Democrat — was and is for me a 'Comrade.' "[106]

With Graf's charming robust personality and easy manner, together with his entree into both émigré and labor circles, it is not difficult to explain his comparatively successful publishing career.[107] Besides the English translations — *Life of My Mother* (1942) and *Prisoners All* (1943) — and some stock of Malik Verlag editions which he had managed to salvage,[108] Graf reprinted three of his earlier works for the American market. *Anton Sittinger* (1941) and *Das bayrische Dekameron* (1939) were issued in editions of 1110 each, [109] and a 1940 reprint of the novel *Bolwieser* is recorded by Walter Berendsohn.[110] After 1948 almost all of Graf's books were produced in Europe with the exception of one volume of poetry, *Der ewige Kalender* (1954), printed in New York in a limited edition. Graf had hoped to reprint many more of his earlier works but his plans were quashed by insurmountable financial difficulties.[111] While Oskar Maria Graf was always in the public eye, his fellow Socialist Josef Luitpold Stern (who wrote under the name of Josef Luitpold) led a retired, almost monastic existence during most of his American sojourn.

Josef Luitpold Stern. A Viennese by birth, Stern soon became deeply committed to Socialism, more specifically to the education of Socialist youth. Stern rapidly made his reputation in this sphere and soon was made director of the Arbeiterhochschule in Vienna, perhaps the educational center of Central European Social Democracy. He was also a leader in the development of standards for public libraries; indeed, to quote Walther Victor, "Stern was the European authority within the labor movement on this subject."[112] Withal, Stern was a prodigiously fertile lecturer, poet, dramatist, and translator (of Walt Whitman among others). The most trying circumstances could not contain his irrepressible spirit. During the months of his internment by the French in 1939 and 1940, Stern composed no less than five collections of lyric poetry which were reproduced in a fine hand by Hugo Priess, a former leader of the Austrian Socialist youth group Rote Falken who was an inmate of another camp, and provided with illustrations by an unnamed artist working in yet a third camp.[113] These lyrics under the title *Das französische Jahr* were published in 1945 in his New York *Selbstverlag* by Stern.

For the greater part of his American exile that lasted from 1940 to

1948, Stern lived and worked in the slums of Philadelphia as librarian of a settlement house. Walther Victor has painted a graphic if overdramatic description of these melancholy surroundings:

> It is an ugly outlying district which withheld any promise of joyousness. Did the sun ever shine, did springtime or the lust for life ever quicken the heart? One cannot believe so. The visitor sees only despairing darkness, crumbling walls, tokens of misery. It is the negro quarter. He enters the "settlement," a humanitarian institution made up of a few old ill-assorted houses; lightless corridors, decay, dust were in evidence despite the painstaking attempt of the good people to make something useful out of the institution. . . . Here is Dr. Stern's room. An iron bedstead, a chair, a table, books, paper, the suggestion of a window. . . . There was the same lump in my throat, the same urge to strike out against this world, the same sense of powerlessness that overcame me when I stepped into his garret in Paris, Boulevard Rochechouart. "Negroes and Italians, in the grey of the slums, and I in their midst, that is now my world," he said to a reporter. . . . He is librarian of the Settlement, manages the children's savings and lends them books to ornament their homes. He receives in return, beside food and lodging, a monthly pittance.[114]

But that by no means was the whole of his life. Besides occasional lecturing commitments, he wrote and by 1945 began once more to publish. In this he liked to compare himself to Upton Sinclair, who was also in his day a Socialist *Selbstverleger* of some notoriety.[115] Back in 1935 Stern had initiated a series of small, thirty-two-page, yellow-covered brochures collectively known as *Die Hundert Hefte*. By 1948 forty-four *Hefte* had been printed, six in the United States dated 1945. Stern also had printed a bilingual selection from his poetry under the title *Sons Like These* (1946).[116] We shall return in the next section to some of the more technical details of Stern's enterprise.

Manufacture, Distribution, and Advertising of Free German Books in the United States

Most Free German books published in this country were also printed here, in many cases by one of the German-American or émigré printers active in the New York area. Those printers who belonged to the New York local of the German-American Typographia[117] frequently advertised their services in the German-American press.[118] Post-1933 émigrés, many of whom turned to job printing for their livelihood,[119] were also responsible for a number of Free German publications. While a few limited editions of Free German books were printed by American presses of note, such as the Plantin Press and the Elm Tree Press, this relationship was not usual. The traditional range of bindings of the German book trade was retained by many émigré publishers. While moderately priced trade editions, such as those of Aurora and Schoenhof, were bound in either cloth or stiff paper, private press editions of a book often were issued in a variety of bindings; half leather, linen, semiflexboard, and *Pappeband* were the more usual materials used.[120] Bookbinding was also a craft in which numerous émigrés were adept, but only rarely was the binder's identity revealed.[121]

Books could be ordered directly from the publisher, the distributing agent, or from one of the émigré bookshops; all made use of announcements and catalogs sent through the mail as well as extensive advertising in the émigré press. Since the demise of the Alliance Book Club in 1941, this particular mode of distribution was no longer a factor although both Wieland Herzfelde and Ernst Willard tried to revive it. Only Pantheon Books, Ungar, Krause, and Schoenhof's Foreign Books were listed in the *Publishers' Trade List Annual,* but neither Ungar nor Krause could be called regular contributors.[122] *Publishers' Weekly* often took notice of Free German books, but with no regularity. As so many émigré publishers evinced a reluctance to handle the details of distribution, these were frequently taken over by one of the larger booksellers. A case in point, Mary Rosenberg's connection with the Pazifische Presse, has already been described. In a like manner Walter H. Perl of the Academic Book Service was entrusted with the sale of Iven Heilbut's volume of verse, *Meine Wanderungen,*[123] and Paul Mueller of Schoenhof's with the general distribution of Aurora books.

The economic situation of the author-publisher was rarely self-sustaining; even Oskar Maria Graf made use of outside help. Like Graf, two other author-publishers, Louis Roemer[124] and Hans Marchwitza,[125] stemmed from the working class and were both closely identified with German radical groups in New York. There is every reason to believe that Marchwitza's two books and Roemer's single volume of verse were, at least in part, subsidized by the Communist Party. The Deutsche Zentral-Buchhandlung, the party bookstore, was charged with the sole distribution of Roemer's *Zeit Gedichte,*[126] which was widely advertised in the Communist press, on isolated occasions in the *Neue Volks-Zeitung* and, strangely enough, in the *Jüdisches Familienblatt* for September, 1938. Fortunately there is extant a detailed description of the working methods of one author-publisher, Josef Luitpold Stern:

> I began my *Hundert Hefte* in exile, actually in November, 1935. Thirty-seven numbers appeared up to November, 1945, thirty-one in Czechoslovakia, six in America. In the penury of my exile years the overriding question for me, as the only publisher of my own works, was

where to obtain the money for printing. The answer came immediately. If I used money to produce one volume and through its sale recouped my expense, I could then transform my re-acquired funds into a new volume; and so forth. At the same time, I retained the standing type used for the *Hefte* and utilized it to produce an (up to now) four volume work, each 300 pages thick [i.e., his collected works that he called the *Sternbild*]. Altogether I sold 38,583 copies in Europe during the years 1935 through 1938 and 3,715 copies in America up to 1945 – a total, therefore, of 42.298 *Hefte*, each 32 pages in length.

Of the collected edition in four volumes, 1792 copies were disposed of during 1937–1938. The volumes were almost exclusively acquired on subscription. In Europe, I sold the *Hefte* in the evening after my lectures, in America they were distributed one-third by colportage, two-thirds by subscription. Behind me stood no organization, no party, no money, nothing but the love of many hearts for "soziale Dichtung."[127]

Prepublication subscription was an expedient forced not only upon the author-publisher but upon most smaller Free German publishers from 1942 to 1947. Barthold Fles, the Johannespresse, the Pazifische Presse, Friedrich Krause, and the Writers Service Center all found subscription the only feasible method of financing many of their books. One newspaper expressed its outrage at this state of affairs: "A number of exiled writers have attempted by means of subscription to issue their own work in 'Selbstverlage' . . . printer, publisher, author and retailer in one, they wander through the land . . . like ordinary salesmen."[128] Even a relatively solvent publisher like Pantheon Books was forced to adopt this method of financing Hermann Broch's *Der Tod des Vergil* (1945). Such, at any rate, is the gist of a letter written by Thomas Mann to Broch indicating that only the lack of 500 additional subscribers was holding up publication of the latter's novel.[129]

To reach the limited audience of émigrés and German Americans, the most logical advertising medium was the German-language press. Communist, Socialist, Austrian, and German-Jewish newspapers alike carried advertisements of books and maintained more or less adequate, if sometimes biased, review columns. Advertisements took the form of brief notices from the publishers, or more often were gratuitously supplied by the paper as reviews or news items. Bookdealers' announcements appeared, as they still do, in the *Aufbau* with great regularity. The Communist press, however, was chary of space for books with a bourgeois taint. Since no survey was made of the conservative German-American press, it is not clear to what extent it aided in the dissemination of Free German literature, although after 1942 some degree of rapprochement was evident.

In the summer of 1944 émigré Willy Pollack, the former Berlin book and art dealer, took over editorial control of the National Weeklies, the largest chain of German-language papers in the United States.[130] The *Aufbau* reported that Pollack wanted to further the production of German-language literature, novels, and short stories without any tendentious background.[131] This indicated a change in policy on the part of the widely circulated chain. It is quite possible that this thaw was accompanied by an increase of both advertisements and reviews of Free German literature. Certainly a few well-disposed papers gave aid and succor to the émigrés, papers such as the *Florida Echo* (Miami Beach), the *Freie Presse für Texas* (San Antonio), and to a lesser extent the *California Staats-Zeitung* (Los Angeles) and the *New Yorker Staats-Zeitung und Herold.*[132]

Another common practice was the inclusion of advertising matter in the book itself or on the book jacket. The notices might offer, as did O. M. Graf in *Das bayrische Dekameron* (1939), books available and books that might be reprinted given sufficient demand. In Walther Victor's *Kehre Wieder über die Berge* (1945) there is appended a list of most of the author's other books, all published in Europe under a variety of imprints and at that time still available from Ernst Willard. Some volumes contain reviews of the author's earlier books; some, such as Aurora's *Morgenroete,* list titles that never saw the light of day. To be sure, the traditional techniques of bookselling such as the circulation of flyers and catalogs were utilized; few have survived the passage of time.[133] The comprehensive lists issued by Krause, Rosenberg, and Schoenhof's Foreign Books, in their capacity as dealers, were another means of disseminating information on new publications. Outside of the German-language press, reviews of Free German books were a rarity, in part because of the language barrier, but also because the very limited size of editions often precluded review copies. Specialized periodicals like the *Journal of English and Germanic Philology* and the *Journal of Central European Affairs* occasionally noted publications falling within their purview.

Free German Publishing — To What End?

A discussion of the aims and ideals that inspired exile publishing might seem redundant at this point; nevertheless it is both possible and prudent to develop this topic in a systematic way. After briefly restating the basic needs which were filled by the publication that went on in the various and widely scattered exile enclaves, several special publishing problems are examined in more detail: books to aid in the Americanization of the new immigrant, books for prisoners of war, and books for postwar Germany.

MEETING BASIC NEEDS

To Maintain the Identity of the German Emigration. From 1933 to the outbreak of the European conflict, and to a lesser degree thereafter, the self-imposed mission of the Free German publisher was to solidify the anti-Nazi front. To this end both German and the languages of the host nations were utilized. Hermann Rauschning's *Die Konservative Revolution* (1941), in both German and English editions, is a good example of the political and polemical literature of this period. To scavenge among the flood of English-language books of this nature is outside the scope of the present study, but the total would be impressive. During the near isolation of wartime America, emphasis shifted to the presentation and reappraisal of the cultural and political heritage of the "other Germany," the land of Heine, Rilke, and Mann—the community of spirit in which the exiles understandably enrolled themselves. Contributing to this end were the reprints and new editions of classic and modern masters; among these publications were the Heine edition reissued by Mary S. Rosenberg, the numerous volumes of Rilke, the Pantheon collection of Stefan George, and the bilingual Hölderlin anthology brought out under the New Directions imprint.[134] The preservation of self-identity was also the most pressing need of the various subgroups within the emigration, whether they were Austrians, Jews, Socialists, or Communists. This was most efficiently done through the medium of the newspaper which served the dual purpose of preserving group unity and facilitating intragroup communication.

To Maintain the Identity of the Individual. For the creative individual, the need to communicate was paramount. Scholars and scientists, not to mention journalists, were impelled to learn English or to have their contributions translated. The poet or novelist, on the other hand, desirous of writing in his native tongue, was faced by the economic facts of émigré life. Those without international reputations had to be content with the transitory medium of newsprint or to publish on their own. Several "Good Samaritans" did attempt to assist younger or relatively unknown authors—publishers such as Barthold Fles, Peter Fisher, and the Writers Service Center of Friderike Zweig. The dedication of Otto Kallir to Richard Beer-Hofmann, who hardly enjoyed an American reputation, was of the greatest importance in the propagation of that author's work both in German and English. But it was indeed blind fortune that favored the venerable Austrian-Jewish dramatist but neglected Heinrich Mann, Alfred Döblin, and Albrecht Schaeffer.

FREE GERMAN PUBLISHERS AND THE
PROCESS OF AMERICANIZATION

The Free German publisher played no really significant role in the

Americanization of the new immigrants. Helping the newcomer to adjust was the self-imposed task of both the *Aufbau*[135] and the *Austro-American Tribune;* it may have been this fact that dampened the prospects of more costly publishing ventures. A few books were indeed aimed at the immigrant audience, in all about ten volumes. As examples we may cite: Robert M. W. Kempner, *Rechte und Pflichten der feindlichen Ausländer* (1942); B. Grossmann, *Taschenbuch über die Vereinigten Staaten für Einwanderer und Ausländer* (1947); and Bruno Russ, *A.B.C. für U.S.A.* (1939).[136] One series that held out much promise, Schoenhof's *Amerika-Bücherei,* unfortunately suffered an untimely demise. In 1945, the Cambridge firm published the first volume of this popular-priced series, *Thomas Jefferson, Auswahl aus seiner Schriften,* hoping to make "American political thinking of stature and value . . . a part of the culture of the German-speaking immigrant."[137] Selections from the writings of Thomas Paine and Abraham Lincoln were also announced but never forthcoming. The availability of Bermann-Fischer and Oprecht books and the rapid recovery of the German publishing industry after 1946 were reasons enough to discourage such projects from flowering on American soil.

REEDUCATION OF THE PRISONERS OF WAR

During World War II in the neighborhood of 400,000 German prisoners were interned in the United States. American authorities, in contrast with their British allies, exhibited a certain diffidence toward the problem of reeducation (or de-Nazification as this was rather negatively termed). A lack of any positive United States program was the spur for lengthy discussions in the émigré press during the winter of 1944.[138] The initial flurry of excitement was caused by reports from some of the camps of Nazi *Fememorde,* the assassination of anti-Nazi prisoners.[139] It also irked the *Neue Volks-Zeitung* that one Nazi camp leader wrote the United States Commandant demanding the removal of that newspaper from the camp library and canteen.[140] Adding to the irritation of many émigrés was the lack of interest shown by American authorities in utilizing the talents of German exiles in the reeducation program. The British made more extensive use of qualified exiles in this sensitive area, a fact well known in the United States.[141]

Belated though it was, government action did follow, and a large-scale program of cultural and political education was begun. Some eighty German-language newspapers were printed and distributed in the many camps that dotted the American countryside. As courses of instruction were developed, more and more German-language publications were sought by camp officials. This turn of events generated an enthusiastic response from Free German publishers and bookdealers in both the

Americas. From Chile the *Deutsche Blätter* solicited gift subscriptions for prisoners of war, while its editors, in an open letter "An die Deutschen Kriegsgefangenen in Nordamerika," attempted to build a certain community of feeling between prisoner and émigré:

> Different fates have led you and us to America, but the cause is the same — National Socialism. . . . Will we come to understand one another, we as Germans in America whether refugees or prisoners? That is the question that demands an answer at this, the most tragic moment in our history.[142]

In the United States, Wieland Herzfelde related the program of the newly founded Aurora Verlag to the prisoner of war problem by emphasizing that:

> With the arrival in this country of hundreds of thousands of German prisoners of war . . . the demands for German books has suddenly risen to an unprecedented height without being met up to now by an adequate increase in the supply of good German books; that is, of books free from any vestige of Nazism. . . . In order to cope, to a modest extent, with the task arising from this situation, a number of writers, from Austria, Germany and Czechoslovakia now living in this country have banded together in a new publishing venture, Aurora Verlag.[143]

The same report added that one of the first Aurora books was to be the anthology *Morgenroete* — "a reader for German prisoners of war." Although announced in 1945, publication was inexplicably delayed for two years — too late, of course, for its original purpose.[144]

Gottfried Bermann-Fischer was the most diligent of his peers in the preparation of reading material for the POW camps. A special series of twenty-four paperbound volumes, *Neue Welt,* was printed with government approval for exclusive sale to prisoners at only twenty-five cents each. The twenty-four titles were selected from a list of forty by a committee of prisoners (a politic move on the part of camp officials) and published in editions of 50,000 each. These books were the prototypes of the pioneer paperback series in post-war Germany, the Fischer-Bücherei.[145] Not resting on these laurels alone, Bermann-Fischer was inspired to hold a competition for the best novel written by a prisoner of war. Perhaps it was a matter of tactful public relations but none of the contest notices in *Der Ruf* (the national POW literary journal) mentioned the name of the émigré publisher. The winning entry, Walter Kolbenhoff's *Von unserem Fleisch und Blut,* was published in Stockholm by Bermann-Fischer on his return to Europe in 1947.

Other Free German books, new and secondhand, were supplied by dealers such as Friedrich Krause and Wieland Herzfelde (Seven Seas Bookshop). Krause claimed to have been supplying POW camps with literature as far back as December, 1943.[146] The Communist publicist F. C. Weiskopf jauntily commented on the prisoner of war trade for readers of *Freies Deutschland* (Mexico City):

> Some days ago I was browsing in a [New York City] book store and the mail just brought orders from the war prisoners camp. What does a camp librarian order? This one (one of the none-too-numerous rare birds) did not want too bad books on his list. Bertolt Brecht: *Private Life of the Master Race;* Agnes Smedley: *Battle Hymn of China;* Paul Merker: *Deutschland Sein oder Nichtsein;* Ernst Sommer: *Revolte der Heiligen;* Ludwig Renn: *Adel im Untergang;* Freiligrath; Herweigh [sic], Heine, Whitman and Willkie.[147]

The government did attempt to screen all books that were distributed to the camps though the resulting regulations were somewhat involved: new books could be sent directly from publisher to camp; older and used books first had to be scrutinized by the camp commandant; books published before 1930 outside the United States had to be sent to the official censor, POW Department, General Post Office, New York.[148] Apparently the camps varied in their acceptance of Communist-sponsored literature. On one occasion the *German American* boasted that an unnamed camp official had ordered 121 copies of its publication *Erziehung vor Stalingrad,* an eye-witness report by the German Communist poet Erich Weinert. It was more usual to find the paper accusing the camps of discrimination against progressive, anti-Fascist literature.

The editors of the *German American* were publicly outraged when in 1944 the paper's application to be circulated in the POW camps was turned down because, and here they quoted from the offending letter, "The Office of Censorship expresses the feeling that the extreme anti-Nazi views expressed in your publication might be more misunderstood than helpful to German prisoners in this country and that it might tend to encourage political dissension within the camp."[149] As of March, 1945, according to Albert Norden, the situation remained largely unchanged:

> Until recently German-language newspapers with subversive content, like the *Neue Volks-Zeitung,* circulated unhindered in the camps, while real anti-Fascist publications were forbidden. I saw in a camp in Trinidad, Colorado, a newspaper for sale under the name of *Der Spiegel* which was completely permeated with the perverted spirit of Nazism. . . . The ban against anti-Fascist books and papers that still is in effect in many camps should be lifted.[150]

BOOKS FOR A NEW GERMANY

In Janus-like fashion Free German publishers faced an expanding market on two fronts: in the United States, the German prisoners of war; in Europe, a defeated Germany starved for intellectual nourishment. The émigrés hopefully prepared to satisfy both demands. The first Aurora catalog issued in 1945 contained the following unambiguous statement of purpose, "The founders of the publishing house foresaw that after the collapse of the Hitler regime Germany and Austria would be afflicted with intellectual as well as material famine and they wanted, true to the great humanistic tradition of German literature, to share in the cultural rebuilding."[151] This utterance pointed in a quite different direction from the statements released to the American press which, if you will recall, emphasized the reeducation of German prisoners of war. Aurora books did enjoy wide circulation in Europe, but only after Herzfelde had shifted his base of operations to Berlin.

Bookdealers too were not hesitant to advertise under the banner of "books for Germany."[152] Ernst Willard with his German Book Club had counted on the long dormancy of the German book trade and proved himself a poor prophet. Far and away the most industrious publisher of German books for Europe was the Bermann-Fischer Verlag, which until 1946 was still directed from New York. While the *Neue Welt* series was printed in the United States, books intended for the continental market were printed in Stockholm. In 1944, Bermann-Fischer declared that "the much discussed problem of the . . . re-education of the German people is essentially a publishing problem."[153] Extending his remarks on that topic in an interview granted to *Publishers' Weekly,* he outlined the future plans of his firm. They were to include the preparation of German editions of important American books—e.g., Wendell Willkie's *One World*—and the issuing of textbooks to be ready for immediate use in liberated Germany. This latter goal was immediately qualified by the statement: "As no one can today prophesy what the educational plans for Germany will be and by whom directed, these books will not be manufactured until they are approved through the official channels."[154]

The textbooks problem was an irritant to many German refugee intellectuals. Fritz Karsen,[155] a former German educator, led the ensuing public debate by taking the position that at least a share in the preparation of new texts should be alloted to qualified émigrés.[156] In this emotionally charged atmosphere, Bermann-Fischer named Professor Karsen to direct a group of émigré scholars and teachers who were authorized to prepare several series of history textbooks and German-language readers for both elementary and secondary schools.[157]

The immediate efforts of the American occupation authorities to provide suitable textbooks were deemed most unsatisfactory by émigré critics; Ludwig Marcuse, for one, sharply castigated the use of outdated and "dangerous" books, actually reprints of texts originally written during the 1920s.[158] The circumstances that led to the adoption of these pre-Nazi texts are described by Marshall Knappen, chief of the Religious Section and deputy chief of the Education Section of the American Military Government:

> The next possibility was the adoption of various texts then actually in the course of preparation for this very purpose by German refugees. Examination of sample manuscripts from these sources showed that excellent work was being done on them. Nevertheless, since reports of the project had already been published, the authorship could not be concealed, and these books would inevitably be open to the same objection as the forced use of refugees as teachers would be. If on later examination local German authorities should decide to use such texts, obviously we would be only too glad to approve these decisions. But at the time is [sic] was believed impractical to gamble that practically all local administrators would so approve these texts. Because German feeling against textbooks by foreigners was believed to be even stronger than it was against those by refugees, a similar objection applied to the suggestion that existing or specially prepared American or English texts should be translated. The difficulties involved in wartime printing forbade us the luxury of reproducing refugee or foreign texts unless they could be generally used.
>
> It was therefore concluded that the least of the evils confronting us was the reproduction of the best available texts from the Weimar period.[159]

The American Military Government was aware of the shortcomings of these texts but felt that their use was an emergency measure to be endured until the Germans themselves could take on the job. In 1949 R. H. Samuel and R. Hinton Thomas caustically commented: "In the British and American Zones the writing of new textbooks is left almost entirely to German textbook committees, which so far have functioned extremely slowly."[160] This policy was not one to appeal to the émigrés who in effect were barred from having their own textbooks used in German schools. Of Bermann-Fischer's planned series of texts, only two could be traced in licensed German editions — both appearing in 1947.[161]

CONCLUSION

The attempt on the part of the émigrés to take upon themselves part of the responsibility for German reeducation parallels the political dreams of the Council for a Democratic Germany. America's postwar policy was as little influenced by the one as by the other. The immediate task of supplying reading matter to those parts of Germany and Austria under United States jurisdiction was taken on by the Office of War Information aided by the Council of Books in Wartime; émigré publishers were not involved.

Under the direction of the Publication Division of the Office of War Information (OWI), an attempt was made to supply current American books to European readers as rapidly as possible.[162] The program was threefold: to publish paperbound translations of American books in various languages; to export American trade books to Europe (the OWI acting either as purchaser or purchasing agent); and to stimulate European publishers to issue informative books about America. The twenty German-language translations which bore the Overseas Editions, Inc. imprint were issued in quantities of 50,000 to 60,000 per title. All Overseas Editions, including books in languages other than German, were printed in New York and added up to a grand total of some 3,500,000 copies. Another series of translations with the Éditions Transatlantique imprint, amounting to about 500,000 copies, was manufactured in London. Most of the German volumes were probably prepared by such émigré writers as Hermann Kesten, translator of Stephen Vincent Benét's *America,* though not all can be properly attributed. In the opinion of Maurice Davie, the émigré writer's "outstanding contribution was in translating into German the American books sent to Europe by the Council on Books under OWI."[163] There was another side to the matter, and émigré publishers did not feel well served by events, their ambitious plans having been wrecked on the shoals of a pragmatic American occupation policy. However, this failure should not overshadow the real and substantial achievement of the Free German publisher in America.

Notes

1. These 353 books and pamphlets are drawn from the listings in Appendix III, which is a tentative checklist only and should not be considered as definitive for the years covered. Criteria for inclusion were American manufacture or an exclusively American imprint. Thus Europa Verlag books bearing the Zürich-New York imprint were considered imports. In some instances publication dates (in particular for undated Ungar reprints) are necessarily only educated guesses. Hence the percentages arrived at in tables 2 and 3 are approximate and are included only to point up general tendencies; no claim is implied of a statistically accurate profile of Free German publishing in the United States.

2. This figure was taken from the U.S. Office of Alien Property Custodian, *Book Republication Program List II (Cumulative)* (Washington, D.C., Dec., 1944). Only ten titles published by Ungar and seven by Mary S. Rosenberg are definitely known to be licensed editions. Probably more such editions were published by Ungar. The leading American publisher of scientific reprints under this program was Edwards Bros., Ann Arbor, Mich.

3. For example, Thomas Mann's open letter to the University of Bonn after his honorary doctor's degree was annulled—*Ein Briefwechsel* (New York: Rotograph Co., 1937)—published in an edition of 10,000 copies.

4. Graf's *Bayrisches Dekameron* and *Anton Sittinger* were reprinted by the author in New York in editions of 1100 each. Letter dated June 1, 1964.

5. Paul Mueller of Schoenhof's Foreign Books which distributed Aurora titles stated they were all issued in editions of 2000 copies (letter, July 13, 1964). The most authoritative bibliography, however, lists many in editions as high as 4000. See Deutsche Akademie der Künste zu Berlin, *Der Malik Verlag* (1967).

6. These three reprints all published in 1945 were: Joseph Roth's *Hiob* and *Radetzkymarsch,* and Kurt Tucholsky's *Das Lächeln der Mona Lisa.* The sole original work of literature was Ernst Waldinger's book of poetry, *Glück und Geduld* (1952).

7. Thomas Mann to Franz Werfel, May 26, 1939, in Thomas Mann, *Briefe, 1937-1947* (Frankfurt am Main: S. Fischer Verlag, 1963), p.94-96.

8. *Aufbau* (N.Y.), Dec. 5, 1941, p.19.

9. See, for example, Karl Kurt Klein, *Literaturgeschichte des Deutschtums im Ausland* (Leipzig: Bibliographische Institut AG, 1939), p.266-78.

10. E.g., Heinrich Conrad Biewirth, *Aus den Leben eines Deutsch-Amerikaners* (Yarmouth, Mass.: Yarmouth Register, 1947).

11. See p.74.

12. One witness among scores was the Austrian writer Oskar Jellinek then living in New York. In a letter to Karel Krejčí (March 30, 1941) he commented: "There are many things here that I sorely miss, but hardly my library, for the mighty Public Library has almost everything I could wish." Krejčí, *Oskar Jellinek Leben und Werk* (Brno: Universita J. E. Purkyne, 1967), p.37.

13. *Aufbau* (N.Y.), Sept. 5, 1947, p.12.

14. Grand Forks, N.D.: The Author, 1953. Quoted material comes from p.91.

15. *Neue Volks-Zeitung,* Aug. 9, 1941, p.2.

16. Kelsen, *Vergeltung und Kausalität* (1941) and Von Mises, *Kleines Lehrbuch des Positivismus* (1939). Both books were printed in Holland by Van Stockum & Zoon. It is doubtful whether the Kelsen work enjoyed much circulation outside of the United States.

17. Franz Werfel, *Poems.* Translated by Edith Abercrombie Snow (Princeton, N.J.: 1945).

18. Several abridgments of dissertations written in German were published during this period but these are of little relevance. Also to be noted is the printing by Hunter College, New York, of Iven Heilbut's lecture, *Die Sendung Hermann Hesses* (1947).

19. John Farrar and Benjamin Huebsch of Viking Press were sponsors of the German American Writers Association to which Schönstedt belonged. *Aufbau* (N.Y.), Dec. 15, 1939, p.13. Schönstedt's novel was first serialized in the Communist weekly *Volksfront* (Chicago).

20. *Deutschamerikanischer Volkskalender* 1938. The contents of this 192-page volume are listed in the *Deutsches Volksecho,* Sept. 11, 1937.

21. Thomas was a former editor of the *Augsburger Volkswille,* ca. 1919 (an organ of the Unabhängige Sozialdemokratische Partei Deutschlands), and a onetime member of the German Reichstag. See *Aufbau* (N.Y.), March 14, 1941, p.1, and Reinhold Grimm, *Bertolt Brecht* (Stuttgart: J. B. Metzlersche Verlagsbuchhandlung, 1961), p.4.

22. Letter from Herman Kormis, May 16, 1964.

23. *Das Antifaschistische Kriegsziel* (New York: Public Voice Publishing Co., Inc., American European Publications, 1939). This thirty-page pamphlet was printed in Stockholm. One pamphlet, *Europäische Umwälzung,* was definitely printed in New York and some of the others may also have been printed there.

24. The *Aufbau* (N.Y.) reported that Bermann-Fischer and the art dealer Aram [sic] intended to establish a German-language publishing house. Nov. 29, 1940, p.10. The American publisher Alfred Harcourt was very influential in giving direction to Bermann-Fischer's American career. See the latter's autobiography, *Bedroht und Bewahrt* (Frankfurt am Main: S. Fischer, 1967), p.224 et passim.

25. *Publishers' Weekly,* Nov. 23, 1940, p.1968; *Aufbau* (N.Y.), March 6, 1942, p.19.

26. Quoted from an interview with Bermann-Fischer, *Aufbau* (N.Y.), Sept. 15, 1944, p.10. Cf. the apparent success of Friedrich Krause in importing Swiss books during the early war years. See p.82.

27. *Publishers' Weekly,* Nov. 23, 1940, p.1968.

28. The publisher was still in Stockholm, but Mann had recently settled in Princeton. *Dieser Friede* was originally titled, "Die Höhe des Augenblicks" and was to have been included in a volume of essays—*Achtung Europa!*—published by Bermann-Fischer in Stockholm. However, separate publication was decided upon. Cf. Mann, *Briefe, 1937-1947,* p.58.

29. Ibid., p.71.

30. *Verse* (Stockholm-New York: Bermann-Fischer Verlag, 1941).

31. Mann, *Briefe, 1937-1947,* p.130.

32. *Aufbau,* Dec. 20, 1940, p.7. *Lotte* was advertised by the Alliance Book Corp. in April, 1940, but it is doubtful if any of the original Stockholm edition was distributed in the United States. Alliance, in any case, ceased distributing Free German books that July. The photographic reprint was probably made in Nov. or Dec., 1940. Copies carry the original title page but with the note "printed in U.S.A." on the verso. These Bermann-Fischer photo reprints were issued in editions up to 5000 copies. See Bermann-Fischer, op. cit., p.226.

33. This is confirmed by an advertisement placed by Harcourt in the *Aufbau* (N.Y.), March 4, 1941, p.14. Hans Bürgin, *Das Werk Thomas Mann: Eine Bibliographie* (Frankfurt am Main: S. Fischer, 1959), makes no mention of an American reprint so it is possible that the edition distributed by Harcourt was the original Stockholm edition.

34. *Aufbau* (N.Y.), Sept. 15, 1944, p.10. The American edition of *Deutsche Hörer,* confirmed by Bermann-Fischer in this interview, is not recorded by Bürgin. *Joseph, der Ernährer* (Bürgin No.66) is an exact reprint of the 1943 Stockholm edition but without the index, p.643-45. There were two American printings, July and Nov., 1944.

35. Bermann-Fischer, op. cit., p.165.

36. Mann, *Briefe, 1937-1947,* p.249.

37. Ibid., p.297.

38. Ibid., p.355.

39. Ibid., p.392.

40. For a biographical sketch of Dagobert Runes, see the *Aufbau* (N.Y.), Aug. 6, 1948, p.7. Before the Alliance Book Corp. was purchased by Ziff-Davis, H. G. Koppell and fellow exile Runes had announced that the first six titles of the fledgling Philosophical Library would appear under their joint imprint. *Publishers' Weekly,* Jan. 24, 1942, p.270. One such volume examined has the name Alliance on the spine but no other indication of joint publication. Runes apparently published only one volume in German, his own poems—*Jordan Lieder* (New York, 1948).

41. For more about Kurt Enoch, who founded the New World Library in 1949 and most recently was in charge of the publishing division of the Times-Mirror Company of Los Angeles, see *Aufbau* (N.Y.), April 29, 1960, p.93, and Frank L. Schick, *The Paperbound Book in America* (New York: Bowker, 1958), p.32-33 et passim.

42. See *Kurt Wolff 1887-1963* (Frankfurt am Main: Heinrich Scheffler, 1963) and Karl H. Salzmann, "Kurt Wolff, der Verleger," *Börsenblatt für den deutschen Buchhandel* (Frankfurt am Main), 14:1729-49 (Dec. 22, 1958). Also, Kurt Wolff, *Autoren Bucher/ Abenteuer* (Berlin: Verlag Klaus Wagenbach, 1965) and Wolff, *Briefwechsel eines Verlegers 1911-1963* (Frankfurt am Main: Heinrich Scheffler, 1966).

43. Pantheon Books was formed in 1942 (although no books were issued until the following year) with financial help from old friend Curt von Faber du Faur (then at Yale) and his stepson Kyrill Schabert.

44. Salzmann, "Kurt Wolff," *Börsenblatt*. . . p. 1747.

45. Wolff also published the English translation. Broch's *Vergil* was originally intended to be published in Amsterdam and the English translation was first spoken for by B. W. Huebsch and the Viking Press, but that was in 1940. The exigencies of the war postponed the appearance of both versions for five years. See Broch's letter to Willa Muir, March 17, 1940 in Broch, *Die Unbekannte Grösse* (Zürich: Rhein Verlag, 1961), p.379–80; his letter to Thornton Wilder of March 6, 1943, in Broch, *Briefe* (Zürich: Rhein Verlag, 1957), p.181–82; also the fascinating correspondence with Kurt and Helene Wolff revealing Broch's great interest in all aspects of the marketing of his book in Wolff's *Briefwechsel*, p.447–60.

46. Salzmann, "Kurt Wolff," *Börsenblatt* . . . , p.1748.

47. *Publishers' Weekly*, Oct. 5, 1940, p.1413.

48. A thumbnail account of Ungar's accomplishments to July, 1945 is given in *Publishers' Weekly*, July 7, 1945, p.30. "The firm has published the book series, Laugh and Learn; Forum of the Nations, a series of books on the history of democratic movements in Germany, Czechoslovakia, and Poland through the centuries; has issued technical books and dictionaries; and has published foreign language textbooks and dictionaries in the European languages as well as in Chinese, Japanese, and other oriental languages."

49. E.g., Hannah Moriarta, *Life in the USA: Information for the Foreign Born* (2 v.; New York: Frederick Ungar, 1945). Each volume contained 160 dialogues and a colloquial American-German vocabulary.

50. In addition to the Ungar reprints, three volumes of Rilke were published by the Johannespresse and one by Herbert Steiner, a total of eighteen volumes.

51. This account of the early history of the Malik Verlag is based largely upon Karl H. Salzmann, "Der Malik Verlag: Verlagsgeschichte als Zeitgeschichte," *Neue Deutsche Literatur*, 4, No.4:88–92 (1956).

52. Cf. Kasimir Edschmid, *Lebendiger Expressionismus* (München: Kurt Desch, 1961), p.258 and Hede Massing, *This Deception* (New York: Duell, 1951), p.44.

53. See H. D. Müller, "Der Malik-Verlag als Vermittler der jungen Sowjetliteratur in Deutschland 1919–1933," *Zeitschrift für Slawistik*, 7, Nr.5:720–38 (1963).

54. Deutsche Akademie der Künste zu Berlin, *Der Malik Verlag*, p.65.

55. Letter dated Sept. 17, 1942, Hermann Kesten, ed., *Deutsche Literatur im Exil: Briefe europäischer Autoren 1933–1949* (München: Verlag Kurt Desch, 1964), p.212–13. Berthold Viertel (1885–1953), a Viennese poet and theatrical director of some note; Ferdinand Bruckner, pseudonym of Theodor Tagger (1891–1958), a dramatist; Friedrich Alexan, pseudonym of Friedrich George, writer, specialist in art history, and co-founder of the Tribune Book and Art Center, New York City.

56. Ernst Bloch (the philosopher), Bertolt Brecht, Ferdinand Bruckner, Alfred Döblin, Lion Feuchtwanger, Oskar Maria Graf, Heinrich Mann, Berthold Viertel, Ernst Waldinger, and F. C. Weiskopf. See *Publishers' Weekly*, July 14, 1945, p.139.

57. Feb. 8, 1946, p.9. Cf. Berendsohn 2:227. All the sponsoring authors shared in the planning of the publishing program. Details of distribution and other technical aspects of publishing were taken on by Paul Mueller of Schoenhof's, Cambridge, Mass.

58. Ruth Fischer makes reference to the "Aurora Company, a German Communist front in New York." *Stalin and German Communism* (Cambridge: Harvard Univ. Pr., 1948), p.608.

59. *Aufbau* (N.Y.), Feb. 8, 1946, p.9.

60. New editions were published of Brecht's *Furcht und Elend des Dritten Reichs* (1948); Seghers's *Der Ausflug der toten Mädchen* (1948); and Waldinger's *Kühle Bauernstuben* (1949). In 1947 a Viennese Aurora Buecherei had already published an edition of Waldinger's volume of poetry. Herzfelde's autobiographical volume *Immergrün,* noted as already published on p.344 of the Aurora anthology *Morgenroete* (1947),

first appeared in print in 1950 as part of the Aurora-Buecherei series. F. C. Weiskopf's survey of German exile literature, *Unter fremden Himmeln,* originally announced by Aurora in New York—*Aufbau* (N.Y.), Nov. 30, 1945, p.11—was published in the Soviet zone by the Dietz Verlag in 1948.

61. Norbert Rothstein, *Die Anmeldung von Ausländer-Vermögen* (1941); Heinrich Heine, *Judisches Manifest* (1946); Edward Kaufmann, *O höre: Gedanken, die immer wieder auferstehn* (1953).

62. E.g. in Sternfeld, *Deutsche Exil-Literatur* and the *Deutsche Bücherverzeichnis 1941-1950.*

63. Letter to the author dated Dec. 16, 1964.

64. Fritz Kahn, *First Aid* (1942). A first and second edition are recorded. "Mr. Krause tells us that he plans a series of 'I see' books by Dr. Fritz Kahn, to be published this month.... The book [*First Aid*] is characterized by a minimum of text and a sequence of illustrations on all phases of first aid." *Publishers' Weekly,* June 13, 1942, p.2210 and June 29, 1942, p.2258.

65. Especially his study, *Ernst Jünger: Die Wandlung eines deutschen Dichters und Patrioten* (1946).

66. See Friedrich Siegmund Schulze, *Die deutsche Widerstandsbewegung im Spiegel der ausländischen Literatur* (Stuttgart: Reclam Verlag, 1947), p.24-26.

67. Four novels in English were published by Doubleday during 1943-1954.

68. Sternfeld, *Deutsche Exil-Literatur,* lists only the English translations. Two other novels, *Die Neue Ordnung* and *Zeugnis des Unsaeglichen,* were announced but never published. Cf. Mueller's prospectus, *Bücher aus dem Schoenhof Verlag* (Cambridge, Mass., 1945). *Heldenplatz* and probably *Der Engel* enjoyed a first printing of 5000 copies.

69. *Austro-American Tribune,* May, 1946.

70. The experiment of a German-American book club for the publishing as opposed to merely the distribution of German-language books had already been tried by Otto Sattler with his Deutschamerikanische Buchgenossenschaft. Only two books ever came out under this imprint and one was Sattler's own, *Lockende Welt* (1931).

71. *Neue Volks-Zeitung,* Jan. 19, 1946, p.2.

72. *Austro-American Tribune,* May, 1946.

73. His international roster of authors was very impressive: John Knittel, Vicki Baum, Richard Llewellyn, Katrin Holland, Bruno Frank, John Bromfield, Peter Lindt—a book by Lindt was actually published by Willard, but not in the framework of the club—Christopher Morley, J. B. Priestley, Romain Rolland, Sinclair Lewis, Stefan Zweig, John Steinbeck, etc. *Neue Volks-Zeitung,* June 15, 1946, p.8.

74. Wilhelm Pfannkuch, "Julius Leopold Korngold," *Die Musik in Geschichte und Gegenwart.* ed. Friedrich Blume, 7, cols. 1629-30 (1958).

75. Max Roden, a minor Austrian poet (nine of whose books were published by the Johannespresse between 1929 and 1937) shared their American exile. In 1950 Roden's *Spiegelungen* was published in Vienna, by the once more European-based Johannespresse.

76. Dating from this period is Emperaire [i.e. Walter Kern], *Asche im Wind und an die Söhne der Sonne, Gedichte* (Zürich: Verlag der Johannespresse, 1938). Beer-Hofmann's wife Paula died in Zürich one month before the voyage to New York.

77. *Aus dem Fragment Paula: Herbstmorgen in Österreich,* published in an edition limited to 575 copies, the first 325 signed. *Paula, Ein Fragment* (1949), was printed at the Elm Tree Press. The Johannespresse also published an English translation of Beer-Hofmann's *Jakobs Traum* with an introduction by Thornton Wilder.

78. First published in a very limited edition of ninety-five copies as the *Jahresgabe* for 1927/28 of the Münchner Gesellschaft der Bücherfreunde.

79. There are two extensive bibliographies: Carolyn Reading, *A Hammer Bibliography*

1930-1952 (Occasional Contributions 45; Lexington, Ky.: Univ. of Kentucky, Margaret I. King Library, Oct., 1952); C. R. Hammer, "A Victor Hammer Bibliography (1930-1955)." *The American Book Collector,* 6:3-12 et passim (Jan., 1956). Articles on Hammer are numerous; e.g. Norman Kent, "The Art of Victor Hammer," *American Artist,* 20:44-49 et passim (June-July-Aug., 1956). Also note a collection of his own writings, *Chapters on Writing and Printing* (Lexington, Ky.: Anvil Pr., 1963).

80. For example, the memorable edition of Hölderlin's *Gedichte,* of which fifty-one copies were printed, was begun in Aurora and completed in Lexington.

81. *Das Antiquariat,* 17, Nr.1/2:21 (1963). Actually Steiner shared the editorial responsibilities for *Corona* with Martin Bodmer during the years 1930-1939.

82. This first edition was limited to 100 copies and was reprinted in 1947 under the Hammer Press imprint in an edition of 120. Recently the text has been made available to a wider public by its inclusion in Steiner's *Begegnungen mit Dichtern* (Tübingen: Rainer Wunderlich Verlag, 1963).

83. Wife and companion in exile of the Franco-German poet Yvan Goll. See *Aufbau* (N.Y.), Jan. 12, 1945, p.12.

84. The Hauptmann-Pinkus relationship has come under close scrutiny. See Fritz Homeyer, *Deutsche Juden als Bibliophilen und Antiquare* (tübingen: J. C. B. Mohr, 1963), p.52-55; Walter A. Reichart and C. F. W. Behl, eds., Max Pinkus (München: Bergstadt Verlag, 1958); Kurt Schwerin, "Max Pinkus, seine Schlesierbücherei und seine Freundschaft mit Gerhart Hauptmann," *Bulletin des Leo Baeck Instius,* 5, Nr. 18:98-125 (1962).

85. Schwerin, op. cit., p.118.

86. Taken from an article first printed in Germany and then reprinted in the *Neue Volks-Zeitung,* Sept. 14, 1946, p.8.

87. Fritz Schlawe, the only recent German commentator who mentions Steiner's work in the United States, terms both *Aurora* and *Mesa* periodicals, a designation not apt for the former, at any rate. *Literarische Zeitschriften, 1910-1930* (Stuttgart: J.B. Metzlersche Verlagsbuchhandlung, 1962), p.31.

88. The only other authentic émigré imprint from California seems to be Friedrich Hollaender, *Emigrantenballade* (Hollywood, *Die Tribüne,* 1939). It has been estimated that ca. 15,000 German Jews alone settled in California including 5000 in Los Angeles, 4000 in San Francisco and 3000 in the Berkeley-Oakland area. *Aufbau* (N.Y.), April 29, 1960, p.137.

89. Gottlieb (1903-1961), known also as a portrait photographer, was until his death the proprietor of Los Angeles' leading musicological bookstore. In earlier days, Guggenheim was a writer on economic affairs for the *Vossische Zeitung* and later succeeded H. G. Koppell as manager of the Deutsche Buchgemeinschaft (1932-1938). Since his arrival in the United States he has made his home in California and has been active in various aspects of publishing. Cf. *Aufbau* (N.Y.), May 29, 1964, p.17.

90. *Aufbau* (N.Y.), Oct. 30, 1942, p.15.

91. At least in the case of Mann's *Thamar,* and probably for the others in the initial set of seven. Bürgin, op. cit., p.38.

92. *Aufbau* (N.Y.), July 7, 1944, p.25.

93. Thomas Mann, *Leiden an Deutschland* (1946); Werfel, *Gedichte aus den Jahren 1905-1945* (1946); Feuchtwanger, *Wahn, oder der Teufel in Boston* (1948); Feuchtwanger, *Narrenweisheit oder Tod und Verklaerung des Jean Jacques Rousseau* (1952). This last publication appeared in a mimeographed, signed edition of 100 copies and was probably prepared to secure American copyright protection for the author.

94. As stated by Miss Rosenberg in a letter of Aug. 22, 1962.

95. Examples can be cited from all countries of refuge. Weiskopf lists a handful,

including one volume of poetry by Eva Priester, *Aus Krieg und Frieden* (London, n.d.) and one of prose, Ulrich Becher, *Das Märchen vom Räuber, der Schutzmann wurde* (Rio de Janeiro, 1943); both were hektographed, the latter was accompanied by a crude linoleum cut. *Unter fremden Himmeln*, p.64–65. In the United States two hektographed publications of more than passing interest are Paul Tillich's *Die politische und geistige Aufgabe der deutsche Emigration* (New York, June 1938) and a volume of poetry by former Expressionist Hans Siemsen, *Wo willst du hin* (New York, ca. 1946).

96. Mimeographed editions of fifty to sixty copies all signed by the author. They are certainly among the major collectors' items of the emigration.

97. Cf. Margaret Nicholson, *A Manual of Copyright Practice for Writers, Publishers and Agents* (New York: Oxford Univ. Pr., 1945), p.118.

98. The mimeographing was done by the firm of Wallenberg & Wallenberg, an émigré concern owned by the sons of the former chief editor of the *BZ am Mittag*. *Aufbau* (N.Y.), Nov. 7, 1947, p.8. Mann mentions this edition in a letter to Ida Herz, dated Oct. 26, 1947: "A mimeographed, signed and bound deluxe edition of 50 has been made here from the original at a price of 60 dollars which was accepted by the Copyright Office. . . ." Thomas Mann, *Briefe 1937–1947*, p.561.

99. F. C. Weiskopf, op. cit., p. 19.

100. "Bertolt Brecht Bibliographie," *Sinn und Form, Zweite Sonderheft Bertolt Brecht* (Berlin: Rütten & Loening, 1957), p.483 – 623.

101. Brecht, *Gedichte 1941–1947*, p.209. Weiskopf's date of 1943 is therefore incorrect.

102. Cf. Appendix III under: R. M. W. Kempner, B. Grossmann, Hans Marchwitza, Hilde Marx, Karl T. Marx, L. Roemer, Weltdemokratische Vereinigung, and Carl Zuckmayer.

103. Until 1948 Graf was the sole distributor of his own publications except for two titles issued by Aurora. Two additional volumes in English were also available during the 1940s: the Alfred Knopf edition of *Prisoners All* (1928) which was reprinted by Graf in 1943 and *The Life of My Mother*, published by Howell, Soskin of New York in 1940.

104. This widely quoted article first appeared in the *Wiener Arbeiterzeitung* and was reprinted with an epilogue in Graf's collected essays, *An manchen Tagen* (Frankfurt am Main: Nest Verlag, 1961), p.14–17.

105. The relation of the Communists to the German American Writers Association, of which Graf was president, is considered in the following chapter. Evidence of his appeal to German-American workers was his weekly column, "Oskar Maria Graf erzählt," that appeared from Dec., 1940 through Sept., 1942 in *Unsere Zeit*, organ of the Föderation Deutscher Arbeiter Klubs.

106. Graf, *An manchen Tagen*, p.17.

107. The dedication to Graf's *Prisoners All*, the popular edition of 1943, reads: "The publication of this book was made possible through the financial assistance of some friends and the subscriptions of progressive German-American workers all over the country. Special gratitude goes to the Nature Friends of Camp Midvale, N.J., the Nature Friends of Camp Boyertown, Pa., and the members of the German-American Congress of Democracy, Detroit. All these have thus visibly demonstrated their determination to stand up for freedom and the great German culture." A Luxus-Ausgabe limited to 250 copies was sold by Graf at five dollars per copy to help finance this popular edition. Cf. *Aufbau* (N.Y.), Nov. 26, 1943, p.8.

108. These Malik editions were: *Der Abgrund* (1936); *Anton Sittinger* (1937), printed in an edition of 3000 copies, as reported by Graf in a letter dated June 1, 1964; and *Bolwieser* (1937), also printed in 3000 copies. Another edition of *Der Abgrund* was published in Moscow by the Verlagsgenossenschaft Ausländischer Arbeiter. The Amelang

catalog *Deutsche Literatur im Exil, 1933–1945* (Frankfurt, 1961) lists the Malik edition and states that it too was printed in Moscow.

109. Letter from Graf, June 1, 1964.

110. Berendsohn 2:239.

111. Cf. *Das bayrische Dekameron* (1939), p.252: "Reprints of the following volumes will be undertaken as soon as sufficient orders are received – *Wir sind Gefangene, Der harte Handel, Die Chronik von Flechtling, Einer gegen Alle, Die Heimsuchung, Kalendergeschichten*. Send card to the author."

112. Walther Victor, *Es kommt aber darauf an, sie zu verändern* (Weimar: Volksverlag, 1962), p.401.

113. Berendsohn 2:86.

114. Victor, op. cit., p.399. Stern later lived at the Quaker College at Pendle Hill, Pa.

115. *Austrian Labor Information,* Feb. 1, 1945.

116. Translated by Louise Salm and priced at one dollar. *Aufbau* (N.Y.), April 27, 1946, p.8. According to the *Austro-American Tribune,* Jan., 1945, the six American *Hefte* were printed by Ernst Willard.

117. Typographia 7 was the New York local. The national organization, founded in 1873, merged with the International Typographical Union in 1894 although still preserving its autonomy until 1940. It published a German-language journal from 1873 to 1940 which, after 1918, was known as the *Buchdrucker-Zeitung* (Chicago).

118. An advertisement in the *Arbeiter,* Oct. 4, 1932 listed the following printers: Philip Bartel, H. Schilling, and John Zeidler. The New York local, at least during the early 1930s, was radically inclined; its *Organisations-Kalender* was regularly carried in the *Arbeiter*.

119. Among these émigré printers were Martin Jahoda, formerly of the Buchdruckerei Jahoda und Siegel, Vienna; F. Kauffmann, former owner of Verlag I. Kauffmann in Frankfurt; Perry Printing, formerly Druckerei Perlstein, Gemeindeblatt-Verlag, Düsseldorf; Salem Press, formerly Druckerei Lentschnitzsky, Mannheim; Paula Schlesinger, formerly of Berlin; and Ernst Willard of Vienna.

120. The many binding variants have, of course, been subjected to no systematic description. For example, Werfel's *Gedichte aus den Jahren 1908–1945* (Pazifische Presse, 1946) exists in at least three bindings: half-leather, full tan cloth, and blue boards with a tan cloth spine.

121. The printer and sometime poet Hans Wolff was responsible for the binding of Walther Victor's *Kehre Wieder über die Berge* (Willard, 1945).

122. A selection of Ungar publications appeared in the 1946 edition, but a listing is absent from the 1947, 1948, and 1949 volumes. Krause too appears only in the 1946 edition while Schoenhof's Foreign Books may be found every year from 1946 through 1949.

123. *Aufbau* (N.Y.), Dec. 4, 1942, p.19. This was one of two volumes published by the author under the imprint Pantheon Editions, not to be confused with Pantheon Books. It was of this book that George N. Shuster wrote: "A ... volume of verse so meritorious that I read the book with genuine amazement. It seems to me that never before in American history has so authentic a German poet made his debut in the New World." *Common Ground,* 3:35 (Winter 1943).

124. Roemer was born in Belgium in 1904, joined the German navy in 1923, and five years thence landed penniless in Canada. Later making his way to New York City he was, from 1934 to its dissolution, first member and then president of the Downtown Arbeiter-Club; subsequently he functioned as educational secretary of the Yorkville Club. His sole publication, a volume of poems entitled *Zeit Gedichte,* appeared in 1938.

125. Hans Marchwitza, today a prominent figure in East German literary circles, came

from an Upper Silesian coal mining family and was primarily known as a writer of proletarian fiction. He came to New York with Eisler, Kantorowicz, Norden, and company in 1941 and there published his only two volumes of poetry, *Untergrund* (1942) and *Wetterleuchten* (1942).

126. See Roemer, *Zeit Gedichte*, p.134.

127. Stern's account has been reproduced several times in Germany, by Weiskopf, op. cit., p.65–66 and Paul E. H. Lüth, *Literatur als Geschichte* (Wiesbaden: Limes Verlag, 1947), 2:417. Lüth's book was the first history of German literature to be published in Germany after the war. Although neither gives the source for the quotation, both obviously drew upon the same original, perhaps one of the *Hundert Hefte*. The present translation is based upon Weiskopf's text.

128. *Solidarität*, July, 1952, p.162.

129. Letter of July 7, 1944, Mann, *Briefe, 1937–1947*, p.371.

130. Among the most important were the *America-Herold und Lincoln Freie Presse*, with a circulation in 1944 of 57,277 and *Die Welt*, "Ein deutschsprachige Monatsschrift für das Amerikanische Heim," whose circulation in 1944 was 16,500. Arndt and Olson, *German-American Newspapers and Periodicals 1732–1955*, p.223, 236. Both papers were published in Winona, Minn.

131. July 7, 1944, p.25. A few months later Pollack was advertising in the *Aufbau* (N.Y.) for German-language manuscripts (Sept. 8, 1944, p.11).

132. It is interesting that the *Staats-Herold Almanach* (New York) for the years 1933–1944 contained not one contribution by an émigré writer. The *Almanach* was published annually by the *New Yorker Staatszeitung und Herold*. In all fairness one must add that the paper did employ émigré journalists.

133. An occasional prospectus, such as the Aurora Verlag flyer on Oskar Maria Graf's *Unruhe einer Friedfertigen* (1947), may itself be an object of historical interest. In it are reproduced letters of commendation by both Heinrich and Thomas Mann, the latter in facsimile.

134. Friedrich Hölderlin, *Poems, German and English* (Norfolk, Conn.: New Directions, 1943).

135. The *Aufbau Almanach* and the *Volkskalender* issued by the Arbeiter Kranken- und Sterbekasse were in part guides for immigrants.

136. The first two titles were published by their authors, the last by the H. K. Publishing Company.

137. *Neue Volks-Zeitung*, Feb. 2, 1946, p.6.

138. Cf. Siegfried Aufhäuser, "Soll man die Kriegsgefangenen erziehen? Eine bisher verpasste Gelegenheit," *Aufbau* (N.Y.) Feb. 4, 1944, p.4; Fritz Karsen, "Kriegsgefangene und Demokratie," *Neue Volks-Zeitung*, May 13, 1944, p.1.

139. "Fememorde in Gefangenenlagern?" *Neue Volks-Zeitung*, Jan. 22, 1944, p.1. The *Femegericht* or vigilante court of medieval Germany was revived in name by the Nazi freebooters during the Weimar Republic and was held responsible for a host of political murders before 1933.

140. "Was deutsche Kriegsgefangenen denken," *Neue Volks-Zeitung*, Jan. 5, 1944, p.3.

141. Paetel, "Deutsche im Exil: Randbemerkungen zur Geschichte der politischen Emigration," *Aussenpolitik*, 6:579 (Sept., 1955).

142. Broadsheet dated "Santiago de Chile, Mitte December 1944."

143. *Publishers' Weekly*, July 14, 1945, p.139. *New York Times*, May 5, 1945, p.3, also reported that Aurora publications were designed principally for German prisoners of war.

144. American officials may have been wary of allowing Aurora books to circulate freely among prisoners for political reasons.

145. Bermann-Fischer, op. cit., p.240–41.

146. *Aufbau* (N.Y.), Dec. 10, 1943, p.16. In 1945 Krause listed the titles most in demand by German prisoners. The first five were El Libro Libre imprints: Theodor Balk, *Das verlorene Manuskript* (1943); Feuchtwanger, *Unholdes Frankreich* (1942); Leo Katz, *Die Totenjäger* (1944); Heinrich Mann, *Lidice* (1943); Paul Merker, *Deutschland—Sein oder Nichtsein* (1944–1945). The other two titles noted were Friedrich Torberg, *Mein ist die Rache* (Pazifische Presse, 1943) and Oscar Meyer, *Von Bismarck zu Hitler* (Krause, 1944). *Publishers' Weekly,* Feb. 10, 1945, p.749.

147. This English translation of an article that originally appeared in the Mexican newspaper, to which Weiskopf regularly contributed, is taken verbatim from Ruth Fischer's periodical, *Network,* 2:13 (July–Aug., 1945). Miss Fischer was indicting the infiltration of Communist literature into the American camps.

148. *Neue Volks-Zeitung,* April 20, 1944, p.3.

149. Feb., 1944.

150. *Die Nation und wir: Ausgewählte Aufsätze und Reden 1933–1964* (Berlin: Dietz Verlag, 1964), 1:289. In its original form an article appearing in the March, 1945 issue of the *Protestant* (N.Y.).

151. Salzmann, *Neue deutsche Literatur,* 4, Nr. 4:92 (1956).

152. Mary S. Rosenberg in the *Neue Volks-Zeitung,* June 21, 1947, p.7.

153. *Aufbau* (N.Y.), Sept. 15, 1944, p.10.

154. *Publishers' Weekly,* Sept. 16, 1944, p.996.

155. Karsen was a noted educational pioneer, a former member of the League of Radical School Reformers. He is often cited for his experimental school for working-class children, the first of its kind in Germany. Karsen taught at New York's City College during part of his American exile.

156. Karsen wholeheartedly supported parallel conclusions reached by a committee of English experts under the chairmanship of classical scholar Gilbert Murray. Cf. the *Neue Volks-Zeitung,* May 27, 1944, p.3.

157. These included Herbert Bloch of Harvard; Julius Lips, formerly at the Cologne Museum of Anthropology, later at Howard University; Frederick Cramer, Professor at Mount Holyoke College; Emmy Heller, Professor of History at Brooklyn College; Helene Wieruszowski, former Librarian at the University of Bonn; and Hugo Bieber, in charge of the volumes on modern history. A series of readers (Lesebücher) was also planned under the direction of Susanne Engelmann of Smith College, Hedda Korsch of Wheaton College, and the novelist Joachim Maass. Texts in chemistry, biology, physics, and mathematics were envisioned for the future. *Publishers' Weekly,* Sept. 16, 1944, p.977, and Dec. 16, 1944. p.2318. Cf. Berendsohn 2:233.

158. *Aufbau* (N.Y.), July 26, 1946, p.4.

159. *And Call It Peace* (Chicago: Univ. of Chicago Pr., 1947), p.64–65.

160. *Education and Society in Modern Germany* (London: Routledge and Kegan Paul, 1949), p.174. For an account of American policies see Henry P. Pilgert, *The West German Educational System* (n.p.: Office of the U.S. High Commissioner for Germany, 1953), p.55–56.

161. A check of the German trade bibliographies for 1945–50 garnered only the following two items: Fritz Karsen, ed., *Geschichte unserer Welt* (v.2 [only]; Berlin: Suhrkamp, 1947); Fritz Karsen, ed., *Lehrbuch der Geschichte* (4 v.; Offenburg: Lehrmittel Verlag, 1947). Both were published as well in Bermann-Fischer Stockholm editions. Offenburg was in the French Zone and, according to F. Roy Willis, the French were much more amenable to using a variety of texts than were the other occupying powers. *The French in Germany* (Stanford: Stanford Univ. Pr., 1962), p.248 et passim. Alfred Döblin

apparently was the liaison between Bermann-Fischer and the French authorities. See Kesten, *Deutsche Literatur im Exil*, p.254.

162. The following account is based on Paul Brooks, "Books Follow the Jeep," *Publishers' Weekly,* Dec. 8, 1945, p.2528–30, and Council on Books in Wartime, *A History of the Council on Books in Wartime* (New York: Country Life Press, 1946).

163. Davie, *Refugees in America,* p.343.

VIII

Plight of the Émigré Author in America

During the late 1930s and early 1940s the United States played host to a whole galaxy of European writers and journalists, personalities as diverse as Maurice Maeterlinck, André Maurois, André Breton, Jacques Maritain, Sigrid Undset, Ferenc Molnar, and the Polish novelist Josef Wittlin. The German-speaking contingent was numerically the most impressive. The daily and periodical press, the publishing, radio, and film industries — in short, all the communications media — were influenced to some extent by these highly self-conscious, ambitious, and talented representatives of a now extinct Central European intelligentsia. The career of the highly articulate Arthur Koestler perhaps epitomizes the end of this class and its integration into either the British, French, or American cultural milieu. Concomitant with this drive toward rapid assimilation was the desire of many artists and writers to maintain as best they could an island of Free German culture in the United States. As the German philosopher Ernst Bloch wrote in 1939: "What is worthy of being called German literature is for now without a home [ohne Volk] . . . and the new center of limited opportunity is for the time being — North America."[1]

It is not often realized to what extent German cultural life of the 1920s was uprooted and transplanted en masse to the United States. An entire literary generation[2] made the crossing, from the Brahmins (Thomas Mann) to Grub Street (Curt Riess, René Kraus), from cabaret poets (Walter Mehring) to onetime Expressionists (Fritz von Unruh,

Albert Ehrenstein), Dadaists (Richard Huelsenbeck), "bourgeois" novelists (Vicki Baum), and the proletarian avant garde (Bertolt Brecht).
Hermann Kesten in one of the best evocations of German émigré
literary life in New York[3] expressed his wonder on seeing so many
familiar faces. Berlin redivivus! At that time too, American "little magazines" were discovering German art of the 1920s, printing with enthusiasm essays on Lehmbruck and Werfel, Rilke, and Kafka. A new
coterie of American disciples gathered together in Los Angeles around
the exiled Brecht; his long-time collaborator Kurt Weill found a new and
financially successful career in the Broadway musical theater. The familiar jagged lines of a Georg Grosz drawing found in a volume of American journalism[4] was not an isolated example of this new and pervasive
artistic stimulus from abroad. All this helped create an image of German
culture in exile that was highly visible to the American public. A lively
German-language cultural life that included newspaper and book publishing, lectures, theatrical presentations, as well as cabaret and nightclub entertaining was also present but largely invisible to non-Germans.
The émigré writer lived, as it were, with one foot tentatively in each
world, a condition that produced an internal conflict not always easily
resolved. The immediate task is to examine the relationship of the
émigré writer to his craft in both these worlds.

A large percentage of the refugee German writers who reached the
United States were part of the last wave of migration that managed to
escape a rapidly collapsing France during 1939 and 1940. Existing
American relief organizations (some 110 of them) naturally shared in the
rescue of writers and journalists but during the crisis year of 1940 a
special effort was called for; to this end the Emergency Rescue Committee was formed under the chairmanship of Frank Kingdon. Although
the Committee was open only to American citizens, a distinguished
group of honorary advisors[5] assisted in the work of aiding writers,
artists, labor leaders, and similarly endangered intellectuals to leave
Europe. Visa recommendations were forwarded to the President's Advisory Committee on Political Refugees, screened and sent on to the State
Department. The American literary world was particularly active in
supporting these rescue actions through various fund-raising campaigns.
One such event was a book auction which was jointly sponsored by the
American Committee for Christian Refugees and the American Jewish
Joint Distribution Committee on behalf of anti-Hilter refugees. Thomas
Mann was chairman of the auction committee that included such emi-
nent bookmen as A. S. W. Rosenbach, Bennett Cerf, and Alfred Knopf.[6]

The American press was also very much aware of the threatened
destruction of Europe's literary elite; for instance, the *New York Herald
Tribune* carried a column headlined "Where Are They?" reporting

weekly on the fate of European authors. Gestures of good will were made by American writers through their organizations and on their own; for example, Carl Van Doren turned over all profits from the German-language rights to his *Benjamin Franklin* (which he refused to grant to any Nazi publisher) to the Joint Distribution Committee.[7] Most of the energies and resources of American writers were funneled through two competing organizations, the Foreign Writers' Committee of the American Center of the P.E.N. and the Communist-sponsored Exiled Writers' Committee, a creation of the ill-fated League of American Writers.

The International P.E.N. Club exhibited throughout those strife-torn decades an admirable concern for the then (and still) endemic problem of refugee authors. The P.E.N. congresses held during that period were showplaces for the anti-Nazi declarations of Free German authors in exile. In 1933 the international congress was held in Ragusa (Yugoslavia), where in the face of hostile questioning by the English delegates, led by International P.E.N. President H. G. Wells, the now completely *judenfrei*[8] Nazi contingent walked out of the meeting in a huff. At that point exiled playwright Ernst Toller rose and delivered a militant anti-Nazi speech that clearly laid out the future ideological position of the P.E.N.

For the duration of the war, England remained headquarters for both the international organization and the Free German P.E.N. group that was officially recognized at the 1934 congress.[9] First international president of the Free German P.E.N. (Schutzverband deutscher Schriftsteller) was Heinrich Mann (1934–1940) then living in Paris; from 1941 to 1947 the office was held by Alfred Kerr. The American branch of the P.E.N. was also deeply concerned with aiding refugee authors and initiated many fund-raising events. The executive secretary of the American Center, Mrs. Jane Hudson, wrote in December of 1945:

> We did not have what could be called a formal program for refugee writers, but we did try to help in all the ways at our disposal. We raised money, both by projects such as a tea in conjunction with Lord & Taylor at which Jules Romains, Maeterlinck, and other prominent refugees spoke, and by an appeal to our membership. . . . We also entertained them in P.E.N. homes, arranged a symposium at New York University at which several of them spoke, etc. Our Foreign Writers' Committee catalogued over 75 of them, and did its best to meet their individual needs.[10]

Affiliated with the American Center was a newly organized European P.E.N. Club in America headed by Jules Romains and Sigrid Undset.[11]

The Exiled Writers' Committee, in contrast to the P.E.N., had very definite political connections. During the early 1930s, the relationship between the American writer and the Communist Party had become more tepid than inspirational, but this changed after 1935 when the spreading unease and fear generated by the nemesis of Hitler gave the party a great boost. Between 1935 and 1939 (the period of the Popular Front), Communist influence among American writers was at its peak and was institutionalized in the League of American Writers. Although the Moscow trials shook the scales from the eyes of most American authors of note, it was the Nazi-Soviet Pact of 1939 that destroyed most of the paper monuments of the Popular Front.[12] The League itself lingered on for a year or more; it was during this period of waning influence that its Exiled Writers' Committee forced itself into the public eye.

The committee came into being sometime during 1939 according to Ralph Roeder (then an active member), and it soon became engaged in some curious activities. One such affair involving Alfred Kantorowicz, then Secretary of the Schutzverband deutscher Schriftsteller in Paris, [13] concerned a large house on the Riviera donated by "an American lady" and offered by the League as a sort of hostel for homeless German writers. According to Davie, the Exiled Writers' Committee "brought a dozen or so writers to this country,"[14] but a careful scrutiny of the evidence belies any claim that the committee actually did succeed in obtaining emergency American visas. Both the President's Advisory Committee and the State Department were insistent on excluding known Communists. The Exiled Writers' Committee, of course, emphatically disagreed with this political discrimination, and Roeder complained that "large numbers of affidavits, some of them submitted by us as long as six weeks ago, have been unaccountably delayed or not even considered."[15] What the League and its committee did accomplish was the procurement of a number of Mexican transit visas enabling many German Communists (Kantorowicz, Gerhard Eisler, Norden, and others) to reach the United States.[16] The committee and its Hollywood affiliate were particularly adept in matters of fund raising; a dinner held at the Hotel Commodore in New York (October 17, 1940) netted $13,200, a similar affair in Hollywood raised an additional $6000.[17]

Once the German writers were safe in America, the League took pains to present them to the public. For example, at the League's last pre-Pact event, the Third American Writers' Congress, a special Exile Writers Benefit reception was held with Professor Harry Slochower of Brooklyn College presiding. The *New York Times* reported in detail the speeches of the day which included Ludwig Renn on "A Writer Without a Country," and Erich Franzen expounding on "The Problem Facing the Exiled Writers."[18] Modest fellowships, of $100 each, were granted by the League to O. M. Graf, the journalist Will Schaber, and the former Nazi turned Communist Bodo Uhse, who went on to Mexico City.[19]

The League, which by the end of 1940 had lost its most respectable names, was dissolved sometime in 1941.

There was yet another body ready and willing to assist the growing number of German intellectuals forced to live in exile. The American Guild for Cultural Freedom, founded in the summer of 1936 by the liberal Austrian Catholic nobleman Prince Hubertus zu Löwenstein, was an organization of sympathetic Americans who wished to help; its aims are best expressed in the Prince's own characteristic prose:

> We believe that our present duty is to cultivate a German territory of the spirit. . . . We appeal not only to the seventy thousand who left Germany during 1933, but also to millions of foreign Germans in all states of the world, to form a united organization. A central authority with supreme powers must be at once instituted. . . . Further, all German organizations should make this cause their own . . . The emigrants as well as the real foreign Germans must realize that today there is no such thing as a Motherland. It is just as if the 'mother country' of a great colonial empire were suddenly to fall into the hands of a foreign power. In that case, the colonies would no longer have any duty towards the new government in their old country, but would have to take over the whole responsibility and representation of their nation.[20]

The Guild was made up of a European and an American Senate. Governor Wilbur L. Cross of Connecticut was given the honorary post of president of the American Senate while two strong-minded liberals, Alvin Johnson and Oswald Garrison Villard, were made executive chairman and treasurer respectively. The European Senate under the presidency of Thomas Mann included twenty-eight representatives of German culture in exile. Before his death, Sigmund Freud held the title of president of the scientific section and the Prince himself acted as general secretary.

Among the aims of the Guild was the most laudable one of aiding émigré writers, scientists, and scholars to continue their work by means of scholarships and grants. Up to the month of September, 1938, the Guild reportedly had awarded more than sixty scholarships totaling $8300.[21] Earlier that same year the *New York Times* listed twelve émigré writers who were recipients of this largess, though of that number only one, Oskar Maria Graf, was to seek asylum in the United States.[22] A very ambitious campaign to raise $200,000 for the assistance of "Jewish, Christian writers, scholars and artists," was initiated by the Guild in December, 1938.[23] A cherished hope of Prince Löwenstein was to encourage and financially aid the émigré writer to both create and publish, and toward that end the Guild arranged a widely advertised contest offering a prize of $5000 for a fictional work in German, 50,000 to 200,000 words in length. Half the amount was promised by the firm of

Little, Brown of New York; the rest was to be made up by the Guild and by simultaneous publication of the selected manuscript by six European publishers.[24] The winning entry out of 177 manuscripts submitted was Arnold Bender's *Es ist später als ihr denkt (It Is Later Than You Think),* a sadly prophetic title. After Bender's work was chosen, several of the countries where it was to be published were already under Nazi occupation and Little, Brown did not care to foot the bill alone. The prize-winning author, it is said, received around $1000 in compensation.[25] One émigré paper saw "the affair of the American Guild" in a quite different light[26] but the true facts of the case are still veiled in obscurity. The activities of the Guild seem to have ceased not long after.

Earning a Living

The economic prospects for the refugee writer were not very cheerful, equally dismal perhaps as those facing the European trained lawyer. With the continental German market gone, the return on the investment of long years of work in the form of royalties was greatly reduced if not completely lost. A number of émigré writers were able to penetrate the American market with translations and many, such as Thomas Mann, Werfel, Feuchtwanger, and Vicki Baum, already possessed a backlog of American editions so that their exile was not especially damaging in a material sense. Oddly enough, one author who emigrated to the United States continued to receive regular royalty payments from the Soviet Union. This was Heinrich Mann. In a letter to Karl Lemke in 1948 he wrote:

> The [Russian] Staatsverlag has granted me, without any application on my part, steady payments for three years. They paid punctually as often as possible, the last two years I was in France, and also the first year of the war in America. The Vice-Consul in San Francisco brought the payment to me; he came every month. The last payment was for my most recent book [*Ein Zeitalter wird besichtigt*]. The Russian edition was paid for before the German edition was published in Sweden. Then my friend the Vice-Consul disappeared into some other diplomatic post and I heard nothing more from this country.[27]

The presence of German and Austrian refugee authors in this country raised the question whether as "stateless" persons they were legally entitled to royalties accruing from American translations of their books. Paradoxically, it was a court decision involving the Austrian-born Adolf Hitler that set the legal precedent in favor of the disenfranchised refugee. The original American publishers of *Mein Kampf,* Houghton Mifflin, brought a successful suit restraining the Stackpole Company from publishing a new edition of the Nazi leader's chef d'oeuvre. Whether or not Hitler was a man without a country, a "staatenloser Deutscher," as he was described on one copyright application, his books were secure in their American copyright.[28]

The problem of earning a living was a difficult one for both the author and his family as Davie reminds us:

> Determination to engage in creative writing thus often worked severe hardships on the author and his family. Rather than retrain—learn a trade, accept a factory post, look for a clerical job, run errands—the author was frequently content to subsist on a small allowance granted by a relief agency. Within the married groups, the spouse frequently became the breadwinner.[29]

Some managed to weather the stormy years without abandoning the practice of their craft, and a few successfully broke into the world of American journalism. The rewards of working for the German-language press (usually on a part-time basis) were not sufficiently large to insure financial independence; while the majority of émigré writers may have preferred some sort of intellectual work—teaching, bookselling, and publishing[30] were especially attractive—a great many were forced into manual labor and even domestic work. Agriculture enticed the brilliantly successful playwright Carl Zuckmayer who spent most of the emigration years on a small Vermont farm. The free-lance journalist and critic Ludwig Marcuse was soon to wear the hood of a dignified professor of philosophy at the University of Southern California. Temporary financial security, at any rate, was the lot of those fortunate enough to obtain one of a variety of grants and fellowships that were available. There were Rosenwald Fellowships[31] distributed by the Emergency Committee in Aid of Displaced Foreign Scholars, and similar grants dispensed by the Refugee Scholars' Fund; the American Committee for Scholars, Writers, and Artists; and the Rockefeller Foundation.

As the war progressed, more and more émigré writers were pulled into government work, serving in the Office of War Information—as did the journalist Leo Lania and the poet Walter Mehring—the Army Specialized Training Program, the Psychological Warfare Service and even in the Office of Strategic Service (OSS). Daniel Lerner has a lot to say on the use of German refugees in the U.S. Psychological Warfare Service, pointing out that they were subject to so much criticism that: "In all of PWS not a single German refugee held a responsible position." He does admit that "their enormous contribution to Sykewar has not been given adequate attention and credit."[32] From 1942 to 1945, service in government as well as in the military temporarily solved for many the problems of earning a living.

Writing for the American Public

For a successful career in American journalism, knowledge of English was a sine qua non. Novelists were not under that pressure if they had either reputation or attractive subject material. It was still a matter of years of hard work for those who did strive for a mastery of their new language. In the meanwhile, the professional translator enjoyed a booming business. One such ambitious entrepreneur advertising in the *Aufbau* offered to "undertake the translation of German manuscripts . . . into English and French for eventual reworking for the films."[33] (The sales value of French film scenarios in 1942 may be open to debate.) The financial and artistic problems arising from the writer's dependence on the professional translator were always a source of constant irritation. Ernst Lothar, although his novels were all written in German, had to supply his prospective publisher with arduously composed resumés in English.[34] Complaints on the quality of the English translations were not infrequent; Zuckmayer's detailed criticism of passages from a proposed English translation of *Der Hauptmann von Köpenick* is characteristic.[35]

Despite the gloomy and carping undertone that gives to many émigré mémoirs a rather melancholy chiaroscuro, there were occasional popular successes outside the charmed circle of Thomas Mann, Werfel, Feuchtwanger, and Vicki Baum. Hermann Kesten, for example, received the not inconsiderable advance of $1200 on his novel *Children of Guernica* from fellow German H. G. Koppell of the Alliance Book Corporation.[36] The Communist author Anna Seghers, then in Mexico City, was probably as astonished as anyone else when her novel *The Seventh Cross* sold 600,000 copies in the United States.[37] To another Communist writer, Walter Schönstedt, went the honor of being the first German to have a short story published in O'Brien's *Best Short Stories* for 1939. The number of Free German novels published in the United States in translation is not accurately known but is probably over 200,[38] and while this collection of fiction included a fair share of potboilers, it is to the credit of American publishers that works of more lasting merit by Brecht, Albert Ehrenstein, Broch, Von Unruh, and others were seen through the presses.[39] In contrast to the novelist, the émigré dramatist found almost no market for his wares whether written in German or English. The German drama had always been neglected on the New York stage and lack of opportunity for performance naturally precluded much chance of publication.

Émigré writers were handicapped by their lack of American experience to draw upon, and so they turned out of necessity to their immediate European past or to more esoteric historical subjects. The very successful writer of popular magazine fiction Martha Albrand (who wrote in German under the name Katrin Holland) was quite at home in English before her arrival in America. Many of her novels, including *No Surrender, Without Orders,* and *Whispering Hill* were serialized in the *Saturday Evening Post*; although she took great care in selecting purely American themes, she always managed to transport her American heroes to Europe on one pretext or another.[40] Hertha Pauli and Maria Gleit[41] inaugurated their American careers by writing children's books in English, which perhaps inspired Varian Fry's comment: "If several of the authors I helped have turned from writing adult books in their native languages to writing juveniles in English, I suppose it must be because it is easier to write for children in a language which is new to you."[42] Some writers did master English well enough to write directly in their adopted tongue; consider Hans Natonek whose novel, *Give Me Joy,* was "a remarkable achievement after only three and one-half years in this country."[43] Hermann Kesten has supplied a brief list of authors who were able to adapt successfully to the English language,[44] to which can be added Joseph Wechsberg of the *New Yorker* and the novelists Stefan Heym and John Kafka.

Scores of German and Austrian newspapermen, editors, and critics sought refuge in this country, but only a few managed to find full-time positions with German-language papers. The more enterprising and career-minded of the younger writers set their sights on the slick magazines and the best-seller lists. One such was the journalist Curt Riess who began during the forties to produce a spate of exposés and sensational reportage that garnered him sharp criticism as well as financial reward.[45] Speaking as a friend rather than a critic, Klaus Mann tried to capture the driving ambition of the man. The scene was New York in 1938 where Riess had been living for four years as American correspondent for a French newspaper.

> Curt Riess, in pre-Hitler Berlin a sports reporter, now writes in French for *Paris-Soir;* he intends as well to write in English, or better in American, about boxers, filmstars, gangsters, generals, spies, dope, politics, and Hitler's love life. "I will be *very* successful, you can count on that!" The contradiction that he seems to expect remains unvoiced. No one doubts that he will make a career. But is there indeed enough success to satisfy this hungry almost wild desire?[46]

Other émigrés tilled the same literary soil; names such as Leo Lania, Kurt Singer, René Kraus, and Stefan Lorant come immediately to mind. In a more serious vein were those commentators from the Socialist and Communist camps who contributed widely to the highbrow monthlies and such left-wing stalwarts as the *Nation* and the *New Republic.* Joachim Joesten was a very industrious journalist (an assistant editor of *Newsweek* magazine during the 1940s) who published on his own several series such as *New Germany Reports* (1947–1950) and the *German Book News* (1947–1949?), both aimed at libraries and designed to make something out of his "inside" information on German affairs.

It is not disingenuous to credit émigré journalists with a healthy share in the shaping of public opinion during the prewar and war years. One need only recall the esteem in which Karl Frank and his American Friends of German Freedom were held and of the undoubted influence of his periodical *In Re: Germany* (1941–1944), the only continuous review in English of books and articles on the German problem.

The arena of exile influence was wide and reached into the highest stages of government as in the case of the economist Gustav Stolper (editor of the *Berliner Börsenblatt* and later of his own widely respected *Deutsche Volkswirtschaft*). A leading member of the Deutsche Demokratische Partei, Stolper was among the first to leave Germany for the United States where, in 1933, he established himself in business and government circles as an authority on European economics (and conversely in Europe as an expert on America). In 1946 he was made economic advisor to the Hoover Commission for Famine Relief, an honorable capstone to a successful career. From 1933 up to his death, Stolper continued to distribute from New York his financial and economic reports (*Berichte*) to subscribers in both Europe and America—English and German editions of 201 consecutive numbers. According to his widow, these reports were widely consulted by officials of many countries and became "during the thirties an element in the molding of European opinion on American affairs."[47]

While some refugee journalists contributed regularly to American journals and some went into government service, others exerted their influence behind the scenes. Hermann Budzislawski, former Communist editor of *Die neue Weltbühne*,[48] became one of the chief advisors to America's most influential columnist, Dorothy Thompson, much to her postwar dismay.[49] Another former German editor, the anti-Communist Willi Schlamm (Budzislawski's immediate predecessor on *Die neue Weltbühne*) occupied an important position in the Time-Life-Fortune organization.[50] The work of Alfred Kantorowicz for the Columbia Broadcasting System, of Ernst Erich Noth for the National Broadcasting Company, as well as the English-language newscasts of Hans Jacob on station WOV (New York City) indicates that radio too made use of émigré talent and experience.[51]

Lecturing, for those who possessed sufficient facility in English, contributed both to the public enlightenment and to the lecturer's pocketbook. American audiences were avid to hear eyewitness reports of the great European tragedy that was slowly unfolding; among the first to assuage this curiosity were former Reichstag deputies Gerhart Seger and

Toni Sender. A feature of *Publishers' Weekly* during the 1930s was a column entitled "Authors on the Rostrum" that recorded the dates and subjects of scheduled lectures. The names that appeared with the most frequency besides the two aforementioned speakers, were Thomas Mann, Erika and Klaus Mann, Emil Ludwig, Peter Drucker, Curt Riess, René Kraus, Franz Werfel, and Hermann Rauschning.

Journalist and novelist Leo Lania toured the country for eight years as a highly successful "lecturer on world affairs," a phase of his career that Lania reviewed with some irony: "Perhaps this was the greatest paradox in my life rich as it was in surprising turns; in my native language I never stood out as a speaker, in the language which I at first could master only with the greatest effort, I achieved immediate recognition and great success as a 'public speaker.' "[52] While the lecture circuit was a professional enterprise with substantial fees involved, émigré authors also participated in English-language educational programs usually connected with libraries, universities, or philanthropic institutions for nominal fees or none at all.[53]

One of the subsidiary figures of the emigration was the literary agent, often himself a refugee, who specialized in handling the works of émigré authors. The end of the war halted this highly specialized service but many agencies had expanded sufficiently to continue in business. Perhaps the agency most closely identified with the German émigrés was that of Barthold Fles, a Dutchman who came to the United States in 1925. At first his agency, established in the early thirties, specialized in foreign authors, but by 1945 he reported that about 90 percent of his business was with American authors.[54] One of his most valuable contributions to émigré literary life was the series of "evenings" he arranged to introduce the newcomers to the intricacies and special problems of the American book world. At these affairs American editors, critics, and writers volunteered to talk on American literature, publishing, journalism, and related themes in a simple, easily understandable English.[55]

There were agencies like the one established by Friedrich Krause, that did *not* specialize in Free German writers. Probably the most successful of all was founded by the former Viennese Franz Horch and now managed by his widow Maria Horch.[56] Then there was Heinrich Mann's agent in America, Paul Kohner,[57] and the Max Pfeffer literary agency which counted among its clients Stefan Heym and Oskar Maria Graf.[58] Several prominent German authors in Mexico City—Anna Seghers, Egon Erwin Kisch, and Otto Katz (former associate of Willi Münzenburg)—were represented by the American Maxim Lieber, who perhaps had other émigré clients in the United States. After the war Lieber was involved in the Hiss-Chambers perjury trial and was called to testify before the House Committee on Un-American Activities.[59]

The German and Austrian directors, actors, musicians,[60] and writers who made up the Hollywood exile colony warrant special attention. The fact is that most émigré authors of international reputation were drawn to Hollywood for one reason or another. Thanks to Warner Brothers and Metro Goldwyn Mayer, a number of these authors were able to emigrate to the United States by being assured of one year contracts as script writers. These contracts (several dozen were issued) were coordinated through the Emergency Rescue Committee. Even a partial list of recipients reads like a literary *Who's Who*: Alfred Döblin, Wilhelm Speyer, Walter Mehring, Alfred Neumann, Alfred Polgar, Bertolt Brecht, Leonhard Frank, Friedrich Torberg, Heinrich Mann.[61] (Werfel and Feuchtwanger turned down similar contracts since they were financially secure.) It was a laudable gesture which, in Thomas Mann's words, "not only enabled these men to emigrate to the United States but also gave them at least certain breathing spell in which to secure the foundations of their existence."[62] However, the reactions of the authors ranged from mild sarcasm to bitterness, since they felt themselves treated as charity cases rather than artists. The contracts of most were allowed to lapse after one year.

Alfred Polgar and Alfred Döblin through their letters, Ludwig Marcuse and Ernst Lothar in their autobiographies, reflect a very natural criticism of the entire Hollywood world of tinsel and celluloid. Marcuse from the vantage of an observer has given us the following resumé:

> Thus Heinrich Mann, Alfred Döblin, Leonhard Frank, Alfred Polgar, Walter Mehring found themselves in the film business; without a knowledge of English, or of film making, full of scorn for the industry—and also without even being asked to undertake anything seriously. Döblin was shown the story of *Mrs. Minniver* [sic] (later one of the great film successes of the war), was told that it was to be made into a pro-English story, and was asked for recommendations . . . and they received the grotesque answer that the material suggested a Chaplinesque treatment.[63]

The physician and novelist Alfred Döblin describing his daily routine at the studio commented: "One does nothing, absolutely nothing! Supposedly we are collaborating on something, but up to now that is only a rumor. We take care of our correspondence, telephone, read newspapers, write on our own—whatever one can do in a sitting position."[64] Alfred Neumann wrote in the same vein of the "$100 per week charity" and the "senseless existence."[65] The attitude is understandable. Perhaps the most pathetic figure in Hollywood was the aged Heinrich Mann who with his wife lived in virtual retirement. It is reported that he refused the financial support of his brother. The unsigned obituary notice in *Das*

Antiquariat (Vienna)[66] draws a melancholy picture of the seventy-year-old author waiting in anterooms for hours in useless attempts to catch the ear of a Hollywood magnate. Émigré Hollywood was plainly divisible into the haves and the have-nots.

The Hollywood experience was, in retrospect, not all that bitter, for financially Hollywood did a lot for more than a few, despite professions to the contrary.[67] It is true, nevertheless, that personal charity was a necessity for many. A committee guided by Liesel Frank, the wife of Bruno Frank, took on the task of caring for the needy. Döblin reported, for instance, that in January, 1942, his income consisted of eighteen dollars a week unemployment insurance and fifty dollars from Frau Frank's committee.[68] Yet life went on as before. In an appealing vignette, Döblin described the festivities occasioned by Heinrich Mann's seventieth birthday:

> When we recently celebrated the 70th birthday of Heinrich Mann at the house of Salke Viertel, everything was as in former times. Thomas Mann pulled out a manuscript from which he read his formal congratulations. Then his brother pulled out his paper and thanked him with equal formality. We sat at dessert, some twenty men and women, and listened to German literature.[69]

German Émigré Literary World

CHANNELS OF COMMUNICATION

Once arrived on these shores, the émigré writer found it extremely difficult to be published in his native language. Although the German-language press did provide some outlet, the number of unpublished manuscripts neared mountainous proportions, if credence be given many contemporary accounts. Weiskopf surmised that as of 1946 about one-half of all German "Emigranten-Literatur" remained unpublished;[70] this state of affairs plagued not only the young and untried but veterans such as Heinrich Mann, Döblin, Zuckmayer, Brecht, Von Unruh, and Albrecht Schaeffer. Döblin wrote of his vain attempt to have Bermann-Fischer (then in New York) publish his *Robinson in Frankreich* (never published under that title) and of his equally unavailing overtures to Fritz Landshoff regarding the second volume of his roman fleuve, *November 1918*.[71] As early as 1938, a novel in manuscript by the German refugee Wolf Weiss found its way into the hands of some American friends. A fragment was printed in the German-American periodical *Gegen den Strom* with the appended notice: "The selection 'Ich gestehe' from the book by the young writer Wolf Weiss is presented at this time with the intention of finding a publisher for it. . . . The manuscript is in New York City and I [the editor, Robert Bek-Gran] am only too willing to give out further details."[72] The plea went unanswered.

The German-American press and certain Latin American émigré journals became the sole repository for most Free German writing that was published from 1941 to 1945. No examination or indexing of these newspapers has yet been undertaken[73] except for the purpose of compiling such author bibliographies as Bürgin's *Thomas Mann* and Nubel's *Bertolt Brecht*. Yet upon such a bibliographical record must rest any hope of fairly assessing the literary life of the German émigrés in America. Apart from purely belletristic contributions, the émigré press printed a mass of reportage, book reviews,[74] and commentary—the work of only a small percentage of the 682 refugeee journalists from Germany and Austria.[75]

It is often overlooked that the author in exile had other means of communication besides the printed word. Although Karl O. Paetel in his brief survey of the German theater in America[76] makes no mention of the theatrical life of the émigrés, the resulting impression that none existed is false, for the theater in formal and informal dress—stage play, musical, cabaret, or dramatic reading—must be considered in any discussion of émigré literary life.

There was already in 1933 a tradition of respect for German revolutionary theater among left-wing groups in the United States. It was the immigrant John Bonn (né Hans Bonn)[77] who during the late 1920s formed a militant German-language ensemble known as the Proletbühne. From this beginning there blossomed an English-language Workers' Laboratory Theater in 1928 and the League of Workers' Theaters (1932-1934) in which John Bonn again was the driving spirit. The didactic propaganda playlet or *Agitprop* introduced in America by the Proletbühne players was quickly picked up by their native-born comrades. Michael Gold, tough-minded prose stylist of the party and leader of the Workers' Drama League (1926-1928) was in his best form when he translated into English *Wer ist der Dümmste (The Biggest Boob in the World)*, a revolutionary play by the young August von Wittfogel (the eminent sinologist, now a United States citizen). This proved to be the League's most applauded production. Another link between the workers' theater movements of Germany and America was the German periodical *Arbeiterbühne und Film*, avidly read on both sides of the Atlantic. After the first half-dozen years of American proletarian theater (during which German revolutionary literature was of seminal importance), the Communists were suddenly checkmated by President Franklin D. Roosevelt's New Deal. In 1936 the experimental theater program of the Works Progress Administration had already attracted many of the left-wing avant-garde, including John Bonn and his German Theatre.[78]

As the émigré colonies in New York City began to grow, new projects for German-language theatrical groups were bruited about. In 1939 the German Jewish Club made plans for its own theater.[79] More prepossessing was the Theater of German Freemen founded by "executives from the Bakery and Confectionary Workers International Union and Butchers Union 174;"[80] their purpose, "the preservation and furthering of German democratic cultural endeavours in America."[81] Plays were to · be given in German—a new piece every month. The composition of the artistic advisory council was impressive: Ferdinand Bruckner, Ferdinand Czernin, Bruno Frank, Manfred George, Fritz Kortner, Erika Mann, Fritz Von Unruh, Franz Werfel, and Carl Zuckmayer. Associated with this council was an organization of playgoers (or workers' theater club) set up by former SPD official Siegfried Aufhäuser. (This venture was modeled directly on the German Freie Volksbühne founded in 1890 as an instrument of SPD *Kulturpolitik*.) Recitations and cabarets were also planned. Austrians in America, among whom were many outstanding actors and directors, often came together to pool their talents; groups like the Wiener Kleinkunstbühne led by Hermann Berghof[82] and Ernst Lothar's short-lived Austrian Theatre.[83] Berendsohn has listed a number of other émigré theatrical groups with a sampling of their repertoires.[84] It was a disheartening fact of life that each new production could expect a run of only three to five nights, so that Bruno Walter spoke truly when, on the demise of Lothar's Austrian Theatre, he commented: "Music is the universal language, German unfortunately is not."[85]

A more direct confrontation of writer and audience was effected through the evening of recitation, an important adjunct to the literary life of the émigrés. One of the reasons for the popularity of this art form was the presence in the United States of two of its most renowned exponents, Ernst Deutsch and Ludwig Hardt. Through this medium the literature of the emigration could be brought to a larger audience. Very frequently local social or cultural clubs sponsored literary evenings which featured authors reading from their own works.

Somewhere between formal stage presentation and the solitary speaker at the lectern stood the cabaret, the satirical review, a form of social and political commentary assiduously cultivated in the German-speaking lands of Europe. It goes without saying that the cabaret was not a vehicle of entertainment destined to thrive in the Third Reich. After 1933, anti-Nazi cabarets were to be found in Vienna as well as in other cities such as Paris, Prague, Moscow, and New York where German exiles were congregated. Erika and Klaus Mann's *Die Pfeffermühle* was particularly well known in America from its tour of the United States in the early thirties.[86] Hollywood was graced with the presence of "Der Elow" (the stage name of Erich Lowinsky), a political satirist of note, and Friedrich Hollaender's *Tingel-Tangel Revue* (in English).[87] Kurt Robitschek's *Kabarett der Komiker, Die Arche, Die Kleine Bühne,*[88] and the more radical *Schiessbude*[89] were others whose names at least have survived. No account would be complete without mention of that indomitable danseuse Valeska Gert and her "off-beat" nightclub the *Bettelbar* (New York) whose story is recorded in one of the more ingratiating memoirs to come out of the emigration.[90]

The radio offered yet another means of communication for both writer and performer. From 1938 on there were a number of stations, mainly in the New York area, that carried German-language programs aimed at the anti-Nazi immigrants and which featured readings and original radio plays written by émigré authors. A number of the older German-language program directors were intransigent or at best unreceptive to a pronounced anti-Nazi point of view, especially before 1942. This conflict of interest was rarely aired in the American and only infrequently in the German-language press, but it was an ever present undercurrent.[91]

One of the first New York stations to broadcast a regular half-hour program for the new immigrants was WEVD (named after Eugene Victor Debs), the largest Jewish station in the country. The program (*Deutsche Refugees für deutsche Refugees*) was started in 1938 with Free German literature a staple ingredient. Karl Jakob Hirsch, among others, wrote a number of anti-Nazi radio plays for WEVD some of which were rebroadcast to Europe.[92] By 1940 the German American Writers Association began sponsoring on WCNW a fifteen-minute program highlighted by interviews with and sketches by German authors in exile.[93] The *Aufbau* went one better and sponsored a full-hour program beginning in 1940 (eleven to twelve midnight) on which much émigré literature was read. Some examples of the scope of this program are quoted by Berendsohn: "Theo Goetz reading from Rilke; Ernst Deutsch and Goetz reading the "Gedankenfreiheit" scene from Schiller's *Don Carlos;* Manfred Furst reading poems of Max Herrmann-Neisse; scenes from Zuckmayer's *Der Hauptmann von Köpenick.*"[94] The SPD-controlled German American Congress for Democracy also sponsored a series of programs which broadcast works by Ernst Noth, Paul Stefan, and Fritz Von Unruh and which was heard throughout New York State and as far afield as Fergus Falls, Minnesota.[95]

The best-known and most durable of émigré programs was the series of interviews and readings presented by the Austrian Peter M. Lindt (111 interviews were collected in book form and published in 1944 under the title *Schriftsteller im Exil).* Lindt began his broadcasting on New York station WBNX, taking over a program formerly run by the "neutral" Georg Brunner.[96] According to a contemporary report, the station asked Lindt to eliminate any anti-Nazi comment from his talks, apparently a wasted effort, for without notice (in April or May, 1944) this program was once again taken over by Herr Brunner, much to the disgust of the *Austro-American Tribune* (May, 1944). However, by 1945 Lindt had joined station WEVD and his familiar program was once again on the air. The widest distribution was granted still another radio series, "We Fight Back," syndicated by nine stations, all in centers of large German-speaking populations: New York, Cincinnati, Chicago, Minneapolis, Milwaukee, Philadelphia, and St. Louis. Under the direction of Ernst J. Aufricht and Manfred George, many celebrities of the literary and political emigration were heard.[97]

It should be clear that the opportunities offered by such diverse media as the newspaper, legitimate theater, cabaret, rostrum, and radio aided in the diffusion of Free German literature among the German-speaking population. The émigré writer was not as restricted or isolated as the limitations of German-language book publishing in the United States would seem to indicate.

Émigré Literary Organizations

The largest and most widely known organization of German émigré writers was the German American Writers Association, otherwise known as the American branch of the Schutzverband deutscher Schriftsteller. (The original SDS, a protective association of German authors in Germany, was established in 1909.) There is even a prehistory to the official founding of the GAWA in 1938. Karl Jakob Hirsch noted that when he arrived in New York in 1935 there was "an association of German writers upon which the early SDS was built."[98] He goes on to comment that the scarcity of professional writers was then so great there were not enough to form an executive committee; they were even forced to elect a physician as chairman. The first public meeting of the GAWA took place on Friday, October 13, 1938; at this time the following slate of officers was elected: Oskar Maria Graf as chairman, a post he held for the life of the organization, Ferdinand Bruckner as second chairman, and Manfred George (Graf's brother-in-law) as secretary.[99]

Graf's inaugural speech outlined the general purposes and specific goals of the GAWA. High priority was given to gaining the support of the German-American public, to making contacts with other organizations, to the sponsoring of lecture tours. and the establishment of a central lecture bureau. Close cooperation with the Deutsch-Amerikanischer Kulturverband was urged, as was the creation of a Free German press service for German-American newspapers to serve as an antidote for international Nazi propaganda. The material success of this latter undertaking (if any) is not known.

During 1939 the membership grew steadily, soon reaching a peak of around 150. The GAWA took part in many anti-Nazi functions and became known to large segments of the American public.[100] One critical observer (Rudolf Brandl) viewed with dismay the political leanings of the association:

> While formally an affiliate of the German-American League for Culture, the Writers Association is actually the brains of the GALC. Although culturally not very severe about its requirements for membership (strange as it sounds – the GAWA includes a contingent of people who are wrestling hard with the German language when it comes to a writing test) it is rendering most valuable services to the Kremlin, and a steady afflux from abroad tends to augment its usefulness to the Soviets. Every word said by George E. Sokolsky in his brilliant article, "Red Ink: What Russia Is Doing to American Books and Movies" (*Liberty*, issue of December 2, 1939) with reference to the political tendencies of the American Writers Congress, applies also to the German American Writers Association.[101]

Brandl's polemic was written in that cold season following the Russo-German treaty of August, 1939; before that cataclysm not much open friction was apparent within the heterogeneous company under the GAWA banner. The fourteen American sponsors[102] of the association, as of January, 1940, were in all honesty supporting a strictly literary (according to its own statutes), politically neutral organization.[103]

Despite GAWA support of several meritorious projects – lectures, literary events and a radio program – strains of dissonance among members rapidly increased in volume. A statement *(Aufruf)* released by the association condemning Hitler but making no mention of his new ally was inserted in the *Volksfront* (Chicago) of September 16, 1939. Intimations of the group's pro-Communist leanings reached honorary president Thomas Mann who felt impelled to ask for an explanation. Rumor had it, wrote Mann, that the association was planning to issue statements denoting both Germany and Russia as peaceful powers *(Friedensmächte)* and England and France as guilty of imperialistic war! Also, he went on, newspapers in Paris and New York have been attacking the GAWA as an agent of Stalin. If there were any shred of truth in the accusation, if any such manifestos were to be issued, he, Mann, would naturally have to sever all connections with the association.[104]

The drama within the GAWA began with the withdrawal of the most determined anti-Communist clique in September, 1939, and reached its climax with the departure (June, 1940) of most of the "bourgeois" anti-Communist liberals. As early as Spring, 1939, recalled Brandl, anti-Soviet remarks by Hermann Borchardt—author of the sardonic anti-Utopia, *The Conspiracy of the Carpenters* (1944)—called down the official wrath of chairman Graf. Brandl, himself, presented a motion to the annual meeting in September entreating all present to "cease every cooperation with Communist papers and organizations. . . . The overwhelming majority refused to even consider a resolution of this kind."[105] One of the leaders of the non-Communist liberal group in the GAWA, Klaus Mann, felt increasingly alienated by the indiscriminately pro-Soviet views of the majority; witness his diary entry for June 28, 1940:

> Many seem to conceive of the war as a kind of imperialistic-capitalist conspiracy, a view which is quite widespread in radical left-wing circles. There, one would only find interest in a struggle against Hitler if the Soviet Union were involved. As long as Moscow and Berlin are allied the Communists find democratic England "at least as bad" as fascist Germany.[106]

A formal letter of resignation signed by Klaus Mann and some of his colleagues—Curt Riess, Martin Gumpert and Hermann Kesten—followed in due course. The letter (quoted in full by Mann) ends with an accurate enough commentary on the then deeply ingrained disunity of the Free German intelligentsia: "In our circles the necessary agreement in moral-political principles and goals is not yet or no longer present. . . . Although we do not at this time wish to cut ourselves loose from a group of exiled German writers, after mature reflection we have had to decide on such a step and herewith announce our resignation."[107] This for all practical purposes may be considered the epitaph of the GAWA.

It is difficult to ascertain how closely some of the long established German-American literary clubs, such groups as the Literarische Gesellschaft of Chicago and the Literarischer Verein of New York, worked with the post-1933 immigrants. One of the very oldest, the Gesellig-Wissenschaftlicher Verein (founded by Carl Schurz) was not only traditionally open to German Jews but took a new lease on life under an émigré president, Peter M. Lindt. Of the other organizations that made their appearance now and then in pages of German-American newspapers,[108] only two warrant more than passing mention: (1) the Writers Service Center and (2) Die Tribüne, Forum für freie deutsche Kultur.

Friderike Winternitz-Zweig, first wife of Stefan Zweig and a personality in her own right, built for herself a new and rich life with roots in both émigré and American circles.[109] Many who remembered her in better days turned to her now for advice and assistance in the trying circumstances of exile. She was instrumental, by virtue of her many contacts in South America, in getting a few books by Heinrich Mann, René Fülöp-Miller, and Hermann Kesten published in Spanish translations.[110] With the help of some American friends, Madame Zweig and a few close associates[111] set up a small organization devoted to aiding refugee writers, artists, and intellectuals — the Writers Service Center. Among the services the new organization hoped to make available were inexpensive translation and copying, assistance in finding employment and lodgings, and a health insurance program.

Under the Writers Service Center imprint, four volumes of poetry by "new" authors were published during 1943 and 1944; costs were partially covered by subscription sale and in part by the authors. Advertisements indicated that the books could be purchased either from the Center or the author. One of the four titles, Alfred Farau, *Trommellied von Unsinn* (1943) was billed in the émigré press as "the volume of poetry ordered by the Brooklyn Public Library for all its branches."[112] In addition to the Center, Frau Zweig founded the American-European Friendship Association which gave wider scope for her good offices.

A different coterie of writers was affiliated with Die Tribüne, Forum für freie deutsche Literatur, founded in the spring or autumn of 1941. Guided by Oskar Maria Graf and Friedrich Alexan, this group retained much of the militant spirit of the old GAWA as a partial review of its activities will illustrate:

> Here, for example, Alfred Kantorowicz read from his Spanish diary "Die vergessene Brigade" and Alex Wedding (pseudonym of Frau F. C. Weiskopf) from her novel of the Peasant's War, "Der Pfeifferhansl." Ferdinand Bruckner's drama of the American Revolution, *Die Toten von Lexington* and his play, *Die Rassen* , were read aloud by actors as were five scenes from Bert Brecht's *Furcht und Elend des Dritten Reichs*. Under the direction of F. C. Weiskopf a Slavic evening was arranged, at which Adolf Hoffmeister's play, *Lidice*, was read, as well as evenings dedicated to German writers in Russia and England.[113]

Paul Tillich, under the sponsorship of the Tribüne, helped celebrate "Goethe Day" on May 18, 1942 and his talk, "Verbanntes Buch-Unzerstörbare Kultur," was printed in the *Aufbau* (N.Y.).[114] The same year saw a slight penetration of America's insensitivity toward the literary pretensions of the "other Germany" in her midst; the occasion, a contest for the five best German-language short stories dealing with the emigration and the fight for freedom with cash awards ranging up to $75.00 (the Modern Age Press of New York sharing the expenses). A jury of five émigrés and two American professors[115] gave the first prize money to one Fritz Zorn, a young writer at the time employed "as a dishwasher in a seaman's hotel at the West Ferry."[116]

With the end of the war the Tribüne underwent a change in decor and reappeared in (of all unlikely places) the subway arcade at New York's Forty-second Street. Here, in July, 1934, Alexan and his colleague Frau Dr. Else Hofmann (former editor of *Oesterreichische Kunst*) opened the Tribune Book and Art Center. These quarters were used for exhibitions (such as a Käthe Kollwitz showing in 1946) and literary evenings[117] until the community of exiled German writers in New York, bereft of its raison d'être, gradually broke up, some individuals remaining in America, others returning to Europe.

Notes

1. Egon Schwarz, ed., *Verbannung: Aufzeichnungen deutscher Schriftsteller im Exil* (Hamburg: Christian Wegner Verlag, 1964), p.181.

2. Not only the literary were included, of course. In music there were: Arnold Schoenberg, Paul Hindemith, Kurt Weill, Bruno Walter; in art, Georg Grosz, Eugen Spiro, Max Beckmann; in architecture, Erich Mendelssohn, Walter Gropius, Mies van der Rohe – and scores of others.

3. *Der Geist der Unruhe* (Köln: Kiepenheuer & Witsch, 1959), p.126.

4. Ben Hecht, *1001 Afternoons in New York* (New York: Viking, 1941).

5. Sigrid Undset, Maurice Maeterlinck, Jules Romains, Jacques Maritain, Thomas Mann, and Hermann Kesten. Cf. Davie, *Refugees in America*, p.113.

6. *Publishers' Weekly,* Nov. 19, 1938, p.1833 and Dec. 3, 1938, p.1978. Rockwell Kent designed the catalog cover.

7. *Publishers' Weekly,* Jan. 14, 1938, p.124.

8. The last freely elected President of the German P.E.N. was the drama critic Alfred Kerr (a Jew) who fled to England in 1933.

9. Now known as the P.E.N. Zentrum deutschsprächiger Autoren im Ausland, London. Needless to say, Thomas Mann occupied the position of honorary president. See Gabriele Tergit (ed.), *Autobiographien und Bibliographien* (London: P.E.N. Zentrum . . . , 1957), p.3–5.

10. Quoted by Davie, op. cit., p.339. The American Center was then presided over by novelist Robert Nathan.

11. The inaugural dinner of the European P.E.N. in America was held on April 30, 1941. The *New York Times* reported that $5,225 was raised to aid the rescue of still stranded authors. May 16, 1941, p.10.

12. The most comprehensive study is Daniel Aaron, *Writers on the Left* (New York: Harcourt, 1961). Cf. Howe and Coser, *The American Communist Party,* p.273–318. Although the great Red scare of the forties and fifties inspired a host of memoirs and apologies, e.g., Granville Hicks, *Where We Came Out* (New York: Viking, 1954), these are not notable either for accuracy or balanced judgments.

13. This was a Popular-Front-oriented association of exiled writers then in Paris (not the same as the Free German P.E.N. though membership overlapped). There was also a branch in the United States, again dominated by the pro-Soviet faction. On the Exiled Writers' Committee of the League of American Writers, see its brochure, *We Must Save Them All: A Report* (New York, ca. Dec., 1940), especially p.11–12.

14. Davie, op. cit., p.113.

15. The League of American Writers, Exiled Writers Committee, op. cit., p.17.

16. Loc. cit.

17. A Committee of Publishers headed by Cass Canfield of Harper's covered operating

expenses for the New York dinner. The $6000 was destined for writers holding Mexican visas and was to pay for their passage on "the Rescue Ship soon to sail from Marseille to Mexico." The Committee claimed to have supplied Mexican visas for thirty-five Germans. Not all were used. Ibid., p.18–22. See also *Publishers' Weekly,* Oct. 5, 1940, p.1408.

18. Other highlights in the *New York Times* report were: O. M. Graf, "The German *Kultur* Heritage — Errors and Gains"; Ernst Bloch, "International Humanism and Anti-Fascist Literature"; Klaus Mann, "The New Synthesis: Europe — America"; Manfred George, "Problems of Organization"; and Walter Schönstedt, "The Roads Towards Victory" (June 5, 1939, p.20).

19. *Publishers' Weekly,* March 23, 1940, p.1226.

20. *After Hitler's Fall: Germany's Coming Reich* (London: Faber & Faber, 1934, p.66–67. See also the Prince's two autobiographical volumes, *Conquest of the Past* (Boston: Houghton, 1938) and *On Borrowed Peace* (Garden City, New York: Doubleday, 1942).

21. Erika and Klaus Mann, *Escape to Life,* p.316.

22. The others were: J. C. Cohn, Hans Flesch-Brunningen, René Schickele, Anna Siemsen, Alfred Wolfenstein, A. M. Frey, Horst Galeky, David Luschnat, Gustav Regler, Paul Zech, and Max Zimmering. *New York Times,* Feb. 6, 1938, Sec.2, p.3.

23. *New York Times,* Dec. 14, 1938, p.19.

24. *Publishers' Weekly,* April 16, 1938, p.1608, and July 2, 1938, p.39. The cooperating publishers were: Albert Bonnier (Stockholm), Gyldendal Norsk Verlag (Oslo), William Collins (London), Querido Verlag (Amsterdam), Albin Michel (Paris), and Sijthoff (Leiden). The judges named were Thomas Mann, Lion Feuchtwanger, Bruno Frank, Alfred Neumann, and Balder Olden.

25. Berendsohn 1:67, based on information obtained from the Prince. Sternfeld, *Exil-Literatur,* cites title as *Es is später denn Ihr wisst.*

26. "Now it was revealed that the Guild had obviously misused the prize money for it declared that the publishers [Little, Brown] had retained the right of veto against the decision and had exercised this right; upon which T. Mann and R. [sic] Frank with sharp protest left the Guild." *Aufbau* (N.Y.), Dec. 29, 1939, p.11.

27. Letter dated June 19, 1948, Heinrich Mann, *Briefe an Karl Lemke und Klaus Pinkus* (Hamburg: Claasen, 1964), p.70–71. The Russian edition of *Ein Zeitalter* was actually never published.

28. The judgment of the Federal Circuit Court of Appeals as quoted in the *New York Times,* June 10, 1939, p.15. Cf. letter by Herbert Reichner in *Publishers' Weekly,* Feb. 18, 1939, p.775.

29. Davie, op. cit., p.336–37.

30. Wieland Herzfelde, for example, was employed as a reader by the firm of Simon and Schuster. The radical journalist Walther Victor was successively employed as assistant Service Manager of the American Book Stratford Press and then for two and one-half years as Knopf's Production Manager. *Publishers' Weekly,* Aug. 14, 1943, p.494, and Dec. 22, 1945, p.2703. Victor had described his experiences at Knopf in "Erfahrungen in einem amerikanischen Verlage," *Ein Paket aus Amerika* (Weimar: Thüringer Volksverlag, 1950), p.86–96.

31. Rosenwald Fellowships were granted to (among others): Ferdinand Bruckner, Albert Ehrenstein, Iven Heilbut, Ruth Fischer, Karl O. Paetel, Robert Pick, and Hans Sahl. Davie, op. cit., p.339.

32. Lerner, *Sykewar* (New York: George W. Stewart, 1942), p.72.

33. *Aufbau* (N.Y.), March 20, 1942, p.20.

34. Ernst Lothar, *Das Wunder des Überlebens* (Hamburg: Paul Szolnay, 1961), p.167.

35. Kesten, *Deutsche Literatur im Exil,* p.235–38.

36. Ibid, p. 138.

37. *Aufbau* (Berlin), 2, No. 9:977 (1946).

38. Cf. Strothmann's statement that 407 volumes of "Schöne Literatur" were translated from the German and published in the U.S. and England during the years 1936-1939 (Tabelle Nr.9). Berendsohn has tabulated that for twelve novelists alone, seventy-five American translations were published during the six years, 1933-1938. (Berendsohn 1:157).

39. E.g., Bertolt Brecht, *A Penny for the Poor* (New York: Hillman-Curl, 1938); Albert Ehrenstein, *Tubutsch* (New York: Profile Pr., 1946).

40. According to Manfred George, "Deutsche Schriftsteller in den USA," *Neue Schweizerische Rundschau*, N.F., 17:315 (1949/1950).

41. Maria Gleit is the wife of Walther Victor. Among her books for children published by Scribner's were: *Pierre Keeps Watch* (1944) and *Katrina* (1945).

42. "What has Happened to Them Since," *Publishers' Weekly*, June 23, 1945, p.2434-37.

43. Barthold Fles, "Attention, Mr. Fry," *Publishers' Weekly* , July 28, 1945, p.307.

44. Kesten listed Robert Neumann, Arthur Koestler, Franz Schoenberner, Klaus Mann, Franz Hoellering, Vicki Baum, Peter de Mendelssohn, Hilde Spiel, Hans Flesch-Brunningen (who wrote in English as Vincent Brun), Ernst Erich Noth, Josef Bornstein, Martin Gumpert, Norbert Mühlen. Erich Mosse. *Der Geist der Unruhe* (Köln: Kiepenheur & Witsch, 1959), p.124.

45. Kesten, *Deutsche Literatur im Exil*, p.219-20; *Das Antiquariat* (Vienna), 6:307 (Sept. 1950).

46. Klaus Mann, *Der Wendepunkt* (Berlin: G. B. Fischer, 1960), p.378.

47. Toni Stolper, *Ein Leben in Brennpunkten unserer Zeit* (Tübingen: Rainer Wunderlich Verlag, 1960), p.352. Another German émigré, Felix Pinner, supplied a similar service. A former chief editor of the *Handelszeitung* of the *Berliner Tageblatt*, Pinner began distributing his German-language *Wirtschaftsanalyse* in 1937. *Aufbau* (N.Y.), Sept. 15, 1939, p.17.

48. Under Budzislawski's editorship the once famous *Weltbühne*, then being issued from Prague, fell completely under Communist control (Walter Ulbricht was a regular contributor). Budzislawski after leaving the United States was given the post of Professor of Journalism at the Karl Marx University, Leipzig. Cf. Alf Enseling, *Die Weltbühne* (Münster: Verlag, C. J. Fahle, 1962), p.36 et passim.

49. See Hans Jacob, *Kind meiner Zeit* (Köln: Kiepenheuer & Witsch, 1962), p.274 et passim for a not always accurate account.

50. The rivalry between the two men apparently carried over into American politics. Hans Jacob recalls in detail the story of how Schlamm had ghostwritten a compromising article for Republican Presidential candidate Thomas E. Dewey which was uncovered by Miss Thompson and her staff and led, following Jacob's account, to Miss Thompson's declaring herself for Roosevelt. Ibid., p.74-78.

51. Kantorowicz, *Deutsche Tagebuch*, 1:285; on Ernst Erich Noth (whose real name was Paul Krantz) see *Neue Volks-Zeitung*, Jan. 23, 1943, p.4; on Hans Jacob, see Jacob, op. cit., p.241.

52. Leo Lania, *Welt im Umbruch* (Frankfurt: Forum Verlag, n.d.), p.336.

53. One such series of lectures on German history and culture was sponsored by the Institute of German Studies of City College of New York. Participants included Gustav Stolper, Karl Korsch (a leading Marxist theorist), Veit Valentin (historian), Erich von Kahler (historian and philosopher), and Rudolf Kayser (literary critic). *New York Times*, Jan. 21, 1940, p.8.

54. *Publishers' Weekly*, July 28, 1945, p.325. Fles may have included as American

authors those German refugees who had already become citizens.

55. The first meeting was held in 1938 and among those participating were Quincy Howe (journalist and radio newscaster), Malcolm Cowley (critic), Whit Burnett (novelist) and Ludwig Lore. *Deutsche Volksecho*, Sept. 24, 1938.

56. *Aufbau* (N.Y.), March 8, 1963, p.19. Horch handled foreign rights both for native American writers such as James Thurber, Upton Sinclair, John Dos Passos, Edna Ferber, and Erskine Caldwell as well as for a number of resident émigrés — e.g. Erich Maria Remarque, Lion Feuchtwanger, Alfred Polgar, and Bruno Walter.

57. *Das Antiquariat* (Vienna), 6:123 (April 1950).

58. *Aufbau* (N.Y.), Nov. 19, 1943, p.9, and Nov. 24, 1944, p.8.

59. *Hearings Regarding Communist Espionage*, 81st Cong., 1st and 2d Sess., 1951, p.3599-3609.

60. With the greatest selectivity we may mention: Max Reinhardt, Billy Wilder, William Dieterle, Peter Lorre, Elisabeth Bergner, Otto Preminger; in music, Arnold Schoenberg and Hanns Eisler. See Hans Kafka, "What Our Immigration Did for Hollywood — and Vice Versa," *Aufbau* (N.Y.), Dec. 22, 1944, p.40.

61. None of these eminent authors enjoyed the slightest success in Hollywood with the exception of Brecht who had the rare distinction of having one of his scenarios actually filmed — Fritz Lang's *Hangmen Also Die*. Two writers not listed, Hans Lustig and Georg Fröschel, were quite successful as film writers. Lustig remained with MGM for eighteen years.

62. Letter to Louis B. Mayer dated Oct., 1941. Thomas Mann, *Briefe, 1937-1947*, p.210.

63. *Mein zwanzigstes Jahrhundert* (München: Paul List Verlag, 1960), p.275.

64. Kesten, *Deutsche Literatur im Exil*, p.172.

65. Ibid., p.224; See also Lothar, op. cit., p.224.

66. *Das Antiquariat* (Vienna), 6:123 (April 1950).

67. E.g., authors who had motion pictures made from their novels or plays included Vicki Baum, Feuchtwanger, Werfel, Bruno Frank, Martin Gumpert, Hans Habe, Stefan Heym, Gina Kaus, Ferenc Molnar, Alfred Neumann, Remarque, Ernst Toller. Berendsohn 2:228-29.

68. Kesten, *Deutsche Literatur im Exil*, p.200.

69. Ibid., p.193.

70. Berendsohn 2:227.

71. Kesten, *Deutsche Literatur im Exil*, p.193, 201.

72. *Gegen den Strom*, 1:16 (June 1938).

73. Berendsohn does give a selected list of sixty-one German authors and the approximate number of their contributions printed in the *Aufbau* up to 1946. Berendsohn 2:208-9.

74. Karl Jakob Hirsch, using the pseudonym Joe Gassner, was the regular book reviewer for the *Neue Volks-Zeitung*. Walther Victor ran a "Bücher und Leser" column in the *German American*.

75. Donald Peterson Kent, *The Refugee Intellectual*, p.15. The figure includes many former luminaries of the Weimar era who died here in relative obscurity. Georg Bernard, one-time editor of the *Vossische Zeitung*, succumbed in New York in 1944; Robert Groetsch, former editor of the *Dresdener Volkszeitung*, at the end of his life was a watchmaker in the same city; Fritz Kummer, for twenty years editor of the world's largest labor newspaper, the *Deutsche Metall-Arbeiter Zeitung* (with a weekly circulation of 1,600,000), was killed in an automobile accident in 1937.

76. "Deutsches Theater in Amerika," *Deutsche Rundschau*, 81:271-75 (1955).

77. See Morgan Y. Himmelfarb, *Drama Was a Weapon: The Left Wing Theatre in New York 1929-1941* (New Brunswick: Rutgers Univ. Pr., 1963), p.12, 24; and Eberhard Brüning, "Probleme der Wechselbeziehungen der amerikanischen und der deutschen

sozialistischen und proletarisch-revolutionären Literatur," *Zur Geschichte der socialistis-chen Literatur 1918-1933* (Berlin: Aufbau Verlag. 1963), p.320-45. Bonn was assisted by two other Germans who came to the United States in the mid-twenties, Anne Howe and Harry Elion.

78. The Proletbühne was still active in 1933, but by 1934 its place was taken by Die Neue Theater-Gruppe. *Der Arbeiter*, Sept. 23, 1934. See also "Ein deutsches Theater im Aufbau," *Neue Volks-Zeitung*, July 18, 1936, p.8, which reported on the progress of a new German theater group made up of members of the White Rats Actors Union and the WPA Deutsche Theatergruppe. For additional information on this group and on the career of its director, John Bonn, see the study by Douglas McDermott based on the Federal Theatre Project Records (WPA) in the National Archives—"The Odyssey of John Bonn: A Note on German Theatre in America," *German Quarterly*, 38:325-34 (May 1965).

79. W. Melnitz, former director of the Neues Theater. Frankfurt am Main, and Kurt Adler (later assistant conductor at the Metropolitan Opera in New York) were members of the organizing committee.

80. *New York Times*, March 16, 1941, p.8.

81. *Neue Volks-Zeitung*, March 8, 1941, p.8.

82. *New York Times*. June 18, 1939, p.2.

83. Lothar, op. cit., p.158-65. The group performed two plays by fellow exiles: Bruno Frank's *Sturm im Wasserglas* and Raoul Auernheimer's *Das ältere Fach*.

84. Refugee Actors Guild; Players from Abroad (Felix G. Gerstmann) ca. 1942; New Yorker Volksbühne (Hans Sonnenthal) ca. 1946; Continental Comedy Theater (Kurt Robitscheck, Joseph Schildkraut, and Walter Mehring—featuring American plays in German translation) ca. 1942-43. Berendsohn 2:213-14. Cf. Kurt Hellmer, "Berlin und Wien am Broadway," *Aufbau* (N.Y.), Dec. 22, 1944, p.55.

85. *Lothar*, op. cit., p.165.

86. Klaus Mann, op. cit., p.280 et passim.

87. See Hollaender's autobiography, *Von Kopf bis Fuss* (München: Kindler, 1965), p.327-29.

88. Berendsohn 2:215.

89. *German American*, Feb. 1, 1945.

90. Valeska Gert, *Die Bettelbar von New York* (Berlin: Arani, 1950). A revision of these memoirs is contained in her latest autobiographical volume—*Ich bin eine Hexe! Kaleideskop meines Lebens* (München: Schneekluth, 1968).

91. In the present study no attempt has been made to investigate the pattern of German-language programming in the Middle West where different circumstances prevailed.

92. *Aufbau* (N.Y.), Nov. 1, 1938, p.2., and K. J. Hirsch, *Heimkehr zu Gott*, p.105.

93. E.g., an interview with Bruno Frank and original sketches by Hans Janowitz and Kurt Juhn were reviewed in the *Aufbau* (N.Y.) for Jan. 12, 1940, p.8.

94. Berendsohn 2:225.

95. *Neue Volks-Zeitung*, June 27, 1942, p.4.

96. Cf. the *New York Times*, June 28, 1942, Sec.8, p.10.

97. Berendsohn 2:225. On the following page Berendsohn lists twenty selected radio dramas broadcast in New York including one "soap opera" series—Peter Martin Lampel, *Die Schulzes Von Yorkville*. A bibliography of Free German radio plays may be considered a *desideratum*.

98. K. J. Hirsch, op. cit., p.107. There was still in 1933 a Nationalverband deutsch-amerikanischer Schriftsteller und Journalisten, and it may be that the association Hirsch speaks of was a remnant of the New York chapter of the Nationalverband.

99. Thomas Mann and Julius Lips were named honorary presidents and an executive body was formed made up of (among others): Paul Tillich, Felix Boenheim (Kurt Rosen-

feld's successor as head of the German American Emergency Conference), Otto Sattler, Gerhart Seger, Stefan Heym, Steffi Kiessler (of the New York Public Library), Erika Mann, and Harry Slochower. *Deutsches Volksecho,* Oct. 15, 1938.

100. See O. M. Graf, "German Writers in America," *New Republic,* April 26, 1939, p. 344–46; Wieland Herzfelde, "German Writers Against Hitler," *Direction* (Darien, Conn.), 2:3 (Dec. 1939).

101. Quoted verbatim from p.17 of Brandl's, *That Good Old Fool, Uncle Sam.*

102. W. H. Auden. Archibald MacLeish, Stephen Vincent Benet, John Farrar, Benjamin Huebsch, Nicholas Murray Butler, Charles Beard, H. V. Kaltenborn, Hendrik Van Loon, Vincent Sheean, Sherwood Anderson, Henry Seidel Canby, John Steinbeck, and George Stevens (the film director). *Aufbau* (N.Y.), Dec. 15, 1939, p.13, and Jan. 19, 1940, p.13.

103. M. George, *Neue Schweizerische Rundschau,* N. F., 17:313 (1949/50).

104. Letter of Nov. 22, 1939, Thomas Mann, *Briefe, 1937–1947,* p.122–23.

105. Brandl, op. cit., p.18.

106. Klaus Mann, op. cit., p. 397.

107. Ibid., p.398. Cf. with the detailed explanation of Gerhart Seger's resignation. Seger had offered a motion *in absentia* at the Sept. 30, 1939 meeting condemning both Hitler and Stalin. He was supported by Brandl, Julius Epstein, and K. J. Hirsch. The vote was thirty-five against, eight for, and seven abstentions. *(Neue Volks-Zeitung,* Oct. 14, 1939, p.2, and Oct. 21, 1939, p.7). The latter issue contains Seger's letter of resignation in full.

108. E.g., The Progressive Literary Club, a new literary society for the nurture of German-language literature in exile *(Austro-American Tribune,* Jan. 1946); The Monday Group of German Writers, later known as the European Writers – Monday Group, a nonpolitical association *(Aufbau* (N.Y.), Nov. 22, 1940, p.8, and Dec. 20, 1940, p.12); the Literarische Gruppe of the New World Club; and the Wendekreis (N.Y.), a cultural organization founded by Social Democrats in the early 1930s.

109. For testimony from her American friends see, Harry Zohn, ed., *Liber Amicorum Friderike M. Zweig* (Stamford, Conn.: Dahl, 1952). See also Friderike Zweig's autobiography, *Spiegelungen des Lebens* (Wien: Hans Deutsch Verlag, 1964).

110. F. Zweig, op. cit., p.258.

111. Dora Edinger, Elisabeth Stoerle, Hedwig Lachmann, and Brigitte Nichols – a daughter of the martyred anarchist philosopher Gustav Landauer and mother of the American theatrical personality Mike Nichols (ibid., p.259 and *Aufbau* (N.Y.), April 23, 1943, p.17).

112. *Austro-American Tribune,* Dec. 1945. Frau Zweig claims that publication of Johannes Urdizil, *Der Trauermantel* (New York: Friedrich Krause, 1945), was sponsored by her organization (op. cit., p.258).

113. Berendsohn 2:216–17.

114. May 29, 1942, p.10.

115. Ferdinand Bruckner, O. M. Graf, Manfred George, Albert Ehrenstein, Friedrich Alexan, Francine Bradley, and Arthur Geismar of New York University.

116. *German American,* Feb. 1943. His story was titled, *Sturz ins Licht.* Second and third prizes were awarded to Hilde Schottländer for *Das Mädchen aus der Dummenschule* and Hans Marchwitza for *Die Familie.* Fourth and fifth prizes went to Warner Shields and Karl Obermann, commendations to Günther Anders and Kurt Pinczower. *(German American,* July, 1942 and Berendsohn 2:216).

117. Berendsohn 2:215.

IX

Epilogue –
German Émigrés in America
after 1945

The German emigration officially ended with the unconditional surrender of the Third Reich. The grim, chaotic months that followed, during which the concentration camps were opened and the four major Allied powers took on the responsibilities of military government, laid bare a Germany with few immediate outward attractions. Many émigrés did make the journey home in the uniform of the United States military or as civilians employed by the occupation forces. Not surprisingly, former politicians and labor leaders were the most importunate in their desire to return, as were a number of publicists and writers. It was not an easy decision to make. Those writers who had made new careers or whose children had become thoroughly assimilated often were loathe to uproot their families; in any case they usually maintained some kind of connection with the Old World. Quite a few of the journalists who remained (such as Kurt Kersten and Karl O. Paetel) were frequent contributors to German and Swiss newspapers and periodicals. The fate of the forty-seven journalists investigated by Kent during the postwar years 1947–1952 seems to have been fairly representative.

> Of the 47 journalists in the study group slightly less than half (23) were able to continue in the field of journalism in the United States. Of those currently earning their livelihood by writing, two were writing in German and finding publishers abroad, two were writing in German for overseas

broadcasts, and three were able to write in German and be translated in English. The remaining fifteen were writing in English.[1]

A conflict of loyalties was not unusual among United States citizens who also happened to be German or Austrian men of letters; sooner or later each had to face his moment of decision,[2] although those who did opt for United States citizenship still remained keenly interested in preserving their cultural heritage. During the 1950s and 1960s the promotion of lectures, public readings and concerts, as well as social and athletic events (not to mention numerous charitable undertakings) was the function of the clubs and organizations that survived.[3]

The German-American press, although its gradual decline was temporarily halted by the influx of new émigrés, relapsed into a permanent state of torpor. From a high of nearly 800 (1893/94), the number of German-language newspapers in 1950 had reached a new low of 50.[4] Only three émigré papers have survived—The *Aufbau,* the *Jewish Way,* and the *German American.* The *Aufbau's* circulation still hovers around the 29,000 mark while the latter two enjoy a paid circulation of only about 2000 each. Almost nothing is left of the once proud German-language Socialist press since the *Neue Volks-Zeitung* ceased publication in 1949.[5] The *Aufbau* still maintains an international readership, remaining the major organ of the surviving German-Jewish immigrants; its format and policies have not altered appreciably although death and old age have remorselessly depleted its staff of contributors. When the present generation of German Jews has departed and with no new wave of immigrants to take their place, the *Aufbau* will be faced with the same problems that caused the demise of the *Neue Volks-Zeitung* and so many other foreign language papers in the United States.

As the situation in Germany slowly improved, the publishing of German-language books in the United States virtually ceased. By 1950 Bermann-Fischer, Herzfelde, and Otto Kallir (temporarily) had returned to Europe, leaving Frederick Ungar and Kurt Wolff to continue as publishers of American trade books. In the bookselling world, the establishments of Paul Mueller and Mary S. Rosenberg still flourished, though Friedrich Krause and H. G. Koppell were forced to seek new fields of endeavour. Retail dealers had to adjust to postwar conditions and, although they continued to supply German books to libraries and individuals, they found it expedient to expand their services—Rosenberg, for instance, added French books to her stock in trade. The major contributions of émigré booksellers after 1945 were in the areas of rare and antiquarian books, imports, and reprints of scholarly books and periodicals.

Remigration[6]

RETURN TO THE WEST

The preparation and implementation of the military occupation has been minutely described in both official and unofficial accounts,[7] but the interesting role played by the former German émigrés has not. During the first six months of the American occupation, émigré journalists in the Psychological Warfare Division (later renamed Information Control) built up a chain of so-called "overt" newspapers—that is, German-language papers openly published and edited by the American authorities. Until the licensing of German-owned papers could get under way, the necessary dissemination of information for the intellectual reawakening of Germany after twelve years of isolation was left to these "overt" publications of the military government. The program began in May, 1945, and by August of that year ten papers were being printed with a combined circulation of 3,785,000.[8] In charge of this stop-gap newspaper empire was the journalist, novelist, and *bon-vivant* Hans Habe.[9] Working with him were Stefan Heym, Joseph Wechsberg, Hans Wallenberg, and other émigrés in uniform.[10]

In line with United States policy of a German press run by Germans, only *Die Neue Zeitung* (Munich) continued to be published after January, 1946, primarily to serve as a model of democratic American journalism. From 1946 to 1953 this paper, under the direction of Hans Wallenberg, was probably the most influential American publication in Germany.[11] The rehabilitation of the German theater was another sphere in which the utilization of former émigrés seemed acceptable. The chief participants in this project were Carl Zuckmayer,[12] who was kept on for one year as special advisor on theatrical affairs in the American zone, and Ernst Lothar, appointed to a similar position in Austria.[13]

The foregoing hardly amounts to an exhaustive description of the role of the émigré in the United States military occupation of Germany, but the historical and biographical accounts published so far shed little more light on the subject. Gottfried Benn's remark on his fellow Germans' "Byzantine obsequiousness towards the émigrés,"[14] or Bruno Brehm's complaint that "he never had an opportunity to speak with an American, only to German émigrés in American uniform,"[15] indicate a lack of enthusiasm for the returned refugees. These and similar suggestions of widespread émigré influence on United States policies were more fiction than fact, and Breitenkamp's allegation that "the refugee group throughout the Military Government organization tended to bring about a turning back of the clock to the days of the Weimar Republic,"[16] cannot be taken too seriously.

The apparently irrevocable rift between Social Democrats and Communists that exerted its baleful influence from 1918 to 1945 was the distinguishing mark of the remigration as well. Depending on their political sympathies, the former exiles were drawn sooner or later to either the American, British, or French Zones in the west or to the Soviet Zone in the east, the embryonic Deutsche Demokratische Republik. The resulting bifurcation of German literary culture was viewed with dismay by western critics.

Hermann Kesten, writing in 1952, went a step further and imposed upon contemporary German letters a fourfold compartmentalization: East German, West German, National Socialist, and Exile literature.[17] This was, in part, a rhetorical device to be demolished by Kesten's belief (shared by other émigrés)[18] in the fundamental unity of German literature — whether written by exiles, members of the "inner emigration," or National Socialists. For these critics, all German literature would be judged in some future time as divergent streams of *one* literary culture. Yet another exile struck a more pessimistic note which at the time seemed to ring true. Wrote Ludwig Marcuse: "The rupture between the Fatherland and the émigrés from Hitler will heal only on the day the last refugee who not only escaped but fought back is dead."[19]

The strangulation of the German economy, ameliorated only by the currency reform of 1948, delayed the return of many émigré writers to the western occupation zones. Alfred Döblin was one of the first remigrants from America to contribute to the reawakening of literary activity in Germany with his periodical *Das Goldene Tor* (1946–1951); he was originally brought over to serve as advisor to the Direction de l'Éducation Publique in the French Zone. By 1950, most of the leading German émigré writers in the United States had returned to Germany either for a visit or for more permanent residence.[20] It is the contention of at least one critic that prior to 1948 the major émigré writers were not published in occupied Germany because: (1) they would not stand to gain anything financially, (2) their copyrights were held by Swiss, Dutch, or Swedish publishers.[21] This is incorrect on several counts. As Marshall Knappen has pointed out, during the first postwar years it was virtually impossible to publish normal-sized books because of the extreme paper shortage; it was equally futile because of currency restrictions to attempt to import German-language publications:

> Here difficult problems of foreign exchange continually beset Lieutenant
> Colonel Waples and his associates. Though lists of suitable Swiss books

were prepared, no method of financing their importation could be devised which could obtain approval. The chief difficulty came from the stringent rules on German foreign trade, which, for the time being at least, seemed to earmark all exportable German civilian funds for the reparation accounts. The same problem presented itself in connection with the payment of royalties for reprinting books by refugee authors living abroad. Consequently, it was necessary to make use of German manuscripts and denazified German publishing houses, in spite of occasional criticism from refugee circles.[22]

Gottfried Bermann-Fischer was anxious, nevertheless, to have his books distributed in Germany to the widest possible audience without delay. To facilitate this, he assigned the rights to his most important Free German books in 1946 to the German publisher Peter Suhrkamp (his former associate at the S. Fischer Verlag prior to 1936).[23] In November, 1947, Bermann-Fischer entered into negotiations with the American Military Government to have printed (in spite of the paper shortage) inexpensive editions of émigré literature in quantities ranging up to 150,000 copies per title.[24] These were published under the aegis of Peter Suhrkamp (imprint S. Fischer) and were available in the American, British and French Zones.

Those two veterans of Free German publishing, Gottfried Bermann-Fischer and Fritz Landshoff, were in the vanguard of the literary remigration. The latter returned to Amsterdam in 1946 to revive the German-language house of Querido after a lapse of six years. During the same year the Allert de Lange Verlag also resumed operations, and as before, the bulk of the publications of both Amsterdam firms was by émigré authors. In 1948 the Bermann-Fischer Verlag moved from Stockholm to Amsterdam where it merged with Querido in April of that year.[25] By the end of April, 1950, the historical cycle was complete, for Bermann-Fischer had returned to Germany and once again was in full legal possession of the name and assets of the S. Fischer Verlag.[26]

The political remigrants to West Germany from America were, in the main, members of the Social Democratic Party who once again took a place in German political life. In 1954 eight of the thirty members of the SPD Executive Committee were former exiles though only one—Max Brauer, former member of the German Labor Delegation in New York and first postwar mayor of Hamburg—was from the American contingent. Other Socialists who returned included former New Beginner Paul Hertz (to a position in the Berlin municipal government) and Rudolf Katz of the *Neue Volks-Zeitung* (as judge and vice-president of the Bundesverfassungsgericht in Karlsruhe).[27] With few exceptions, such as former Reichstag members Toni Sender, Gerhart Seger, and Wilhelm Sollmann, as well as the former leader of the Austrian Revolutionary

Socialists Josef Buttinger, émigré political and labor leaders did not tarry in the United States.

THE JOURNEY EAST

The gathering places were New York City and Mexico City where the small resident colonies of KPD members plus some nonparty sympathizers began preparations for their imminent journey to Berlin. The Mexican contingent almost in toto booked passage on a Soviet ship that sailed in July of 1946,[28] but their associates in New York were hampered by government red tape. Almost before the victory celebration had subsided, sixteen[29] of the American group petitioned for immediate passage back to Germany. The *German American* not surprisingly came out in support of the petitioners urging its readers to write to the State Department on their behalf.[30] Finally, on November 11, 1946, after a year and a half of patient waiting, the first boatload of émigrés bound for Berlin departed from New York harbor. It was a curiously assorted group: there was the Communist publicist and veteran of the Spanish Civil War, Alfred Kantorowicz and his wife; Max Schroeder from the staff of the *German American;* the Hans Marchwitzas; Horst Baerensprung, former general secretary of the Reichsbanner (the paramilitary organization founded by the SPD in 1924); and the venerable Jakob Walcher, colleague of Karl Liebknecht and Rosa Luxemburg.[31] Other luminaries followed somewhat later.[32] Lion Feuchtwanger and Heinrich Mann, though charter members of the East German literary pantheon, were either unwilling (the case with Feuchtwanger) or unable to leave their California homes. The nearly eighty-year-old Mann was apparently agreeable to such a move but was never offered any sort of financial security, not even passage money. "If I had the dollars," he wrote to Karl Lemke on March 3, 1949, "I would have tried to emigrate."[33]

Of all the human links between the United States and Communist Germany forged during the emigration years, there is none more interesting than novelist and journalist Stefan Heym, practically the last of a once dynamic breed of German-American radicals. Heym entered the United States in 1935 when only twenty-two years of age and almost immediately received a stipend from the University of Chicago to study literature.[34] On February 20, 1937, the then twenty-four-year-old Heym was entrusted with the direction of the Communist Party of America's German-language organ, the *Deutsches Volksecho,* a job he held for the life of the paper, a little over two years. At the same time he was perfecting an admirable command of the English language that enabled him to write and publish four very successful novels between the years 1942 and 1951 — *Hostages* (1942), *Of Smiling Peace* (1944), *The Crusaders* (1948) and *The Eyes of Reason* (1951). As an officer in the

United States Army, Heym supervised the publishing of *Der Ruf,* the literary journal for the German prisoner of war camps in the United States, then later took part in the occupation of Germany.

In 1953 Heym fled to the Deutsche Demokratische Republik and with bitter words renounced both his American citizenship and officer's commission.[35] His subsequent literary production—one novel, two volumes of short stories, and four of essays (as of 1965)—has not been overly impressive, but he has managed to periodically incur the wrath of the Ulbricht regime for real or imagined ideological sins. Even a dramatic adaptation of *Tom Sawyer* brought down upon him an official reprimand, as Jürgen Rühle reports somewhat facetiously, because it told the story of a boy who stole prunes: "If the children saw that, the Party feared, they would all go out and steal prunes"[36]—and prunes, Rühle reminds us, were state property. Although in 1959 Heym was awarded the Nationalpreis für Kunst und Literatur, the following year he once again fell into disfavor, this time for his collection of short stories *Schatten und Licht* (1960)—a book "unusual for the entire post-Stalin era" in its frank treatment of East German realities;[37] for that transgression the critic Günter Ebert denied to Heym any claim to be called a "socialist" writer.[38] Five years later (as reported by the *Aufbau* (N.Y.) of March 26, 1965) another clash occurred between author and state; this time government officials prevented Heym from fulfilling a speaking engagement in West Germany, allegedly for some un-Ulbrichtian remarks on the 1953 workers' rebellion found in the manuscript of his latest novel. It would be pleasant to think that Heym may have owed some of his intransigence to his American experience.

A Final Assessment

From the German point of view, the literary accomplishments of the anti-Nazi émigrés are far more significant than their political activities. In the balance of German history, for example, the chronicle of the Social Democrats in exile does not weigh heavily; on the contrary, it has been called "a tale of failure and frustration, of shattered hopes and bitter strife."[39] The same impotence may be ascribed to all other political groups in exile, with the possible exception of the Communists (and in the final analysis, only the Ulbricht clique from Moscow enjoyed any lasting success). Events in Germany from 1933 to 1945 ran their course with little meaningful involvement on the part of the political exiles in America or elsewhere. The halfhearted attempt of the Council for a Democratic Germany to assume the mantle of a government in exile was presumptuous; this study has already reiterated Karl O. Paetel's opinion that an organization completely ignorant of the July, 1944 conspiracy against Hitler had no moral or political legitimacy to represent the German people. The self-assurance of the SPD-in-exile that it alone was the legally elected representative of German Socialism, and that after the war it would be called to account for its stewardship was equally ill-founded. As Edinger has pointed out, the postwar SPD "refused to be bound by any of the manifestoes, statements, or actions of the Sopade and failed to formalize the mandate which the exiled leaders had claimed during the 1933–1946 interregnum." The new SPD made it quite clear that it had "no formal links with the past."[40]

On the other hand, the emigration and, in particular, the émigré press was of the greatest significance in the history of German-American radicalism. It was the émigrés of 1933 who took command of the Socialist press (Seger, Stampfer, Katz), the Communist and pro-Communist press (Heym, Martin Hall, Gerhart Eïsler et al.), and who wielded great influence in anti-Nazi and labor organizations. It was these émigrés who, whether they wrote articles or gave lectures, were respectfully received by the American public as experts on all things European. Yet while the emigration gave intellectual leadership to German-American radicalism, it provided few workers to build up the German-language labor unions. So it was that these unions remained dominated by rank and file immigrants of an earlier day, at least on the shop level. The influx of left-wing writers and journalists gave to the German-American radical press that vitality and breadth without which it could not have carried on through the 1940s. The rejuvenating effect of the emigrant journalist on a rather pedestrian and stodgy *Neue Volks-Zeitung* has been described by Karl Jakob Hirsch when he had just been taken on as book and motion picture reviewer:

> This paper, which has existed in New York since the year 1878 has a readership that cares not the slightest for any pretense to literary quality. It was amusing to hear that my predecessor on the paper was forced to spend her last years in bed and had to copy all her criticism from the American papers. The public was quite satisfied too. One of the older editors commented: "What, you're going to the movies yourself? God knows you don't need to!"
> I mention this tragi-comic episode only to show what little future there is for literary work in the German press of America.[41]

Certainly no one could foresee that in five years many of the finest German journalists and writers would be contributing to these same German-American papers.

The achievements of Free German publishers in the United States also warrant recognition. It is not important that the great expectations of a German-American literary renaissance remained unfulfilled; these were highly unrealistic in any case. What will remain of importance are the several hundred volumes of German literature, including first editions of major authors, and the even greater amplitude of the journal literature. To determine the relative merit of this body of literature must be the task of future critics blessed with the advantage of sufficient historical distance. One of the chief aims of this study has been the unraveling of the tangled and often obscure history of the Free German book trade in America. Inextricably a part of such an investigation was found to be the relationship of the newer émigrés to the older German Americans. While the achievements of the émigré press and book trade may be evaluated as part of German or Austrian history — or in the case of the *Aufbau*, as one of the last products of the German-Jewish tragedy — they may also be seen as an important chapter in German-American history. This is most clearly illustrated by the German-language radical and Socialist press: *Der Arbeiter,* the *Deutsches Volksecho,* the *Neue Volks-Zeitung,* et al. In the pages of these newspapers émigré intellectuals of the Left joined forces with the German-American worker and for twelve years shared a common fate. That these twelve years also witnessed the end of German-American socialism as a political and cultural force (part of the almost complete failure of American socialism as a viable political movement) only adds a final touch of historical irony.

Notes

1. Kent, *The Refugee Intellectual*, p.138.

2. This state of mind has been candidly discussed by Ernst Lothar, *Das Wunder des Uberlebens,* p.239–46 A similar problem is treated in Heinrich Fraenkel's *Farewell to Germany* (London: B. Hanison, 1959).

3. Among these may be mentioned the New World Club, the American Federation of Jews from Central Europe, the Jewish Club of 1933 (Los Angeles), and United Help, Inc., founded in 1955 to assist Nazi victims in the United States through social and welfare programs. Also worthy of note are the Austrian Forum and Austrian Institute (New York City), the latter supported by the Austrian government. The Leo Baeck Institute in New York cannot be overlooked, although the emigration period does not fall within its special field of interest.

4. Wittke, *German-Language Press in America*, p.208, 282. In 1930 the figure was 172; in 1939, 181.

5. Only *Solidarität,* the organ of the Arbeiter Kranken- und Sterbekasse (now the Workmen's Benefit Fund) is still being published in both English and German editions.

6. This useful term was coined by Alfred Vagts in his study of those German emigrants to America (of all periods) who returned to their land of origin — *Deutsch-Amerikanische Rückwanderung* (Beihefte zum Jahrbuch für Amerikanstudien 6. Heft; Heidelberg: Carl Winter, 1960).

7. The Historical Division of the Office of the U.S. High Commissioner for Germany has published a host of detailed studies. Most pertinent to the present discussion is Henry P. Pilgert, *Press, Radio and Film in West Germany 1945–1953* (1953). Marshall Knappen. *And Call It Peace* (1947) is a candid account of the workings of the military

government in the fields of education, religion, and cultural affairs by an insider—a necessary supplement to the official histories. See also, Albert Norman, *Our German Policy: Propaganda and Culture* (New York: Vantage Pr., 1951).

8. Pilgert, op. cit., p.15.

9. Habe was born Jean Bekessy. Cf. his autobiography, *Ich stelle mich* (München: Verlag Kurt Desch, 1954), p.478 et passim. Habe claims to have controlled eighteen newspapers (p.478) while Pilgert mentions only ten. See also Habe, *Im Jahre Null: Ein Beitrag zur Geschichte der deutschen Presse* (München: Verlag Kurt Desch, 1966).

10. *Aufbau* (N.Y.), July 20, 1945, p.7.

11. Three "overt" periodicals were also sponsored by the Americans: *Heute*, a pictorial news magazine; the more intellectual *Amerikanische Rundschau*; and the *Neue Auslese*, a joint British-American digest magazine.

12. *Aufbau* (Berlin), 2, No. 9:973 (1946).

13. Lothar, op. cit., p.297.

14. This was written in a letter to Johannes Weyl dated June 10, 1946. Gottfried Benn, *Ausgewählte Briefe* (Wiesbaden: Limes Verlag, 1957), p.101.

15. Quoted in Breitenkamp, *The U.S. Information Control Division and Its Effects on German Publishers and Writers: 1945 to 1949*, p.18. Brehm was a popular National Socialist novelist.

16. Ibid, p.43.

17. See Kesten's *Der Geist der Unruhe*, p.116–34.

18. E.g., Graf, *An manchen Tagen*, p.17–47.

19. Marcuse, *Mein zwanzigstes Jahrhundert*, p.178.

20. As of 1952, Kesten notes sixteen writers who left America for West Germany: Leonhard Frank, Alfred Döblin, Wilhelm Speyer, Fritz von Unruh, Alfred Neumann, Walter Mehring, Heinrich Hauser, Carl Zuckmayer, Ferdinand Bruckner, Friedrich Torberg, Albrecht Schaeffer, Karl Jakob Hirsch, Adrienne Thomas, Joachim Maass, Erich Franzen, and Hans Sahl. *Der Geist der Unruhe*, p.121.

21. Breitenkamp, op. cit., p.91.

22. Knappen, op. cit., p.159–60. Douglas Waples was officer in charge of book publications for the U.S. Information Control.

23. Suhrkamp, who from 1936 to 1950 managed the S. Fischer Verlag, Berlin, after the Nazis appropriated the firm from its legal owners, showed himself to be one of the most gallant and honorable of all German publishers during the Hitler years. This naturally contributed to the universally high esteem in which he was held after 1945. Cf. Curt Vinz and Günter Olzog, eds., *Dokumentation deutschsprachiger Verlage* (München: Günter Olzog Verlag, 1962), p.69.

24. *Aufbau* (N.Y.), Nov. 28, 1947, p.14.

25. Salzmann, *Börsenblatt für den deutschen Buchhandel* (Leipzig), 116, Nr. 23:187 (1949).

26. Bermann-Fischer/Querido Verlag, Amsterdam, and S. Fischer Verlag, Vienna (founded in 1947) were both incorporated in the new S. Fischer Verlag, Frankfurt am Main. On the rupture between Bermann-Fischer and Peter Suhrkamp (who wanted to retain control of the old S. Fischer Verlag) see Bermann-Fischer's account, *Bedroht und Bewahrt*, p.318–24.

27. Cf. Friedrich Stampfer, "Heimkehr aus der Emigration," *Neue Volks-Zeitung*, Aug. 16, 1947, p.7 (on the plight of returning politicians). Edinger gives a balanced judgment on the influence of the SPD remigrants in the new Germany (*German Exile Politics*, p.243).

28. *New York Times*, July 22, 1946, p.5. On board, among others, were Paul Merker, the journalist Alexander Abusch, and Walter Janka, later the director of the Aufbau Verlag, Berlin.

29. They were: Philip Daub, Gustav A. Deter, Maria Deter, Gerhard Eisler, Lisa Kirbach, Ernst Kruger, Lore Kruger, Hans Marchwitza, Albert Norden, Herta Norden, Karl Obermann, Albert Schreiner, Emma Schreiner, Max Schroeder, Else Steinfurth, and Alfred Zahn *'German American,* June 15, 1945). Cf. *The Network,* 2:16 (May, 1945).

30. *German American,* April 15, 1946.

31. A lengthy description of this long voyage home can be found in Kantorowicz, *Deutsches Tagebuch,* 1, 193-212.

32. E.g., Ernst Bloch, Bertolt Brecht (via Switzerland), Walther Victor, and Maximilian Scheer who became the chief editor of *Ost und West* (Berlin), a periodical founded in 1947 by Alfred Kantorowicz. Scheer's American impressions were published in two books: *Begegnungen in Europa und Amerika* (Berlin: Alfred Kantorowicz Verlag, 1949) and *Die Reise war nicht geplant* (Berlin: Aufbau Verlag, 1957). It is worth noting at this point that East Germany's conception of the United States was at first largely determined by the writings of former émigrés such as Scheer, Norden, Schreiner, Heym, Victor, and Weiskopf.

33. Heinrich Mann, *Briefe an Karl Lemke und Klaus Pinkus,* p.96. See also Kantorowicz, *Deutsches Tagebuch,* 1, 136-38, where letters from Feuchtwanger and Mann are reproduced. Cf. Kantorowicz, *Deutsche Schicksale: Intellektuelle unter Hitler und Stalin* (Wien: Europa Verlag, 1964), p.131-52.

34. *Aufbau* (N.Y.), Oct. 9, 1942, p.9. According to this report, Stefan Heym was born Hellmuth Fliegel in Chemnitz, Germany, in the year 1913. His two original German-language plays, *Die Hinrichtung* (1935) and *Gestern/Heute/Morgen* (1937) date from his American period, the latter play indeed having a German-American background.

35. Jürgen Rühle, *Literatur und Revolution* (Köln: Kiepenheuer & Witsch, 1960), p.305.

36. Ibid., p.306.

37. Martin Jänicke, *Der dritte Weg: Die antistalinistische Opposition gegen Ulbricht seit 1953* (Köln: Neuer deutscher Verlag, 1964), p.195.

38. Ibid., p.196.

39. Edinger, op. cit., p.247.

40. Ibid., 241-42.

41. Karl Jacob Hirsch, *Heimkehr zu Gott,* p.104.

Appendix I

Retail Distributors of
Free German Publications
in the United States
1933-1950

Listed are those book dealers who as part of their trade bought and sold Free German publications; omitted are the so-called international book dealers such as G. E. Stechert and Brentano's. Biographical information is given if available. Besides the German-American press itself, use was made of such compilations as the *American Book Trade Directory* and Scott Adams, ed., *The O.P. Market* (1943). Dates following the dealer's name indicate approximately the years of bookselling activity in the United States. Unless otherwise indicated, place of business is New York City.

Arthur M. Adler. 1942- .

Alliance Book Corporation. 1939–1940. Organized by H.G. Koppell, Alliance distributed the publications of Bermann-Fischer, Querido, and Allert de Lange (among others) in the United States. Retail sales were also part of the program of the Alliance Book Club.

Anhalt's Buchhandlung, Chicago. 1938–1942. These were years during which the firm advertised in various New York papers.

Arbeiter Buchhandlung. 1928–1935. The official distributor of German-language Communist literature, it was operated by the newspaper of the same name. There were two stores in New York and "branches" in Milwaukee, Philadelphia, and Chicago.

Aufbau Bücherdienst. 1939–1941. The German-Jewish newspaper offered to supply all Free German books as part of their personal book service—any book old or new. The service was apparently given up after 1941.

Bookfair. ca. 1944. Advertised only in the *Austro-American Tribune*.

Bookshop, ca. 1941. Located at 1614 Second Ave., New York City.

A. Bruderhausen. ? - 1943? An older firm dating from the pre-1933 era. Although not advertising in the émigré press, Bruderhausen is designated as a "Free German" specialist in *The O.P. Market.*

Deutsche Zentralbuchhandlung. 1935-1941. The authorized outlet for German-language Communist publications.

Franz F. Feigl. ca. 1944.

Philip Feldheim. 1943?-1965. Specialized in Jewish books and was for a time United States representative of the Schocken Publishing House, Tel-Aviv.

Theo Feldman. 1938-1957.

Peter Thomas Fisher. 1939-1945? Fisher was born and educated in Vienna where his father, Oskar Fischer, was a well-known bookseller. The younger Fisher (he anglicized the name) started a bookselling service of his own in this country ca. 1939. In 1958 he joined the New York Graphic Society as sales and promotion manager, and in 1963 was made manager of the Harcourt, Brace & World bookstore in New York.

German American. May, 1941-1945? This radical German-language newspaper distributed its own publications and those of El Libro Libre (Mexico City).

Fred S. Gottschalk. ca. 1936. Advertised in the *Aufbau*—modern books in English, French, and German as well as a lending library service.

Helen Gottschalk. 1941-1945?

Felix Kauffmann. 1939-1945? [d. 1953]. Former owner of the Frankfurt publishing firm of I. Kauffmann and of the Druckerei Lehrberger & Co. in Rödelheim. He was professionally active in New York both as printer and bookseller (specializing in Judaica).

Kerekes Bookstore. 1933-1943.

Andrew Kertesz. 1934-1938? A specialist in anti-Fascist literature. He was the representative of the Münzenberg group of German-language publishers operating in Paris (Éditions du Carrefour and in 1938 Éditions Sebastian Brant) and Basel (Universumbücherei).

H. Felix Kraus. 1945-1948? In 1946, made United States agent for the Büchergilde Gutenberg and other Swiss firms.

Friedrich Krause. 1938-1952. Proprietor of the Zentrale freier deutschen Bücher and American agent for Oprecht and Europa Verlag, he also distinguished himself as a publisher of Free German books.

Gregory Lounz. 1942-

Moderne Deutsche Buchhandlung. 1932-1969. The leading German Socialist bookstore in New York, Herman Kormis, owner.

Leo Mohl, Colorado Springs. 1942-1964? Mohl was formerly associated with Hugo Heller of Vienna.

Oscar Neuer. 1943-1950.

Walter Perl. 1941-1950? His bookshop went under the name of Academic Book Service.

Paul S. Rapaport, Cincinnati. 1942-1945? In 1942 Rapaport represented *Austrian Labor*

Information in Cincinnati. As of 1945, he was advertising in the Austro-American press as an agent for periodical subscriptions.

Alfred Rose, Kew Gardens, New York. 1941-1950?

K. N. Rosen. ca. 1942.

Mary S. Rosenberg. 1939-   . Publisher and bookseller, her firm now deals in both German and French periodicals and books, new and antiquarian.

Schoenhof's Foreign Books, Inc., Cambridge, Mass. ?-   . This long-established firm, previously known as the Schoenhof Book Company, was managed by Paul Mueller, former owner of W. Mueller, Vienna, from December, 1941 to his death sometime in 1965. The firm was purchased in January, 1945 by French & European Publications, Inc. (I. Molho and V. Crespin) of New York City who, in 1940, founded the Free French publishing house, Editions de la Maison Française, Inc.

Seven Seas Bookshop. 1944-1946. The proprietor of this book (and stamp) store was Wieland Herzfelde, guiding spirit behind the Aurora Verlag, New York, and former owner of the Malik Verlag and Buchhandlung in Berlin.

Transbooks Company, Inc. 1946-1950? Transbooks was organized in 1946 by Eric Kaufmann (formerly with Karl Block, Berlin) and Frederick Sussman (formerly with the Kiepenheuer Verlag and after 1933 with Querido). The firm was the American agency for the revived Querido Verlag in Amsterdam after the war.

Frederick Ungar. 1942-

Van Riemsdyck's Book Service. 1934-1952? A specialist in Dutch literature, Van Riemsdyck was one of the first commercial distributors of Free German books in New York, advertising occasionally in the *Neue Volks-Zeitung*.

Volksbuchhandlung Verbrannter Bücher. 1935. No such bookstore actually existed in New York. It was most probably a name invented for propaganda purposes, appearing only once in the German-American press—as the sponsor of a Hanns Eisler evening in 1935. See *Der Arbeiter*, March 21, 1935.

Williams Book Store, Boston, Mass. 1941-1945? The German and European section of this established bookstore was built up in 1941 by Paul Mueller, later the manager of Schoenhof's Foreign Books. In 1943 another émigré was in charge, Willy Pollack, a former Berlin art and book dealer (Reuss und Pollack).

Zionist Book Shop. ca. 1942. The owner was Wolf Sales, formerly of Berlin.

Free German and Free Austrian Newspapers and Periodicals in the United States 1933-1950 — A Checklist

The following list includes those German-language newspapers and other publications of a periodic nature which were openly anti-Nazi; staffed wholly or in part by émigré journalists, or devoted to émigré interests. Relevant English-language publications are also listed. If ascertainable, volume numbers will be given along with inclusive dates. Bibliographical documentation (source of information or location of files) has been provided for each publication. Sources most frequently used are: *Union List of Serials* (ULS), Arndt and Olson, *German-American Newspapers and Periodicals 1732–1955*, and A. C. Breycha-Vauthier, *Die Zeitschriften der österreichischen Emigration 1934–1946*.

General Periodicals in German

[*Berichte*]. Nos. 1–201; 1933–1946. New York. irregular.

Economic and financial analyses supplied on a subscription basis in both English and German editions by the economist Gustav Stolper.

Source: Toni Stolper, *Ein Leben in Brennpunkten unsere Zeit* (Tübingen, 1960), p.352.

Blätter der Dritten Front; Briefe an die Freunde in Deutschland. 1947–1950. Forest Hills, New York. irregular.

A circular letter (Rundbrief) dealing with the political situation in Germany distributed by Karl O. Paetel to his friends in Germany. Total circulation never amounted to more than 200 copies.

Source: Letter from Paetel dated Dec. 29, 1963.

Buchklub in Amerika Magazin. May, 1946. New York. monthly.

The short-lived house organ of the German book club created by Ernst Willard of the Willard Publishing Company.

Source: Austro-American Tribune, May, 1946.

Deutsche Gegenwart. Jahrgang I–II; 1947–1948. Forest Hills, New York. monthly.

A journal on current events edited and published by Karl O. Paetel. Its purpose was to report the real situation in Germany to American readers.

Source: Arndt and Olson.

Welt-Spiegel. November 1946–1954? New York. monthly.

Title varies: November 1946–August 1947, *Social Scientific Society Gesellig-Wissenschaftlicher Verein Monthly Bulletin;* September 1947–1954? *Welt-Spiegel: Monatsschrift fuer Literatur, Kunst, Musik, Theater, Film, Wissenschaft, Politik und Wirtschaft.* The Social Scientific Society was founded in 1870 by Carl Schurz and Dr. Abraham Jacobi. During the thirties and early forties it suffered a rapid decline in membership. The appointment, in 1946, of the Austrian émigré Peter M. Lindt as both president of the society and editor of the *Welt-Spiegel* gave new life to the venerable organization.

Source: Arndt and Olson.

[*Wirtschaftsanalyse; Korrespondenz*]. 1937–1940? New York. irregular.

Economic and financial analyses (similar to Gustav Stolper's *Berichte*) distributed by Felix Pinner.

Source: Aufbau (N.Y.), Sept. 15, 1939, p.17.

[Title not known]. February–March, 1945? Fort Ontario, New York. irregular.

A periodical issued by internees at Fort Ontario. In 1944, 982 refugees were admitted to the United States outside of the regular immigration procedure and placed in an emergency refugee shelter at Fort Ontario near Oswego, New York, where they remained until 1946. The group consisted of many nationalities but primarily of Yugoslavs and Austrians. A camp periodical was produced under the editorship of Bernard Guillemin, formerly of Berlin. The first hektographed issue (in German) was about eighty pages in length. A second issue printed in Serbo-Croatian and devoted to the problems of Yugoslavia was also offered for sale to the American public.

Source: Aufbau (N.Y.), Feb. 23, 1945, p.6.

General Periodicals in English

Center of Information Pro Deo. *Correspondence.* Jan. 15, 1942–1943? New York. irregular.

Source: ULS.

Center of Information Pro Deo. *Forum.* April–June, 1943? New York. monthly.

A journal of Catholic opinion. The *Forum* of the CIP (as it was called in the émigré press) published a number of speeches and letters on the German question. Contributors included Friedrich Wilhelm Foerster, Emil Ludwig, and Goetz Briefs. The CIP was actually a Catholic information center that had its roots in the International Press Congress held at Cologne in 1928. Under the direction of Hein Hoeben (murdered by the Nazis according to the *Aufbau* report), a Catholic press agency existed in Germany until 1936. In that year it was moved to Brussels and Breda (Belgium), in 1940 to Lisbon and then to New York.

Sources: ULS; *Aufbau* (N.Y.), March 19, 1943, p.15.

Council for a Democratic Germany. *Bulletin.* V.1, nos. 1–5; Sept., 1944–May, 1945. New York. irregular.

Organ of the Council which was the last attempt to form a Free German front in the United States.

Source: ULS.

Decision; a Review of Free Culture. V.1–3, no. 1/2; Jan., 1941–Jan./Feb., 1942. New York. quarterly.

An international literary review edited by Klaus Mann.

Source: ULS.

European Reports. Nos. 1–2; 1945. Elmhurst, N. Y. irregular.

A bulletin of current events edited and published by Joachim Joesten. Superseded by *New Germany Reports.*

Source: ULS.

German Book News; Periodical Reports on German Publishing. May, 1947–1949? New York. monthly.

A news service on postwar German publishing compiled by Joesten and aimed primarily at public and college libraries.

Source: ULS.

International Science. V.1, no. 1; May, 1941. New York.

An English-language journal published by the New World Club. Only one issue appeared.

Source: ULS.

Mesa. Nos.1–4; Autumn, 1945–Autumn, 1955. Aurora, N. Y.; Lexington, Ky. irregular.

A finely printed literary periodical. Published by Herbert Steiner and printed by Victor Hammer, *Mesa* was a lineal descendant of Steiner's famous literary periodical of the thirties, *Corona.* The five published numbers contain contributions in several languages.

Source: ULS.

The Network; Information Bulletin on European Stalinism. V.1–3, no. 3; Jan., 1944–Dec., 1945. New York. monthly.

A strongly anti-Communist news and "scandal sheet" which during this period dealt mainly with former German Communists in the United States. Edited by Ruth Fischer, a former leader of the KPD. Superseded by *Russian State Party Newsletter on Contemporary Communism.* New York. March, 1946–March, 1947.

Source: ULS.

New Germany Reports. Nos.1–15? 1947–1950? Elmhurst, N. Y. irregular.

A survey of events in postwar Germany edited and published by Joachim Joesten. It supersedes *European Reports.*

Source: ULS.

News Background, Inc. Confidential Reports. 1943–1944? New York. irregular.

A numbered pamphlet series on current events published by Joachim Joesten.

Source: ULS.

News Background Reports. 1941–1945? New York. irregular.

A numbered pamphlet series on current events which was published by Kurt D. Singer.

Source: ULS.

TNT. 1942? New York. monthly?

A periodical that wanted to combine the distinctive features of *Simplizissimus, Punch,* and *La Vie Parisienne*. The art director was Erich Godal. His collaborators included E. Gondör, a former artist for the Ullstein publishing empire; Ludwig Wronkow, the *Aufbau* staff cartoonist, and many American artists.

Source: Aufbau (N.Y.), Jan. 24, 1941, p.6.

Zig Zag. March, 1946–1947? New York. monthly?

A periodical devoted to aspects of New York life. It was started by members of the *Aufbau* circle (including Hans Hacker, Gerda Avon, Therese Pol, and Ruth Karpf).

Source: Aufbau (N.Y.), Feb. 28, 1947, p.11.

The German-Jewish Press

Aufbau. Jahrgang 1– , Dec. 1, 1934–. New York. weekly.

A newspaper published in German and English in the interests of the German-Jewish community, primarily the post–1933 immigrants. It began as the *Nachrichtenblatt* of the German-Jewish Club, Inc. (later known as the New World Club) and soon developed into the leading newspaper of the German-Jewish emigration. Rudolf Brandl was editor from 1937 to 1939 but the paper's great expansion and success began with the appointment of Manfred George to that post in 1939. In 1941 the *Aufbau* absorbed the California German-language paper, *Neue Welt*.

Source: Arndt and Olson.

Aufbau Almanach. 1941. New York. annual.

A collection of information and articles for the benefit of the new immigrants. Apparently only one volume was published. Edited by M. Citron and subtitled: *The Immigrant's Handbook*.

Source: Arndt and Olson.

Congregation Habonim, Inc. *Bulletin*. 1940– . New York.

Bulletin of the largest post-1933 German-Jewish congregation in America. It was first published entirely in German; later articles in English were added. Since 1963 published entirely in English.

Source: ULS.

The Cosmopolitan News. ca. 1939. Baltimore, Md. monthly.

Mitteilungsblatt of the Phönix Club and official organ of the New Hebrew Cosmopolitan Society, the *Cosmopolitan News* was a typewritten newsletter containing mostly club news.

Source: Aufbau (N.Y.), Oct. 1, 1939, p.12.

Deutsch-Israelitische Kultusgemeinde. *Bulletin*. 1927–1933? New York. irregular.

Organ of the Deutsch-Israelitische Kultusgemeinde, New York. The congregation was established in the late 1920s and after 1927 was led by Rabbi Max Malina. It was the first German-Jewish community founded in the United States after World War I. Most of its membership came from post-1919 immigrants; it was not well supported by the older German Jews.

Source: Jüdisches Familienblatt, Jan. 15, 1939.

Jewish Way. V.1– , Feb. 15, 1939– . New York. monthly.

A newspaper devoted to the interest of the German Jews published in English and German. From Sept. 1940 through 1948 published semi-monthly. Title varies: Feb.,

1939–Feb., 1940, *Our Way in America;* March–May, 1940 and Jan. 16–May 3, 1942, *Way in America;* July, 1940–Dec., 1941, *Way in America and Neues jüdisches Gemeindeblatt.* Edited at various times by Julius Kollensher, Adolph Weiss, Aaron J. Weiss, Julius Becker, Max Oppenheimer, and Alice Oppenheimer.
Source: Arndt and Olson.

Jüdischer Zeitgeist. 1930–1937. New York. monthly.
A newspaper devoted to the interests of the German-Jewish community published and edited by Max Malina. A precursor of the *Jüdisches Familienblatt.* Rabbi Malina, in Oct. of 1931, was also made associate editor of the *Jewish Chronicle* (Bronx, N.Y.).
Source: Jüdisches Familienblatt, Sept. 7, 1939.

Jüdisches Familienblatt. Sept., 1937–Feb., 1939. New York. monthly.
Successor to the *Jüdischer Zeitgeist.* Edited and published by Rabbi Malina (associate editor was Willy Aron). The paper claimed to be "an organ for all Jews, one that fights against the unfortunate passion for assimilation" (Sept. 1, 1937, p.4).
Source: New York Public Library.

Jüdisches Gemeindeblatt für den Zusammenschluss zur Einheitsgemeinde. Nov., 1938–Sept., 1939. New York. monthly.
Organ of the Synagogengemeinde Washington Heights, New York. Superseded by the *Neues jüdisches* [sic] *Gemeindeblatt.*
Source: ULS.

Neue Welt. 1933–1941. Los Angeles. monthly.
Bulletin of the Jewish Club of Los Angeles. Edited by Leopold Jessner. In 1941 merged with the *Aufbau* and thereafter appeared as a special supplement called the *Westküste.*
Source: Aufbau (N.Y.), Oct. 1, 1939, p.12.

Neues jüdisches [sic] *Gemeindeblatt.* Oct., 1939–June, 1940. New York. monthly.
A community newspaper that merged with the *Jewish Way* in July, 1940.
Source: Jewish Way, July 24, 1940; copy in New York Public Library.

New Currents; a Jewish Monthly. V.1–3, no.3; March, 1943–March, 1945. New York. monthly.
A journal on Jewish affairs published by the American Committee of Jewish Writers, Artists, and Scientists, Inc. The sponsoring committee included Albert Einstein and Sholem Asch. The advisory board consisted of Waldo Frank, Howard Fast, Lion Feuchtwanger, Leo Huberman, and Albert Maltz. Many German-Jewish émigrés were contributors. No issues were published Oct.–Dec., 1943.
Source: ULS.

The Searchlight. 1936. New York. bi-weekly.
A journal on the Jewish question edited by the German-American writer Eugene F. Grigat. *The Searchlight* lasted for only a few numbers; it was probably supported by the American Jewish Congress which was behind some of Grigat's other publications.
Source: Neue Volks-Zeitung, May 15, 1936, p.10.

The Austrian Émigré Press

Austria. Jahrgang 1, nos.1–7; April–Dec., 1941. New York. monthly.
A Roman Catholic journal printed largely in English and published by the Aus-

trian-American League. No issues were published in Aug. and Sept., 1941. Supersedes the League's *Mitteilungen.*
Source: Arndt and Olson.

Austria. 1944-1952? New York. monthly.
A paper of conservative democratic opinion at one time claiming to be the organ of the Austrian colony in America. In 1944 it was presented as the organ of the Christliche-sozialistische Partei of Hans Rott. The editor was Octave Otto Günther (who also edited a periodical of the same name from New York during 1909-1914). After 1945 editions of *Austria* were published in New York, Graz, and Vienna.
Source: Arndt and Olson.

Austrian Bulletin in the United States. Nos.1-4; May-Sept., 1941. Tenafly, N. J. irregular.
A mimeographed journal on Austrian affairs published by the Austro-American Center. The editor was E. K. Winter.
Sources: ULS; Breycha-Vauthier.

Austrian Democratic Review. June, 1941-Jan., 1944. New York. monthly.
A newspaper for Austrian émigrés sponsored by Austrian Action (chairman, Ferdinand Czernin). Title varies: June, 1941-Jan., 1942, *Austrian Action;* Feb., 1942, *Mitteilungsblatt der Austrian Action: Free Austrian Movement;* March, 1942-May, 1943, *Oesterreichische Rundschau.*
Source: Arndt and Olson.

Austrian Jewish Representative Committee Affiliated with the World Jewish Congress. *Bulletin.* 1944-1947. New York. monthly?
Source: Jacob Robinson and Philip Friedman, *Guide to Jewish History under Nazi Impact* (New York: YIVO Institute for Jewish Research, 1960), p.303.

Austrian Labor Information. Nos. 1-37; April 20, 1942-May 1, 1945. New York. monthly.
The German-language organ of the Austrian Labor Committee (Austrian Social Democrats in exile). Edited by Otto Leichter. Beginning with the May 1, 1944 issue, a new supplement was added—*Freie Tribuene des internationalen Sozialismus.* The editor, Wilhelm Ellenbogen, presided over a permanent staff of contributors that included Hugo Fernandez Artucio, Desider Benau, Theodor Dan, Paul Hertz, Paul Keri, and Siegfried Taub. This was the only attempt during the emigration (after 1941) at a German-language international Socialist periodical of any pretensions.
Source: Arndt and Olson.

Austrian Labor News. Nos.1-40; Feb., 1942-Dec. 1, 1945. New York. monthly.
An English-language journal published by the Austrian Labor Committee, in large part a translation of *Austrian Labor Information.*
Source: ULS.

Austrian Republic. V.1-3, no.3; 1946-April, 1948. New York. monthly.
The organ of the Friends of Austrian Labor (formerly American Friends of Austrian Labor), Adolf Sturmthal, chairman.
Source: ULS.

Austro-American Tribune, see *Forum and Tribune.*

Donau Echo. 1942-1943? Toronto, Canada. monthly?
Organ of the monarchist Free Austrian Movement, the *Donau Echo* had moved to

Canada from Brussels. The editor was Wilhelm Wunsch and the paper was distributed in the United States.
Source: Breycha-Vauthier.

Forum and Tribune. V.1–7, no.10; April 25, 1942–July, 1949, New York. monthly.
A newspaper for Austrians in America. Title varies: April 25, 1942–June 15, 1943, *Freiheit fuer Oesterreich;* July, 1943–Aug. 1, 1948, *Austro-American Tribune.* Published by the Assembly for a Democratic Austrian Republic until July, 1944; afterward by the Austro-American Tribune, Inc. Edited by William Green and Alfred Hornik.
Source: Arndt and Olson.

Frei-Österreich. 1944–1945? New York. monthly?
Mitteilungen of the Free Austrian Movement (monarchist).
Source: Breycha-Vauthier.

Freie österreichische Jugend. Jahrgang 1–2, no.12; Dec., 1941–Jan., 1943. New York. monthly.
A newspaper for young people. Published by Austrian Action, Inc. in Dec., 1941; afterward by the Free Austrian Youth Committee. Superseded by *Young Austro-American.*
Source: Arndt and Olson.

Freiheit fuer Oesterreich, see *Forum and Tribune.*

Liberation. V.1–3, no.9; June, 1941–Feb., 1944. Ottawa, Canada; New York. monthly.
A Free Austrian newspaper originally devoted to the monarchist cause. Title varies: June, 1941–June, 1943, *Voice of Austria.* Beginning with the April, 1943 issue the newspaper was published in New York. In July, 1943, it changed its name to *Liberation* although continuing the same volume numbering and fulfilling subscriptions placed earlier for the *Voice.* The new owner was Antoine Gazda, an American industrialist in Rhode Island. The paper was no longer monarchist in tone as Otto of Habsburg had withdrawn his financial support which had influenced the views of the paper when it was published in Canada under the editorship of Franz Klein.
Sources: Arndt and Olson; *Aufbau* (N.Y.), March 15, 1944, p.9.

News of Austria. 1941–1942? Washington, D.C. monthly.
Organ of the Free Austrian Council; a mimeographed paper.
Source: Breycha-Vauthier.

Oesterreichische Rundschau, see *Austrian Democratic Review.*

Young Austro-American. March, 1943–1955? New York. monthly.
A newspaper for young people. Title varies: March, 1943–June, 1943, *Jugend im Kampf.* Published by the Free Austrian Youth Council through June, 1943, then by the Austro-American Youth Council. It was issued as a supplement to the *Austro-American Tribune.*
Source: Arndt and Olson.

The Free German Socialist Press

Der Anti-Faschist. Jan., 1938–Nov., 1939? New York. monthly.
An anti-Nazi publication aimed at the non-Communist German-American worker. It was sponsored by the Club Deutscher Antifaschisten (who also supported the journal *Gegen den Strom),* a group of dissident members of the Deutscher Arbeiter Klub who

had left that Communist-controlled organization. The editor, as noted in the Feb., 1938, issue, was Karl Maison.
Source: The author's collection.

Arbeiterwohlfahrt USA. *Bulletin.* 1945–1946? New York. irregular?
Organ of the Arbeiterwohlfahrt USA, a German workers' aid organization in America. One of the members of the last elected SPD executive committee was Marie Juchacz, best known as the founder of the German Arbeiterwohlfahrt. Living in Paris, she was unable to take part in exile political activities until the Sopade was relocated there in 1938. At that time she joined with Paul Hertz in pressing for a unification, a concentration of all German Socialists (including the Austrians and the New Beginners). The SPD refused to abandon its "mandate" from the German people and declined to form any new organization or even to share its trusteeship with any other group. The friction and acrimony generated during these last Parisian days of 1938–1940 lasted until the end of the war. When Marie Juchacz arrived in New York she was, because of her past association with the New Beginners, refused any opportunity to work with the German Labor Delegation, although she would gladly have done so. Frau Juchacz and some friends then formed their own small association. At the end of the war she set up a new welfare operation designed to supply food and clothing to needy workers in Germany. At this point, the German Labor Delegation felt obliged to welcome back the new Arbeiterwohlfahrt USA into the SPD fold. Besides the *Bulletin,* the Arbeiterwohlfahrt USA published a *Rundbrief* (which may have been merely a German-language version of the former).
Sources: Jahrbuch der Sozialdemokratische Partei Deutschlands (Hanover: Vorstand der SPD, 1947), p.124–25; Fritzmichael Roehl, *Marie Juchacz und die Arbeiterwohlfahrt* (Hanover: Dietz, 1961), p.181 et passim; Edinger, *German Exile Politics,* p.216.

Deutschamerikanische Volks-Kalender. 1938–1939. New York. annual.
A determinedly anti-Nazi yearbook or almanac (each volume ca. 200p.) with many articles written by émigrés. Published by the Arbeiter Kranken- und Sterbekasse.
Source: Deutsches Volksecho, Aug. 7, 1937; Sept. 11, 1937; Dec. 24, 1938.

Gegen den Strom. Jahrgang 1–2, no.12; March, 1938–Nov., 1939. New York. irregular.
An independent German-American Socialist periodical, critical of both the Communists and the Social Democrats. The editor and publisher was Robert Bek-Gran, a former functionary of the CPA German Section. The venture was supported primarily by the Club Deutscher Antifaschisten. *Gegen den Strom* was not the organ of the Deutsch-Amerikanischer Kulturverband as Arndt and Olson (p.365) state, but on the contrary, a bitter foe of that organization.
Source: Arndt and Olson.

I.B. Berichte. 1939–1940. London, Oslo, New York. irregular.
Issued by the New Beginners (sometimes referred to as their *Inlands-Berichte).*
Sources: Kurt Klein, "Der sozialistische Widerstand gegen das Dritte Reich dargestellt an der Gruppe 'Neu Beginnen' " (unpublished Ph.D. dissertation, Univ. of Marburg, 1957); Jürgen Reimer, "Quellen und Materialen zur politischen Emigration und zum innerdeutschen Widerstand gegen das Dritte Reich," *Internationale wissenschaftliche Korrespondenz zur Geschichte der deutschen Arbeiterbewegung,* 5:18 (Dec., 1967); Sternfeld, *Deutsche Exil-Literatur.*

In Re: Germany. V. 1–4, no.2/3; Feb., 1941–March, 1944. New York. monthly.
A critical bibliography of books and magazine articles on Germany. Published by the Research and Information Service of the American Friends of German Freedom. This

organization was the creation of Karl Frank (using the alias Paul Hagen), the leader of the New Beginners in the United States.
Source: ULS.

Inside Germany Reports. Nos.1–26; April 15, 1939–May, 1944. New York. irregular.
A newsletter reporting on conditions within Germany. Published by the American Friends of German Freedom.
Source: ULS.

Kampfsignal. Jahrgang 1–3, no.6; Dec. 3, 1932–Nov. 15, 1934. New York. irregular.
A radical Socialist paper. Published by the Kampfsignal Publishing Association: Hermann Gund, chairman; August Burkhardt, treasurer; Selmar Schocken, secretary. Schocken, who had previously been labor editor of the *New Yorker Volkszeitung,* was editor of the *Kampfsignal* until May, 1933. Gund and Burkhardt were top officials of the Amalgamated Food Workers, which, with the Arbeiter Kranken- und Sterbekasse, was one of the chief financial supports of the paper.
Source: Arndt and Olson.

Letters on German Labor. Nos.1–2; July 15–Sept. 9, 1943. New York. irregular.
A publication of the German Labor Delegation in the United States.
Source: ULS.

Neue Volks-Zeitung. Jahrgang 1–18, no.32; Dec. 17, 1932–Aug. 6, 1949. New York. weekly.
A conservative Social Democratic newspaper in the German language (successor to the *New Yorker Volkszeitung*). It was consistently anti-Nazi and anti-Communist. After Gerhard Seger was made editor in May, 1936, the paper became the American voice of the SPD in exile.
Source: Arndt and Olson.

New Essays. V.1–6, no.4; Oct., 1934–Winter, 1943. Chicago: New York. monthly; quarterly.
Organ of the Council Communists. Title varies: Oct., 1934–Dec., 1937, *International Council Correspondence* (Chicago); Feb., 1938–Winter, 1942, *Living Marxism* (New York). The *International Council Correspondence* was a mimeographed monthly; its successors were printed and appeared quarterly. The Council Communists "considered themselves the only true Marxists and fought the Communist Party, Trotskyists, and Socialists alike. Its chief editor was Paul Mattick, and its adherents came mainly from among German refugees." The émigré Karl Korsch, a highly regarded Marxist theorist, was the most important contributor to this journal.
Source: Walter Goldwater, *Radical Periodicals in America 1890–1950* (New Haven: Yale Univ. Library, 1964), p.17.

Sänger Zeitung. 1925–1944? Chicago; New York. irregular.
Organ of the Arbeiter Sänger von Amerika. This was not, of course, an émigré newspaper. However, the year 1942 is of special interest in the present context, for it was during these twelve months that the émigré journalist Walther Victor reigned as editor of the *Sänger Zeitung.* It was in that year, too, that the place of publication shifted to New York. Victor shook up the staid German-American organization considerably with his militant radicalism and emphasis on the class struggle. He wrote in the Sept., 1942, issue that during the preceding eight months he and his wife had written "not less than thirty-three articles not counting any short pieces and notices." The proletarian singers accepted the class struggle placidly but revolted when Victor denigrated the musical abilities of one of their choir directors, imputing to him Nazi

sympathies as well. The swell of opposition forced Victor to resign as editor. In this case, the symbiotic relationship of émigré leadership and German-American readership was not a success.
Source: Arndt and Olson.

Sozialistische Informationsbriefe. 1939. New York. irregular.
The German-language bulletin of the New Beginners. The last two issues were published by Karl Frank in the United States (previous issues were published in Paris and London).
Source: Kurt Kleim, "Der sozialistische Widerstand gegen das Dritte Reich dargestellt an der Gruppe 'Neu Beginnen,' " p.256.

Unser Wort. Oct., 1940–1941? New York. monthly.
This is a continuation of the Trotskyite monthly newspaper of the same name published in Paris during the thirties. The New York edition continued the old numbering side by side with the new; e.g., the Dec., 1940 issue is numbered Nr.2 (101). The American editor was Dale Edwards.
Source: The author's collection.

The German-American Communist Press

Der Arbeiter. Jahrgang 1–11, no.7; Sept. 15, 1927–Feb. 13, 1937. New York. weekly.
The German-language newspaper of the American Communist Party. Title varies: Sept. 15–Dec. 11, 1927, *Mitteilungsblatt der deutschen Sprachfraktion, German Language Bureau;* Jan.–June 15, 1928, *Kommunistisches Mitteilungsblatt.* At first a semi-monthly (irregular) publication, it began to appear weekly after Jan., 1930. Published by the Arbeiter Publishing Co. Superseded by the *Deutsches Volksecho.*
Source: Arndt and Olson.

Deutsch-Amerikanischen Klubs U.S.A. *Mitteilungsblatt.* May, 1934–1938? New York. irregular.
Organ of the Föderation der Deutsch-Amerikanischen Klubs U.S.A., German-American workers' clubs under the control of the CPA. Title varies: May, 1934–April, 1935, Deutsche Arbeiter-Klubs. *Mitteilungsblatt;* May, 1935–March, 1937, Deutsch-Amerikanische Arbeiter-Klubs. *Mitteilungsblatt;* May, 1935–Jan., 1937, published as a supplement to *Der Arbeiter.* The volume and issue numbering is very confused.
Source: The author's collection.

Der Deutsch-Amerikanische Kulturverband. *Mitteilungsblatt.* 1935–1936? New York. irregular.
Official bulletin of the Deutsch-Amerikanische Kulturverband.
Source: Der Arbeiter, Oct. 6, 1935, p.3.

Der Deutsche-Amerikanische Kulturverband [for the Eastern District]. *Mitteilungsblatt.* Nov. 1939–1940? New York; Philadelphia. irregular.
Bulletin of the DAKV eastern district. Because the DAKV organized on the basis of regional branches, it is possible that other local bulletins were distributed.
Source: Volksfront (Chicago), Nov. 18, 1938.

Deutsche Zentralbücherei. [*Mitteilungsblatt*]. Feb., 1936? New York.
The proposed bulletin of the Buchgemeinschaft der deutschen Antifaschisten. When

on Sept. 15, 1935, *Der Arbeiter* announced the founding of a German Communist book club, it promised that from Feb. 1, 1936, a bi-monthly bulletin would be distributed free to members. In all probability this undertaking was never carried out, for in the March 21, 1936 issue of *Der Arbeiter* a column appeared with the title – "Mitteilungen der Deutschen Zentralbücherei."
Source: Der Arbeiter, Sept. 15, 1935.

Deutsches Volksecho. Jahrgang 1–3, no.37; Feb. 20, 1937–Sept. 16, 1939. New York. weekly.

The official German-language newspaper of the Communist Party in continuation of *Der Arbeiter;* the *Deutsches Volksecho* with its tabloid format was a more popularly written publication. Stefan Heym was editor for the duration of the paper's existence. The issues of Jan. 1 and Jan. 8, 1938, were titled: *Deutsches Volksecho und Deutsch-Kanadische Volkszeitung.* With the assistance of the Deutsch-Kanadischer Volksbund of Toronto, a special page was begun under the rubric, "Deutsch-Kanadischen Nachrichten." Although the subtitle soon disappeared from the masthead, Canadian news continued to be printed intermittently. There was also a German-language paper published by the Canadian Communist Party, *Die Volksstimme* (Toronto), that flourished ca. 1944 and was probably distributed in the United States. The *Volksecho* merged with the *Volksfront* (Chicago) in Oct., 1939.
Source: Arndt and Olson.

Die Einheitsfront. Jahrgang 1, no.1; Aug., 1934. New York.

The stillborn bulletin of Antifaschistische Aktion, a national federation of anti-Nazi German-American labor groups that soon fell under Communist control. The editor for this one issue was Otto Durick.
Source: Arndt and Olson.

The German American. V.1; May, 1942– New York. monthly.

A bilingual newspaper aimed at the German-American worker which for a number of years was under Communist influence. From May 1, 1946, through 1949 it was published twice a month. Originally sponsored by the German American Emergency Conference (founded by Kurt Rosenfeld), the *German American* was vehemently anti-Nazi, but it was also dominated by the Communist Party and thus was a successor to the *Arbeiter*, the *Deutsches Volksecho*, the *Volksfront*, and *Unsere Zeit*. Its aboveboard editors were two German-American labor leaders: Rudolf Kohler and Gustav Faber. Behind the scenes the real direction of the paper lay in the hands of émigré Communists such as Gerhard Eisler, Albert Norden, and Albert Schreiner.
Source: Arndt and Olson.

German American Emergency Conference. *Bulletin.* March–April, 1942. New York. monthly.

The predecessor of the *German American.*
Source: Unsere Zeit, Sept., 1942.

Germany Today. V. 1–2, no.11; June 21, 1945– Dec. 7, 1946. New York. semi-monthly.

An English-language newsletter on Germany. Published by the German American Inc., it contained mostly propaganda for the Communist Free Germany movement. Editors: June 21, 1945–Sept. 7, 1946, Albert Norden; Sept. 21–Dec. 7, 1946, Alfred Zahn. After Dec. 7, 1946, "Germany Today" continued to appear as a section of the parent *German American.*
Source: ULS.

Das neue Leben. Nos.1–3; June–Aug., 1939. New York. monthly.

A German-American newspaper for young people sponsored by the CPA (joined by the Naturfreunde and various sports clubs) and published by the German Youth Association. The first issue was printed, the last two mimeographed reportedly in editions of 1000 copies each *(Volksfront,* Sept. 9, 1939). Superseded by *Youth Outlook.*
Source: The author's collection.

Schiffahrt. March 1937–July 1939? New York. irregular.
A clandestine news bulletin aimed at members of the German seamen's trade union. Subtitled in 1937: *Organ des Gesamtverbandes der Arbeitnehmer der öffentlichen Betriebe-Sektion, Schiffahrt und verwandte Betriebe.* The dateline in 1937 reads: Hamburg, New York, Bremen. The publication was anti-Nazi and pro-Russian, probably Communist in origin. Printed on very thin paper, it could be easily smuggled aboard ship. The Feb., 1938 issue gives as its editorial address a post office box in New York City. The newspaper was for sale at most American harbors. Readers were asked: "At least once a month to write to the editor about everything that has happened to them on board and about everything discussed by their comrades at ship's mess" *(Schiffahrt,* Feb., 1938).
Source: Arndt and Olson.

Die Stimme. June–August, 1933? New York. irregular.
Organ of the Arbeitsgemeinschaft proletärischer Freidenker. This was a Communist-sponsored rival to the *Freidenker* (Milwaukee), the journal of the Free Thought League of North America.
Source: Der Arbeiter, June 13, 1933.

Unsere Zeit. V. 1–3, no.9; Jan., 1940–Sept., 1942. New York. monthly.
Bulletin of the Federation of German American Clubs, U.S.A. This is the successor, after some lapse of time, to the *Mitteilungsblatt* of the Deutsch-Amerikanische Klubs, U.S.A. The readers of *Unsere Zeit* were urged to buy the *German American,* and after Sept., 1942, subscriptions to *Unsere Zeit* were completed by the latter paper.
Source: The author's collection.

Victory Committee of German American Trade Unionists. *Action Bulletin.* 1945. New York. irregular.
A bulletin of news of interest to the German-American worker. The Victory Committee was a Communist front organization that drew its members from the German-language unions in New York City and vicinity. The Committee also sponsored a regular feature page in the *German American* called "The Union Spotlight."
Source: German American, July 1, 1945.

Volksfront. V. 1–6, no.52; Jan., 1934–Dec. 30, 1939. Chicago. weekly.
A German-language anti-Nazi newspaper, actually the Midwestern voice of the Communist Party of America. Edited jointly by Erich von Schroetter and the émigré journalist "Martin Hall." Beginning in 1937 the *Volksfront* appropriated for itself the title of official organ of the Deutsch-Amerikanischer Kulturverband. Published by the Cultural Front Press Association. It absorbed the *Deutsches Volksecho* on Oct. 20, 1939.
Source: Arndt and Olson.

Youth Outlook. Jahrgang 1, nos. 1–2? Nov.–Dec., 1939? New York. monthly.
A newspaper for young people written in German and English. It superseded *Das neue Leben* which had been abruptly terminated following the Nazi-Soviet Pact in Aug., 1939. *Youth Outlook* was predictably anti-British, anti-French, and anti-war. It was published by the German-American Youth Federation, an affiliate of the Deutsch-Amerikanischer Kulturverband.
Source: The author's collection.

Free German Books and Pamphlets Published in the United States 1933–1954 — A Checklist

It has proven impossible to locate and examine all the publications listed below so that, in place of a full-fledged bibliography, a checklist must for the moment suffice. The source of my information concerning any hitherto unrecorded title or edition is included when such publications have not been available for inspection (although obviously this is no clear proof of existence). Data on suppositious publications and titles announced but never published are also included. With few exceptions only German-language and bilingual books and pamphlets are listed, arranged first by publisher and then alphabetically by author.

Aldus Buch Compagnie, *see* Verlag der Aldus Buch Compagnie.

Alliance Book Corp. New York.

> Alliance Book Club. *Deutsche Bücher*. 1938.
>> A prospectus.

> Alliance Book Corp. *Freie deutsche Literatur*. 1938.
>> Publisher's announcement.

Alliance Book Corp. and Longmans Green & Co. New York, Toronto.
> At least thirteen Alliance titles bear this joint imprint. All were printed in Europe except where otherwise indicated.

> Alexander, Edgar. *Deutsches Brevier*. 1938. 263p.

> Gumpert, Martin. *Dunant: Der Roman des Roten Kreuzes*. 1938. 324p.

> Horvath, Ödön von. *Ein Kind unserer Zeit*. 1938. 212p.

> Körmendi, Franz. *Der Irrtum*. 1938. 450p.

> Ludwig, Emil. *Quartett*. 1938. 393p.

> Mann, Heinrich. *Die Vollendung des Königs Henri Quatre*. 1938. 823p.

Mann, Thomas. *Achtung, Europa! Aufsätze zur Zeit.* 1938. 191p.
This first edition was printed in the United States as was the later Stockholm (Bermann-Fischer) edition. See Bürgin, *Das Werk Thomas Mann: Eine Bibliographie*, p.36.

———— *Dieser Friede.* 1938. 28p.
Printed in the United States. The true first edition according to Bürgin (p.36) was the Bermann-Fischer edition published in Stockholm but also printed in the United States.

Silone, Ignazio. *Die Schule der Diktatoren.* 1938. 324p.

Valentin, Veit. *Weltgeschichte.* 2v. 1938.

Zernatto, Guido. *Die Wahrheit über Österreich.* 1938. 330p.

Zweig, Arnold. *Versunkene Tage.* 1938. 222p.

Zweig, Stefan. *Ungeduld des Herzens.* 1939. 443p.

American Association for a Democratic Germany. New York.
The last metamorphosis of Karl Frank's (New Beginners) American organization.

American Association for a Democratic Germany. *Der neue Kampf um die Freiheit: Briefe und Dokumente Berliner Sozialisten* (Schriftenreihe für ein demokratisches Deutschland, No.1). 1946.

———— *Some Recent Information on Anti-Nazi Developments among German Youth.* 1945.

———— *They Fought Hitler First: A Report on the Treatment of German Anti-Nazis in Concentration Camps from 1933–1939.* 1945.
Hagen, Paul [i.e., Karl Frank]. *Erobert, nicht befreit: Das deutsche Volk im ersten Besatzungsjahr* (Schriftenreihe für ein demokratisches Deutschland, No.2. [1946]

———— *Four Horsemen over Germany.* Nov., 1945.

———— *From the Rubble Up.* Dec., 1945.
Memorandum über die Anti-Hagen Kampagne. 1 Feb. 1945.
A mimeographed pamphlet.

American Friends of German Freedom. New York.
Karl Frank's original organization of American sympathizers.

American Friends of German Freedom. *Germany Tomorrow.* 1940.

———— *Norway Does Not Yield.* 1941.

Hagen, Paul [i.e., Karl Frank]. *Deutschland nach Hitler; um die Vollendung der demokratischen Revolution.* 1943. 54*l*.
Mimeographed by Hagen probably for private distribution. Published in English as *Germany after Hitler.* New York: Farrar & Rinehart. [1944]
Zur Abwehr der Angriffe gegen Paul Hagen. 1941.
Pamphlet also published in English as *Replies on the Attacks on Paul Hagen.* 1941.

Antifaschistische Aktion. New York.
An anti-Nazi front organization formed by the German-American Left ca. 1933–34. It soon became dominated by the Communists.

[Seger, Gerhart] *Wer hat das Reichstagsgebäude in Brand gesteckt?* 1933. 4p.
Attributed to Seger by Herman Kormis.

Arbeitsgemeinschaft der fortschrittlichen deutschsprachigen Vereins von Chicago. Chicago.

Arbeitsgemeinschaft der fortschrittlichen deutschsprachigen Vereins von Chicago. *An die Deutschen Amerikas.* [1938]
   Broadsheet in German and English.

Aufbau Verlag. New York.
   The imprint used by the German-Jewish newspaper *Aufbau.*

Aron, Willy. *Assimilation und Nationalismus: Ein Briefwechsel mit Constantine Brunner.* 1935. 4*l.*
   Cover title: " 'Sonderdruck' *Aufbau, New York, 1935.* "

George, Manfred. *Das Wunder Israels. 1949.* 40p.

_____ *Das Wunder Israels.* 1954. 63p.

Aurora Verlag. New York.
   A cooperative publishing house with pronounced left-wing sympathies. It was managed by Wieland Herzfelde and can be considered a continuation of his Malik Verlag. Paul Mueller of Schoenhof's Foreign Books (sole distributor of Aurora publications in the United States) has stated that all Aurora books were issued in editions of 2000 copies. However, the most recent source – Deutsche Akademie der Künste zu Berlin, *Der Malik-Verlag* (1967) – gives varying figures. These appear below:

Aurora Verlag. *Oskar Maria Graf, Unruhe um einen Friedfertigen.* 1947.
   A prospectus for Graf's book containing letters of commendation from Heinrich and Thomas Mann.

Bloch, Ernst. *Freiheit und Ordnung: Abriss der Sozial-Utopien.* [1945] 160p.
   This edition listed in the *Deutsche Bibliographie 1945–50.*

_____ *Freiheit und Ordnung: Abriss der Sozial-Utopien.* 1946. 190p.
   This edition held by the Library of Congress. 3000 copies published.

/Brecht, Bertolt. *Furcht und Elend des Dritten Reiches.* 1945. 112p.
   3000 copies published.

/Bruckner, Ferdinand [i.e., Theodor Tagger]. *Simon Bolivar.* 1945. 158p.
   1600 copies published.

/ Döblin, Alfred. *Sieger und Besiegte: Eine wahre Geschichte.* 1946. 110p.
   4000 copies published.

/ Feuchtwanger, Lion. *Venedig (Texas) und vierzehn andere Erzählungen.* 1946. 175p.
   4000 copies published.

/ Graf, Oskar Maria. *Der Quasterl.* 1945. 81p.
   3000 copies published.

_____ *Unruhe um einem Friedfertigen.* 1947. 474p.

✓*Morgenröte: Ein Lesebuch.* 1947. 351p.
   An anthology "herausgegeben von den Gründern des Aurora Verlages." Introduction by Heinrich Mann. Cloth $3.50. Student ed. $2.50.

Seghers, Anna. *Der Ausflug der toten Mädchen.* 1946. 127p.
   4000 copies published.

Viertel, Berthold. *Der Lebenslauf.* 1946. 111p.
   1500 copies published.

Waldinger, Ernst. *Die kühlen Bauernstuben.* 1946. 111p.
   1500 copies published.

Weiskopf, Franz Carl. *Die Unbesiegbaren: Berichte, Anekdoten, Legenden 1933-1945.* 1945. 47p.
>3000 copies published.

(Aurora Verlag. N.Y.)
>Books announced but never published in the United States.

Alexan, Friedrich S. [i.e., Friedrich George]. *Der Wohltäter.*
>Cited in *Der Malik-Verlag* (p.69).

Brecht, Bertolt. *Gedichte im Exil 1933-1947.*
>Cited in *Morgenröte,* p.341.

Broch, Hermann. *Die Bücherverbrennung.*
>Cited in *Publishers' Weekly,* July 14, 1945, p.139.

Grosz, Georg. *Unter den gleichen Sonne.*
>Cited in *Publishers' Weekly,* July 14, 1945, p.139. Listed in *Der Malik-Verlag* (p.69) as *Unter der selben Sonne.*

Heartfield, John. *Faschistenspiegel.*
>Cited in *Publishers' Weekly,* July 14, 1945, p.139. Listed in *Der Malik-Verlag* (p.69) as *Krieg im Frieden.*

Herzfelde, Wieland. *Immergrün.*
>Listed as already published in *Morgenröte,* p.344. *Immergrün,* a short autobiographical work, was first published by the Aufbau Verlag of Berlin in 1950. For further details see Herzfelde, "Wie 'Immergrün' entstand," *Unterwegs* (Berlin: Aufbau Verlag, 1961), p.7-9.

———— *Vogel Rock.*
>Cited in *Books Abroad,* 19:139 (Spring, 1945).

Marchwitza, Hans. *Acht Ruten Land.*
>Listed in *Der Malik-Verlag* (p.69).

Weiskopf, Franz Carl, and Pinthus, Kurt. *Geschichte der deutschen Literatur im Exil.*
>See *Der Malik-Verlag* (p.69). Announced in the *Aufbau* (N.Y.) of Nov. 30, 1945 (p.11) as Weiskopf, *Unter fremden Himmeln,* the title under which it was published by the Dietz Verlag of Berlin in 1948.

Zoff, Otto. *Österreichische Novelle.*
>Cited in *Der Malik-Verlag* (p.69).

Zweig, Arnold. *Neue Erzählungen.*
>Cited in *Der Malik-Verlag* (p.69).

Bermann-Fischer Verlag. New York.
>Listed here are books actually published and printed in the United States, including photographic reprints of some of Bermann-Fischer's Stockholm editions.

Beer-Hofmann, Richard. *Verse.* Stockholm-New York: 1941. 51p.
>"Copyright, 1941 . . . Manufactured in the USA." A limited printing of 100 signed copies on Archer Bütten was also issued.

Bücherreihe "Neue Welt."
>An inexpensive series of paperbound books (25¢ each) issued in 1945 for German prisoners of war. They are listed in order by volume number.
>
>1. Benét, Stephen Vincent. *Amerika.*
>2. Willkie, Wendell. *Unteilbare Welt.*
>3. Conrad, Joseph. *Der Freibeuter.*
>4. Hemingway, Ernest. *Wem die Stunde schlägt.*

  5. Werfel, Franz. *Das Lied von Bernadette.*
  6. Curie, Eve. *Madame Curie.*
  7. Roth, Joseph. *Radetzkymarsch.*
  8. Frank, Leonhard. *Die Räuberbande.*
  9. [Einstein, Alfred, ed.]. *Die schönsten Erzählungen deutscher Romantiker.*
 10. Mann, Thomas. *Achtung, Europa! Aufsätze zur Zeit.*
 11. Zuckmayer, Carl. *Der Hauptmann von Köpenick.*
 12. [Einstein, Alfred, ed.]. *Briefe deutscher Musiker.*
 13. Remarque, Erich Maria. *Im Westen nichts Neues.*
 14. Mann, Thomas. *Der Zauberberg.* Erster Bd.
 15. ———— *Der Zauberberg.* Zweiter Bd.
 16. Heine, Heinrich. *Meisterwerke in Vers und Prosa.*
 17. Werfel, Franz. *Die vierzig Tage des Musa Dagh.* Erster Bd.
 18. ———— *Die vierzig Tage des Musa Dagh.* Zweiter Bd.
 19. Zweig, Arnold. *Der Streit um den Sergeanten Grischa.*
 20. Baum, Vicki. *Liebe und Tod auf Bali.*
 21. Mann, Thomas. *Lotte in Weimar.*
 22. Zuckmayer, Carl. *Ein Bauer aus dem Taunus.*
 23. Scott, John. *Jenseits des Ural.*
 24. Saroyan, William. *Menschliche Komödie.*

Mann, Thomas. *Bekenntnisse des Hochstaplers Felix Krull: Der Memoiren erster Teil.*
S. Fischer: 1954. 228p.
  A limited mimeographed edition produced in New York for the author and his publisher, Bermann-Fischer, in order to protect Mann's American copyright by fulfilling the demands of the manufacturing clause. This is a true first edition. See Bürgin, op. cit., p.48.

———— *Deutsche Hörer.* ca. 1942. 152p.
  A photo reprint of the 1942 Stockholm edition. See the *Aufbau* (N.Y.), Sept. 15, 1944, p.20.

———— *Dieser Friede.* Stockholm: 1938. 28p.
  The verso of the title page reads: "Printed in the U.S.A." The first edition. Another edition released in the United States by Alliance.

———— *Doktor Faustus: Das Leben des deutschen Tonsetzers Adrian Leverkühn, erzählt von einem Freunde.* 1947. 754p.
  Mimeographed by the firm of Wallenberg & Wallenberg in an edition of fifty copies—an American-made first edition to protect the author's copyright. These volumes originally sold for $60 each. See Bürgin, op. cit., p.41.

———— *Der Erwählte.* S. Fischer: 1951. 315p.
  A numbered and signed edition of 60 copies mimeographed in New York by Wallenberg & Wallenberg. Bürgin, op. cit., p.45.

———— *Joseph, der Ernährer.* 1944. 642p.
  A photo reprint of the Stockholm edition. The verso of the title page reads: "Printed in the United States of America. First Edition July 1944. Second Edition November 1944." The binding is similar to the Stockholm edition. The reprint lacks the index, p.643–45.

———— *Lotte in Weimar.* 1940. 450p.
  A photo reprint of the Stockholm edition. Verso of the title page reads: "Printed in USA." See also Thomas Mann, *Briefe: 1937–1947*, p.297.

Werfel, Franz. *Jacobowsky und der Oberst.* 1945. 141p.
  A photo reprint of the Stockholm edition. Verso of title page reads: "Printed in the U.S."

Bruno Blau. Sunnyside, Long Island, N.Y.

Blau, Bruno. *Das Ausnahmerecht für die Juden in den europäischen Ländern, 1933–1945 (Teil I Deutschland).* 1952. 142p.
No more published. A second edition was published in Düsseldorf (1954).

√ Bertolt Brecht. Santa Monica, Calif.(?)
Brecht, Bertolt. *Gedichte im Exil.* 1944.
A limited photocopied edition of Brecht's original typescript.

Congregation Habonim. New York.

Strauss, Eduard. *Aufsaetze und Anmerkungen 1919–1945.* 1946. 108p.
Strauss was one of the founders of this congregation and these essays were collected in honor of his 70th birthday. Introduction by Leo Baeck.

Council for a Democratic Germany. New York.

A last and futile attempt (1944–45) to form a broadly based Free German front in the United States.

Council for a Democratic Germany. *A Declaration of the Council for a Democratic Germany.* 1944.
A mimeographed pamphlet. A German-language version has also been reported. On this and other publications of the Council, see Karl O. Paetel, *Vierteljahrshefte für Zeitgeschichte,* 4:286–301 (July, 1956).

——— *Denkschrift über den Wiederaufbau einer Gewerkschaftsbewegung in Deutschland.* July 14, 1944.
There also exists an English version of this pamphlet under the title *The Reconstruction of the Trade Union Movement in Germany.*

——— *Erklärungen an die Mitglieder und Freunde des Rates für ein demokratisches Deutschland.* Okt., 1945.
A mimeographed pamphlet.

——— *Memorandum: Emergency Measures in Germany.* April 7, 1945.
A pamphlet sent to various public figures.

——— *Preliminary Material of the Council for a Democratic Germany.* April, 1944.
A mimeographed pamphlet.

——— *Rede des Chairman Paul Tillich, Zusammenkunft der New Yorker Unterzeichner der Deklaration des "Council for a Democratic Germany."* June 17, 1944.
A mimeographed pamphlet.

Samuel Curl, Inc. New York.

Mehring, Walter. *No Road Back.* 1944. 163p.
Poems in German and English of the Berlin cabaret poet and satirist. Tr. by S. A. De Witt. Illus. by Georg Grosz.

Der Deutsch-Amerikanische Kulturverband. New York, Chicago.

The DAKV was founded in 1935 to coordinate the German-American cultural front against Nazism. It considered itself as spokesman for all Free Germans in America but by 1938 was under Communist Party control. After 1938 the headquarters of the Verband was moved from New York to Chicago, although a strong New York branch as well as other smaller regional branches still functioned.

Der Deutsch-Amerikanische Kulturverband. *Bleibt eurer Muttersprache treu!* [1935?] 4p.
The newspaper *Solidarität* (Oct., 1935, p.353) attributed this pamphlet to Gerhart Seger.

_____ *The Case of Mr. Killinger*. Chicago: 1937. 6p.

Manfred von Killinger was German Consul in San Francisco. This pamphlet was probably prepared by the San Francisco regional group of the DAKV.

_____ *Die erste Nationalkonvention des Deutschamerikanischen Kulturverbandes abgehalten vom 28. bis 30. Mai 1938 in Chicago*. Chicago: 1938. 16p.

_____ *Für Frieden. Freiheit und Kultur! . . . Der Deutsch Amerikanische Kulturverband ruft auf zum Deutschen Tag*. New York: 1936.
Broadsheet.

_____ *Programm Deutscher Tag veranstaltet unter den Auspizien des Deutsch-Amerikanischen Kultur-Verbandes*. [New York] 1935. 16p.

_____ *Verfassung des Deutsch-Amerikanischen Kultur-Verbandes*. New York: [ca. 1935] 4p.

_____ *Vorbereitendes Komitee zur Gruendung eines Deutsch-Amerikanischen Kulturverbandes*. New York: Sept., 1935.
A mimeographed broadsheet signed by the secretary of the organizing committee, Herman Kormis.

_____ *Was ist und was will der Deutschamerikanische Kulturverband?* New York: [1937] 4p.

_____ *Was man den Nazis antworten soll*. Chicago: 1937. 8p.

_____ [Title not known. 1941]
Cited in Alfred Kantorowicz, *Vom moralischen Gewinn der Niederlage*, p.210.

Hall, Martin [i.e., Hermann Jacobs]. *Martin Niemoeller: The Fate of a German Minister*. Chicago: 1938. 8p.

Ludwig, Emil. [Title not known. 1936]
Text of a speech given on German Day in San Francisco, Dec., 1936. Cited in the *Neue Volks-Zeitung*, Jan. 11, 1936, p.4.

Mann, Thomas. *Thomas Manns Bekenntnis für ein freies Deutschland: Rede die am 21. April 1937 in New York gehalten wurde*. New York: 1937. 4p.
A hitherto unrecorded pamphlet.

Norden, Albert. *The Thugs of Europe*. [New York] 1942.

Deutscher Freiheits-Bund. New York.

Deutscher Freiheits-Bund. *The War of the "Little Hitlers": Der Krieg der "kleinen Hitler."* 1935. 19p.
A pamphlet in English and German. Listed in Hans Gittig, ed., *Bibliographie zur Geschichte des antifaschistischen Widerstandes*. Berlin: Deutsche Staatsbibliothek, 1959. Nr.947.

Deutscher Arbeiter Club, Inc. New York.

Deutscher Arbeiter Club, Inc., *Erstes Stiftungsfest*. Dec., 1933. 16p.

Éditions de la Maison Française, Inc. New York.

One of the most important Free French publishing houses. It was founded in 1940 by the proprietors of French and European Publications, Inc., I. Molho and V. Crespin (who in 1945 bought control of Schoenhof's Foreign Books, Cambridge, Mass.).

Maritain, Jacques. *Durch die Katastrophe (À travers le désastre)*. Collection "Voix de France." 1941. 73p.

Farrar & Rinehart. New York.

Böttner, Karl [i.e., Karl Jakob Hirsch]. *Felix und Felicia: Eine Sommergeschichte.* Herausgegeben von A. J. F. Zieglschmid. 1938. 288p.

Schönstedt, Walter. *Das Lob des Lebens.* 1938. 371p.
  Farrar published the German original and the English translation *(In Praise of Life)* in the same year. A German edition was also released in 1938 by Europa Verlag in Zürich.

Ruth Fischer. New York.

Fischer, Ruth. *Öffentliche Erklärung.* 1944.
  A pamphlet distributed on the street by friends of Ruth Fischer prior to a meeting of the Council for a Democratic Germany. It accused the Council of being a front for the Stalinists. See Karl O. Paetel, *Vierteljahrsheft für Zeitgeschichte,* 4:295 (July, 1956).

Peter Thomas Fisher. New York.

Cohn, Ruth C. *Inmitten aller Sterne.* 2d ed. 1952.
  The first edition was published by Theo. Gaus' Sons in 1949.

Gilbert, Robert. *Meine Reime, deine Reime: Berliner, Wiener und andere Gedichte mit 10 Illustrationen von Fritz Eichenberg.* 1946. 206p.
  Printed by the Profile Press of New York. Designed by Fred Siegle.

Barthold Fles. New York.

Herrmann-Neisse, Max. *Letzte Gedichte.* 1942. 252p.
_____ *Mir bleibt mein Lied.* 1942. 184p.
  Both volumes by the German émigré poet who died in England in 1941 were edited and published under the direction of his widow. The title pages carry the London imprint of Barmerlea Book Sales.

Sahl, Hans. *Die hellen Nächte: Gedichte aus Frankreich.* 1942. 73p.
  With a woodcut by Hans Alexander Mueller. Printed by the Spiral Press of New York.

Viertel, Berthold. *Fürchte dich nicht! Neue Gedichte.* 1941. 183p.

Föderation Deutsch-Amerikanischer Klubs. New York.
  Formerly the Föderation Deutsch-Amerikanische Arbeiter Klubs.

Federation of German-American Clubs. *Nazi-Taten und das Deutsche Volk: Was alle Deutsch-Amerikaner wissen muessen.* 1942. 47p.

Friedrich Wilhelm Foerster. New York.

Foerster, Friedrich Wilhelm. [Title not known] 1943.
  A mimeographed three-page letter arguing in favor of a hard peace for Germany; a criticism of Karl Frank's views. Cited in Paetel, *Vierteljahrshefte für Zeitgeschichte,* 4:292–93 (July, 1956).

Freedom Publishing Co. New York.
  Founded by Stephen Naft, the editor of *Living Age.* Stephen Naft (1878–1956), born Siegfried Nacht (and who also wrote under the name Arnold Roller), was long active in the United States as a publicist for anarcho-syndicalism. Max Nomad, his brother, was better known to the American public.

Rauschning, Hermann. *Die konservative Revolution.* 1941. 301p.

Freidenkerbund von Nordamerika. Milwaukee, Wis.

The traditionally radical Freidenkerbund also published the German-language newspaper *Freidenker* from 1872 to 1942.

Hartwig, Theo. *Der Faschismus in Deutschland.* 1933. 40p.

Theo. Gaus' Sons, Inc. New York.

Printers and publishers.

Cohn, Ruth C. *Inmitten aller Sterne.* 1949. 24p.
A second edition was published by Peter Thomas Fisher, 1952.

Wolff, Hans. *In den silbernen Nächten: Gedichte.* 1950. 40p.
This publisher also issued Wolff's *Auch der Herbst kommt wieder* in 1958 (39p.).

The German American. New York.

The radical pro-Communist newspaper founded by Kurt Rosenfeld's German American Emergency Conference in 1942.

Eisler, Gerhard. *Eisler Hits Back.* 1947.
Pamphlet. The *German American* also distributed Eisler's *My Side of the Story* (1947), a publication of the Civil Rights Congress.

German American. *Einige Fragen an Herrn Schumacher.* [1948?]
Pamphlet. Cited in the *German American,* Jan. 21, 1948.

_____ *Ja, dem deutschen Volk muss geholfen werden.* [1947]
Pamphlet. Cited in the *German American,* Oct. 7, 1947.

_____ *The Red Army Speaks to the German Soldier: Special Supplement of the German American.* 1943.

_____ *The Signs of Awakening: German Underground Speaks.* 1943.
The manifesto of the Rhineland Conference in English and German versions.

_____ *Special Supplement: Original Leaflets Circulated by the Red Army among German Soldiers on the Russian Front.* [1943?]

_____ *What Will Happen with Germany? The Creation of the National Committee Free Germany: The Manifesto and Its Significance.* 1943. 32p.
Text in German and English. Included is a long list of German-American supporters of the committee.

Weinert, Erich. *Erziehung vor Stalingrad.* 1943. 46p.
With an introduction by Oskar Maria Graf.

German American Emergency Conference. New York.

German American Emergency Conference. *Bericht von der Konferenz.* 1942.
Cited in *Unsere Zeit,* April, 1942.

German Communists Workers Library Publishers. New York.

No German-language publications with this imprint have been traced. See Workers' Library Publishers, p.215.

Central Committee of the Communist Party of Germany. *Destroy Hitler! Free Germany!* 1942.

The German-Jewish Publishers of America. New York.

The corporate name adopted by a group of scholars, writers, and rabbis who joined together to publish the essays and other writings of Willy Aron. Aron was the associate editor of the *Jüdisches Familienblatt.*

Aron, Willy. *A Bibliographical Essay, Containing an Account of Books, Treatises, Essays and Articles Written by Willy Aron; Also Extracts From a Philosophical Correspondence Between Albert Einstein and Willy Aron Relating to the Problems of Space and Time, and Spinoza's Cogitato et Extensio.* 1935. 10p.
> Text in German.

German Labor Delegation in the U.S.A. New York.
> The official representative of the German Social Democratic Party in the United States.

German Labor Delegation in the U.S.A. *Programm der Landeskonferenz deutschsprachiger Sozialdemokraten und Gewerkschaftler in den U.S.A. 1943.*
> Broadsheet. The meeting held on July 3–4, 1943, was sponsored by the German-Language Branch of the Social Democratic Federation of America, the German Labor Delegation in the U.S.A., and the *Neue Volks-Zeitung.*

_____ *What Is to Be Done with Germany?* 1945.
> Pamphlet.

Oskar Maria Graf. New York.

Graf, Oskar Maria. *Anton Sittinger.* 1941. 387p.
> A reprint edition of 1100 copies.

_____ *Bayrisches Dekameron.* [1939] 251p.
> A reprint edition of 1100 copies.

_____ *Bolwieser.* 1940.
> It is questionable if this novel of Graf's was ever reprinted in the United States. Berendsohn lists it (2:239) but Graf in a letter to the author made no mention of this particular edition.

_____ *Der ewige Kalender: Ein Jahresspiegel mit Zeichnungen von Anna Maria Jauss.* 1954. 46p.

_____ *Prisoners All.* 1943. 442p.
> The English translation by Margaret Green was originally published in 1928 by Alfred Knopf. Graf reissued it in a numbered and signed edition of 250 copies at $5. The proceeds helped him to print a "Volksausgabe" to be sold for $2.50.

B. Grossmann. New York.

Grossmann, B. *Taschenbuch über die Vereinigten Staaten für Einwanderer und Ausländer.* 1947. 80p.
> Cited in the *Aufbau* (N.Y.), April 25, 1947, p.8.

H. K. Publishing. New York.

Russ, Bruno, ed. *A.B.C. für U.S.A.* 1939. 89p.
> Contributors included Arthur Rundt and Rudolf Elias. Cited in the *Aufbau* (N.Y.), June 1, 1939, p.14.

Hagen, Paul [i.e., Karl Frank]. New York.

Hagen, Paul. *Erklärung an die Mitglieder und Freunde des Council for a Democratic Germany.* 1945.
> A five-page mimeograpned manuscript, dated Oct. 18, 1945, in which Frank announces his resignation from the Council.

_____ [Title not known] 1943.
> A six-page mimeographed letter, dated Feb. 24, 1943, replying to Friedrich Wil-

helm Foerster's open letter on the German problem (see p.197). See Paetel, *Viertel-jahrshefte für Zeitgeschichte*, 4:292–93 (July, 1956).

Hammer Press. Aurora, N.Y.

The several imprints used by the Austrian artist and printer Victor Hammer in the United States, including books printed for Herbert Steiner, have been kept in one alphabet. Only Hammer's German-language publications are included in this listing. For more complete information, see Carolyn Reading, *A Hammer Bibliography*.

Hauptmann, Gerhart. *Die Finsternisse, Requiem: With an Essay by Walter A. Reichart.* 1947. 28p.

The publication of the 400 copies of this first edition was financed by Herbert Steiner. A short prospectus was also printed by the Hammer Press.

Hölderlin, Johann Christian Friedrich. *Gedichte, Entwürfe zu Gedichten und Bruch-stücke aus den Jahren MDCCXCVI–MDCCCIV.* Lexington, Ky.: Druck der Stam-peria del Santuccio, 1949. 256p.

The colophon reads: "Druck der Stamperia del Santuccio begonnen in sommer 1946 vollendet im herbst 1949 in den Vereinigten Staaten von Amerika Elftes Werk." The printing was begun in Aurora, N.Y. and completed at Lexington. This edition was limited to 51 copies which sold at $100 each.

Kredel, Fritz. *Blutiger Kehraus, 1917.* Aurora, N.Y.: Hammerpresse, 1948. 171p.

An introduction was furnished by Curt Faber du Faur. The edition was limited to 152 copies.

Rilke, Rainer Maria. *Briefe an eine Freundin 1918–1925* (The Aurora Series, 6). Edited by Richard von Mises. Aurora, N.Y.: Wells College Pr., 1944. 36p.

This edition was limited to 100 copies.

Steiner, Herbert. *Begegnung mit Stefan George* (The Aurora Series, I). Aurora, N.Y.: Wells College Pr., 1942. 16p.

This edition was limited to 100 copies.

―――― *Begegnung mit Stefan George.* Aurora, N.Y.: Hammer Press, 1947. 16p.

This second edition was limited to 120 copies.

Harwig, Gerhard. Danbury, Conn.

Harwig, Gerhard. . . . *als Obstfarmer in Connecticut.* [Sept., 1945. 171*l.* variously num-bered. Mimeographed]

Selections from letters containing his impressions of America. Copies were given only to intimate friends who would read "without boredom." "Should any stranger mistakenly pick up these letters," writes the author, "then may he first make his peace with Heaven."

Hunter College. New York.

Heilbut, Iven George. *Die Sendung Hermann Hesses.* 1947.

A lecture given by Heilbut who was a member of the Hunter College faculty.

Information and Service Associates. New York.

The Anti-Defamation League of New York used this imprint on its German-language publications.

Jelenko, Eduard W. *Judenhass-Menschenhass: Anklagen und Widerlegungen im Lichte der Wahrheit.* [1933] 31p.

Mann, Heinrich. *Ihre ordinäre Antisemitismus.* 1934. 12p.

Reprinted from Mann's *Der Hass* (Amsterdam: Querido, 1933).

Noyes, William Albert. *A Letter to a Hitlerite: Brief an einem Nationalsozialisten.* 1934. 15p.
> The text of this pamphlet is in English and German. A note on the title page reads: "Reprinted from *The Johns Hopkins Alumni Magazine,* March, 1934."

Institute of Social Research. New York.
> The former Institut für Sozialforschung, under the direction of Max Horkheimer, was forced to leave the University of Frankfurt in 1933. The Institute was reestablished in New York under the auspices of Columbia University. The research of the Institute was published in the German-language *Zeitschrift für Sozialforschung* (Paris), 1932–1939. This journal was continued by *Studies in Philosophy and Social Science* (New York) which expired after the Oct., 1942 issue.

Horkheimer, Max and Adorno, Theodor W. *Philosophische Fragmente.* 1944. 319p.
> Hektographed. A later edition appeared under the altered title—*Dialektik der Aufklärung: Philosophische Fragmente* (Amsterdam: Querido Verlag, 1947).

Johannespresse, *see* Verlag der Johannespresse.

I. Kauffmann. New York.
> I. Kauffmann Verlag (Frankfurt a. M.) was an important German publisher of Judaica, Hebraica, and Orientalia. The last owner, Felix Kauffmann, fled to the United States in 1939. He was active both as bookseller and printer.

Lazarus, Paul. *Die jüdische Gemeinde Wiesbaden, 1918–1942: Ein Erinnerungsbuch.* 1949. 36p.

Robert M. W. Kempner. Philadelphia.
> Kempner, before 1933, was an official in the Ministry of the Interior in Berlin. After 1939 he was connected with the University of Pennsylvania and perhaps is best known as a member of the American legal staff at the Nuremberg Trials.

Kempner, Robert M. W. *Rechte und Pflichten der "feindlichen Ausländer."* [1942].
> A bilingual publication distributed by Kurt Grossmann in New York. Cited in the *Aufbau* (N.Y.), Jan. 9, 1942, p.7.

Hans Felix Kraus. Tenafly, N.J.
> A young Austrian-Jewish painter who entered the American booktrade just after the end of World War II. In 1946 he was made the United States representative of the Büchergilde Gutenberg. A number of titles bearing the Kraus imprint and dated 1946 are listed in the Deutsche Bücherverzeichnis but these all were publications of the Büchergilde Gutenberg. Some of these are listed below:

Bromfield, Louis. *Der grosse Regen.* 1946. 613p.

Grimm, Jakob. *Die Bremer Stadtmusikanten.* 1946. 28p.

Heye, Arthur. *Meine Brueder in stillen Busch, in Luft und Wasser.* 1946.

Friedrich Krause. New York.
> One of the leading importers and publishers of Free German books in the United States.

Goerdeler, Carl F. *Politisches Testament* (Dokumente des anderen Deutschland, 1.) 1945. 70p.

Juhn, Kurt. *Der Hexenhammer.* 1944. 32p.
> Illustrated by Erich Godal in an edition of 500 copies.

Langerhans, Heinz. *Deutsche Märtyrer in Konzentrationslagern.* 1945.
Advertised before publication as Band IV of the Dokumente des anderen Deutsch-land. Paetel's *Deutsche innere Emigration* was actually published as volume IV of that series. Although listed by Sternfeld, *Deutsche Exil-Literatur 1933–1945,* there is no other proof that the book was indeed published.

Lehmann-Haupt, Hellmut, ed. *Neue deutsche Gedichte* (Dokumente des anderen Deutschland, 3). 1946. 46p.

Meyer, Oscar. *Von Bismarck zu Hitler: Erinnerungen und Betrachtungen.* 1944. 238p.

Osborn, Max. *Der bunte Spiegel: Erinnerungen aus dem Kunst-, Kultur- und Geistesle-ben der Jahre 1890 bis 1933.* 1945. 280p.
Introduction by Thomas Mann.

Paetel, Karl O., ed. *Deutsche innere Emigration* (Dokumente des anderen Deutschland, 4). 1946. 115p.

————— *Ernst Jünger: Die Wandlung eines deutschen Dichters und Patrioten* (Doku-mente des anderen Deutschland, 2). 1946. 76p.

Perl, Walter H. *Thomas Mann 1933–1945: Vom deutschen Humanisten zum ameri-kanischen Weltburger.* 1945. 64p.

Rosenthal von Grotthuss, Alfred. *Kein dritter Weltkrieg.* 1945. 211p.

Die schönsten deutschen Lieder zum Singen und Spielen. 2v. 1944–1945.

Schwarz, Paul. *Die Aussenpolitik des Dritten Reichs.* 1945.
Listed only in Berendsohn 2, otherwise unverified.

Urzidil, Johannes. *Der Trauermantel: Eine Erzählung aus Adalbert Stifters Jugend und Kindheit.* 1945. 69p.
Three editions were offered on subscription: (1) a "bibliophile edition;" copies 1–25 bound in leather and signed, (2) a "Sonderausgabe," copies 26–100, signed, (3) an "allgemeine Ausgabe." Cited in the *Aufbau* (N.Y.), Jan. 5, 1945, p.7.

Labor Conference To Combat Hitlerism. New York.

Labor Conference To Combat Hitlerism. *Arbeiter deutscher Abstammung!* [ca. 1935]
Broadsheet printed on both sides.

Frederick Paul Lowell. New York.

Lowell, Frederick Paul. *Anders als die Andern: Ein Hamburg-Altonaer Sittenbild.* 1943. 251p.
Vignettes from the sexual underworld of Hamburg. The author warns in his preface (p.8), ". . . this book should not be read by children entering puberty."

Josef Luitpold, *see* Josef Luitpold Stern.

The Macmillan Co. New York.

Vagts, Alfred. *Deutschland und die Vereinigten Staaten in der Weltpolitik.* 1935. 2v.
Set, printed, and bound in Great Britain.

Thomas Mann, *see* Bermann-Fischer Verlag.

Hans Marchwitza. New York.

Marchwitza, Hans. *Untergrund.* 1942.
A collection of his poems.

————— *Wetterleuchten: Gedichte.* 1942. 32p.
Both volumes were printed by the Zeidler Press of New York.

Hilde Marx. New York.

> Marx, Hilde. *Berichte.* 1951. 96p.
> Poems from the years 1938–1951.

Karl T. Marx. New York.

> Marx, Karl T. *Der Feigling, Urlaub vom Jenseits, Ephrata Legende, Couleur in Dings-kirchen, Das Ferkel, und andere Geschichten.* [1942] 125p.
> Printed at the Stuyvesant Press.

Neue Welt Publishers. Chicago.

> [Damit, Hans.] *Truth and Facts About the Third Reich (Series, no 1* [and only?]). 1936. 32p.
> There was also a German-language edition.

New Directions. Norfolk, Conn.

> Hölderlin, Friedrich. *Some Poems of Friedrich Holderlin.* 1943. 32p.
> Tr. by Frederic Prokosch. German and English texts.
> Rilke, Rainer Maria. *Poems from The Book of Hours "Das Stundenbuch."* 1941. 31p.
> Tr. by Babette Deutsch. German and English texts.

Pantheon Books. New York.

> The American trade publishing house of Pantheon Books was founded in 1942 by Kurt Wolff and Kyrill Schabert. The company became a division of Random House in June, 1961.

> Broch, Hermann. *Der Tod des Vergil.* 1945. 522p.
> Faber du Faur, Curt von, ed. *Tausend Jahre deutscher Dichtung.* 1949. 488p.
> George, Stefan. *Poems.* 1943. 253p.
> A bilingual edition introduced by Ernst Morwitz, tr. by Carol North Valhope [pseud.] and Morwitz.

Pantheon Editions. New York.

> The imprint adopted by Iven George Heilbut for his own publications.

> Heilbut, Iven George. *Francisco and Elizabeth.* 1942. 23p.
> _____ *Meine Wanderungen: Gedichte.* 1942. 71p.
> Distributed by Walter H. Perl's Academic Book Service (*Aufbau* (N.Y.), Dec. 4, 1942, p.19) and later by Storm Publishers of New York.

Paramount Printing and Publishing Co. New York.

> Farkas, Karl. *Zurueck ins Morgen.* [1946. 78 unnumbered pages.]
> A Viennese cabaret artist of some repute, Farkas emigrated to the United States in 1939 or 1940. This volume of occasional poetry contains numerous illustrations by "FM."

Pazifische Presse. Los Angeles.

> The Pazifische Presse was started by Ernst Gottlieb and Felix Guggenheim for the purpose of producing finely printed editions of those German émigré writers of note who settled in the Los Angeles area. Mary S. Rosenberg of New York took on the distribution of all Pazifische Presse books and indeed covered all publishing costs for the last four titles issued. The first seven volumes (1942–43) were issued in editions of 250 of which copies 1–150 were signed and bound in half leather. All but Feucht-wanger's *Narrenweisheit* were printed at the Plantin Press of Los Angeles.

Döblin, Alfred. *Nocturno*. 1943. 55p.

Feuchtwanger, Lion. *Narrenweisheit oder Tod und Verklaerung des Jean Jacques Rousseau*. 1952. 293p.
>   Issued in only 100 typescript copies to secure American copyright protection.

_____ *Wahn oder der Teufel in Boston: Ein Stück in 3 Akten*. 1948. 108p.
>   This edition bore the joint imprint of Pazifische Presse and Mary S. Rosenberg. Selected by the American Institute of Graphic Arts as one of the fifty books of the year in 1948.

Frank, Bruno. *Sechzehntausend Francs*. 1943. 53p.

Frank, Leonhard. *Mathilde*. 1943. 40p.

Mann, Thomas. *Das Gesetz: Erzählung*. 1944. 79p.
>   500 numbered copies of which 1-250 were signed.

_____ *Leiden an Deutschland: Tagebuchblätter aus den Jahren 1933 und 1934*. 1946. 90p.
>   500 numbered copies of which 1-250 were signed.

_____ *Thamar*. 1942. 54p.

Neumann, Alfred. *Gitterwerk des Lebens*. 1943. 65p.

Torberg, Friedrich [i.e., Friedrich Kantor-Berg]. *Mein ist die Rache*. 1943. 62p.

Werfel, Franz. *Gedichte aus den Jahren 1908-1945*. 1946. 167p.
>   Copies 1-250 were signed and bound in half leather. The ordinary edition exists in at least two binding variants: (1) tan full cloth and (2) blue boards with tan cloth spine. Chosen by the American Institute of Graphic Arts in 1946 as one of the fifty books of the year.

_____ *Die wahre Geschichte vom wiederhergestellten Kreuz*. 1942. 49p.

Max Pfeffer. New York.
>   Pfeffer, an émigré from Vienna, operated a literary agency in New York.

Schubert, Hans. *In einer kleinen Bank*. [1945?]

Siegelberg, Mark. *Fremde Erde*. 1941.
>   Both these items are undoubtedly mimeographed acting versions of plays. See Berendsohn 2:242.

Philosophical Library. New York.
>   An English-language house founded by Dagobert Runes. While living in Vienna, Runes, with the aid of the Austrian Socialist Party, published a tract accusing Austrian Catholic theologians of being harbingers of anti-Semitism. A sentence of 60 days in prison persuaded Runes to emigrate. He arrived in New York in 1931 and with a sharp eye for the market, began to issue several English-language periodicals including *The Modern Thinker* and *The Modern Psychologist*. The first Philosophical Library imprint, the *Dictionary of Philosophy* (1942), was a success and the firm has flourished since. See Kurt Lubinski, "Ein dichtenden Verleger," *Aufbau* (N.Y.), Aug. 6, 1948, p.7-8.

Runes, Dagobert D. *Jordan Lieder: Frühe Gedichte*. [1948] 31p.

George Posner. New York.
>   Drucker, Erich. *Gedichte*. 1946.
>>   Listed in Berendsohn 2:238. This is perhaps identical with the volume of Drucker's poetry published by the Verlag für sozialistische Dichter (see p.214).

Princeton University Press. Princeton, N.J.

Werfel, Franz. *Poems*. 1945. 119p.
> Tr. by Edith Abercrombie Snow with a foreword by Franz Werfel.

Public Voice Publishing Co. New York.

> Max Sievers, leader of the Deutscher Freidenkerverband and editor of the independent Socialist newspaper *Freies Deutmchland: Organ der deutschen Opposition* (Antwerp), established the Public Voice Company as his American distributing agency. Toward the end of 1939 and under the direction of Wendelin Thomas, the New York group published a series of pamphlets in continuation of the then defunct *Freies Deutschland*. Consequently most of the pamphlets issued carried the series title *Schriftenreihe "Freies Deutschland."*

Das antifaschistische Kriegsziel: Eine Stimme der deutschen Opposition. [1939] 31p.
> Printed in Stockholm. The other pamphlets were probably all printed in New York.

Debatten um ein Kriegsziel. [1940]. 12p.

Europäische Umwälzung. June, 1940. 32p.
> Printed in New York.

Jugend im Dritten Reich. [April, 1940]
> This title does not appear on the list of available pamphlets that is printed on the back cover of *Europäische Umwälzung*. It is, however, advertised in the June, 1940 issue of *Solidarität*.

Kriegswirtschaftliche Halbjahrsbilanz des Dritten Reich. [1940] 16p.

Der sonderbare Krieg. [1940] 8p.

Wohin? — der innere Kriegsschauplatz. [1940]

Reynal & Hitchcock. New York.

> Frank, Bruno. *Zwölftausend: Schauspiel in drei Akten, und Nina: Komödie in drei Akten*. Boston, New York: Published for Reynal & Hitchcock by Houghton Mifflin Co. [1943] 195p.
> A text edition; Anthony Scenna, ed.

Joachim Ringelnatz, *see* Gerhard Schulze.

Rudolf Rocker. Crompond, N.Y.

> Rocker, the well-known and highly respected libertarian anarchist — leader of the English Yiddish labor movement, although not himself a Jew — came to the United States before World War II. He spoke often before German-American organizations, and his friends financed several English translations of his writings.

> Rocker, Rudolf. *Zur Betrachtung der Lage in Deutschland: Die Möglichkeiten einer freiheitlichen Bewegung*. New York, London, Stockholm. 1947. 36p.
> The text is dated Crompond, N.Y., Jan., 1947. The booklet was printed in Stockholm with the help of the Sveriges Arbetares Centralorganisation and the Internationale Arbeiter-Assoziation (p.4).

Louis Roemer. New York.

> Roemer, Louis. *Zeit Gedichte*. [1938] 134p.
> This book was distributed and probably financed by an official Communist Party agency, the Deutsche Zentral-Buchhandlung of New York.

Mary S. Rosenberg. New York.

> Most of the publications that appeared with Miss Rosenberg's imprint were reprints licensed by the U.S. Alien Property Custodian.

Frank, Philipp, and Mises, Richard von, eds. *Die Differential- und Integralgleichung-en der Mechanik und Physik*. 2v. 2d ed. 1943.
  A reprint of the Vieweg & Sohn edition of 1930–1935.

Guggisberg, Hans, ed. *Lehrbuch der Gynäkologie*. 1946.

Hamann, Richard. *Geschichte der Kunst*. 1945.

Heine, Heinrich. *Jüdische Manifest: Eine Auswahl aus seinem Werken, Briefen und Gesprächen*. Edited by Hugo Bieber. 1946. 315p.
  The first edition of this collection was published under the title *Confessio Judaica* (Berlin: Welt-Verlag, 1925).

Irk, Sigmund, and Justi, Eduard. *Praktische Physik*. 1944.
  Reprint of the 17th Teubner edition of 1935.

Kaufmann, Edward. *O höre: Gedanken, die immer wieder auferstehen*. [1953] 59p.
  Printed at the Manzsche Buchdruckerei, Vienna.

Klemperer, Otto. *Einführung in die Elektronik*. 1944.

Kohlrausch, Friedrich. *Praktische Physik*. 1944.

Rothstein, Norbert. *Die Anmeldung von Ausländer-Vermögen*. 1941.
  Cited in the *Aufbau* (N.Y.), Sept. 24, 1941, p.6.

Schmidt, Heinrich. *Philosophisches Wörterbuch*. 1946.
  Reprint of the well-known Kröners Taschenausgabe.

Werfel, Franz. *Schönste Gedichte*. 1946.
  This citation appears in both Sternfeld, op. cit., and the *Deutsches Bücherver-zeichnis* for 1941–1950. Miss Rosenberg reported that this is an incorrect entry for Werfel's *Gedichte aus den Jahren 1908–1945*, published by the Pazifische Presse and distributed by herself. The confusion arose, she believed, from her advertising copy which included the phrase, "Werfel's best poems by his own choice."

Rotograph Co. New York.

Mann, Thomas. *Ein Briefwechsel*. 1937. 4p.
  The author's copy is a folio pamphlet with six columns of printed text. Bürgin, op. cit., p.35, describes the New York edition as an octavo eight-page pamphlet. It seems most likely that there were two different printings.

William Salloch. New York.

Mann, Thomas. *Tonio Kröger*. 1944.
  A reprint cited in Berendsohn 2:240.

Sängerzeitung. *see* Verlag der Sängerzeitung.

Schocken Books. New York.

  Schocken Books was organized in 1946 with Theodore Schocken as president. The editor at that time was Hannah Arendt.

Brod, Max. *Franz Kafka: Eine Biographie*. 2d ed. [1947] 287p.
  The first edition was published in Prague (1937).

Kafka, Franz. *Gesammelte Schriften*. Herausgegeben von Max Brod. 7v. 1947–1952.

Wolfskehl, Karl. *1933: A Poem Sequence*. [1947] 123p.
  In German and English.

Schoenhof Verlag. Cambridge, Mass.

  Paul Mueller, former owner of Muellers Buchhandlung in Vienna, and later on the staff of the Williams Book Store in Boston, became manager of Schoenhof's Foreign Books in 1941, a position he held until his death in 1964.

Fontane, Theodor. *Irrungen, Wirrungen.* 1945. 183p.
Cited in *Books Abroad,* 20:237 (Spring 1946).

Jefferson, Thomas. *Auswahl aus seiner Schriften.* Übersetzt und herausgegeben von Walter Grossmann (Amerika-Bücherei, Bd. 1). 1945. 128p.
The first printing consisted of 5000 copies.

Kalécko, Mascha. *Verse für Zeitgenossen.* 1945. 63p.

_____ *Verse für Zeitgenossen.* 1948. 63p.
A reprint of the 1945 edition.

Lothar, Ernst. *Der Engel mit der Posaune.* 1946. 634p.

_____ *Heldenplatz.* 1946. 406p.
Two other novels of Ernst Lothar were announced but never published. These were *Die neue Ordnung* and *Zeugnis des Unsaeglichen.*

Maritain, Jacques. *Von Bergson zu Thomas von Aquin.* Übersetzt von Edward M. Morris. 1945. 296p.

1000 Worte Spanisch. [ca. 1945]
This is a photolithographic reprint of a popular language course published by Ullstein in Germany before 1933. It was probably intended for use by emigrants going to Latin America.

Schreyer-Pisarsky. New York, Vienna.

Schreyer, Isaac. *Psalm eines einfachen Mannes: Gedichte 1911-1947.* [1950] 95p.
Printed in Vienna at the Manzsche Buchdruckerei. The poems are introduced by Ernst Waldinger who, with Schreyer's widow, was probably responsible for the publication of this volume.

Gerhard Schulze. Leipzig.

Ringelnatz, Joachim [i.e., Hans Botticher]. *Betrachtungen über dicke und dünne Frauen.* Philadelphia auf Kosten guter Freunde in 100 Exemplaren gedruckt im Jahre 1940/41.
This is a fictitious Free German imprint. The 6 unnumbered leaves are a facsimile edition of the author's manuscript dated July 30, 1923. It was actually printed by Gerhard Schulze in Leipzig. Copies without any imprint also exist. See Werner Kayser and Hans Peter des Coudres, *Joachim-Ringelnatz-Bibliographie* (Hamburg: Dr. Ernst Hauswedell & Co., 1960), p.19-20.

Hans Siemsen. New York.

Siemsen, Hans. *Wo willst du hin?* [ca. 1946]
A mimeographed volume of poetry by the former German expressionist writer.

Arnold Stein Printing Co. New York.

Pappenheim, Bertha. *Prayers: Gebete.* Tr. into English by Dr. Estelle Forchheimer. [1946. 29p.]
A bilingual collection of simple prayers published by friends and former students of Bertha Pappenheim who died in New York in 1936. Frau Pappenheim, born in 1859, was the founder of the Jüdisches Frauenbund and a pioneer in social work.

Josef Luitpold Stern. New York.

Stern, under the nom de plume Josef Luitpold, published 6 volumes (32p. each) of the series *Die hundert Hefte* during his stay in the United States. This series was started in 1935 when Stern still resided in Vienna. Probably all the items listed below were printed by Ernst Willard of New York.

[Stern], Josef Luitpold. *Die Europäischen Tragödie.* 1946.
    A cycle containing at least two related plays, *Michael Servetus* and *Georg Forster*, published in three Hefte each. The six sold for $2.50. *Neue Volks-Zeitung,* April 27, 1946, p.8.

────── *Das französische Jahr, erster Teil: Der Sanger von Montmartre* (Die hundert Hefte, Bd.19). 1945.

────── *Das französische Jahr, zweiter Teil: Die steinerne Orgel* (Die hundert Hefte, Bd.20). 1945.

────── *Die goldene Schwelle* (Die hundert Hefte, Bd.22). 1945.

────── *Der Herzdoktor: Erzählungen* (Die hundert Hefte, Bd.50). 1945.

────── *Sons Like These.* Translated by Louise Salm. 1946. 64p.
    An anthology in English and German.

────── *Unter dem Huf* (Die hundert Hefte, Bd.?). 1945.
    Cited in the *Austro-American Tribune,* Feb., 1945.

────── *Das Zauberspiel* (Die hundert Hefte, Bd.7). 1945.

Storm Publishers. New York.

    Storm Publishers was founded in Sept., 1946 by Alexander Gode von Äsch, then head of Crowell's reference and foreign department (before that an instructor of German and French at the University of Chicago). The first publication of the new firm was an English version of Fritz von Unruh's novel *Der nie verlor (The End Is Not Yet).* Only one German-language title bears the Storm imprint.

Weinberg, Berthold. *Deutung des politischen Geschehens unserer Zeit, entwickelt aus einer Wesenbetrachtung der Voelker und der allgemeinen Bewegung der Zeit.* 1951. 236p.
    Introduction by Thomas Mann.

Otto Strasser. New York.

    Although Strasser never resided in the United States, his followers managed to publish several brochures in New York using a variety of imprints.

Fairbanks, Douglas, Jr., and Strasser, Otto. *Hitler's Shadow over South America.* Brooklyn: Free German Movement, 1942.

Strasser, Otto. *Free Germany against Hitler.* Brooklyn: P.O. Box 64, Kensington Sta., 1941. 15p.

────── *Hitlers Sturz durch die Frei-Deutschland Bewegung.* New York: Free Europe Radio Station, 1941. 16p.
    The German edition of the preceding. A Spanish version was also prepared and distributed throughout South America.

Paul Tillich. New York.

Tillich, Paul. *Die politische und geistige Aufgabe der deutschen Emigration.* Juni, 1938. Hektographed.

Trans-Ocean Publishers. Chicago.

Reich, Hanns Leo. *Das ist mein Wien: Notizen einer Sehnsucht.* 1953. 80p.

Illustrated. Printed by Krause Printing, Chicago. Reich (1902–59), who left Austria for the United States in 1934, was a man of many talents—actor, director, film writer (he spent 1934–36 in Hollywood), poet, journalist (occasional book reviews for the *Chicago Sun*), and radio personality. While in Chicago, Reich presented a daily radio program (1936–59), the Wiener Radio Stunde, over two local stations. He also worked for the OWI during World War II. Reich was awarded the Silver Emblem of Merit of the Republic of Austria in 1956 "for bringing Austrian news and culture to the American people."

Die Tribüne. Hollywood, Calif.

Hollaender, Friedrich. *Emigrantenballade*. 1939.
　　Cited in Sternfeld, op. cit.

Triton Verlag. New York.

Farkas, Karl. *Farkas entdeckt Amerika*. 1941.
　　A Viennese cabaret artist of some repute, Farkas emigrated to the U.S. in 1939 or 1940. Publication of this book of verse was noted in the *Aufbau* (N.Y.), July 18, 1941, p.6.

Frederick Ungar. New York.

The former Viennese publisher Friedrich Ungar arrived in New York in the autumn of 1940 and soon became the most prolific of all Free German publishers in the United States. The overwhelming majority of his titles were inexpensive reprints of literary texts which carried no printed notice of licensing or original copyright. Each volume reprinted by the authority of the U.S. Alien Property Custodian bears a statement to that effect on the title page. These latter publications were usually of a scientific or scholarly nature. Exact information concerning the scope of the Ungar list has been very difficult to obtain, most of the volumes being unaccounted for in any bibliographical compilation (and attempts to enlist the assistance of the publisher have been in vain). Thirty-one titles are listed on the dust jacket of Rilke's *Erste Gedichte,* for example, and an advertisement in the *Aufbau* mentions twenty dictionaries, none by title, of which twelve have still eluded identification. The sum total of titles both known and unknown is 110.

Ahrens, Lothar. *Dictionary of Aeronautics*. 1944. 562p.
　　Licensed reprint of the *Taschenwörterbuch Flugwesen, fünfsprachig.*

Bartsch, Rudolf. *Schwammerl*. 1946. 78p.
　　Cited in the *Deutsche Bücherverzeichnis 1941–1950 Nachtrag.*

Busch, Wilhelm. *Die fromme Helene*. [1946?] 113p.

―――― *Max und Moritz*. [1949]

―――― *Neues Wilhelm Busch Album*. [1946] 314p.

―――― *Wilhelm Busch Album* [1946?]

Claudius, Matthias. [Title not known. 1946?]
　　Cited in the *Aufbau* (N.Y.), Dec. 21, 1945, p.6.

Dictionaries. [Twelve dictionaries, titles not known. ca. 1945]
　　Cited in the *Aufbau* (N.Y.), Dec. 21, 1945, p.6.

Dostojewski, Fedor. *Brevier*. [1947?]
　　Tr. by A. Eliasberg.

Drei Bücher der Liebe. [1946].
　　Cited in the *Aufbau* (N.Y.), Dec. 21, 1945, p.6.

Duden Pictorial Encyclopedia in Five Languages: English, French, German, Italian and Spanish Containing 30,000 Words Explained by Pictures. 1944.
A newly prepared (licensed) edition in larger format combining in one volume the 5 separate Duden picture vocabularies in the 5 languages indicated.

Ganghofer, Ludwig. *Der Herr Gott Schnitzer von Ammergau; Der Jäger von Fall, Hochlandsgeschichten.* 1948. 230p.

_____ *Die Trutze von Trutzberg.* 1948. 429p.

Gaspey-Otto-Sauer. [Five grammars, titles not known. 1946?]
Cited in the *Aufbau* (N.Y.), Dec. 21, 1945, p.6.

George, Stefan. *Ausgewählte Gedichte.* 1945.

Girschner, Otto. *Repetitorium der Musikgeschichte.* [1945?]

Goethe, Johann Wolfgang von. *Faust I.* [1946?]

_____ *Faust II.* [1946?]
This and the preceding are reprints of the Insel edition.

_____ *Der Weisheit letzter Schluss: Ein Goethe-Brevier.* Herausgegeben von Robert Lohan. 1944. 30p.

Grillparzer, Franz. *Der letzte Klassiker: Ein Grillparzer-Brevier.* Herausgegeben von Robert Lohan. 1945. 27p.

Grimm, Jakob. *Grimms Märchen neu erzählt.* 1944.

Der grosse Duden. 1949. 1007p.
With German and English index.

Hamilton, Louis. *Handbuch der englischen und deutschen Umgangssprache.* 1943. 256p.
Later published by Langenscheidt in Berlin (5. Auflage, 1947).

Hamsun, Knut. *Sklaven der Liebe.* 1946. 191p.

_____ *Viktoria.* 1946. 191p.
These two Hamsun volumes both listed in the *Deutsche Bücherverzeichnis* may be one and the same publication.

Heine, Heinrich. *Buch der Lieder.* [1946]

Hesse, Hermann. *Eine Bibliothek der Weltliteratur.* 1945. 22p.
A licensed reprint of the Reclam edition.

Hoffmann, Heinrich. *Struwelpeter.* [1946?]

Kant, Immanuel. *Ein Kant Brevier.* 1945. 28p.
Edited by Franz Gellner.

Kästner, Erich. *Fabian.* 1945. 82p.

_____ *Gesang zwischen den Stühlen.* 1944. 109p.

_____ *Herz auf Taille* [1946?] 111p.
Reprint of the Curt Weller edition of 1929 (licensed).

_____ *Lärm im Spiegel.* [1946?] 110p.

_____ *Ein Mann gibt Auskunft.* 1944. 110p.
Licensed reprint of the Deutsche Verlagsanstalt edition, 1930.

Keller, Gottfried. *Die drei gerechten Kammacher. Kleider machen Leute.* [1946?] 31p.

Kleinlogel, Adolf. *Rahmenformeln: Gebrauchsfertige Formeln für alle statischen Grössen zu allen praktisch vorkommenden Einfeld-Rahmenformeln aus Eisenbeton, Stahl oder Holz.* [1944]
A licensed reprint of the 1939 German edition published by Ernst & Sohn, Berlin.

Kleist, Heinrich von. *Die Marquise von O. und andere Erzählungen.* [1946?] 21p.

Körber, Heinrich. *Psychoanalyse: Die Freudsche Lehrer in ihrer Theorie und Anwendung.* [1945]

Krueger, Gustav. *Englische Synonymik: Sammlung sinnverwandter englischer Wörter.* [1945] 224p.

Lagerlöf, Selma. *Die schönsten Geschichte der Lagerlöf.* [1946?]

Lohan, Robert, ed. *Amerika, du hast es besser.* 1946. 376p.

———— *Es war einmal: Sechs schöne Märchen neu erzählt.* 1944. 80p.

———— *Living German Literature.* 3v. 1946.

   A historical anthology of German literature with vocabulary. V.1 first published in 1944 as *German Life in Literature.*

———— *Sprechen und Reden: Ein Handbuch fur alle, die durch das Wort wirken wollen oder müssen.* [1946?] 222p.

   The *Deutscher Bücherverzeichnis* cites this language manual with the date ca. 1936. It was probably one of Ungar's Viennese publications issued in 1936 which he either brought with him to New York or reprinted there. Another edition of this same work was published in Zürich by Rascher in 1938 (272p.).

Löns, Hermann. *Das zweite Gesicht.* [1946?]

Meyrink, Gustav. *Des deutschen Spiessers Wunderhorn.* [1946?]

Morgenstern, Christian. *Galgenlieder.* [1946?] 96p.

———— *Der Gingganz.* [1946?]

———— *Palma Kunkel.* [1946?]

———— *Palmström.* [1946?]

Moriarta, Hannah. *Life in the U.S.A.: Information for the Foreign Born.* 2v. [1945]

Muret-Sanders enzyklopädisches englisch-deutsch und deutsch-englisch Wörterbuch. 2v. [1944]

Nestroy, Johann Nepomuk. *Das ist klassisch.* Herausgegeben von Egon Friedell. 1946. 24p.

   Probably a reprint of the 1922 edition, *Das ist klassische: Ein Nestroy Brevier.*

Nietzsche, Friedrich. *Also sprach Zarathustra.* Herausgegeben von A. Baumler. [1947?]

Nock, Samuel Albert. *Spoken American: Conversations in American on American Subjects.* Edited by H. Mutschmann. [1945]

Paechter, Heinz. *Nazi Deutsch: A Glossary of Contemporary German Usage.* 1944. 128p.

   In association with Bertha Hellman, Hedwig Paechter, and Karl O. Paetel.

Rilke, Rainer Maria. *Aufzeichnungen des Malte Laurids Brigge.* [1947?] 394p.

   The copy of this reprint examined contained additional matter not indicated on the title page: *Kleine Schriften, Die Weise von Liebe und Tod des Cornet Christoph Rilke, Maurice de Guérin, Der Kentaur, Gedichte aus fremden Sprachen.* There may exist copies of this reprint containing only the *Aufzeichnungen.*

———— *Ausgewählte Gedichte.* [1947] 79p.

   There was also a 1948 printing.

———— *Das Buch des Bilder.* [1942?] 173p.

———— *Duineser Elegien.* [1944?] 40p.

   "Photolithographed by the Murray Printing Company, Cambridge, Massachusetts."

———— *Erste Gedichte.* [1947?] 161p.

   There was also a 1948 printing.

Rilke, Rainer Maria. *Die frühen Gedichte*. [1943?] 44p.
A later printing (ca. 1947) is recorded.

―――― *Gedichte aus fremden Sprachen*. [1947?]

―――― *Geschichten vom lieben Gott*. [1942?] 179p.

―――― *Kleine Schriften*. [1944?] p.215–307.
Photoreprint made from Rilke's *Ausgewählte Werke* (Insel, 1938).

―――― *Neue Gedichte*. [1947?]

―――― *Der neuen Gedichte anderer Teil*. [1947?]

―――― *Die Sonette an Orpheus*. [1944?] 61p.
"Photolithographed by the Murray Printing Company, Cambridge, Massachusetts."

―――― *Das Stundenbuch*. [1947?]

―――― *Die Weise von Liebe und Tod des Cornet Christoph Rilke*. [1942?] 28p.

Roth, Joseph. *Hiob*. [1945] 74p.

―――― *Radetzkymarsch*. 1945. 146p.

Schaber, Will, ed. *Thinker vs. Junker*. 1941. 282p.

―――― ed. *Die vier Freiheiten*. 1946. 162p.

―――― ed. *Weinberg der Freiheit*. 1946. 499p.
The German version of *Thinker vs. Junker*.

Schiller, Johann Christoph Friedrich von. *Seid umschlungen Millionen: Ein Schiller-Brevier*. Herausgegeben von Robert Lohan. 1945. 27p.

Schlomann, Alfred, ed. *Technologisches Wörterbuch: Gewerbe, Industrie, Technik und ihre wissenschaftlichen Grundlagen*. 3v. [1944]

Die schönsten Gedichte. [1946?]
Cited in the *Aufbau* (N.Y.), Dec. 21, 1945, p.6.

Schopenhauer, Arthur. *Aphorismen zur Lebensweisheit*. [1946?]

―――― *Metaphysik der Geschlechtsliebe*. [1946?]

―――― *Über die Weiber*. [1946?]

―――― *Über Schriftstellerei und Stil: Über Leser und Bücher: Über Sprache und Worte*. [1946?]

Shakespeare, William. *Shakespeare Brevier*. Gesammelt und eingeleitet von Rudolf Presber. [1946?] 32p.

Der Sprach-Brockhaus: Deutsche Bildwörterbuch für Jedermann. [1944]
A licensed reprint of the 1936 edition.

Tolstoi, Leo. *Krieg und Frieden*. [1946] 2v. in 1.
The double-column text fills a folio of 318 pages; German translation by Ernst Strenge.

Tucholsky, Kurt. *Das Lächeln der Mona Lisa*. [1946?]

Waerden, Bartel Leendert van der. *Handbuch der Schwefelsäurefabrikation*. 3v. [1944]

Waldinger, Ernst. *Glück und Geduld*. 1952. 139p.

Wiechert, Ernst. *Der Dichter und die Jugend*. [1946] 24p.

Witham, W. Tasker. *Americans as They Speak and Live: 15 Dialogues in English and German Portraying Representative American Scenes*. [1945] 157p.
German version by Robert Lohan. Illustrated by Harry Roth.

Zahn, Ernst. *Vier Erzählungen aus den "Helden des Alltags."* [1946?] 23p.

Albert Unger. New York.

Baerwald, Richard. *Okkultismus, Spiritismus und unterbewusste Seelenzustände.* [1945?] 125p.
An apparently unauthorized reprint of the 1920 edition published by B. G. Teubner (Leipzig) in its series *Natur und Geisteswelt* (Nr.560).

Klemperer, Paul. *Aus meiner Mappe.* 1944. 101p.
"Manufactured in the United States of America by Ernst Willard."

The University of Chicago Press. Chicago.

Bergsträsser, Arnold, ed. *Deutsche Beiträge zur geistigen Überlieferung.* 1947. 251p.

Kelsen, Hans. *Vergeltung und Kausalität.* [1941] 542p.
Published in The Hague by W. P. Van Stockum & Zoon. The Univ. of Chicago Pr. acted as American agent.

Mises, Richard von. *Kleines Lehrbuch des Positivismus: Einführung in die empiristische Wissenschaftsauffassung* (Library of Unified Science, v.1). 1939.
Also published by W. P. Van Stockum & Zoon with the Univ. of Chicago Pr. acting as American agent.

Unser Wort. New York.

A Trotskyite newspaper edited by Dale Edwards (see p.187, Appendix II).

David, H. *Die internationale Arbeiterbewegung und der Neue Weltkrieg.* Herausgegeben im Verlag von *Unser Wort.* Dale Edwards, P.O. Box 173, Sta. D, New York. [1940?] 26p.
Mimeographed with printed cover.

Verlag der Aldus Buch Compagnie. New York.

The Aldus Buch Compagnie was an Amsterdam firm (Abraham Horodisch) that published art books in German and English. The New York imprint was probably adopted for commercial reasons.

Horodisch, Abraham. *Alfred Kubin als Buchillustrator.* 1949. 51, 99p.
In 1950 an English translation was published under the Aldus imprint and distributed by the bookdealer George Efron.

Verlag der Johannespresse. New York.

The Johannespresse was the imprint used by Otto Kallir, the close friend of the Austrian-Jewish writer, Richard Beer-Hofmann. One publication announced by the Johannespresse—Annette Kolb's *König Ludwig II und Richard Wagner (Aufbau* (N.Y.), Oct. 13, 1944, p.6)—was actually issued in 1947 by the Querido Verlag of Amsterdam.

Beer-Hofmann, Richard. *Aus dem Fragment Paula: Herbstmorgen in Österreich.* 1944. 61p.
325 copies were printed of which 75 were on Strathmore Text Paper, numbered and signed by the author.

_____ *Jacob's Dream.* 1945. 188p.
An English translation of *Jaakobs Traum* with an introduction by Thornton Wilder. This version was also issued in 1947 under the imprint of the Jewish Publication Society.

Beer-Hofmann, Richard. *Paula: Ein Fragment.* 1949. 247p.
Printed by the Elm Tree Press for members of the Richard Beer-Hofmann Gesellschaft.

Rilke, Rainer Maria. *Briefe an Baronesse von Oe* [Rilke im Jahre 1896, Bd.2]. 1945. 70p.
I.e., Baronesse Láska von Oestéren.

_____ *Briefe, Verse und Prosa aus dem Jahre 1896* [Rilke im Jahre 1896, Bd.3]. 1946. 109p.

_____ *Ewald Tragy* [Rilke im Jahre 1896, Bd.1]. 1944. 71p.
A special numbered edition of 100 of these three volumes of Rilke were issued in addition to a regular trade edition.

Verlag der Sängerzeitung. Chicago.

Die blutigen Februarkämpfe in Oesterreich und Wien: Sonderabdruck. 1934.
A collection of articles taken from the pages of the *Sängerzeitung.* Profits were to go to charity. Cited in the *Neue Volks-Zeitung,* April 28, 1934, p.13.

Verlag für sozialistische Dichter. New York.

Drucker, Erich. *Aus fernen Ländern: 24 Sonette um Deutschland.* 1945. 30p.
See the Erich Drucker entry on p.204 under George Posner.

Eric M. Warburg. New York.

Warburg, Max M. *Aus meinen Aufzeichnungen.* Herausgegeben von Hugo Bieber. [1950] 158p.

Weltdemokratische Vereinigung. New York.

Reynold, H. F. *Adolph Hitler: Der letzte "grosse" Antisemit* (Blau-Silber Heft, No.1). März/April, 1939.
According to Herman Kormis (letter of June 10, 1964), the Weltdemokratische Vereinigung never existed. "Reynolds [sic] is an assumed name for a fellow from Washington Heights. I forgot his name. No other number appeared."

Willard Publishing Co. New York.

Before his arrival in the United States, Ernst Willard (formerly Ernst Wilhartitz) was owner of the Frisch Verlag, Vienna. He was active in New York both as printer and publisher.

Farau, Alfred [i.e., Friedrich Farau Hernfeld]. *Wo ist die Jugend, die ich rufe?* [1946] 87p.

Hirsch, Helmut. *Amerika, Du Morgenröte: Verse eines Flüchtlings.* 1947. 48p.

Klemperer, Paul. *World Mosaic of Atoms (Genie und Verstand retten die Welt): Trilogie.* 1946.
This pamphlet cited in Sternfeld, op. cit., also noted in the *Catalogue of Copyright Entries* as *Worldmosaic of atoms.*

Korngold, Julius. *Posthumous Erinnerungen.* 1946.
Cited in the *Aufbau* (N.Y.), Feb. 1, 1946, p.9.

Lindt, Peter M. *Schriftsteller im Exil: Zwei Jahre deutsche literarische Sendung am Rundfunk in New York.* 1944. 192p.

Ludwig, Emil. *How To Treat the Germans.* 1943. 96p.

Luise Kautsky zum Gedenken: Nachrufe von Friedrich Adler und Olga Lerda-Olberg.

Bericht aus Amsterdam: Annie van Scheltema, aus Birkenau: Lucie Adelsberger.
Briefe aus und über Buchenwald von Benedikt Kautsky. [1945] 40p.
  Cited in Berthold, *Exil-Literatur 1933–1945,* p.114.
The Quarter Library. "A collection of popular books on interesting war and postwar topics."
  No.1. Ludwig, Emil. *On Roosevelt.*
  No.2. Arnstein, Rudolf. *Concerning the Coming Peace.*
  No.3. Hofmannsthal, Emilio von. *Attention, Legislators! Fifty Billions Spurned!*
  No.4/5. *The Western Frontier of Russia.* Published under the auspices of the Association of Officers and Men formerly of the Russian Army, Inc., P. Konovaloff, Lt. General, Chairman.
    These booklets selling at 25¢ were probably published ca. 1944. They are advertised on the dust wrapper of Lindt (see above), which also informs us that other titles will follow.

Victor, Walther. *Kehre wieder über die Berge.* 1945. 351p.

Wolff, Hans. *Lied des Lebens.* 1945. 40p.
  Karl Vollmoeller supplied the introduction to this book of poems.

Workers' Library Publishers. New York.
  Very likely this imprint is a variant of German Communists Workers Library Publishers.

An Appeal of the German Communists: Destroy Hitler! Free Germany! 1942.
  Cited in *The Network,* May, 1945.

Merker, Paul. *Whither Germany.* 1943.

Writers Service Center. New York.
  The Center was organized by Friderike Zweig for the purpose of aiding German émigré writers and artists in the United States. Four volumes of poetry by young or little-known writers were published under its imprint.

Boerner [-Bronstein], Lola. *Unzeitgemässe Gedichte.* 1943. 47p.

Farau, Alfred [i.e., Friedrich Farau Hernfeld]. *Das Trommellied vom Irrsinn.* 1943. 61p.

Nussbaum, William. *Überfahrt.* 1943.

Sachs, Lessie. *Tag und Nacht.* 1943. 31p.
  Introduction by Heinrich Mann.

Carl Zuckmayer. New York.
  Zuckmayer, Carl. *Carlo Mierendorff: Porträt eines deutschen Sozialisten.* 1944.
    A memorial address given by Zuckmayer on March 12, 1944. Appearing first in this form, the address has been reprinted several times: *Deutsche Blätter,* 2:3–12 (Heft 6, 1944); *Die Wandlung,* 1:1089–1105 (Dec., 1946); Karl O. Paetel, ed., *Deutsche innere Emigration* (New York: Friedrich Krause, 1946).

Selected Bibliography
of Works Consulted

Newspapers and Periodicals

The American German Review. 1934–1965.

Das Antiquariat (Vienna). 1950–1965.

Der Arbeiter (N.Y.). 1927–1937.

Aufbau (Berlin). 1945–1950.

Aufbau (N.Y.). 1934–1965.

Austrian Labor Information (N.Y.). 1942–1945.

Austrian Labor News (N.Y.). 1942–1945.

Austro-American Tribune (N.Y.). 1943–1948.

Books Abroad. 1933–1950.

Bulletin des Leo Baeck Instituts. 1957–1967.

Council for a Democratic Germany (N.Y.). *Bulletin.* 1944–1945.

Deutsche Blätter (Santiago de Chile). 1943–1946.

Deutsches Volksecho (N.Y.). 1937–1939.

Freiheit für Oesterreich (N.Y.). 1942–1943.

Gegen den Strom (N.Y.). 1938–1939.

The German American (N.Y.). 1942–1948.

In Re: Germany (N.Y.). 1941–1946.

Jewish Way (N.Y.). 1939–1950.

Journal of Central European Affairs. 1941–1950.

Jüdisches Familienblatt (N.Y.). 1937–1939.

Jüdisches Gemeindeblatt für den Zusammenschluss zur Einheitsgemeinde (N.Y.). 1938–1939.

Kampfsignal (N.Y.). 1932–1934.

Leo Baeck Society of Jews from Germany (N.Y.). *Yearbook.* 1956–1966.

The Network (N.Y.). 1944–1945.

Neue Volks-Zeitung (N.Y.). 1932–1949.

Neues Jüdisches Gemeindeblatt (N.Y.). 1939–1940.

Das Neues Leben (N.Y.). 1939.

New York Times. 1933–1950.

Österreichische Rundschau (N.Y.). 1942–1943.

Publishers' Weekly. 1933–1950.

Sänger Zeitung (N.Y.). 1942.

Der Schweizer Buchhandel. 1946–1950.

Solidarität (N.Y.). 1933–1943.

Staats-Herold Almanach (N.Y.). 1936–1947.

Unsere Zeit (N.Y.). 1940–1942.

Volksfront (Chicago). 1939.

Weltspiegel (N.Y.). 1946–1950.

Wiener Library Bulletin. 1946–1965.

Youth Outlook (N.Y.). 1939.

Books

Aaron, Daniel. *Writers on the Left*. New York: Harcourt, 1961.

Adams, Scott, comp. *The O.P. Market: A Subject Directory to the Out of Print Book Trade*. New York: Bowker, 1943.

Alexander, Robert J. *Communism in Latin America*. New Brunswick: Rutgers Univ. Pr., 1957.

American Friends Service Committee. *Refugee Facts*. Philadelphia: 1939.

Arndt, Karl J. R., and Olson, May E. *German-American Newspapers and Periodicals 1732-1955*. Heidelberg: Quelle & Meyer, 1961.

Austrian Centre (London). *Five Years*. London: 1944.

Bauer, Otto. *Die illegale Partei*. Paris: Éditions "La Lutte Socialiste," 1939.

Baum, Vicki. *Es war alles ganz anders*. Berlin: Verlag Ullstein, 1962.

Beer-Hofmann, Richard. *Gesammelte Werke*. Frankfurt am Main: S. Fischer Verlag, 1963.

Bek-Gran, Robert. *Apologia Pro Vita Mea*. [Printed as manuscript], 1926.

_____ *Vom Wesen der Anarchie*. Nürnberg: Verlag "Der Bund," 1920.

Benn, Gottfried. *Ausgewählte Briefe*. Wiesbaden: Limes Verlag, 1957.

Bentwich, Norman. *The Rescue and Achievements of Refugee Scholars*. The Hague: Nijhoff, 1953.

Berendsohn, Walter A. *Die humanistische Front. Teil 1: Von 1933 bis zum Kriegsausbruch 1939*. Zürich: Europa Verlag, 1946.

Bergsträsser, Ludwig. *Geschichte der politischen Parteien in Deutschland*. 10th ed. (Deutsches Handbuch der Politik, Bd. 2). München: G. Olzog, 1960.

Bermann-Fischer, Gottfried. *Bedroht und Bewahrt*. Frankfurt am Main: S. Fischer, 1967.

Berthold, Werner (ed.). *Exil-Literatur 1933-1945: Eine Ausstellung aus Beständen der Deutschen Bibliothek*. Zweite Auflage. Frankfurt am Main: 1966.

Bischoff, Ralph F. *Nazi Conquest Through German Culture*. Cambridge, Mass.: Harvard Univ. Pr., 1942.

Brandl, Rudolf. *That Good Old Fool, Uncle Sam: A Refugee Sounds a Warning*. New York: 1940.

Brecht, Bertolt. *Gedichte 1941-1947: Gedichte im Exil, in Sammlungen nicht enthaltene Gedichte, Gedichte und Lieder aus Stücken*. Frankfurt am Main: Suhrkamp Verlag, 1964.

Breitenkamp, Edward Carlton. *The U.S. Information Control Division and Its Effects on German Publishers and Writers: 1945 to 1949*. Grand Forks, N.D.: 1953.

Breycha-Vauthier, A. C. *Die Zeitschriften der österreichischen Emigration 1934-1946* (Biblos-Schriften Bd.26). Wien: Österreichische Nationalbibliothek, 1960.

Brill, Hermann. *Gegen den Strom,* Offenbach: Bollwerk Verlag, 1946.

Broch, Hermann. *Briefe.* Zürich: Rhein Verlag, 1957.

———— *Die Unbekannte Grösse.* Zürich: Rhein Verlag, 1961.

Budzinski, Klaus. *Die Muse mit der scharfen Zunge: Vom Cabaret zum Kabarett.* München: Paul List Verlag, 1961.

Bürgin, Hans. *Das Werk Thomas Mann: Eine Bibliographie.* Frankfurt am Main: S. Fischer, 1959.

Buttinger, Josef. *In the Twilight of Socialism: A History of the Revolutionary Socialists of Austria.* New York: Praeger, 1953.

Cannon, James P. *The First Ten Years of American Communism.* New York: Stuart, 1962.

———— *The History of American Trotskyism.* New York: Pioneer Publishers, 1944.

Communist Party of America, New York State Committee. *Proceedings of the Tenth Convention.* New York: 1938.

Council on Books in Wartime. *A History of the Council on Books in Wartime.* New York: Country Life Pr., 1946.

Crawford, Rex, ed. *The Cultural Migration.* Philadelphia: Univ. of Pennsylvania Pr., 1953

Davie, Maurice R. *Refugees in America.* New York: Harper, 1947.

Deutsch, Julius. *Ein weiter Weg.* Zürich: Amalthea, 1960.

Deutsche Akademie der Künste zu Berlin. *Der Malik-Verlag 1916-1947.* Berlin: 1967.

Deutsche Blätter (Santiago de Chile). *An die Deutschen Kriegsgefangenen in Nordamerika.* Santiago de Chile: Deutsche Blätter, Mitte Dezember, 1944.

Deutsche Nationalbibliographie Ergänzung I; Verzeichnis der Schriften die nicht angezeigtdurften. Bearbeitet und herausgegeben von der Deutschen Bücherei in Leipzig. Leipzig: Verlag des Börsenvereins der deutschen Buchhändler, 1949.

Draper, Theodore. *American Communism and Soviet Russia.* Compass Books. New York: Viking, 1963.

———— *The Roots of American Communism.* Compass Books. New York: Viking, 1963.

Drechsler, Hanno. *Die Sozialistische Arbeiterpartei Deutschlands.* Meisenheim am Glan: Anton Hain, 1965.

Dressler, Helmut. *Werden und Wirken der Büchergilde Gutenberg.* Zürich: Büchergilde Gutenberg, 1947.

Drews, Richard, and Kantorowicz, Alfred, eds. *Verboten und verbrannt.* Berlin: Heinz Ullstein-Helmut Kindler Verlag, 1947.

Duggan, Stephen. *The Rescue of Science and Learning.* New York: Macmillan, 1948.

Edinger, Lewis J. *German Exile Politics.* Berkeley: Univ. of California Pr., 1956.

Edschmid, Kasimir. *Lebendiges Expressionismus.* München: Kurt Desch, 1961.

Einsiedel, Heinrich, Graf von. *I Joined the Russians*. New Haven: Yale Univ. Pr., 1953.

———— *The Shadow of Stalingrad*. London: Wingate, 1953.

Eisler, Gerhard, Norden, Albert, and Schreiner, Albert. *The Lesson of Germany*. New York: International Publishers, 1945.

Enseling, Alf. *Die Weltbühne* (Studien zur Publizistik, Bd. 2). Münster: Verlag C. J. Fahle, 1962.

Esslin, Martin. *Brecht: The Man and his Work*. Garden City, N.Y.: Doubleday, 1960.

Fischer, Ruth. *Stalin and German Communism*. Cambridge, Mass.: Harvard Univ. Pr., 1948.

Foerster, Friedrich Wilhelm, and T. H. Tetens. *Open Letter to the "Loyal Americans of German Descent."* New York: 1943.

Fontana, Oskar Maurus. *Wiener Schauspieler*. Wien: Amandus Ed., 1948.

Fraenkel, Heinrich. *Farewell to Germany*. London: B. Hanison, 1959.

———— *The Other Germany*. London: Drummond, 1942.

Fry, Varian. *Surrender on Demand*. New York: Random, 1945.

Frye, Alton. *Nazi Germany and the American Hemisphere 1933–1941*. New Haven: Yale Univ. Pr., 1967.

Gerson, Louis L. *The Hyphenate in Recent American Politics and Diplomacy*. Lawrence, Kansas: Univ. of Kansas Pr., 1964.

Gert, Valeska. *Die Bettlerbar von New York*. Berlin-Grunewald: Arani, 1950.

Glanz, Rudolf. *Jews in Relation to the Cultural Milieu of the Germans in America up to the Eighteen Eighties*. New York: 1947.

Glazer, Nathan. *The Social Basis of American Communism*. New York: Harcourt, 1961.

Goetz, Curt, and Martens, Valérie von. *Wir wandern, wir wandern: Der Memoiren dritter Teil*. Stuttgart: Deutsche Verlags-Anstalt, 1963.

Goldschmidt, Alfons. *On Economics You Are Wrong* (S E L Publications, No. 1). New York: 1936.

Goldwater, Walter. *Radical Periodicals in America 1890–1950*. New Haven: Yale Univ. Library, 1964.

Graf, Oskar Maria. *An manchen Tagen*. Frankfurt am Main: Nest Verlag, 1961.

———— *Das bayrische Dekameron*. New York: Im Selbstverlag, 1939.

———— *Prisoners All*. New York: O. M. Graf, 1943.

Grayson, Gary Travers. *Austria's International Position 1938–1953*. Genève: Droz, 1953.

Grigat, Eugene F. *Old Glory or Swastika*. Brooklyn, New York: AFA Publishing Co., 1935.

Grimm, Reinhold. *Bertolt Brecht*. Stuttgart: J. B. Metzlersche Buchhandlung, 1961.

Gross, Babette. *Willi Münzenberg*. Stuttgart: Deutsche Verlagsanstalt, 1967.

Habe, Hans [i.e., Jean Bekessy]. *Ich stelle mich*. München: Verlag Kurt Desch, 1954.

──── *Im Jahre Null: Ein Beitrag zur Geschichte der deutschen Presse*. München: Verlag Kurt Desch, 1966.

Halperin, S. William. *Germany Tried Democracy: A Political History of the Reich from 1918 to 1933*. New York: Crowell, 1946.

Hammer, Victor. *Chapters on Writing and Printing*. Lexington, Ky.: Anvil Pr., 1963.

Hammer, Walter. *Hohes Haus in Henkers Hand: Rückschau auf die Hitlerzeit, auf Leidensweg und Opfergang deutscher Parlamentarier*. Zweite durchgearbeitete und erweiterte Auflage. Frankfurt am Main: Europäische Verlagsanstalt, 1956.

Hawgood, John A. *The Tragedy of German-America*. New York: Putnam, 1940.

Hecht, Ben. *1001 Afternoons in New York*. Illustrations by George Grosz. New York: Viking, 1941.

Heinrich Heine Club, ed. *Heines Geist in Mexico*. Mexiko: Heine-Club, 1946.

Herzfelde, Wieland. *John Heartfield: Leben und Werk*. Dresden: VEB Verlag der Kunst, 1962.

──── *Unterwegs: Blätter aus fünfzig Jahren*. Berlin: Aufbau-Verlag, 1961.

Hicks, Granville. *Where We Came Out*. New York: Viking, 1954.

Hiller, Kurt. *Köpfe und Tröpfe*. Hamburg: Rowohlt, 1950.

──── *Rote Ritter: Erlebnisse mit deutschen Kommunisten*. Gelsenkirchen: Ruhr-Verlag, 1951.

Himmelfarb, Morgan Y. *Drama Was a Weapon: The Left Wing Theatre in New York 1929-1941*. New Brunswick: Rutgers Univ. Pr., 1963.

Hirsch, Karl Jakob. *Heimkehr zu Gott*. München: Verlag Kurt Desch, 1946.

Hirshler, Eric E. (ed.). *Jews from Germany in the United States*. New York: Farrar, 1955.

Hollaender, Friedrich. *Vom Kopf bis Fuss*. Müchen: Kindler, 1965.

Homeyer, Fritz. *Deutsche Juden als Bibliophilen und Antiquare* (Schriftenreihe wissenschaftlicher Abhandlungen des Leo Baeck Instituts, 10). Tübingen: J. C. B. Mohr, 1963.

Howe, Irving, and Coser, Lewis. *The American Communist Party*. New ed. New York: Praeger, 1962.

Jacob, Hans. *Kind Meiner Zeit*. Köln: Kiepenheuer & Witsch, 1962.

Jänicke, Martin. *Der dritte Weg: Die antistalinistische Opposition gegen Ulbricht seit 1953*. Köln: Neuer deutscher Verlag, 1964.

Jarmatz, Klaus. *Literatur in Exil*. Berlin: Dietz, 1966.

Kamman, William Frederic. *Socialism in German American Literature*. Philadelphia: Americana Germanica, 1917.

Kantorowicz, Alfred. *Deutsche Schicksale: Intellektuelle unter Hitler und Stalin.* Durchgesehen und ausgewählt von Günther Nenning. Wien: Europa Verlag, 1964.

———— *Deutsche Schicksale: Neue Porträts.* Berlin: Alfred Kantorowicz Verlag, 1949.

———— *Deutsches Tagebuch.* 2v. Berlin: Kindler, 1959–1961.

———— *Porträts: Deutsche Schicksale.* Berlin: Chronos-Verlag, 1947.

———— *Vom moralischen Gewinn der Niederlage.* Berlin: Aufbau-Verlag, 1949.

Katalog der Rilke-Sammlung Richard von Mises. Bearbeitet und herausgegeben von Paul Obermüller und Herbert Steiner unter Mitarbeit von Ernst Zinn. Frankfurt am Main: Insel-Verlag, 1966.

Kayser, Werner, and Des Coudres, Hans Peter. *Joachim-Ringelnatz-Bibliographie.* Hamburg: Dr. Ernst Hauswedell & Co., 1960.

Kent, Donald Peterson. *The Refugee Intellectual.* New York: Columbia Univ. Pr., 1953.

Kesten, Hermann (ed.). *Deutsche Literatur im Exil: Briefe europäischer Autoren 1933–1949.* München: Verlag Kurt Desch, 1964.

———— *Der Geist der Unruhe.* Köln: Kiepenheuer & Witsch, 1959.

———— *Meine Freunde die Poeten.* München: Kindler, 1959.

Klein, Karl Kurt. *Literaturgeschichte des Deutschtums im Ausland.* Leipzig: Bibliographische Institut AG, 1939.

Kloss, Heinz. *Um die Einigung des Deutschamerikanertums.* Berlin: Volk und Reich Verlag, 1937.

Knappen, Marshall. *And Call It Peace.* Chicago: Univ. of Chicago Pr., 1947.

Koestler, Arthur. *The Invisible Writing.* New York: Macmillan, 1954.

Koszyk, Kurt. *Zwischen Kaiserreich und Diktatur: Die Sozialdemokratische Presse von 1914 bis 1933* (Deutsche Presseforschung, Bd. 1). Heidelberg: Quelle & Meyer, 1958.

Krejčí, Karel. *Oskar Jellinek Leben und Werk.* Brno: Universita J. E. Purkyne, 1967.

Kurt Wolff: 1887–1963. Herausgegeben von den Verlage Heinrich Scheffler, Frankfurt am Main und Günther Neske, Pfullingen. Frankfurt am Main: Ludwig Oehms, 1963.

Kutzbach, Karl August. *Autorenlexikon der Gegenwart: Schöne Literatur.* Bonn: H. Bouvier, 1950.

Landmann, George Peter. *Stefan George und sein Kreis.* Hamburg: Dr. Ernst Hauswedell, 1960.

Lania, Leo [i.e., Lazar Herrmann]. *Welt im Umbruch.* Frankfurt am Main: Forum Verlag, 1955.

Laqueur, Walter Z. *Young Germany.* New York: Basic Books, 1962.

Latein-Amerikanisches Komitee der Freien Deutschen. *Deutsche, wohin?* Mexiko, D.F.: Verlage "El Libro Libre," 1944.

The League of American Writers. Exiled Writers Committee. *We Must Save Them All: A Report.* New York: ca. Dec., 1940.

Lens, Sidney. *Left, Right & Center: Conflicting Forces in American Labor.* Chicago: Regnery, 1949.

Lerner, Daniel. *Sykewar.* New York: George W. Stewart, 1942.

Lewis, Flora. *Red Pawn: The Story of Noel Field.* Garden City, N.Y.: Doubleday, 1965.

Lindt, Peter M. *Schriftsteller im Exil: Zwei Jahre deutsche literarische Sendung am Rundfunk in New York.* New York: Willard Publishing Co., 1944.

Link, Werner. *Die Geschichte des Internationalen Jugend-Bundes (IJB) und des Internationalem Sozialistischen Kampf-Bundes (ISK)* (Marburger Abhandlungen zur politischen Wissenschaft, Bd. 1). Meisenheim am Glan: Anton Hain, 1964.

Löwenstein, Prinz Hubertus zu. *After Hitler's Fall: Germany's Coming Reich.* London: Faber & Faber, 1934.

_____ *Conquest of the Past.* Boston: Houghton, 1938.

_____ *On Borrowed Peace.* Garden City, New York: Doubleday, 1942.

Lothar, Ernst. *Das Wunder des Überlebens.* Hamburg: Paul Szolnay, 1961.

Lüth, Paul E. H. *Literatur als Geschichte.* 2 v. Wiesbaden: Limes Verlag, 1947.

Malina, Max. *Deutsche Juden in New York nach dem Weltkriege.* New York: 1931.

Mann, Erika, and Mann, Klaus. *Escape to Life.* Boston: Houghton, 1939.

Mann, Heinrich. *Briefe an Karl Lemke und Klaus Pinkus.* Hamburg: Claasen, 1964.

Mann, Klaus. *Der Wendepunkt.* Berlin: G. B. Fischer, 1960.

Mann, Thomas. *Briefe 1937 - 1947.* Herausgegeben von Erika Mann. Frankfurt am Main: S. Fischer Verlag, 1963.

_____ *Letters to Paul Amann 1915 - 1952.* Middletown, Conn.: Wesleyan Univ. Pr., 1960.

Marcuse, Ludwig. *Mein zwanzigstes Jährhundert.* München: Paul List Verlag, 1960.

Massing, Hede. *This Deception.* New York: Duell, 1951.

Matthias, Erich. *Sozialdemokratie und Nation.* Stuttgart: Deutsche Verlags-Anstalt, 1952.

Melzer, Joseph (ed.). *Deutsch-Jüdisches Schicksal: Wegweiser durch das Schrifttum der letzten 15 Jahre, 1945 - 1960.* Köln: Joseph Merlzer Verlag, 1960.

_____ *Wegweiser durch das Schrifttum: Deutsch-Jüdisches Schicksal.* Nachtrag 1960 - 1961. Köln: Joseph Melzer Verlag, 1961.

Merkl, Peter H. *The Origin of the West German Republic.* New York: Oxford Univ. Pr., 1963.

Mohler, Armin. *Die konservative Revolution in Deutschland 1918-1932.* Stuttgart: Friedrich Vorwerk Verlag, 1950.

Morgenröte: Ein Lesebuch. Herausgegeben von den Gründern des Aurora Verlages. New York: Aurora Verlag. 1947.

Morgenthau, Hans J. *The Tragedy of German-Jewish Liberalism* (The Leo Baeck Memorial Lectures, 4). New York: Leo Baeck Institute, 1961.

Nicholson, Margaret. *A Manual of Copyright Practice for Writers, Publishers, and Agents.* New York: Oxford Univ. Pr., 1945.

Norden, Albert. *Die Nation und wir: Ausgewählte Aufsätze und Reden 1933-1964.* 2v. Berlin: Dietz Verlag, 1964.

Norman, Albert. *Our German Policy: Propaganda and Culture.* New York: Vantage Pr., 1951.

Paetel, Karl O. *Jugendbewegung und Politik.* Bad Godesberg: Voggenreiter Verlag, 1961.

Park, Robert E. *The Immigrant Press and Its Control.* New York: Harper, 1922.

Pfeiler, William K. *German Literature in Exile* (University of Nebraska Studies, New Series, 16). Lincoln: Univ. of Nebraska Pr., 1957.

Pilgert, Henry P. *Press, Radio and Film in West Germany 1945 - 1953.*[N.p.]: Historical Division . . . Office of the U.S. High Commissioner for Germany, 1953.

Pochmann, Henry A. *Bibliography of German Culture in America to 1940.* Madison: Univ. of Wisconsin Pr., 1954.

Pross, Helge. *Die deutsche akademische Emigration nach den Vereinigten Staaten: 1933 - 1941.* Berlin: Duncker & Humblot, 1955.

Radio Bremen. *Auszug des Geistes: Bericht über eine Senderreihe* (Bremer Beiträge, 4). Bremen: Verlag B. C. Heye, 1962.

Reading, Carolyn. *A Hammer Bibliography 1930 - 1952* (Occasional Contributions, 45). Lexington, Ky.: Margaret I. King Library, Univ. of Kentucky, Oct., 1952.

Reichart, Walter A., and Behl, C. F. W. (eds.). *Max Pinkus.* München: Bergstadt Verlag, 1958.

Reynolds, Lloyd G., and Killingsworth, Charles C. *Trade Union Publications.* 3v. Baltimore: Johns Hopkins Pr., 1944 -1945.

Richter, Fritz. *Wenn du drüben bist. . . Geschichte eines Schlesiers in Amerika.* Stuttgart: Behrendt Verlag, 1949.

Ritter, Gerhard. *The German Resistance: Carl Goerdeler's Struggle Against Tyranny.* London: George Allen & Unwin, 1958.

Ritzer, Walter. *Rainer Maria Rilke Bibliographie.* Wien: Verlag O. Kerry, 1951.

Robinson, Jacob, and Friedman, Philip. *Guide to Jewish History under Nazi Impact* (YIVO Institute for Jewish Research: Bibliographical Series, No.1). New York: YIVO Institute for Jewish Research, 1960.

Roehl, Fritzmichael. *Marie Juchacz und die Arbeiterwohlfahrt.* Hanover: Dietz Verlag, 1961.

Roemer, Louis. *Zeit Gedichte.* New York: L. Roemer, 1938.

Rogge, O. John. *The Official German Report: Nazi Penetration 1924-1942, Pan-Arabism 1939-Today.* New York: Yoseloff, 1961.

Rosenberg, Arthur. *Entstehung und Geschichte der Weimarer Republik.* Herausgegenben von Kert Kersten. Frankfurt am Main: Europäische Verlagsanstalt, 1955.

Roth, Guenther. *The Social Democrats in Imperial Germany*. Totowa, New York: Bedminster Pr., 1963.

Rothfels, Hans. *The German Opposition to Hitler*. Chicago: Regnery, 1962.

Rühle, Jürgen. *Literatur und Revolution*. Köln: Kiepenheuer & Witsch, 1960.

Samuel, R. H. and Thomas, R. Hinton. *Education and Society in Modern Germany*. London: Routledge & Kegan Paul Ltd., 1949.

Saposs, David J. *Communism in American Unions*. New York: McGraw-Hill, 1959.

Sattler, Otto. *Lockende Welt: Erinnerungen an Landstrasse, Meere und ferne Länder*. Herausgegeben von der Deutschamerikanischen Buchgenossenschaft. New York: The Cooperative Press, 1931.

Schauer, Georg Kurt. *Deutsche Buchkunst 1890 bis 1960*. 2 v. Hamburg: Maximilian-Gesellschaft, 1963.

Scheer, Maximilian. *Begegnungen in Europa und Amerika*. Berlin: Alfred Kantorowicz Verlag, 1949.

_____ *Die Reise war nicht geplant*. Berlin: Aufbau Verlag, 1957.

Scheurig, Bodo. *Freies Deutschland*. München: Nymphenburger Verlagshandlung, 1961.

Schick, Frank L. *The Paperbound Book in America*. New York: Bowker, 1958.

Schiller-Nationalmuseum, Marbach A.N. *Albrecht Schaeffer 1885–1950: Gedächtnisausstellung zum 75. Geburtstag des Dichters* (Sonderausstellungen des Schiller-Nationalmuseums, Katalog Nr.8). Marbach: 1961.

_____ *Expressionismus: Literatur und Kunst 1910–1923*. Herausgegeben von Bernhard Zeller (Sonderausstellungen des Schiller-Nationalmuseums, Katalog Nr.7). Marbach: 1960.

Schlawe, Fritz. *Literarische Zeitschriften: 1910–1930*. Stuttgart: J. B. Metzlersche Berlagsbuchhandlung, 1962.

Schlösser, Manfred (ed.). *An den Wind geschrieben*. Zweite Ausgabe. Darmstadt: Agora, 1961.

Schüddekopf, Otto Ernst. *Linke Leute von Rechts*. Stuttgart: W. Kohlhammer Verlag, 1960.

Schulze, Friedrich Siegmund. *Die deutsche Widerstandsbewegung im Spiegel der ausländischen Literatur*. Stuttgart: Reclam Verlag, 1947.

Schwarz, Egon, and Wegner, Matthias, eds. *Verbannung: Aufzeichnungen deutscher Schriftsteller im Exil*. Hamburg: Christian Wegner Verlag, 1964.

Seger, Gerhard. *Reisetagebuch eines deutschen Emigranten*. Zürich: Europa Verlag, 1935.

Selznick, Philip. *The Organizational Weapon*. Glencoe, Ill.: Free Pr., 1960.

Shannon, David A. *The Socialist Party of America: A History*. New York: Macmillan, 1955.

Sinn und Form: Sonderheft Hanns Eisler. Berlin: Rütten & Loening, 1964.

Smith, Arthur Lee. *The Deutschtum of Nazi Germany and the United States.* The Hague: M. Nijhoff, 1965.

Soffke, Günther. *Deutsches Schrifttum im Exil (1933-1950): Ein Bestandsverzeichnis* (Bonner Beitrage zur Bibliotheks- und Bücherkunde, Bd. 11). Bonn: H. Bouvier, 1965.

Spolansky, Jacob. *The Communist Trail in America.* New York: Macmillan, 1951.

Stampfer, Friedrich. *Erfahrungen und Erkenntnisse: Aufzeichnungen aus meinem Leben.* Köln: Verlag für Politik und Wirtschaft, 1957.

Sternfeld, Wilhelm, and Tiedemann, Eva. *Deutsche Exil-Literatur 1933-1945: Eine Bio-Bibliographie.* Heidelberg: Verlag Lambert Schneider, 1962.

Stolper, Toni. *Ein Leben in Brennpunkten unserer Zeit.* Tübingen: Rainer Wunderlich Verlag, 1960.

Strasser, Otto. *Exil.* München: Otto Strasser, 1958.

Strothmann, Dietrich. *Nationalsozialistische Literaturpolitik.* Bonn: H. Bouvier, 1960.

Tartakower, Arieh, and Grossmann, Kurt. *The Jewish Refugee.* New York: Institute of Jewish Affairs, 1944.

Tergit, Gabriele, ed. *Autobiographien und Bibliographien.* London: P.E.N. Zentrum Deutschsprachiger Autoren im Ausland, 1957.

Tjaden, K. H. *Struktur und Funktion der "KPD-Opposition" (KPO): Eine organisations-soziologische Untersuchung zur "Rechts"-Opposition im deutschen Kommunismus zur Zeit der Weimarer Republik* (Marburger Abhandlungen zur Politischen Wissenschaft, Bd. 4). Meisenheim am Glan: Anton Hain, 1964.

U.S. Bureau of the Census. *Historical Statistics of the United States, 1960.*

U.S. Congress, House, Committee on Un-American Activities. *Hearings Regarding Communist Espionage.* 81st Cong., 1st and 2d Sess., 1951.

────── *Investigation of Communist Activities in the New York City Area,* Part 6. 83d Cong., 1st Sess., 1953.

────── *Organized Communism in the United States.* 83d Cong., 1st Sess., 1953.

U.S. Congress, Senate, Committee on the Judiciary. *Communist Activities among Aliens and National Groups.* 2 v. 81st Cong., 2d Sess., 1950.

U.S. Office of Alien Property Custodian. *Book Republication Program List II (Cumulative).* Washington, D.C.: Dec., 1944.

Vagts, Alfred. *Deutsch-Amerikanische Rückwanderung* (Beihefte zum Jahrbuch für Amerikastudien, Heft 6). Heidelberg: Carl Winter, 1960.

Victor, Walther. *Ein Paket aus Amerika.* Weimar: Thüringer Volksverlag, 1950.

────── *Es kommt aber darauf an, sie zu verändern* (Ausgewählte Schriften, Bd.3). Weimar: Volksverlag, 1962.

────── *Ich kam aus lauter Liebe in die Welt* (Ausgewählte Schriften, Bd. 2). Weimar: Volksverlag, 1961.

────── *Kehre wieder über die Berge.* New York: Willard Publishing Co., 1945.

Vinz, Curt, and Olzog, Günter (eds.). *Dokumentation deutschsprachiger Verlage.* München: Günter Olzog Verlag, 1962.

Vollmer, Bernhard. *Volksopposition im Polizeistaat: Gestapo- und Regierungsberichte 1934-36* (Quellen und Darstellungen zur Zeitgeschichte, 2). Stuttgart: Deutsche Verlagsanstalt, 1957.

Wacker, Helga. *Die Besonderheiten der deutschen Schriftsprache in den USA* (Duden-Beiträge. Sonderreihe. Die Besonderheiten der deutschen Schriftsprache im Ausland, 14). Mannheim: Bibliographisches Institut, 1964.

Wallenberg, Hans. *Report on Democratic Institutions in Germany.* New York: American Council on Germany, Inc., 1956.

Weber, Hermann, ed. *Der deutsche Kommunismus: Dokumente.* Köln: Kiepenheuer & Witsch, 1963.

Wegner, Matthias. *Exil und Literatur: Deutsche Schriftsteller im Ausland 1933 -1945.* Frankfurt am Main: Athenäum Verlag, 1967.

Weinert, Erich. *Das Nationalkomitee "Freies Deutschland" 1943 -1945.* Berlin: Rütten & Loening, 1957.

Weiskopf, Franz Carl. *Reportagen* (Gesammelte Werke, Bd.7). Berlin: Dietz Verlag, 1960.

_____ *Uber Literatur und Sprache* (Gesammelte Werke, Bd.8). Berlin: Dietz Verlag, 1960.

_____ *Unter fremden Himmeln: Ein Abriss der deutschen Literatur im Exil 1933 -1947.* Berlin: Dietz Verlag, 1948.

White, Lyman Cromwell. *300,000 New Americans.* New York: Harper, 1957.

Widmann, Hans. *Bibliographien zum deutschen Schrifttum der Jahre 1939-1950.* Tübingen: Niemeyer, 1951.

The Wiener Library, London. *Catalogue Series.* 4v. London: Vallentine, Mitchell, 1960-1963.

Wille, Werner, ed. *Aufrecht zwischen den Stühlen: K.O.P. Grüsse zum 50. Geburtstag am 23. November 1956 für Karl O. Paetel.* Nürnberg: Druckhaus Nürnberg, 1956.

Willis, F. Roy. *The French in Germany.* Palo Alto: Stanford Univ. Pr., 1962.

Wittke, Carl. *The German-Language Press in America.* Lexington: Univ. of Kentucky Pr., 1957.

_____ *Refugees of Revolution.* Philadelphia: Univ. of Pennsylvania Pr., 1952.

Wolff, Kurt. *Autoren/Bücher/Abenteuer.* Berlin: Verlag Klaus Wagenbach, 1965.

_____ *Briefwechsel eines Verlegers 1911 -1963.* Frankfurt am Main: Heinrich Scheffler, 1966.

Zohn, Harry, ed. *Liber Amicorum Friderike M. Zweig.* Stamford, Conn.: Dahl, 1952.

Zohner, Alfred (ed.). *Das Josef-Luitpold Buch.* Wien: Verlag der Wiener Volksbuchhandlung, 1948.

Zweig, Arnold. *Juden auf dem deutschen Bühne.* Berlin: Welt-Verlag, 1928.

Zweig, Friderike M. *Spiegelungen des Lebens.* Wien: Hans Deutsch Verlag, 1964.

Articles

Ahrend, R. K. "Die Einheitszeitung," *Gegen den Strom* 1:7-8 (March 1938).

Albrechtova, Gertrude. "Zur Frage der deutschen antifaschistischen Emigrationsliteratur im tschechoslowakischen Asyl, " *Historica* 8:177-233 (1963).

"Arbeitsfeld und Arbeitsplan des Deutsch-Amerikanischen Klubs St. Louis, Mo.," *Mitteilungsblatt der Deutsch-Amerikanischen Klubs U.S.A.* 5:2-4.

Aufhäuser, Siegfried. "Soll man die Kriegsgefangenen erziehen? Eine bisher verpasste Gelegenheit," *Aufbau* (N.Y.), Feb. 4, 1944.

Bell, Daniel. "The Background and Development of Marxian Socialism in the United States," Donald Drew Egbert and Stow Persons, eds., *Socialism and American Life* (Princeton: Princeton Univ. Pr., 1952), 1:215 -405.

Berendsohn, Walter A. "Emigrantenliteratur 1933-1947," *Reallexikon der deutsche Literaturgeschichte,* Werner Kohlschmidt and Wolfgang Mohr, eds., 1:366-43 (1958).

———. "Probleme der Emigration aus dem Dritten Reich," *Aus Politik und Zeitgeschichte* (Bonn), Aug.8, 1956, p.497-512, and Aug. 15, 1956, p.513-26.

Bielefeld, Fred. "Unser Club," *Aufbau Almanach* (New York, 1941), p.30 -33.

Brandl, Rudolf. "Der 'Kulturverband' und seine Sippe," *Gegen den Strom* 2:9-25 (Oct.-Nov., 1939).

Brenner, Hildegard. "Deutsche Literatur im Exil 1933-1947," in Hermann Kunisch and Hans Hennecke, eds., *Handbuch der deutschen Gegenwartsliteratur* (1965), p.677-94.

Brooks, Paul. "Books Follow the Jeep," *Publishers' Weekly,* Dec. 8, 1945, p. 2528 -30.

Brown, F. "For Improving the Work of the Party among the Foreign-Born Workers," *The Communist* (New York) 13:700-10 (July, 1934).

Brüning, Eberhard. "Probleme der Wechselbeziehungen zwischen der amerikanischen und der deutschen sozialistischen und proletarischrevolutionären Literatur," *Zur Geschichte der sozialistischen Literatur 1918 -1933* (Berlin: Aufbau Verlag, 1963), p.320 -45.

Carew Hunt, R. N. "Willi Muenzenberg," *St. Antony's Papers* 9:72-87 (1960).

Cunz, Dieter. "Rise and Fall of the German Americans in Baltimore," *Common Ground* 7:61 -71 (Spring 1947).

"Ein deutsche Theater im Aufbau," *Neue Volks-Zeitung,* July 18, 1936.

"Die deutschen Emigration nach 1933: Ihr Einfluss auf das amerikanische Geistesleben," *Frankfurter Allgemeine Zeitung,* May 27, 1964.

Eisele, Ernst. "Der deutsche Buchhandel in Amerika," German American Conference, *Sitzungsberichte und Erläuterungen* (New York, 1932), p.29 -31.

Erler, Fritz. "Die Rolle der Gruppe Neu Beginnen," *Politische Studien* 6, Nr.69:43-45 (1956).

"Fememorde in Gefangenenlagern? " *Neue Volks-Zeitung,* Jan. 22, 1944.

Fles, Barthold. "What Has Happened to Them Since? Reply," *Publishers' Weekly,* July 28, 1945, p.307.

"Foreign-language Press: 1,047 Immigrant Newspapers Talking to More than Six Million Readers in Thirty-Eight Different Languages," *Fortune* 22:90–93 (Nov. 1940).

"Freies Deutschland," *Wiener Library Bulletin* 7:7 (April 1953).

Friedrich, Carl J. "Foreign Language Radio and the War," *Common Ground* 3:65–72 (Autumn, 1942).

Fry, Varian. "What Has Happened to Them Since: Writers I Helped Escape from France," *Publishers' Weekly*, June 23, 1945, p.2434-37.

George, Manfred. "Deutsche Schriftsteller in den USA," *Neue Schweizerische Rundschau*, N.F., 17:312–16 (1949/1950).

_____ "Die Stimme der Immigration: Notizen über den '*Aufbau*,'" in American Federation of Jews from Central Europe, *Twenty Years . . . 1940–1960* (New York, 1961), p.77 –85.

_____ "Ueber den *Aufbau*," *Aufbau Almanach* (New York, 1941), p.6 –9.

Glanz, Rudolf. "German Jews in New York City in the 19th Century," *YIVO Annual of Jewish Social Science* 11:9–38 (1956/1957).

Graf, Oskar Maria. "German Writers in America," *New Republic* (April 26, 1939), p.344 –46.

Gross, Babette. "The German Communists' United-Front and Popular-Front Ventures," in Milorad M. Drachkovitch and Branko Lazitch, eds., *The Comintern: Historical Highlights* (New York: Praeger, 1966), p.111–38.

Grossmann, Kurt R. "What Happened to the German Jews? A Balance Sheet," in American Federation of Jews from Central Europe, *Ten Years . . . 1941 –1951* (New York, 1951), p.41 –49.

Gruber, Helmut. "Willi Münzenberg: Propagandist For and Against the Comintern," *International Review of Social History* 10, pt. 2:188–210 (1965).

Hahn, Hugo. "The Religious Situation of Our Generation," in American Federation of Jews from Central Europe, *Twenty Years . . . 1940 –1960* (New York, 1961), p.86 –89.

Hammer, C. R. "A Victor Hammer Bibliography (1930 –1955)," *The American Book Collector* 6:3–12 et passim (Jan., 1956).

Heimann, Eduard. "The Refugee Speaks," *Annals of the American Association of Political and Social Scientists* 203: 106–13 (May 1939).

Hellmer, Kurt. "Wandlungen der Oesterreichischen Monarchisten," *Aufbau* (N.Y.), March 17, 1944.

Herzfelde, Wieland. "German Writers against Hitler," *Direction* (Darien, Conn.) 2:1–3 (Dec., 1939).

Hirsch, Felix E. "Gerhart Seger: In the Tradition of Carl Schurz," *American-German Review* 33:26–27 (April/May, 1967).

Hirsch, Julius, and Hirsch, Edith. "Berufliche Eingliederung und wirtschaftliche Leistung der deutsch-juedischen Einwanderung in die Vereinigten Staaten (1934 –1960)," in

American Federation of Jews from Central Europe, *Twenty Years . . . 1940-1960* (New York, 1961), p.41 -70.

Holborn, Louise W. "Deutsche Wissenschaftler in den Vereinigten Staaten in den Jahren nach 1933," *Jahrbuch für Amerikastudien* 10:15- 26 (Heidelberg: Carl Winter, 1965).

Huebsch, B. H. "Culture in Exile," *Saturday Review of Literature,* July 2, 1938, p.17.

Jurkowski, Werner. "Geschichte und Aufgaben der Naturfreunde in USA," *Deutsche Volksecho* (New York), July 8, 1939.

Karsen, Fritz. "Kriegsgefangene und Demokratie," *Neue Volks-Zeitung,* May 13, 1944.

Katz, Rudolf. "Der New Yorker Stalin-Coup," *Neue Volks-Zeitung,* May 6, 1944.

"Kein Deutschland Komitee in USA: Ein Dementi Thomas Manns," *Aufbau* (N.Y.), Dec. 3, 1943.

Kent, Norman. "The Art of Victor Hammer," *American Artist* 20:44- 49 et passim (June, 1956).

Klaus, Erwin H. "Die fortschrittliche deutschamerikanische Bewegung," *Aufbau Almanach* (New York, 1941), p.73 -82.

Kloss, Heinz. "German-American Language Maintenance Efforts," in J.A. Fishman, ed., *Language Loyalty in the United States* (The Hague: Mouton, 1966), p.206- 52.

Krause, Friedrich. "Das freie deutsche Buch in U.S.A., " *Aufbau* (N.Y.), Dec. 5, 1941.

Kuehl, Michael. "Die exilierte demokratische Linke in U.S.A.," *Zeitschrift für Politik* 4:273-89 (July, 1957).

Liepmann, Heinz. "German Authors Write in Exile," *New York Times Sunday Book Review,* Oct. 23, 1936.

Lore, Ludwig. "German Socialism Underground," *New Republic,* Aug. 15, 1934, p.8 -9.

Lowenstein, Ludwig. "Die Entwicklung des 'New World Club,'" in American Federation of Jews from Central Europe, *Twenty Years . . . 1940 -1960* (New York, 1961), p.71 -76.

McDermott, Douglas. "The Odyssey of John Bonn: A Note on German Theatre in America," *German Quarterly* 38:325- 34 (May, 1965). .

Maier-Hultschin, J. C. "Nochmals: Neubeginnen," *Politische Studien* 6, Nr.70:47- 49 (1956).

_____ "Struktur und Charakter der deutschen Emigration," *Politische Studien* 6, Nr.67:6- 22 (1955).

Mann, Klaus. "Report on German Writers," *Saturday Review of Literature,* July 17, 1937, p.18.

Marcuse, Herbert. "Der Einfluss der Emigration auf das amerikanische Geistesleben: Philosophie and Soziologie," *Jahrbuch für Amerikastudien* 10:27- 33 (Heidelberg: Carl Winter, 1965).

Mareg, E. W. "Geschichte der Deutschen Arbeiterklubs," *Gegen den Strom* 1:3-4 (April 1938); 1:9 - 11 (May 1938); 1:12 -14 (June 1938); 1:12 -14 (Aug. 1938).

Müller, H. D. "Der Malik-Verlag als Vermittler der jungen Sowjetliteratur in Deutschland 1919 -1933," *Zeitschrift für Slawistik* 7, Nr., 5:720-38 (1963).

Nubel, Walter. "Bertolt Brecht Bibliographie," *Sinn und Form: Zweite Sonderheft Bertolt Brecht* (Berlin: Rütten & Loening, 1957), p.483-623.

Oehme, Walter. "Brecht in der Emigration," *Neue deutsche Literatur,* 11, Nr.6:180 -85 (1963).

_____ "Der Funke blieb lebending: Die antifaschistische deutsche Literatur in der Pariser Emigration," *Neue Deutsche Literatur* 11, Nr.12:167-71 (1963).

Paetel, Karl O. "Bibliographie der Zeitschriften und Zeitungen des deutschen politischen Exils 1933 -1945, " *Politische Studien* 9:425-31 (June, 1958).

_____ "Das deutsche Buch in der Verbanning," *Deutsche Rundschau* 76:755-60 (Sept., 1950).

_____ "Die deutsche Emigration der Hitlerzeit," *Neue politische Literatur* 5:465-82 (June, 1960).

_____ "'Deutsche Gegenwart' in den U.S.A.," *Börsenblatt für den deutschen Buchhandel* (Frankfurt am Main), 15:1007-11 (Aug. 25, 1959).

_____ "Deutsche im Exil: Randbemerkungen zur Geschichte der politischen Emigration," *Aussenpolitik* 6:572-85 (Sept., 1955).

_____ "Deutsches Theater in Amerika," *Deutsche Rundschau* 81:271 -75 (1955).

_____ "Das National-Komitee 'Freies Deutschland,' ' *Politische Studien* 6, Nr.69:7-26 (1956).

_____ "Die Presse des deutschen Exils 1933 -1945," *Publizistik* Nr.4:241 -53 (June-Aug., 1959).

_____ "Zum Problem einer deutschen Exilregierung," *Vierteljahrshefte für Zeitigeschichte* 4:286 -301 (July, 1956).

Pate, George W. "Free Germans in the United States," *The Christian Science Monitor,* Nov. 14, 1942, p.5 et passim.

Pfannkuch, Wilhelm. "Julius Leopold Korngold," *Die Musik in Geschichte und Gegenwart,* ed., Friedrich Blume, 7:Col. 1629-30 (1958).

Reichardt, Hans J. "Neu Beginnen," *Jahrbuch für die Geschichte Mittel- und Ostdeutschlands* 12:150-88 (1963).

Reimer, Jürgen. "Quellen und Materialien zur politischen Emigration und zum innerdeutschen Widerstand gegen das Dritte Reich," *Internationale wissenschaftliche Korrespondenz zur Geschichte der deutschen Arbeiterbewegung* 5:1-38 (Dec., 1967).

Roeder, Ralph. "Exiles and the League," *Saturday Review of Literature,* Oct. 19, 1940, p.7.

Rosenstock, Werner. "Jewish Emigration from Germany," in Leo Baeck Institute of Jews from Germany, *Year Book* 1:373-90 (New York, 1956).

Roucek, Joseph. "Foreign-Language Press in World War II," *Sociology and Social Research* 27:462-71 (July, 1943).

Salzmann, Karl H. "Amsterdam als Verlagsort der deutschen Emigration," *Börsenblatt für den deutschen Buchhandel* (Leipzig) 116, Nr.23:186–87 (1949).

_____ "Kurt Wolff, der Verleger," *Börsenblatt für den deutschen Buchhandel* (Frankfurt am Main) 14:1729–49 (Dec. 22, 1958).

_____ "Der Malik-Verlag: Verlagsgeschichte als Zeitgeschichte," *Neue deutsche Literatur* 4, Nr.4:88–92 (1956).

Sander, Wilhelm. "Auslandsgruppen der SPD," *Jahrbuch der Sozialdemokratische Partei Deutschlands* (Hanover: Vorstand der SPD, 1947), p.121–26.

Scheyer, Ernst. "Geistiges Leben in der Emigration," *Jahrbuch der Schlesischen Friedrich-Wilhelms Universität zu Breslau* (Würzburg) 5:271–95 (1960).

Schlag, Wilhelm. "A Survey of Austrian Emigration to the United States," in Otto Hietsch, ed., *Österreich und die angelsächsische Welt* (Wein: Braumüller, 1961), p.139–96.

Schleimann, Jorgen. "The Organization Man: The Life and Work of Willi Münzenberg," *Survey: A Journal of Soviet and East European Studies* 55:64–91 (April, 1965).

Schmidt, Hannes. "Unsere Emigrante," *Gegen den Strom* (New York) 1:12–13 (May, 1938).

Schwerin, Kurt. "Max Pinkus, seine Schlesierbücherei und seine Freundschaft mit Gerhart Hauptmann," *Bulletin des Leo Baeck Instituts* 5, Nr.18:98 –125 (1962).

Shuster, George N. "Dr. Brüning's Sojourn in the United States (1935–1945)," in Ferdinand A. Hermens and Theodor Schieder, eds., *Staat, Wirtschaft und Politik in der Weimarer Republik: Festschrift für Heinrich Brüning* (Berlin: Duncker & Humblot, 1967), p. 449–66.

_____ "Those of German Descent," *Common Ground* 3:31–35 (Winter, 1943).

Stampfer, Friedrich. "Heimkehr aus der Emigration," *Neue Volks-Zeitung,* Aug. 16, 1947, p.7.

Steiner, Herbert. "Corona," *Akzente* 10:40–49 (Feb. 1963).

Sternfeld, Wilhelm. "Die Emigrantenpresse," *Deutsche Rundschau* 76:250–59 (April, 1950).

_____ "Press in Exile: German Anti-Nazi Periodicals 1933 –1945," *Wiener Library Bulletin* 12:31 (1949); 14:5 (1950).

Stock, E. "Washington Heights' 'Fourth Reich': The German Émigrés' New Home," *Commentary* 11:581–88 (June, 1951).

Stourzh, Gerald. "Bibliographie der deutschsprachigen Emigration in den Vereinigten Staaten, 1933–1963: Geschichte und Politische Wissenschaft," *Jahrbuch für Amerikastudien* 10:232–66 (Heidelberg: Carl Winter, 1965).

_____ "Die deutschsprachige Emigration in den Vereinigten Staaten: Geschichtswissenschaft und Politische Wissenschaft," *Jahrbuch für Amerikastudien* 10:59–77 (Heidelberg: Carl Winter, 1965).

Svehla, J. "Von Schweizer Verlegern und Buchhändlern," *Der Schweizer Buchhandel* 6:334 –37 (June 15, 1948).

Walter, Hans-Albert. "Die Helfer im Hintergrund: Zur Situation der deutschen Exilverlage 1933 -1945," *Frankfurter Hefte* 20:121 -32 (Feb., 1965).

————— "Klaus Mann und 'Die Sammlung,' Porträt einer Literaturzeitschrift im Exil (II)," *Frankfurter Hefte* 22:49 -58 (Jan., 1967).

————— "Leopold Schwarzschild and the *Neue Tage-Buch," Journal of Contemporary History* 1, Nr.2:103- 16 (1961).

————— "Der Streit um die 'Sammlung,' Porträt einer Literaturzeitschrift im Exil (I)," *Frankfurter Hefte* 21:850 -60 (Dec., 1966).

"Was deutsche Kriegsgefangenen denken," *Neue Volks-Zeitung,* Jan. 5, 1944.

Weiskopf, Franz Carl. "Respectable Development: Free Book Publishing House, El Libro Libre," *Saturday Review of Literature* Feb. 5, 1944, p. 18.

White, Marjorie Taggert. "Europe's Press in Exile," *Saturday Review of Literature,* July 17, 1943, p.3 -5.

Wilk, Gerard H. "Yorkville, Twenty Years After," *Commentary* 17:41- 48. (Jan.. 1954).

Wischnitzer, Mark. "Die jüdische Wanderung unter der Naziherrschaft 1933 -1939," Heinz Gänther, ed., *Die Juden in Deutschland 1951/52 -1958/59* (Hamburg: Gala Verlag, 1959), p.95 -136.

Bookdealers' and Publishers' Catalogs

Allert de Lange. *Herbsterscheinungen, 1938.* Amsterdam: 1938.

Alliance Book Club. [*Prospectus*]. New York: 1939.

Alliance Book Corporation. *Freie deutsche Literatur.* New York: 1939.

Almanach für das freie deutsche Buch. Prag: Kacha Verlag, 1935.

Antiquariat Amelang. *Deutsche Literatur im Exil.* Frankfurt am Main: 1961.

————— *Deutsche Literatur im Exil zweite Folge.* Frankfurt am Main: 1962.

Éditions Nouvelles Internationales. [*Catalog*]. Paris: 1938.

Europa Verlag. *Verlagsverzeichnis Europa Verlag, Verlag Oprecht.* Zürich-New York: Ausgabe Frühjahr, 1948.

Fischer Verlag. *Vollständiges Verzeichnis aller Werke, Buchserien und Gesamtausgaben mit Anmerkungen zur Verlagsgeschichte 1886- 1956.* Frankfurt am Main: S. Fischer, 1956.

Friedrich Krause, Publisher and Bookseller. *Catalogue Number 31.* New York: Winter 1945/1946.

————— *Freie deutsche Literatur! Auslieferung fuer Amerika.* New York: 1939.

————— *Neuerscheinungen Fruehjahr und Sommer 1939.* New York: 1939.

Fünf Jahre freies deutsches Buch. Paris: Strauss, 1938.

Gerd Rosen Buchhandlung. *Die deutsche Literatur seit 1890*. Compiled by R. F. Krummel. Berlin: 1961.

Malik Verlag. *Neue Bücher aus dem Malik Verlag*. Prag: Sommer, 1935.

Michael Kacha Verlag. [*Prospectus*]. Prag: ca. 1935.

Oprecht und Helbling Bücherstube und Versandbuchhandlung. *Bücher 1938*. Zürich: 1938.

—— *Bücher 1939*. Zürich: 1938.

Proszenium Theater Antiquariat. *Verfemte Kultur: Erste-vierte Folge*. Kemnath: 1963–1965.

Querido Verlag. *Gesamt Katalog*. Amsterdam: 1938.

Schoenhof Verlag. *Bücher aus dem Schoenhof Verlag*. Cambridge, Mass.: 1945.

Verlag Julius Kittls Nachfolger. *Herbst 1934*. Mährisch-Ostrau: 1934.

—— *Neuerscheinungen 1938*. Mährisch-Ostrau: 1938.

Verlag Oprecht-Europa Verlag. [*Catalog*]. Zürich-New York: 1939.

Verlagsanstalt "Graphia." [*Catalog*]. Karlsbad: 1938.

Unpublished Manuscripts and Other Sources

Alperin, Robert Jay. "Organization in the Communist Party USA 1931–1938." Unpublished Ph.D. dissertation, Northwestern Univ., 1959.

Berendsohn, Walter A. "Die humanistische Front: Teil 2." Unpublished manuscript ca. 1948 on deposit at the Deutsche Bibliothek, Frankfurt am Main.

Dickson, Paul. "Das Amerikabild in der deutschen Emigrantenliteratur seit 1933." Unpublished Ph.D. dissertation, Ludwig Maxmilians-Universität, Munich, 1951.

Freund, J. Hellmut. S. Fischer Verlag GmbH Lektorat. Letters dated April 1, 1964 and Feb. 23, 1965.

Graf, Oskar Maria. Letter dated June 1, 1964.

Hertz, Paul. *Paul Hertz Papers*. On microfilm. Hoover Institution Library. Stanford Univ., Stanford, Calif.

Jacobsen, Claire. "The German Petty Bourgeoisie in Transition: Imperial Germany and Yorkville, U.S.A." Unpublished Ph.D. dissertation, Columbia Univ., 1958.

Kleim, Kurt. "Der sozialistische Widerstand gegen das Dritte Reich dargestellt an der Gruppe 'Neu Beginnen.'" Unpublished Ph.D. dissertation, Univ. of Marburg, 1957.

Kormis, Herman. Seventeen letters written between May, 1964 and May, 1965.

Levi, Anna S. "Views Regarding the Adjustment of the Germans in the United States as Revealed by the German-American Press (available in New York City), 1925–1939." Unpublished master's dissertation, Graduate School of Jewish Social Work, New York, 1940.

Mueller, Paul. Letter dated July 13, 1964.

Paetel, Karl O. Letter dated Dec. 29, 1963.

Rappaport, Ruth. "A Selective Guide to Source Materials on German Jews in the U.S. from 1933 to the Present Time." Unpublished report dated May 19, 1958, Univ. of California, School of Librarianship.

Rosenberg, Mary S. Letters dated Aug. 22, 1962 and Dec. 16, 1964.

Rumpel, H. Letter dated April 1, 1964 on behalf of Mrs. E. Oprecht of the Europa Verlag, Zürich.

Wetzel, John Charles. "The American Rescue of Refugee Scholars and Scientists from Europe 1933-1945." Unpublished Ph.D. dissertation, Univ. of Wisconsin, 1964.

Index